Serial Murder and the Psychology of Violent Crimes

SERIAL MURDER
AND THE
PSYCHOLOGY
OF VIOLENT CRIMES

Edited by

Richard N. Kocsis, PhD

Forensic Psychologist

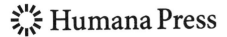 Humana Press

Editor
Richard N. Kocsis, PhD
Forensic Psychologist in Private Practice
Sydney, Australia

ISBN: 978-1-58829-685-6   e-ISBN: 978-1-59745-578-7

Library of Congress Control Number: 2007933143

Printed on acid-free paper

9 8 7 6 5 4 3 2 1

springer.com

Dedication

Ezt a könyvet szeretett apám és megboldogult anyukajanak tiszteletére és megemiékezésére irtam.

About the Editor

RICHARD N. KOCSIS, PhD, is a forensic psychologist in private practice. He is the author/co-author of close to 90 scholarly publications (articles, book chapters, etc.) on the topics of criminal profiling, serial violent offenders, and their criminal investigation. He has served as an expert consultant to law enforcement, emergency, and prosecution agencies, as well as private law firms. In addition to his clinical and forensic work, he has held various academic positions in the areas of forensic psychology and criminology, including Lecturer in Investigations (Policing). In 2000, he was awarded the Australian Museum's prestigious *Eureka* prize for critical thinking in recognition of his scientific research in the area of criminal profiling.

Preface

The 21ST CENTURY: THE AGE OF SERIAL VIOLENT CRIME

Despite technological and societal advances, crimes of an inexplicably violent nature still permeate contemporary civilizations throughout the world. The very existence of such aberrations, despite the passage of time over the centuries and the supposed evolution of our societies, suggests that some of the most basic instincts inherent to humanity may fundamentally relate to its proclivity for violence. Far from being manifestations of the modern era, serial violent crimes bear an uncanny resemblance to a number of ancient mythological creatures. These similarities raise suggestions that such creatures may have been attempts by ancient cultures to account for the abhorrent crimes. A series of seemingly unrelated brutal murders featuring the excessive mutilation of victims, with indications of body parts having been consumed and/or blood having been drunk, provided inspiration for folklore creatures such as werewolves or vampires. Similarly, the demonic spirits known as incubi that would rape women may be the ancient world seeking to account for serial rapists. Moving beyond these mythological examples, identifiable vignettes of serial violent crimes can be found in history, such as the Roman emperor Nero, who is well chronicled for his madness and delight in starting fires.

Serial violent crimes in contemporary society no longer typically invoke any relation with the supernatural but are, instead, now more notionally explained by labels such as serial murder, serial rape, or serial arson. However, what is more difficult to reconcile than the simple labeling of these behaviors is their continued manifestation. Whereas perhaps some argument may be advanced that serial violent crimes were an artifact of barbaric and/or less evolved societies, the basis for this rationale seems to be undermined by the observation of these crimes in contemporary and arguably progressive societies of the modern era. That is, despite the supposed evolution of modern civilization in fostering compassion, human rights, and equality among races, cultures, and religions, these crimes of extreme serial violence continue to emerge and, instead of being assuaged or diminished by the human race's ascent into greater civility, appear to be increasing in their prevalence.

Perhaps even more perplexing than the continued existence of these crimes is the unique and yet contradictory ways in which contemporary societies perceive these crimes. In contrast to the almost habitual high-volume crimes such as burglary or assault, the singular occurrence of one of these serial sexually violent crimes strikes immeasurable fear into a community. Paradoxically, despite the fear these crimes generate, they also attract an almost insatiable, albeit morbid, fascination by the public, with popular media depictions of these crimes and their investigation featured as mainstream ingredients for contemporary film, television, and literature.

Beyond the origins and impact of serial violent crimes, the investigation and apprehension of individuals who perpetrate these crimes pose one of the greatest challenges for modern-day law enforcement even in cases where direct eye witnesses to the crime exist. In many circumstances, the typical criminological factors that characterize many of the more common manifestations of murder (e.g., the existence of some prior knowledge of or acquaintance between the victim and the offender) are not present. The absence of these factors renders criminal investigations surprisingly difficult, as the motivational dynamics and purpose for the crime are internalized in the offender's own mind and are therefore not necessarily discernible from the evident situational factors of the crime. *Serial Murder and the Psychology of Violent Crimes* also examines the inherent danger of inaccurately analyzing information that exists about a violent crime and how this may adversely impact upon a criminal investigation.

Given the difficulties these serious crimes pose to law enforcement and the obtuse psychological factors inherent to their perpetrators, it is surprising that few books are available (in contrast to the plethora of popular culture and true crime literature) that examine these crimes and/or their perpetrators in a scientifically dispassionate context. It is with these goals in mind that *Serial Murder and the Psychology of Violent Crimes* has been assembled, with scholars from around the globe contributing their collective knowledge in an attempt to understand the mechanisms that characterize these offenders and, through such understanding, aid or enhance procedures for the investigation of serial violent crimes in the future.

Richard N. Kocsis, PhD

Contents

Notes on Contributors

BRUCE A. ARRIGO, PhD, is Professor of Crime, Law, and Society in the Department of Criminal Justice at the University of North Carolina at Charlotte, USA. He holds additional faculty appointments in the Psychology Department and the Public Policy Program. Dr. Arrigo has written extensively in the areas of criminal and legal psychology. His recent books in these areas include *Criminal Behavior: A Systems Approach* (Prentice Hall, 2006) and *The Psychology of Lust Murder* (Academic Press, 2006). Dr. Arrigo is an elected Fellow of the American Psychological Association and an elected Fellow of the Academy of Criminal Justice Sciences.

RAY BULL, PhD, is Professor of Forensic Psychology at the University of Leicester. His major research topic is investigative interviewing. In 1991 he was commissioned by the Home Office (together with a Law Professor) to write the first working draft of the *Memorandum of Good Practice on Video Recorded Interviews with Child Witnesses for Criminal Proceedings*. He was part of the small team commissioned by the Home Office in 2000 to write the 2002 government document *Achieving Best Evidence in Criminal Proceedings: Guidance for Vulnerable or Intimidated Witnesses, Including Children* (ABE). During 2002/2003 he led the small team commissioned by government to produce an extensive training pack relating to ABE. In 2004 he was commissioned by the Scottish Executive to draft guidance on the taking of evidence on commission. In 2005 he received a Commendation from the London Metropolitan Police for "innovation and professionalism whilst assisting a complex rape investigation." He has authored and co-authored a large number of articles in quality research journals and has co-authored and co-edited many books including *Investigative Interviewing: Psychology and Practice* (1999; a second edition is now being written). In recognition of the quality and extent of his research publications he was awarded a higher doctorate (Doctor of Science) in 1995.

JEFFREY B. BUMGARNER, PhD, is an associate professor of criminal justice at Texas Christian University in Ft. Worth, Texas. He earned a BA in political science from the University of Illinois (Urbana-Champaign), an MA in public administration from Northern Illinois University, and a PhD in training and organization development from the University of Minnesota. He has several years of experience in local and federal law enforcement as a patrol officer, criminal investigator, and trainer. He has authored several works on police practice and professionalism. Books he has authored include *Profiling and Criminal Justice in America* and *Federal Agents: The Growth of Federal Law Enforcement in America.*

KATHY E. CHARLES, BSC, PhD, is a Research Fellow at Glasgow Caledonian University where she is working an applied/forensic project investigating individual differences in unfamiliar face processing and recognition. Her first degree was a BSc (Hons) Psychology with Sociology from the University of Leicester (2001). She moved to Glasgow Caledonian University in 2002 to take up a fully funded PhD scholarship in Forensic Psychology. While working on her PhD she gained other work experiences including undergraduate and adult teaching, working with adult offenders, and volunteering with older long-term psychiatric patients. She completed her PhD in 2006.

VINCENT EGAN, BSC, PhD, is Director of the postgraduate forensic psychology courses at Glasgow Caledonian University. He holds a BSc (Hon) degree in Psychology from the University of London (1984), a PhD from the University of Edinburgh (1991), and a Doctorate in Clinical Psychology from the University of Leicester (1996). Professor Egan is a Chartered Forensic and Chartered Clinical Psychologist and an Associate fellow of the British Psychological Society with more than 60 publications.

JAMES ALAN FOX, PhD, is the Lipman Family Professor of Criminal Justice at Northeastern University. Among his 16 books are several on serial murder co-authored with Jack Levin. In addition to the area of serial homicide, Fox also specializes in mass murder, workplace violence, juvenile violence, capital punishment, and crime measurement. He has published and lectured widely on these topics. He is also a fellow with the Bureau of Justice Statistics of the United States Department of Justice.

JEFFREY L. GELLER, MD, MPH, received degrees from Williams College, the University of Pennsylvania School of Medicine, and the Harvard University School of Public Health. Dr. Geller completed his residency and fellowship at the Beth Israel Hospital and Harvard Medical School. Currently Dr. Geller is Professor of Psychiatry at the University of Massachusetts Medical School (UMMS). Dr. Geller has spent his career focusing on the delivery of psychiatric care and treatment of those with the greatest needs and fewest resources. He has done this through his current position as Director of Public Sector Psychiatry at UMMS; as a consultant to many U.S. states, to the U.S. Department of Justice, and to the FBI; through a Robert Wood Johnson Health Policy Fellowship; and through work in the American Psychiatric Association. Dr. Geller is the author of more than 90 articles in refereed journals and scores of book reviews and opinion pieces. He is the coauthor of the book, *Women of the Asylum.*

HELINÄ HÄKKÄNEN, PhD, is a forensic psychologist and Academy Research Fellow at the Finnish National Bureau of Investigation. She is the group leader of the Forensic Psychology Research Group at the Department of Psychology, University of Helsinki, where she also holds an adjunct professorship. She has published several scientific and general articles dealing with offender profiling and violent crime issues. Dr. Häkkänen has assisted the police in several arson, rape, and homicide investigations and has lectured on offender profiling at the university and to the police administrations in different countries. Her current research interests include offender profiling, behavior and personality in war crimes, risk assessment, personality and psychopathic features of violent offenders, and investigative interviewing. Her work is funded by the Academy of Finland.

ERICA P. HODGES, MS, is a Mississippi State University graduate in Clinical Psychology. She concentrated on forensic psychology where she researched media influences of guilty verdicts, juror decisions in violent murder cases, profiling accuracy, and serial sexual homicides. During the summer she is a clinical supervisor in Windsor, New Hampshire at Wediko Children's Services. Currently she resides in Tel Aviv, Israel.

CLIVE HOLLIN, PhD. Alongside his various academic appointments at the universities of East London, Birmingham, and Leicester, Professor Hollin has worked as a psychologist in both the Prison Service and the Youth Treatment Service and as a Clinical Scientist with Rampton Hospital Authority. In 1998, he was the recipient of the Senior Award for distinguished contribution to the field of Legal, Criminological, and Forensic Psychology presented by the Division of Criminological and Legal Psychology of The British Psychological Society. He is currently Head of the School of Psychology at The University of Leicester where he holds a personal chair as Professor of Criminological Psychology. He has published more than 200 academic papers and 17 books, including *Psychology and Crime: An Introduction to Criminological Psychology.* He edits the academic journal *Psychology, Crime, & Law.*

KRISTINE M. JACQUIN, PhD, is an Associate Professor of Psychology at Mississippi State University. Her research in the forensic psychology area examines criminal profiling accuracy, the causes and prevention of reactive relational aggression, and juror decisions in violent crime cases. As a licensed clinical psychologist, Dr. Jacquin consults with clients, attorneys, courts, and agencies on a variety of forensic and neuropsychological issues.

JACK LEVIN, PhD, is the Irving and Betty Brudnick Professor of Sociology and Criminology and director of the Brudnick Center on Conflict and Violence at Northeastern University in Boston, Massachusetts. He has authored or coauthored 27 books, including *Mass Murder: America's Growing Menace, Killer on Campus, Hate Crimes Revisited, The Will to Kill: Making Sense of Senseless Murder, Domestic Terrorism, The Violence of Hate,* and *Extreme Killing: Understanding Serial and Mass Murder.* Levin has published numerous articles in professional journals including *Criminology, Journal of Applied Psychoanalytic Studies, American Behavioral Scientist, Journal of Social Issues, Justice Quarterly,* and *Journal of Interpersonal Violence.*

JANET MCCLELLAN, is currently a PhD candidate at Northcentral University in Arizona and assistant professor at SUNY Canton in the Criminal Investigation Department. McClellan has an extensive background in public service including as a police officer, police chief, investigator, correction official, and chief executive of the Kansas Violent Sexual Predator Maximum Security Facility.

LEONARD I. MORGENBESSER, PhD, is a part-time adjunct faculty member in the MA (Social Policy) and BA (Criminal Justice) programs of Empire State College (SUNY) and is also in his 32nd year of full-time consecutive service with the State of New York Department of Correctional Services in Albany/Headquarters (Division of Program Planning, Evaluation, and Research). His research interests include sexual assault of elderly victims in institutions (i.e., nursing homes) and in the community, a topic he has studied in collaboration with Professor Ann Wolbert Burgess, DNSc, RNCS, FAAN of Boston College Nursing School. He serves on various journal editorial boards including *Journal of Child Sexual Abuse, Criminal Justice and Behavior,* and *International Journal of Offender Therapy and Comparative Criminology.* Dr Morgenbesser serves on various boards including The Restorative Justice/Crime Victims Committee of The American Correctional Association, and The New York State Chapter Executive Board of ATSA (Association for Treatment of Sexual Abusers). Dr Morgenbesser resides in Albany, NY (capital city of New York State) and may be reached at Leonard.Morgenbesser@esc.edu/.

GEORGE B. PALERMO, MD, MSc Crim, graduated from the University of Bologna Medical School, Bologna, Italy, and was trained in general medicine and psychiatry in the United States. He holds a MS in Criminology from the University of Rome, La Sapienza. He is a Diplomate of the American Board of Psychiatry and Neurology in Psychiatry and a Diplomate of the American Board of Forensic Examiners and of Forensic Medicine. He is Clinical Professor of Psychiatry at the Medical College of Wisconsin, and Professor Adjunct of Criminology and Law Studies at Marquette University, in Milwaukee, Wisconsin.

IAN SALE, MD, graduated from the University of Tasmania Clinical School of Medicine and undertook postgraduate training in psychiatry in Adelaide, South Australia. In recent years he pursued an interest in forensic and medicolegal psychiatry. In Tasmania he participated in police training and exercises with police negotiators. He is Director of Training for postgraduate training in psychiatry and a medical member of the state's Forensic Tribunal.

LOUIS B, SCHLESINGER, PhD, is Professor of Forensic Psychology at John Jay College of Criminal Justice, City University of New York and a Diplomate in Forensic Psychology of the American Board of Professional Psychology. He has published numerous articles, chapters, and eight books on homicide, sexual homicide, and criminal behavior.

HANNAH SCOTT, PhD, is an Associate Professor in the Faculty of Criminology, Justice, and Policy Studies at the University of Ontario Institute of Technology in Oshawa, Ontario, Canada. She has taught and conducted research in both the United States and Canada. Her current interests are in the areas of victimology, gender issues, homicide, criminological theory, and statistics. She also has a keen interest in Crime Prevention Through Environmental Design (CPTED) modeling and the mapping of crime patterns. She has published in a number of academic journals on subjects including sexual assault among Aboriginal and non-Aboriginal peoples, violence by men, and women's fear of crime. Her book is called *The Female Serial Murderer: A Sociological Study of Homicide and the 'Gentler Sex'* (Mellen Press). Dr. Scott has taught at both the graduate and undergraduate level. At the graduate level she has taught both Criminological Theory and Victimology. At the undergraduate level she has taught Criminological Theory, Victimology, Organized Crime, Statistics, Introduction to Canadian Criminal Justice, Deviance, and Sociology. She received her PhD in Sociology from The University of Alberta, Edmonton, Alberta, Canada.

STACEY L. SHIPLEY, PsyD, is Chief Psychologist on the Social Learning Rehabilitation Unit at North Texas State Hospital, Maximum Security Hospital in Vernon, Texas. Dr. Shipley specializes in forensic evaluations and violence risk assessment, evaluating or treating individuals adjudicated by the courts as not guilty by reason of insanity or incompetent to stand trial for felony offenses, and the treatment of maternal filicide offenders. She has published in the areas of psychopathy, women and crime, maternal filicide, homicide, and serial offenders. Her books include *The Female Homicide Offender* (2004) and *Introduction to Forensic Psychology, 2nd edition* (2005), both coauthored with Bruce A. Arrigo.

RONALD TURCO, MD, is a forensic psychiatrist practising in Portland, Oregon. He is an Associate Clinical Professor of Psychiatry at the Oregon Health Sciences University and teaches classes on geopolitics and psychoanalysis. He has authored more than 150 technical articles in psychiatry and psychoanalysis and four books. Dr. Turco is Past President of the American Academy of Psychoanalysis and the American Society of Psychoanalytic Physicians. He has been an active member of numerous homicide task forces, works with the Oregon State Police and is a consultant to government agencies. He has been instrumental in the apprehension of three serial killers and many homicide perpetrators. In 1981 he was involved in the largest manhunt and criminal investigation in Oregon history, resulting in the capture of the I-5 killer. He is a consultant in international terrorism with The American Academy of Psychoanalysis.

PETER J. VAN KOPPEN, PhD, is a senior researcher at the Netherlands Institute for the Study of Crime and Law Enforcement (NSCR) at Leiden, The Netherlands; Professor of Law and Psychology at the Department of Law of Maastricht University; and Professor of Law and Psychology at the Department of Law of the Free University Amsterdam. He was formerly Professor of Law and Psychology at the Department of Law of Antwerp University, Belgium. He is a psychologist. He studied law in Groningen, Amsterdam, and Rotterdam. He now serves as president of the European Association for Psychology and Law. Peter van Koppen's research encompasses the broad area of social science research in law.

JESSICA WOODHAMS, PhD, is a lecturer in Forensic Psychology at the University of Leicester. Prior to commencing her post at Leicester in 2002, she worked as a crime analyst for the London Metropolitan Police, specializing in the analysis of stranger sexual crime. Jessica's major research topics reflect her previous employment. She has conducted and continues to conduct applied research into investigative techniques for sexual and nonsexual crimes, the behaviors of offenders and victims during adult and juvenile sexual offenses, and the identification of false allegations. She has advised police forces on the development of databases for linking crimes and local youth offending teams working with juvenile sexual offenders. She has written a number of research articles and book chapters on her research topics and has presented her findings at both national and international conferences.

PART I

THE PSYCHOLOGY
OF SERIAL VIOLENT CRIMES

Chapter 1

Normalcy in Behavioral Characteristics of the Sadistic Serial Killer

Jack Levin and James Alan Fox

Abstract

Sadistic serial killers have been widely diagnosed as sociopaths who are lacking in empathy and inordinately concerned with impression management. We propose instead that many of the behavioral characteristics thought to be distinctive of these serial murderers are actually shared widely with millions of people who never kill anyone. By focusing so much on sociopathic characteristics, researchers may have downplayed the importance of the existential processes—compartmentalization and dehumanization—that permit serial killers to rape, torture, and murder with moral impunity. Moreover, by uncritically accepting the sociopathic designation, researchers may have ignored the interaction between sadism and sociopathy that causes empathy to be heightened rather than diminished.

INTRODUCTION

In popular culture, as in serious writing on the topic, serial killers are frequently characterized as "evil monsters" who share little, if anything, with "normal" human beings. This image is represented, for example, in the title of Robert Ressler's insightful book, *Whoever Fights Monsters* and Carl Goldberg's *Speaking With the Devil: Exploring Senseless Acts of Evil*, just as it is in the cinematic depiction of serial killer Aileen Wuornos in the popular film *Monster*. The same image is reinforced by excessive media attention to grisly crimes

From: *Serial Murder and the Psychology of Violent Crimes*
Edited by: R. N. Kocsis © Humana Press, Totowa, NJ

involving Satanic human sacrifice, the sexual torture of children, and acts of cannibalism and necrophilia.

In the professional literature, a similar impression of the sadistic serial killer is encouraged by researchers and authors who focus on certain characteristics that have been widely regarded as psychologically distinctive of sadistic serial killers—in particular, their lack of empathy for the pain and suffering of victims, their inordinate concern with impression management to maximize personal pleasure, and their lack of remorse.

Those who seek to understand sadistic serial murderers may have accepted uncritically the conventional professional wisdom depicting sadistic serial killers as suffering from a personality disorder variously labeled as sociopathy, psychopathy, or antisocial personality *(1,2)*. A closer examination of this kind of psychopathology suggests, first, that at least some sadistic killers may not require possession of an antisocial personality disorder to kill with moral impunity. Instead, they are able to overcome the forces of conscience in the same way as most other human beings—by compartmentalizing and dehumanizing their victims. Moreover, some characteristics attributed to serial killers and widely regarded as part and parcel of a personality disorder may actually overlap with abilities shared by millions of other human beings. Indeed, these "distinguishing characteristics" are hardly distinguishing at all from the vast majority of human beings who never kill any member of their own species. Finally, certain characteristics associated with sociopathy and found in sadistic serial killers may be profoundly modified in the presence of sexual sadism. In particular, their empathy may be heightened rather than reduced.

SOCIOPATHY AND SERIAL MURDER

Mental health specialists seem to agree that the sadistic serial killer tends to be a *sociopath*, which is a disorder of personality or character rather than of the mind. He lacks a conscience, feels no remorse, cares exclusively for his own pleasures in life, and lacks the ability to empathize with the suffering of his victims. Other people are seen by the serial killer merely as tools to fulfill his own needs and desires, no matter how perverse or reprehensible they may be *(3–5)*.

In the literature, the term sociopath is often employed interchangeably with psychopath and antisocial personality disorder. Initially, the word psychopath was widely used by psychiatrists and psychologists to identify the syndrome of character traits involving an impulsive, reckless, and selfish disregard of others. During the 1950s, however, the psychiatric profession recommended the use of the diagnostic term "sociopath," in part to distinguish the psychopathic personality from the much more serious psychotic disorders. Then, during the late 1960s, psychiatrists once again proposed a change in terminology, replacing both the sociopathic and psychopathic diagnoses with the antisocial personality disorder (APD). Some experts in psychopathology maintain fine distinctions among the three diagnostic categories, even offering various subtypes for each *(6)*. To understand sadistic serial murder, however, these differences are not particularly important because the fundamental characteristics prevalent among these offenders are, for the most part, common to all three terms.

Presentation of Self

Usually as an aspect of their presumed sociopathic disorder, serial killers are often characterized as being extremely skillful at impression management. They are seen as unusually capable of looking and acting beyond suspicion, of appearing to be more innocent than a truly innocent person, of being able to lure their victims with charm and cunning.

For example, Derrick Todd Lee, the 34-year-old man who raped and murdered a number of women in the area of Baton Rouge, stayed on the loose at least in part because he was able socially to blend in so well. To many he came across as "friendly" and "charming." He cooked barbeque and led a Bible study group. Those who got to know him informally regarded him as more a preacher than a killer. Green River Killer Gary Ridgway, who in 2004 was convicted for the deaths of 48 prostitutes in Washington State, brought his young son with him to a crime scene to look "fatherly" and give his victim a false sense of security. John Wayne Gacy, who brutally murdered 33 men and boys, was regarded by his suburban Chicago neighbors as a gregarious chap. He often played the part of a clown at children's birthday parties and organized get-togethers for the people on his block. Gacy frequently lured victims to his home by offering to interview them for a job with his construction company.

Even if serial killers seem to be skillful at presentation of self, they are certainly not alone in their concern for projecting an image that is acceptable to others. Sociologist Erving Goffman *(7)* long ago suggested that managing the impression that we wish to convey to others was a normal, healthy human characteristic. In fact, *successful* individuals in many legitimate occupations seem to have a particular knack for using self-awareness to their personal advantage. This is true, for example, of effective politicians who come across as "one of the guys," of skillful actors who base their entire professional lives on their ability to stage a character, and of sales personnel who are able to convince their clients that they really do have their best interests at heart.

Even in the most mundane areas of everyday life, normal people stage a character. Goffman distinguished between the *frontstage* where the performance is given from the *backstage* region where it is rehearsed. In a restaurant, for example, the wait staff stages a scene in the dining area by their cordial and hospitable demeanor with customers. In the kitchen, however, the same waiters complain about their working conditions and swap unflattering stories about their experiences with customers.

The difference between serial killers and other "successful" people may lie not so much in the greater effectiveness of the serial killers at impression management as a means to an end but in their greater willingness to torture and kill as a result of employing the tactic. When individuals use techniques of self-presentation for benign purposes in everyday life, it escapes our attention; or we might characterize our friends and family members in a complimentary way, emphasizing their polite manners, attractive smile, or charming style. When a serial killer is polite and charming for the purpose of luring his victims, however, we characterize him as inordinately manipulative and devious.

In a diagnostic sense, is the serial killer who flatters his victims into modeling for his photo shoots any different in his manipulative skills from the sales clerk who wants to convince a shopper to buy the most expensive dress on the rack? Does the serial killer who kisses his wife goodbye as he goes off to troll the streets for prostitutes to rape and murder really differ in his role-playing behavior from the loving family man who brutally mistreats his employees at work but loves his family? It may be a different playing field—but a similar game.

Compartmentalization

Serial killers typically target absolute strangers *(8)*. On a practical level, this creates a more difficult challenge for law enforcement without the benefit of knowing the motivation or the relationship between victim and killer. This may be only half of the story, however.

Compartmentalization is a psychological facilitator that serial killers use to overcome or neutralize whatever pangs of guilt they might otherwise experience *(9)*. It may be an immense exaggeration to suggest that most serial killers are totally lacking in human warmth and concern. Instead, they may be able to compartmentalize their moralistic predilections by constructing at least two categories of human beings—their circle of family and friends, whom they care about and treat with decency, and individuals with whom they have no relationship and therefore victimize with total disregard for their feelings.

For example, Hillside Strangler Kenneth Bianchi clearly divided the world into two camps. The individuals toward whom he had no feelings including the twelve women he brutally tortured and killed. Ken's inner circle consisted of his mother, his common-law wife, and his son, as well as his cousin Angelo

Buono, with whom he teamed up for the killings. Bianchi's wife Kelli Boyd once told investigators: "The Ken I knew couldn't ever have hurt anybody or killed anybody. He wasn't the kind of person who could have killed somebody."

It could be argued, of course, that Bianchi was simply manipulating his spouse in order to appear innocent. However, it is also a compelling interpretation that he compartmentalized human beings in a manner that was not very different from the way that normal people compartmentalize others in everyday life.

Indeed, the killer can take advantage of the normalcy of compartmentalization, when he interacts with those in his inner circle. For example, despite his conviction on 33 counts of murder, John Wayne Gacy was seen by those in his community as a rather decent and caring man. Lillian Grexa, who had lived next door to Gacy while he was burying victims in the crawl space underneath his house, remained supportive, even writing to him on death row. "I know they say he killed 33 young men," explained Grexa, "but I only knew him as a good neighbor...the best I ever had."

Thus, the compartmentalization that allows killing without guilt may really be an extension of this existential phenomenon. An executive might be a heartless "son of a bitch" to all his employees at work but a loving and devoted family man at home. A harsh disciplinarian at home can be highly regarded by his friends and acquaintances. Similarly, many serial killers have jobs and families, do volunteer work, and kill part-time with a great deal of selectivity. A sexual sadist who may be unmercifully cruel in his treatment of a stranger he meets in a bar might not dream of harming his family members, friends, or neighbors.

According to psychiatrist Robert Jay Lifton (10), the Nazi physicians who performed ghoulish experiments at Auschwitz and other concentration camps compartmentalized their activities, attitudes, and emotions. Through the extreme psychological process known as "doubling," any possible feelings of guilt were minimized because the camp doctors developed two separate and distinct selves—one for doing the dirty work of experimenting with and exterminating inmates and the other for living the rest of their lives outside the camp. In this way, no matter how sadistic they were on the job, they were still able to see themselves as gentle husbands, caring fathers, and honorable physicians.

Just as it was with the Nazi concentration camp doctors, the process of compartmentalization operates to the advantage of a serial murderer who kills for profit, that is, he robs and then executes to silence the eyewitnesses to his crimes. Like a hitman for the mob, he kills for a living yet otherwise leads an ordinary family life. In a similar way, a sexual sadist who may be unmercifully brutal to a hitchhiker or a stranger he meets at a bar might not dream of hurting family members, friends, or neighbors.

Lifton argues that physicians may be more susceptible to doubling than are the members of many other professional groups. To practice medicine objectively, they must become accustomed to dealing mundanely with the biological basics of humanity—blood, internal organs, and corpses. As a result, doctors learn to develop a "medical self." They become desensitized to death and learn to function under demands that would be abhorrent to most laypeople. A few medical practitioners may even develop a fondness for the pain and suffering of their patients. Beginning with his residency in Ohio State University's medical school in 1983, Michael Swango poisoned to death as many as 60 hospital patients under his care. Writing in his diary, Swango explained the pleasure that he received from killing: He loved the "sweet, husky, close smell of indoor homicide." It reminded him that he was "still alive."

Dehumanization

Compartmentalization is aided by another universal process: the capacity of human beings to *dehumanize* "the other" by regarding outsiders as animals or demons who are therefore expendable. Serial killers have taken advantage of this process in the selection of their victims: They often view prostitutes as mere sex machines, gays as AIDS carriers, nursing home patients as vegetables, and homeless alcoholics as nothing more than trash. By regarding their victims as subhuman elements of society, the killers can delude themselves into believing that they are doing something positive rather than negative. They are, in their minds, ridding the world of filth and evil. This was apparently the collective thinking of German citizenry during the 1930s and 1940s, when stereotyping Jews as "vermin" helped to justify an "eliminationist anti-Semitism."

The behavior of a serial killer after his capture provides some insight into his level of conscience and his use of dehumanization. Genuine sociopaths almost never confess after being apprehended. Instead, they continue to maintain their innocence, always hoping beyond hope to get off on a technicality, to be granted a new trial, or to appeal their case to a higher level.

A few sociopathic serial killers have confessed to their crimes, not because they were remorseful but because they considered it in their best interest to do so. For example, Clifford Olson, who raped and murdered eleven children in Vancouver, British Colombia, decided that the police "had the goods on him." He decided, therefore, that he might as well turn his defeat into an advantage. Olson confessed to murder and led the police to the bodies of his victims in exchange for a $100,000 "ransom." Olson was later asked to reveal information about other missing children, not for a fee but for the sake of the worried parents. In true sociopathic fashion, he responded, "If I gave a shit about the parents, I wouldn't of killed the kid."

By contrast, serial killers who possess a conscience may confess to their crimes, even if it is no longer self-serving to do so. So long as they are still on the loose and alone with their fantasies and private thoughts, they are able to maintain the myth that their victims deserved to die. After being caught, however, they are forced to confront the disturbing reality that they had killed human beings, not animals, demons, or objects. At this point, their victims are *rehumanized* in their eyes. As a result, these serial killers may be overcome with guilt for the sadistic crimes they committed and freely confess.

Not unlike sadistic serial killers, soldiers in combat learn psychologically to separate the allies from the enemy, treating the latter as less than human. As a result, countless normal and healthy individuals who would never dream of killing for fun have slaughtered the enemy in combat. They are not, in their minds, killing human beings—only "gooks," "krauts," or "kikes." While in the midst of combat, they continue to hold dehumanized images. After returning home, however, they typically adopt prevailing attitudes toward the members of the same groups with whom they now live at peace. At the end of the Cold War, for example, we easily modified our thinking about the "red peril" and "the evil empire," viewing Russians as our allies rather than our mortal enemy. After World War II, the negative image of our Japanese opponents—"the yellow peril"—quickly dissipated.

Similarly, it is easy to argue that brutal terrorists who target civilians and government officials are sociopaths whose lack of conscience makes possible doing the most despicable things to their innocent victims. Yet the dehumanization process may mean much more than an absence of conscience in facilitating a terrorist who kills civilians. Arab terrorists refer to Jews and Christians as "pigs" and "dogs." Their terrorist acts may be more altruistic than selfish, designed to give them a place of honor in their religious community and to influence changes in policy they regard as detrimental to their national interests.

Lack of Empathy

During the 1930s, social philosopher George Herbert Mead *(11)* identified "role taking" as a basic human quality, whereby an individual is able to adopt the viewpoint of another person. Initially, the child takes one role at a time. He may, for example, "put himself in the shoes" of his father or mother, his teacher, his siblings, and his close friends. Later, according to Mead, the maturing child comes to develop a consistent self-concept as he is able to define himself from the viewpoint of the entire language community, or "the generalized other."

Many serial killers apparently share the role-taking ability, even if they use it to enhance the pleasure they derive from inflicting pain and suffering on their victims. Indeed, role-taking ability has been shown to take the form of a continuum rather than a dichotomous variable, along which any given individual's degree of empathy can be located. Thus, there are some individuals whose empathy is so profound and broad that they commiserate with the plight of starving children on the other side of the world. Many individuals are closer to the middle of the continuum, identifying with the grief of victims in proximity to them but emotionally oblivious to the pain and suffering of most strangers. At the other end of the continuum, however, there may also be millions who are completely lacking in empathy. They may not be serial killers, but they are insensitive to human tragedy. They may not kill, but they are more than willing to cheat, swindle, lie, womanize, make unethical business decisions, or sell someone a bad used car.

Hare *(5)* estimates that at least 1% of the population consists of what he refers to as "subclinical psychopaths." They are not repeat killers but possess the characteristics usually associated with individuals who kill for pleasure. Subclinical psychopaths are, instead, charming men who use women for sex and money, only to then abandon them; con artists who engage in insider-trading and illegal market timing as stock brokers and money managers; individuals who are HIV-positive and still have unprotected sex; and salesmen who make vastly exaggerated claims about their products. Psychopaths are neighbors, coworkers, bosses, and dates. Some are sadistic serial killers.

We believe that lack of empathy is one characteristic of sadistic killers that has been accepted far too uncritically by psychologists and criminologists alike. Many investigators have indeed argued, based on superficial familiarity with serial murder cases, that sadistic serial killers are incapable of appreciating their victims' pain and suffering. It has been reported that serial killer Henry Lee Lucas once compared his attitude toward killing humans to our concern for squashing a bug—no big deal. Similarly, Hillside Strangler Kenneth Bianchi boasted that "killing a broad" meant nothing to him. Yet as we shall argue below, "killing a broad" meant everything to him.

In the case of repeat killers for whom murder is instrumental, the lack of empathy may truly be essential for avoiding apprehension. Profit-motivated serial killers, for example, may not enjoy the suffering of their victims but still take their victims' lives for the sake of expediency. During the 1970s, for example, Gary and Thaddeus Lewington committed a series of ten armed robberies around central Ohio during which they took their victims' wallets and then cavalierly shot each one in the head. Twenty years later, Sacramento landlady Dorothea Puente, with moral impunity, poisoned to death her nine elderly tenants so she could steal their social security checks. In October 2002, DC snipers John Allen Mohammad and Lee Boyd Malvo dispassionately shot and killed ten innocent victims to further their demands for 10 million dollars in ransom—pay up or perish. For them, the physical distance from the victims they gunned down with a long-range rifle aided in inoculating them against any tendency to empathize. The victims were merely and literally targets of opportunity. In addition, they apparently saw Americans as "the enemy," which only aided them in dehumanizing their victims chosen at random.

For sadistic serial killers, however, murder is an end in itself, making the presence of empathy—even intensely heightened empathy—important in two respects. First, their crimes require highly tuned powers of *cognitive* empathy to capture their victims. Killers who do not understand their victims' feelings would be incapable of conning them effectively. For example, Theodore Bundy understood all too well the sensibilities of female college students who were taken in by his feigned helplessness. He trapped attractive young women by appearing to be disabled and asking them for help. In Calaveras County, California, serial killers Leonard Lake and Charles Ng gained entry into the homes of their victims by answering classified ads in the local newspaper, pretending that they wished only to purchase a camcorder or furniture. Milwaukee's cannibal killer Jeffrey Dahmer met his victims in a bar and lured them to his apartment, where they expected to party, not to be murdered.

Second, a well-honed sense of *emotional* empathy is critical for a sadistic killer's enjoyment of the suffering of his victims. For sadistic objectives to be realized, a killer who tortures, sodomizes, rapes, and humiliates must be able to both understand and experience his victim's suffering. Otherwise, there would be no enjoyment or sexual arousal. Thus, he feels his victim's pain, but he interprets it as his own pleasure. Indeed, the more empathic he is, the greater his enjoyment of his victim's suffering.

In the literature of psychology as well as criminology, lack of empathy—along with a manipulative and calculating style, an absence of remorse, and impulsiveness—is frequently regarded as a defining characteristic of the sociopathic or antisocial personality disorder. Yet Heilbrun *(12)* came to quite a different conclusion from his interviews of 168 male prisoners. He found two kinds of sociopath—those who had poor impulse control, low IQ, and little empathy (the Henry Lee Lucas type) and those who had better impulse control, high IQ, sadistic objectives, and heightened empathy (the Theodore Bundy type). In fact, the most empathic group of criminals in Heilbrun's study was comprised of intelligent sociopaths with a history of extreme violence, particularly rape, a crime occasionally involving a sadistic component.

According to Heilbrun, violent acts inflicting pain and suffering are more intentional than impulsive. In addition, empathic skills promote the arousal and satisfaction of sadistic objectives by enhancing the criminal's awareness of the pain being experienced by his victim. Because the subjects in Heilbrun's study were surveyed within months of their scheduled parole hearing dates, it is certainly possible that at least some of the observed differences could represent systematic response error. That is, perhaps the more intelligent subjects, anticipating their upcoming parole review, were more apt to feign empathy through their responses. Thus, IQ differences may have produced artificial differences in empathy responses.

Whether methodological concerns were partially responsible, Heilbrun's finding of empathic sadistic sociopaths was all but ignored in the literature—that is, until recently, when psychiatrists began to question the commonly held view that antisocial types necessarily lack the ability to feel their victims' pain. Instead, psychiatrists noted that in many cases they possess, as Glen Gabbard *(13)* wrote in *Psychiatric News*, "tremendous powers of empathic discernment—albeit for the purposes of self-aggrandizement."

We suggest it is in the *interaction* between sexual sadism and sociopathy that empathy becomes both heightened and perverted. Sociopaths lack empathy; sadists require empathy. When both disorders are present together, sociopathic empathy is profoundly modified. One disorder enhances the other, making possible the sadistic thrills that many serial killers seek.

CONCLUSION

Many individuals who live conventional lives are able to satisfy their sadistic needs in a socially acceptable way. Business leaders have been known to wheel and deal, hire and fire; some teachers are unnecessarily tough on their students; and parents can be harsh and threatening in their child-rearing practices. For various reasons, serial killers lack whatever it takes to achieve a position of dominance in the legitimate system. Had serial killer Theodore Bundy ever completed his law degree, he might have been able to kill them—figuratively, of course—inside the courtroom, rather than on the streets. If Aileen Wuornos had been blessed with the opportunity for a decent childhood, she might have become an aggressive entrepreneur rather than a deadly highway prostitute.

Sadism has even found a prominent position in popular culture. Many prime-time television series now owe their staying power to the sadistic impulses they exploit on the tube. Audience members find tremendous enjoyment in viewing horrified contestants who devour worms and insects on NBC's *Fear Factor*;

Donald Trump who exclaims without nuance, "You're fired" on his wildly popular series; *The Apprentice*; *American Idol's* Simon Cowell who brutally insults a contestant; Ann Robinson who refers to a losing player as "the weakest link"; contestants who backstab one another or eat rodents on an episode of *Survivor*; and aspiring singers lacking any talent who are deceived and humiliated for the sake of a laugh on the WB's contest, *Superstar USA*.

In their capacity for committing extreme violence against innocent victims, serial killers obviously differ qualitatively from the average person. Few members of society would be able to torture and kill multiple victims (although the sadistic impulse is probably much more pervasive than we would like to think). In terms of their underlying psychology, however, serial murderers may not differ from normal people as much as we have been led to believe.

An alternative possibility is that the sociopathic designation has been incorrectly applied to sadistic serial killers. If they really do not differ from other people qualitatively in terms of their ability to project a public image of themselves, their ability to compartmentalize and dehumanize, and their empathy for the suffering of victims, they may not be the extreme sociopaths we have believed them to be. This does not mean that the psyche of the serial murderer is like that of normal people, only that we have been looking in the wrong place for the important differences.

REFERENCES

1. Levin, J., & Fox, J. A. (1985). *Mass Murder: America's Growing Menace.* New York: Plenum Press.
2. Palermo, G. B., & Kocsis, R.N. (2005). *Offender Profiling: An Introduction to the Sociopsychological Analysis of Violent Crime.* Springfield, IL: Charles C Thomas.
3. Harrington, A. (1972). *Psychopaths.* New York: Simon & Schuster.
4. Magid, K., & McKelvey, C.A. (1988). *High Risk: Children Without a Conscience.* New York: Bantam Books.
5. Hare, R. D. (1993). *Without Conscience: The Disturbing World of the Psychopaths Among Us.* New York: Pocket Books.
6. Samenow, S. (2004). *Inside the Criminal Mind.* New York: Random House.
7. Goffman, E. (1959). *The Presentation of Self in Everyday Life.* Garden City, NY: Doubleday.
8. Fox, J. A., & Levin, J. (2005). *Extreme Killing: Understanding Serial and Mass Murder.* Thousand Oaks, CA: Sage.
9. Fox, J. A., & Levin, J. (1994). *Overkill: Serial and Mass Exposed.* New York: Plenum Press.
10. Lifton, R. J. (1986). *The Nazi Doctors: Medical Killing and the Psychology of Genocide.* New York: Basic Books.
11. Mead, G. H. (1934). *Mind, Self, and Society.* Chicago: University of Chicago Press.

12. Heilbrun, A. B. (1982). Cognitive models of criminal violence based upon intelligence and psychopathy levels. *Journal of Consulting and Clinical Psychology*, 50, 546–557.

13. Gabbard, G. O. (2003). *American Psychiatric Association's Institute on Psychiatric Services*. Boston: APAIPS.

Chapter 2

Compulsive-Repetitive Offenders
Behavioral Patterns, Motivational Dynamics
Louis B. Schlesinger

Abstract

This chapter examines the compulsive repetitive offender, specifically individuals who commit crimes repetitively because of an internal sexual drive. Topics of sexual motivation, problems in terminology, and historical context are reviewed, along with a presentation of sexual murderers, traditional sex offenders, and individuals who engage in other sexually motivated antisocial acts. The important role of fantasy, planning, personality traits, and the usefulness of treatment are also covered.

INTRODUCTION

Individuals who commit crimes repetitively and in a similar way have been present since premodern times. Various types of recurring antisocial acts that are sexually motivated have also been recorded for centuries. Among these acts are homicide, arson, voyeurism, exhibitionism, rape, and child molestation. Numerous individuals have been apprehended for such crimes, have served lengthy prison sentences, and upon release have committed the same offense against the same type of victim in almost identical fashion. Thus, repetitive

From: *Serial Murder and the Psychology of Violent Crimes*
Edited by: R. N. Kocsis © Humana Press, Totowa, NJ

offenders, especially those who commit crimes in a ritualistic fashion, which provides them with sexual gratification, have always been a major criminal-justice problem.

BACKGROUND FOR UNDERSTANDING THE COMPULSIVE-REPETITIVE OFFENDER

Two aspects of research into repetitive offenders have generated some controversy. These aspects need to be analyzed before the history, behavioral and motivational patterns, and treatment of repetitive offenders are discussed.

Sexual Motivation

Individuals who repetitively and similarly commit crimes–specifically when internal forces push them to kill, rape, expose themselves, set fires, or molest children–do so because of abhorrent sexual drives (1). The vast majority of psychiatric, psychological, and criminal-investigative practitioners and researchers agree that such internally driven offenses are sexually motivated (e.g., 2–8). These offenders have a serious disturbance in the sexual area, and they achieve gratification through various forms of acting out, including violence (9). After a period of engaging in deviant sexual fantasy—usually for a number of years—offenders begin to act their fantasies out by engaging in sexually sadistic behaviors (perhaps directed toward animals), setting fires, molesting children, and the like (10). These offenders have an inner urge to act on their disturbed sexual fantasies; and once they kill or rape or set fires, they typically repeat the behavior until apprehended.

In many cases, the compulsive-repetitive offender does not display an overt manifestation of genitality, which has led a few researchers (e.g., 11–14) to question whether the underlying motivation for these offenders is actually sexual. For example, with regard to the compulsive-repetitive murderer, Egger (15) has stated that "sex is only an instrument used by the killer to obtain power and domination over his victim . . . [the sexual aspect] frequently present in [these] murders . . . is not the central motivating factor for the killer, but merely an instrument used to dominate, control, and destroy the victim" (p. 30). However, genital contact or ejaculation is not necessary for sexual satisfaction, a conclusion held widely for many years by authorities on sexual behavior (e.g., 16,17). In fact, even in normal sexual relations, genital involvement is not necessary to achieve sexual arousal. The act of kissing, for example, is sexually stimulating, but the mouth is not a genital organ; it is, rather, the opening to the digestive system. Certainly many other forms of sexual arousal (e.g., various fetishes) also have nothing to do with direct genital stimulation.

For compulsive-repetitive offenders, their antisocial behavior—be it killing, torture, molestation, firesetting, or rape—is eroticized and sexually gratifying.

Problems with Terminology

Since the early 1980s, the term "serial" has become the popular and accepted adjective for describing individuals who kill or rape in a repetitive fashion. The adjective is a good one because it describes what the offender is doing—specifically, killing, raping, molesting, or setting fires in a series. It is much easier to understand than the term "compulsive," which has several psychological meanings. For instance, compulsive has been used as a label for various forms of mental disorders, such as "compulsive personality" and "obsessive-compulsive neurotic." However, the individual with a compulsive personality or an obsessive-compulsive disorder is totally different from the compulsive-repetitive offender.

Although serial may be easier to understand than compulsive, it may not necessarily be the best adjective to describe repetitive offenders because it raises several notable problems in classification *(18)*. For example, individuals who kill a series of people for profit (e.g., contract killers) have different underlying motivations than do those who are driven to kill for sexual gratification. Similarly, the repetitive arsonist may set a series of fires, but his motivation may be anger, revenge, or perhaps profit through the collection of insurance money. Even the individual who "exposes" himself on various occasions may do so for purposes of group affiliation, such as when college students engage in "streaking." Moreover, the number of victims necessary for a person to qualify as a serial offender (e.g., *2,3,5*, or *10*) is totally arbitrary and usually has little to do with the drive to act out in a repetitive way. For example, the offender's intelligence, degree of planning, geographical mobility, postoffense conduct, type of victim, investigative problems encountered, as well as the uncontrollable variable of luck, all contribute to the total number of victims, some of whom may never be linked to the offender.

Thus, the serial nature of the crime often has more to do with circumstances outside the offender than with the underlying dynamics motivating his criminal conduct. If, for example, the BTK killer in Topeka, Kansas *(19)* had been apprehended after his first or second homicide, he would not have had the opportunity to kill 10 people. He would still have been the same individual with the same inner compulsion to kill; he just would not have been labeled a serial killer. Accordingly, of the two terms, compulsive describes more accurately than serial the offender's main motivating force—that is, an urge to act out.

COMPULSIVE-REPETITIVE HOMICIDAL OFFENDERS

Premodern Interest

The compulsive-repetitive sexually motivated murderer is by no means a modern phenomenon. Cases of compulsive-repetitive homicide, have been documented, for example, as far back as 15th century France, where Gilles de Rais *(20)* managed to kidnap, torture, sexually molest, and kill about 150 to 800 children during an 8-year period. Rais killed his victims after torturing, sodomizing, decapitating, and dismembering them. He sometimes dressed victims in fine clothes and had intercourse with the bodies while they were dying. At his trial it was disclosed that he kept the heads of those children he considered "particularly beautiful." One of Rais's underlings testified in court that Rais had taken more pleasure in seeing the body parts pulled from his victims and watching them die in a torturous manner than in having sex with them.

Because of the vicious nature of such acts—especially the seemingly gratuitous violence, including torture, cannibalism, dismemberment, and disembowelment—premodern people believed that a supernatural force, such as a vampire or werewolf (rather than a man), must have been responsible. The belief in lycanthropy—the idea that humans have the capacity to turn into wolves—was fairly widespread during the 16th century *(21)*. One offender, Gilles Garnier, who sexually attacked, murdered, cannibalized, and strangled many children, used lycanthropy—considered a valid medical phenomenon—as a defense at his 1573 trial *(21)*. Perhaps one of the most notorious premodern examples of a compulsive murderer was Jack the Ripper, who terrorized the Whitechapel section of London during the late 1880s *(22)*. He was called Jack the Ripper because he supposedly sent letters to the press proclaiming, "I am down on whores and shan't quit ripping them until I do get buckled." This offender, who killed between five and nine prostitutes, has never been definitively identified.

At the same time Jack the Ripper was active, Richard von Krafft-Ebing published the first scientific study of sexual deviation, including sexually motivated murder and other sexually motivated antisocial acts. His classic 1886 text, *Psychopathia Sexualis (23)*, had a major influence at the time and was referenced by all turn-of-the-century scholars including Freud *(16)*. A careful reading of Krafft-Ebing's book reveals that a great deal of what we currently know about the compulsive-repetitive offender was first described by him during the 19th century. For instance, Krafft-Ebing provided his theory of why such offenders were almost always male. He theorized that men have an inborn aggressive character that becomes excessively developed; they are essentially a throwback to primitive man, who used violence to obtain female partners for propagation. He also described how these offenders frequently lie, manipulate, and take trophies and souvenirs from the crime scene. He found them to use ligatures, torture their victims for prolonged periods of time, to have previously engaged in animal cruelty, and to target prostitutes, make frequent use of pornography, humiliate and degrade their victims, and engage in signature-like ritualistic behavior. Krafft-Ebing also found that such offenders frequently had wives and girlfriends, whom they did not harm, but the men found greater sexual satisfaction in murder than in their (nonaggressive) sexual relations.

Krafft-Ebing also pointed out the important relationship of fantasy, the compulsion to kill, and the sexual stimulation achieved by the violence. He described the case of an individual who knifed women in the genital region and ejaculated the instant he stabbed them. Here, Krafft-Ebing found the stabbing to be "an equivalent for coitus" (p. 73). He believed that the sexually stimulating aspect of the offender's behavior is primarily a feeling of power and control over the victim. "The idea that she might feel the power I had over her is what is sexually arousing' (p. 76)... [that] she is completely in his power... the impulse to complete subjugation of the woman" (p. 78).

Interest During the First Half of the 20th Century

During the early years of the 20th century, a number of compulsive-repetitive murder cases were reported and studied in substantial detail. Peter Kürten, who terrorized Düsseldorf, Germany during the 1920s *(24)* through murder, arson, assault, and rape, is a case in point. Kürten had sex with his sisters, engaged in sex with animals, and frequently watched his father rape his mother. After serving time in prison for assorted offenses (including committing his first murder at age 9), he attacked 29 people and killed several. For a period of 5 years Kürten's compulsion to kill was overwhelming; he attacked men, women, and children by knifing, choking, and cutting their throats. The varied behavioral patterns and large number of victims led the police to believe initially that the crimes were committed by more than one offender. Kürten was preoccupied with fire, burned down a number buildings, and experienced sexual excitement while watching the flames. He was also a vampire, gaining sexual gratification through drinking the blood of his victims.

Perhaps one of the most bizarre cases in the annals of crime is that of Albert Fish, who operated in New York during the 1920s *(25,26)*. Although he looked like a gentle grandfather, Fish was not only a compulsive murderer but a sadist, masochist, pedophile, and cannibal. One of his most heinous crimes was the abduction, murder, dismemberment, and cannibalization of a 12-year-old girl. The case remained unsolved for 6 years until Fish wrote a graphic letter to the victim's mother, describing how he killed the child. The police then traced the stationary the letter was written on to Fish. Prior to his execution, a radiograph of his abdominal area showed 24 sewing needles around his bladder that he had inserted to gain masochistic gratification.

During the 1940s, William Heirens—who had a fetish for female underwear and committed numerous home burglaries to obtain the object of his fetishistic desire—terrorized Chicago (27). On occasion, he would urinate and defecate on the premises, behavior typical of many fetish burglars (28). Heirens was suspected of having committed hundreds of burglaries before he was arrested for the murder of two adult women and the abduction of a 6-year-old girl; he had cut the girl into pieces and deposited the body parts in sewers and garbage cans around the Chicago area. The Heirens case is particularly instructive as it illustrates the strength of his underlying compulsion. For instance, he wrote, "Catch me before I kill more, I can't control myself" on the bathroom mirrors of his victims. Heirens also developed headaches and he sweated profusely when he attempted to contain the compulsion to kill: "I resisted for about two hours. I tore sheets out of the place and went into a sweat. I would take out plans and draw how to get into certain places. I would burn up the plans. Sometimes this helped" (29, p. 120).

Interest During the Modern Era

During the latter half of the 20th century a number of high profile cases generated additional psychological and psychiatric interest in the problem of the compulsive-repetitive offender. For example, Edward Gein (30)—on whom Alfred Hitchcock's main character in *Psycho* was based—dug up corpses from local cemeteries, killed and disemboweled women, fashioned soup bowls from victims' skulls, upholstered chairs with human skin, and collected female genitalia in a box. Gein told investigators that he enjoyed dressing up in a vest made of human skin. Amateur photographer Harvey Glatman (25), dubbed the "Lonely Hearts Killer," put ads in newspapers for "models" whom he then raped and murdered. Ted Bundy (31) became well known for his murder of about 40 women over a wide geographical area. One of the most widely known compulsive-repetitive offenders during this period was Albert DeSalvo, commonly called the Boston Strangler (32). DeSalvo began his career as a voyeur, progressed to sexual molestation and rape, and then, within an 18-month period, is alleged to have killed 13 women. He used a similar abduction technique in all his crimes. He would knock on potential victims' doors posing as a photographer or repairman. When he entered, he overpowered the women and molested, raped, or killed them.

During the late 1950s and 1960s there was some scientific interest in the study of the compulsive-repetitive offender (e.g., 33–36). Revitch (37) completed one of the first descriptive studies of 43 adult men and adolescent boys who attacked women, including 9 murderers. He found that 30 (69%) of these subjects had previously committed offenses, only 3 of which were overtly sexual; 12 of the 30 offenses (40%) were burglaries.

Ressler and colleagues *(5)* carried out the first systematic, large-scale, empirically based investigation of the sexually motivated murderer in coordination with the FBI. These investigators studied a nonrandom sample of 36 sexual murderers and described their personality traits and crime scene patterns. They looked into the offenders' childhoods, prior criminal acts, *modus operandi* (MOs), and techniques used to avoid apprehension. The authors noted, in particular, the importance of the offenders' sexual fantasies in connection with their crimes. "The fantasies reflect their actions based on their beliefs and patterns of reasoning. . . . These men murder because of the way they think" (p. 43).

Following this study, the technique of psychological profiling—which had been inspired 20 years earlier by Brussel *(38)*—was refined and used regularly by the FBI as an investigative aid. Profiling involves assessing the crime scene, specifically as to its level of organization (which reflects the level of offender planning) and then drawing a description of the unknown offender's personality and likely behavior patterns based on characteristics of offenders who have left similar crime scenes *(39)*. Hazelwood and Douglas *(40)* distinguished organized from disorganized crime scenes (i.e., those without much physical evidence and those with a lot of physical evidence) and linked these patterns to various personality traits and behavioral characteristics of offenders.

Experience has demonstrated, however, that the practice of psychological profiling is much more complicated than simply matching a list of crime scene indicators with corresponding personality and behavioral traits. Most crime scenes are neither highly organized nor highly disorganized; instead, they typically present a mixed picture *(9)*. Some investigators *(41)* have argued that the FBI approach to profiling is not "scientific" enough in that it relies too heavily on an investigator's experience rather than on empirical validation. Notwithstanding the lack of strong and consistent empirical support for profiling, however, researchers *(42)* have demonstrated some level of accuracy, particularly when the technique is used by profilers experienced in the process.

NONHOMICIDAL COMPULSIVE-REPETITIVE OFFENDERS

Traditional Sex Offenders

In addition to the compulsive-repetitive sexually motivated murderer, the traditional compulsive-repetitive sexual offender (i.e., one who commits sex offenses such as child molestation, exhibitionism, or rape) has also plagued society for centuries *(43)*. Sex offenders, as a group, have been researched extensively since the mid-1940s, with voluminous studies denoting their personality and behavioral characteristics as well as their response to various treatment approaches *(44–46)*. The general conclusion from the numerous studies is that sex offenders comprise a heterogeneous group who target different types of victims (children, adults), engage in different types of sexual behavior (molestation, sexual assault), come from all walks of life (including the clergy), and more than any other type of criminal, pose a high risk for repetition *(44,47)*.

The crimes of this group of offenders are considered particularly disturbing because they target society's most vulnerable individuals, specifically women and children. In the United States following World War II, special legislation was enacted—generally referred to as sexual-psychopath laws—to combat the problem. Because sexual offending was believed to be a result of specific psychological problems that could not be addressed in prison, specialized centers were created, staffed by mental health professionals, to provide treatment to these individuals. Those sex offenders who were deemed compulsive-repetitive and whose problems presumably stemmed from psychological conflicts were sent to these treatment centers, whereas those who committed sexual crimes as a result of situational factors were sent to prison.

Some states (such as New Jersey) required a special release process, above and beyond that of the parole board. A team of mental health specialists would evaluate the offender after a period of treatment; and only if he was deemed no longer a threat would there be a recommendation to the parole board for his release *(48)*. Over the years, however, particularly beginning in the 1980s, numerous sex offenders in the United States were released from treatment programs only to recommit the exact offense—often in the same fashion and targeting the same type of victim. These repeat offenders gained a great deal of public attention and outrage. Thus, the release of sex offenders became a political issue; and by the early 1990s many of the U.S. sex-offender programs, which were often free-standing facilities, were closed or moved to a section of the state penitentiary, where little use was made of mental health professionals' ability to provide therapy or predict recidivism.

During the early 1990s, the sexual-psychopath laws were again amended as a result, in large part, of the case of 7-year-old Megan Kanka, a New Jersey girl who was raped and murdered by a twice-convicted sex offender who was residing in her neighborhood. This case led to the Megan's Law amendment to the Jacob Weterling Act, which required that all states develop a registry of sex offenders who had targeted children. In addition, states must notify the communities of offenders' whereabouts. The type and method of notification vary widely among and within states, so not all sex offenders are handled similarly. Generally, their level of risk to reoffend is assessed by various subjective or objective measures, or both (e.g., *49*), and the community notification proceeds accordingly. Since these measures were taken, several high-profile cases in the United States of children who were murdered by released sex offenders have resulted in even further sexual-psychopath legislation; some of these laws totally bar sex offenders from living in certain communities.

Sexually Motivated Antisocial Acts

Another group of offenders also act out in a compulsive-repetitive fashion. While their antisocial acts are also sexually motivated, these are not traditional sex offenders. For example, Revitch *(50)* described burglaries that are sexually motivated. Schlesinger and Revitch *(51)* found a direct connection between sexually motivated burglary and sexual homicide with obvious investigative implications. Specifically, these researchers noted that if a woman was abducted or killed in her home, the chance that the offender had previously committed a burglary was about 77%, a finding that can easily narrow the field of unknown suspects. More recently, Schlesinger and colleagues *(52)* replicated this study and found a 63% likelihood that an offender who entered a victim's residence to abduct, rape, or kill her had been previously arrested for burglary.

Arson is another crime that, in many instances, is sexually motivated. Lewis and Yarnell *(53)* found the compulsive-repetitive firesetter (pyromaniac) to have "a sadistic drive sexually colored" (p. 437). This connection was also noted by Fras *(54)* years later. However, some investigators (e.g., *55*) have not found sexual motives in any of their repetitive firesetters. Such researchers seem to be looking for overt genitality, which is extremely rare. Instead, pyromaniacs' sexual motivation typically becomes apparent only after extensive contact with these offenders. Here, as noted above, the sexual dynamic is manifested in an eroticization of the feelings of power and control the offenders experience by setting fires.

CHARACTERISTICS OF COMPULSIVE-REPETITIVE OFFENDERS

Important Role of Fantasy

Common to all compulsive-repetitive sexually motivated offenders—but especially offenders who plan their crimes—is a rich fantasy life that leads to future acting out. Beres *(56)* defined fantasy as a "group of symbols synthesized into a unified story ... it may be a substitute for action or it may prepare the way for later action" (p. 328). In their comprehensive review of the literature on sexual fantasy, Leitenberg and Henning *(57)* found that sexual fantasies, commonly experienced by both men and women, fall into four general categories: conventional heterosexual imagery; scenes involving sexual power and irresistibility; images of varied settings, practices, and positions; and images of submission or dominance in which some level of physical force is involved or implied. Deviant sexual fantasies involving force or abnormal sexual stimulation play a significant role in sexually motivated crimes. The importance of fantasy in sexual crimes was stressed by Hazelwood and Warren *(58)*, who found that "fantasy is the link between the underlying motivations for sexual assaults and the behavior exhibited during the crime" (p. 137).

Not everyone who has deviant fantasies commits a sexually motivated offense. In fact, a large proportion of the noncriminal and nonpsychiatric population also report deviant sexual fantasies, including homicidal fantasies *(59,60)*, but do not act on them. For instance, Grendliner and Byrne *(61)* found that 54% of men who never committed a sexual assault fantasized about having forced sex with a partner. Briere and Runtz *(62)* found that 21% of male undergraduate students acknowledged an abnormal sexual attraction to children, and 9% admitted to having had specific sexual fantasies about children; however, all these individuals denied acting on their fantasies. Similarly, Crepault and Couture *(63)* reported that 61% of their nonoffender adult male sample had fantasies in which they "sexually initiated" a young girl; 33% fantasized raping a woman; 12% fantasized being humiliated; and 5% fantasized having sex with an animal. None of these men acted out their fantasies.

Although not all individuals who have deviant sexual fantasies act out, many do. In their study of the relationship between sadistic fantasy and criminally sadistic behavior, MacCulloch and colleagues *(64)* found that 81% of their subjects committed sadistic crimes as an outgrowth of recurring sadistic masturbatory fantasies. However, these authors also recognized that not all individuals who harbor such fantasies ultimately act out. The main problem, the authors acknowledged, is the inability to distinguish the critical features differentiating these two groups. Several other investigators *(65,66)* have found that sexual crimes such as rape and child molestation have multiple causes, with deviant sexual fantasy being just one.

Compulsion to Act

If deviant sexual fantasies are not sufficient for determining whether an individual has committed a crime, the question then arises as to why some individuals act on their disturbed fantasies and others do not. Revitch and Schlesinger *(6,7)* concluded that those individuals who act out their fantasies do so because of an inner compulsion. In many cases, the compulsion is so strong that an attempt to resist it results in anxiety and somatic manifestations. Although an offender can describe his fantasies simply by reporting his thoughts, a compulsion is more abstract and difficult to explain. Offenders, therefore, often do not attempt a description of an inner drive to act out, and many examiners also overlook the importance of the underlying compulsion when they evaluate such subjects. Schlesinger *(9)* concluded that a tension state develops as a consequence of intense fantasies and results in a compulsion to act, often criminally. Following the act, the offender returns to his premorbid state, and the cycle repeats itself; the result is multiple (or serial) offenses, committed particularly by those who plan their crimes.

Meloy *(67)* attempted to determine the factors that contribute to the behavioral acting out of deviant sexual fantasies. He proposed a "structuring" of sexual fantasy that provides the offender with "certain positive reinforcements prior to, or between his [crimes], which would reset with the high arousal of the actual [sexual crime] and would have less propensity to extinguish over time" (p. 9). In fact, in addition to a behavioral-psychodynamic component, Meloy *(67)* argues there may also be a physiological ingredient. A neurobiological substrate underlying compulsive-repetitive offenses was first theorized by Krafft-Ebing *(23)* and was supported years later by MacLean *(68)*, who, in cases of primate aggression, pointed to an anatomical interconnection between sex and violence. Miller *(69)* has argued that an abnormality in the temporal lobe limbic mechanism is the foundation for the "driven quality" of the compulsive offender's urge to act.

IMPORTANCE OF PLANNING WITH COMPULSIVE-REPETITIVE OFFENDERS

Compulsive-repetitive offenders of all types (i.e., murderers, traditional sex offenders, and those who commit other sexually motivated antisocial acts) can be envisioned as falling on a hypothetical spectrum. On one end are those who plan their crimes in detail and release their compulsion with such care that they are often not apprehended for long periods of time. On the other end are those individuals who act out their inner compulsion in an unplanned, impulsive, spontaneous fashion. Because the latter group of offenders leave a great deal of evidence at the crime scene, they are often arrested after their first or second offense. In between these extremes lie the majority of compulsive offenders, who exhibit a mixture of both planning and spontaneity in their criminal conduct.

Personality as an Intervening Variable

Whether an offense is planned or spontaneous is not a result of the offender's fantasies or even his compulsion to act out; rather, it is a result primarily of his personality. Personality is thus an intervening variable between an offender's inner life and the way the crime is committed *(9)*. People who have reasonably intact personalities, with little overt disturbance, direct their lives in an orderly fashion. When such individuals commit crimes, they are likely to do so with some degree of planning and logic. For example, if such an individual has a compulsion to kill, he is likely to plan the homicide in an orderly way. Compulsive-repetitive offenders who commit planned crimes typically have psychopathic, sociopathic, narcissistic, antisocial, and other personality disorders that do not disorganize their thinking and behavior. They may be manipulative and deceptive, but they are not distracted by overt psychopathological symptoms (e.g., hallucinations and delusions) that interfere with the ability to behave in a methodical fashion.

Conversely, compulsive-repetitive offenders who act in an unplanned, impulsive, spontaneous fashion do not do so because of different types of fantasies or a different type of inner compulsion to act out. Instead, they have more overt disturbance, usually falling within the borderline, schizotypal, or schizoid spectrum of personality disorders, which results in a decreased ability to carefully plan. Individuals with these disorders do not necessarily act out spontaneously all the time; however, to a large degree, they do lack the controls necessary to contain their behavior. Thus, when their fantasies build to a point where the compulsion becomes overbearing, they may act out in an impulsive, high-risk manner that is likely to get them apprehended. Such offenders are distracted by their symptoms and lack the inner resources necessary to plan much of their behavior, including their criminal behavior.

Sometimes compulsive-repetitive offenders who do not plan are profoundly mentally ill, suffering from schizophrenia. When these individuals have an underlying compulsion to act out, they do so in a disorganized, spontaneous fashion, primarily because the severe symptoms of their mental illness makes planning impossible for them. An exception to this rule is found in the paranoid form of schizophrenia because here the psychopathological symptoms do not disorganize the underlying character structure, and the individual is able to act in a highly planned way. In addition, individuals with reasonably intact personalities can also act in an impulsive manner if they have an impulse-control disorder or if they are under the influence of substances. Bradford and colleagues *(70)* commented on the well known disinhibiting effects of substances and their relation to criminal behavior.

Thus, the compulsive offender's personality (or mental illness) does not cause him to commit his crimes; the drive to commit an offense is a result of an inner compulsion fueled by the offender's fantasy life. The offender's personality (or psychopathology) simply shapes and influences how the compulsion is carried out. Because planning is often necessary to elude law enforcement, it is easy to see why many compulsive-repetitive offenders with multiple victims (i.e., serial offenders) usually do not have major psychiatric illnesses that result in disorganized thinking. Compulsive-repetitive offenders with a major mental disorder that results in thought disorganization are usually unable to plan their crimes; their apprehension is thus much quicker, and they have fewer victims.

Behavior Patterns of Those Who Plan Their Crimes

Compulsive-repetitive offenders who plan their crimes often engage in ritualistic behavior at the crime scene; this behavior is referred to as personation or signature: "The offender often invests intimate meaning into the [crime] scene in the form of body positioning, mutilation, items left, or other symbolic gestures" (*71*, p. 354). Such repetitive ritualistic acts, which often serve as the offender's "calling card" (*72,73*), have little to do with the perpetration of the offense itself; instead, they are an outgrowth of the offender's longstanding deviant fantasies. The purpose of the ritualistic behavior is to provide psychosexual gratification, which the offense itself (e.g., homicide, rape, molestation) does not allow the perpetrator to achieve. Hazelwood and Warren (*74*) noted that "a pervasive and defining fantasy life and a carefully developed and executed set of crime scene behaviors" (p. 267) are outgrowths of the imaginations of individuals who engage in ritualistic crimes.

Behavior Patterns of Those Who Do Not Plan Their Crimes

Hazelwood and Warren (*74*) also describe the impulsive offender as someone who "invests little or no planning in his crimes. Instead, he acts impulsively, takes little or no measures to protect his identity, and is seemingly oblivious to the risk involved in committing the crimes" (p. 270). These researchers found impulsive offenders' fantasies to be as undifferentiated as their behavior: Such individuals are generally unaware of the fantasies underlying their actions; and if they do describe their fantasies, they typically report them in simplistic and concrete terms, usually involving simple victim characteristics and demographics. If such an offender has a pornography collection, according to Hazelwood and Warren, it usually lacks a specific theme, as his fantasies are as undifferentiated as the pornography he reads. Impulsive offenders who do not plan their crimes do not usually seek out a particular type of victim because any victim will do. Adolescents and very young adults—whose development is not yet complete—typically commit unplanned crimes, behaving in a spontaneous, impulsive fashion. Myers and Blashfield *(75)* and Myers *(76)* conducted extensive studies of adolescents who committed sexual murders. These researchers found that juvenile offenders were typically behaviorally disorganized, and their crimes were impulsive, unplanned, or poorly planned, occurred in their own neighborhoods, and involved known (typically older) victims.

TREATMENT AND INTERVENTION

Since the 1950s, traditional sex offenders have been exposed to a variety of treatments, the effectiveness of which is questionable. For instance, Grossman and colleagues *(77)* found that many studies purporting to measure the success of treating traditional sex offenders were flawed. They did note, however, that the various treatment approaches seemed to decrease future offending to some extent with some individuals, but one could not rely on the results of the treatments. Over the years, various treatment modalities have been employed, including individual and group therapy, aversion therapy, covert sensitization, masturbatory reconditioning, cognitive restructuring, relapse prevention, hormonal therapies, castration, and even surgical intervention to remove brain centers connected with sexual arousal *(77)*. Depending on the offender's motivation, level of deviance, and level of accompanying antisocial thinking, some of these treatments seem to have some benefit. However, none of these therapies alter sexual arousal patterns; rather, they help offenders identify triggers for acting out and teach them how to manage such stress.

The psychotherapeutic treatment of the compulsive-repetitive murderer or potential murderer—including compulsive-repetitive offenders who have engaged in other sexually motivated antisocial acts—remains virtually unstudied. These individuals do not go to a treatment center; instead, they are incarcerated in prison, where treatment is sporadic if available at all. Other individuals who have a potential to commit a compulsive homicide or sexually motivated antisocial act *(10)*, and who display some behavioral indicators (e.g., killing cats, firesetting, unprovoked assaults on females), are often hospitalized usually out of desperation or lack of a more acceptable immediate alternative. These hospitalizations are typically brief and unproductive. In fact, when the treatment staff at the hospital confront such an individual, they are not sure what they are treating, as there is no overt psychosis and often no behavioral display while the person is in the hospital unit. If potential offenders do present with a psychosis (which is rather rare) or, more often, anxiety, depression, or other symptoms, they are treated with medication, discharged, and referred for outpatient psychotherapy.

However, outpatient psychotherapy of the potential compulsive-repetitive offender is itself problematic. In particular, many therapists refuse to treat violent or potentially violent individuals on an outpatient basis because of liability concerns, stemming in part from cases such as Tarasoff v. Regents *(78)*. As a result, "legal standards that were developed to protect citizens, in actuality may result in less protection, because patients are again being shunned by practitioners due to the fear of legal entanglements" *(79,* p. 177).

Specialized forensic centers are desperately needed to provide evaluation and treatment of these pathological offenders and potential offenders. These centers should focus on research, study, and teaching and should be connected to medical schools and graduate schools of psychology and criminology. Such a model would provide an excellent opportunity for practitioners to gain clinical experience with this population of offenders and potential offenders, as well as to engage in research and provision of training. Although the government devotes vast resources to the apprehension, legal disposition, and incarceration of such offenders, it expends relatively little on prevention, treatment, or scientific study of the problem. The proposed model would be one further step to protect society from a subgroup of dangerous individuals about whom we desperately need to learn more.

REFERENCES

1. Schlesinger, L. B., & Revitch, E. (Eds.) (1997). *Sexual Dynamics Of Anti-social Behavior* (2nd ed). Springfield, IL: Charles C Thomas.
2. Grubin, D. (1994). Sexual murder. *British Journal of Psychiatry*, 165, 624–629.
3. Lunde, D. T. (1976). *Murder And Madness*. San Francisco: San Francisco Book Co.
4. Myers, W. C., Reccoppa, L., Burton, K., & McElroy, R. (1993). Malignant sex and aggression: an overview of serial sexual homicide. *Bulletin of the American Academy of Psychiatry and Law*, 21, 435–451.
5. Ressler, R. K., Burgess, A. W., & Douglas, J. E. (1988). *Sexual Homicide: Patterns and Motives*. New York: Free Press.
6. Revitch, E., & Schlesinger, L. B. (1981). *Psychopathology of Homicide*. Springfield, IL: Charles C Thomas.
7. Revitch, E., & Schlesinger, L. B. (1989). *Sex Murder and Sex Aggression*. Springfield, IL: Charles C Thomas.
8. Warren, J., Hazelwood, R. R., & Dietz, P. E. (1996). The sexually sadistic serial killer. *Journal of Forensic Sciences*, 41, 970–974.

9. Schlesinger, L. B. (2004). *Sexual Murder: Catathymic and Compulsive Homicides.* Boca Raton, FL: CRC Press.
10. Schlesinger, L. B. (2001). The potential sex murderer: ominous signs, risk assessment. *Journal of Threat Assessment,* 1, 47–72.
11. Egger, S. A. (1990). *Serial Murder: An Elusive Phenomenon.* Westport, CT: Praeger.
12. Levin, J., & Fox, J. A. (1985). *Mass Murder.* New York: Plenum.
13. Storr, A. (1972). *Human Destructiveness.* New York: Basic Books.
14. West, D. J. (1987). *Sexual Crimes and Confrontation: a Study of Victims and Offenders.* Brookfield, VT: Gower.
15. Egger, S. A. (2002). *The Killers Among Us* (2nd ed.). New York: Prentice Hall.
16. Freud, S. (1961). Three essays on the theory of sexuality. In: Strachey, J. (Ed. & Trans.), *The Standard Edition of the Complete Psychological Works of Sigmund Freud* (Vol. 7, pp. 130–243). London: Hogarth Press (original work published 1905).
17. Socarides, C. W. (1988). *The Preoedipal Origin and Psychoanalytic Therapy of Sexual Perversions.* New York: International Universities Press.
18. Schlesinger, L. B. (2004). Classification of antisocial behavior for prognostic purposes: study the motivation, not the crime. *Journal of Psychiatry & Law,* 32, 191–219.
19. Beattie, R. (2005). *Nightmare in Wichita.* New York: Penguin Books.
20. Benedetti, J. (1972). *Gilles De Rais.* New York: Stein & Day.
21. Hill, D., & Williams, P. (1967). *The Supernatural.* New York: Signet.
22. Begg, P., Fido, M., & Skinner, K. (1991). *Jack the Ripper A-Z.* London: Headline.
23. Von Krafft-Ebing, R. (1886). *Psychopathia Sexualis* (C. G. Chaddock, Trans.). Philadelphia: F. A. Davis.
24. Wilson, C., & Pitman, P. (1962). *Encyclopedia of Murder.* New York: Putnam.
25. Nash, J. R. (1973). *Bloodletters and Badmen: A Narrative Encyclopedia of American Criminals.* New York: Evans.
26. Schechter, H. (1990). *Deranged.* New York: Pocket Books.
27. Freeman, L. (1956). *Catch Me Before I Kill More.* New York: Pocket Books.
28. Schlesinger, L. B. (2000). Serial burglary: a spectrum of behaviors, motives, and dynamics. In: Schlesinger, L. B. (Ed.), *Serial Offenders: Current Thought, Recent Findings* (pp. 187–206). Boca Raton, FL: CRC Press.
29. Kennedy, F., Hoffman, H., & Haines, W. A. (1947). A study of William Heirens. *American Journal of Psychiatry,* 104, 113–121.
30. Schechter, H. (1989). *Deviant.* New York: Pocket Books.
31. Rule, A. (1988). *The Stranger Beside Me.* New York: Signet.
32. Rae, G. W. (1967). *Confessions of the Boston Strangler.* New York: Pyramid Press.
33. Guttmacher, M. S. (1960). *The Mind of the Murderer.* New York: Farrar, Straus & Cudahy.
34. Brittain, R. P. (1970). The sadistic murderer. *Medicine, Science, and Law,* 10, 198–207.

35. Bromberg, W. (1961). *The Mold of Murder: A Psychiatric Study of Homicide*. New York: Grune & Stratton.
36. Revitch, E. (1957). Sex murder and sex aggression. *Journal of the Medical Society of New Jersey*, 54, 519–524.
37. Revitch, E. (1965). Sex murder and the potential sex murderer. *Diseases of the Nervous System*, 26, 640–648.
38. Brussel, J. S. (1968). *Casebook of a Crime Psychiatrist*. New York: Grove Press.
39. Ressler, R. K., Burgess, A. W., Douglas, J. E., Hartman, C. R., & D'Agostino, R. B. (1986). Sexual killers and their victims: identifying patterns through crime scene analysis. *Journal of Interpersonal Violence*, 1, 288–308.
40. Hazelwood, R. R., & Douglas, J. E. (1980). The lust murderer. *FBI Law Enforcement Bulletin*, 49, 1–5.
41. Canter, D., Alison, L. J., Alison, E., & Wentink, N. (2004). The organized/ disorganized typology of serial murder: myth or model? *Psychology, Public Policy and Law*, 10, 293–320.
42. Pinizzotto, A. J., & Finkel, N. J. (1990). Criminal personality profiling: an outcome and process study. *Law and Human Behavior*, 14, 215–233.
43. Brancale, R., Ellis, A., & Doorbar, R. (1952). Psychiatric and psychological investigation of convicted sex offenders. *American Journal of Psychiatry*, 102, 17–21.
44. Schlesinger, L. B. (Ed.) (2000). *Serial Offenders: Current Thought, Recent Findings*. Boca Raton, FL: CRC Press.
45. Apfelberg, B. (1944). A psychiatric study of 250 sex offenders. *American Journal of Psychiatry*, 100, 762–773.
46. Araji, S. K. (2000). Child sexual abusers: a review and update. In: Schlesinger, L. B. (Ed.), *Serial Offenders: Current Thought, Recent Findings* (pp. 23–50). Boca Raton, FL: CRC Press.
47. Abel, G. G., Becker, J. V., Cunningham-Rathner, N., Rouleau, J. L., & Murphy, W. O. (1987). Self-reported sex crimes of non-incarcerated paraphilias. *Journal of Interpersonal Violence*, 2, 3–25.
48. Vuocolo, A. B. (1969). *The Repetitive Sex Offender*. Menlo Park, NJ: Quality Printing.
49. Witt, P. H., Del Russo, J., Oppenheim, J., & Ferguson, G. (1996). Sex offender risk assessment and the law. *Journal of Psychiatry & Law*, Fall, 343–377.
50. Revitch, E. (1978). Sexually motivated burglaries. *Bulletin of the American Academy of Psychiatry and Law*, 6, 277–283.
51. Schlesinger, L. B., & Revitch, E. (1999). Sexual burglaries and sexual homicide: clinical, forensic, and investigative considerations. *Journal of the American Academy of Psychiatry and Law*, 27, 227–238.
52. Schlesinger, L. B., Pinizzotto, A., & Pakhomou, S. (2004). Burglary and sexually motivated homicide. *Sex Offender Law Report*, 5, 21–23.
53. Lewis, N.D.C., & Yarnell, H. (1951). *Pyromania (Pathological Firesetting)*. Nervous and Mental Disease Monographs, No. 82. New York: Collidge Foundation.
54. Fras, I. (1997). Firesetting (pyromania) and its relationship to sexuality. In: Schlesinger, L. B., & Revitch, E. (Eds.). *Sexual Dynamics of Anti-social Behavior* (2nd ed., pp. 188–202). Springfield, IL: Charles C Thomas.

55. Geller, J., Erlen, J., & Pinkus, L. (1986). A historical appraisal of America's experience with "pyromania": a diagnosis in search of a disorder. *International Journal of Law and Psychiatry*, 9, 201–229.

56. Beres, D. (1960). Perception, imagination, and reality. *International Journal of Psychoanalysis*, 41, 327–334.

57. Leitenberg, H., & Henning, K. (1995). Sexual fantasy. *Psychological Bulletin*, 117, 469–496.

58. Hazelwood, R. R., & Warren, J. I. (1995). The relevance of fantasy in serial sexual crime investigation. In: Hazelwood, R. R., & Burgess, A. W. (Eds.), *Practical Aspects of Rape Investigation* (2nd ed., pp. 127–138). Boca Raton, FL: CRC Press.

59. Kendrick, D. T., & Sheets, V. (1993). Homicidal fantasies. *Etiology and Sociobiology*, 14, 231–246.

60. Crabb, P. B. (2000). The material culture of homicide fantasies. *Aggressive Behavior*, 26, 225–234.

61. Grendliner, V., & Byrne, D. (1995). Coercive sexual fantasies of college men as predictors of self-reported likelihood to rape and overt sexual aggression. *Journal of Sex Research*, 23, 1–11.

62. Briere, J., & Runtz, M. (1989). University males' sexual interest in children: predicting potential indices of pedophilia in a non-forensic sample. *Child Abuse and Neglect*, 13, 65–67.

63. Crepault, C., & Couture, M. (1980). Mens' erotic fantasies. *Archives of Sexual Behavior*, 9, 565–581.

64. MacCulloch, M. C., Snowden, P. J., Wood, P., & Mills, H. E. (1983). Sadistic fantasy, sadistic behavior, and offending. *British Journal of Psychiatry*, 143, 20–29.

65. Finkelhor, D., & Araji, S. (1986). Explanations of pedophilia: a four factor model. *Journal of Sex Research*, 22, 145–161.

66. Marshall, W. L., Laws, D. R., & Barbaree, H. E. (1990). *Handbook of Sexual Assault: Issues, Theories and Treatment of the Offender*. New York: Plenum.

67. Meloy, J. R. (2000). The nature and dynamics of sexual homicide: an integrative review. *Aggression and Violent Behavior*, 5, 1–22.

68. MacLean, P. D. (1962). New findings relevant to the evolution of psycho-sexual functions of the brain. *Journal of Nervous and Mental Disease*, 135, 289–301.

69. Miller, L. (2000). The predator's brain: neuropsychodynamics of serial killing. In: Schlesinger, L. B. (Ed.), *Serial Offenders: Current Thought, Recent Findings* (pp. 135–166). Boca Raton, FL: CRC Press.

70. Bradford, J., Greenberg, D. M., & Motayne, G. G. (1992). Substance abuse and criminal behavior. *Psychiatric Clinics of North America*, 15, 605–622.

71. Douglas, J. E., Burgess, A. W., Burgess, A. G., & Ressler, R.K. (1992). *Crime Classification Manual*. San Francisco: Jossey-Bass.

72. Keppel, R. D. (1997). *Signature Killers: Interpreting the Calling Cards of the Serial Murderer*. New York: Pocket Books.

73. Keppel, R. D. (2000). Investigation of the serial offender: linking cases through M.O. and signature. In: Schlesinger, L. B. (Ed.), *Serial Offenders: Current Thought, Recent Findings* (pp. 121–134). Boca Raton, FL: CRC Press.

74. Hazelwood, R. R., & Warren, J. I. (2000). The sexually violent offender: impulsive or ritualistic? *Aggression and Violent Behavior*, 5, 267–279.
75. Myers, W. C., & Blashfield, R. (1997). Psychopathology and personality in juvenile sexual homicide offenders. *Journal of the American Academy of Psychiatry and Law*, 25, 497–508.
76. Myers, W. C. (2002). *Juvenile Sexual Homicide*. San Diego: Academic Press.
77. Grossman, L. S., Martis, B., & Fichtner, C. G. (1999). Are sex offenders treatable? A research review. *Psychiatric Services*, 50, 349–361.
78. Tarasoff v. Regents of the University of California. 17 Cal. 3d 425, 551 P.2d 334, 131 Cal. Rpt. 14 (1976).
79. Schlesinger, L. B., & Revitch, E. (1990). Outpatient treatment of the sex murderer and potential sex murderer. *Journal of Offender Counseling, Services, and Rehabilitation*, 15, 163–178.

Chapter 3

Serial Juvenile Sex Offenders and Their Offenses

Jessica Woodhams, Clive Hollin, and Ray Bull

Abstract

In light of the dearth of literature specifically on serial juvenile sex offenders, this chapter considers the findings of research with juvenile sex offenders and juvenile repeat sex offenders with respect to what this might tell us about juvenile serial sex offending and its investigation. The chapter reports on different types of juvenile sex offenders: those that offend against younger children and those that offend against their peers or adults; those that assault as a group compared to those who assault alone; and juvenile sex offenders who target strangers as victims, a group that may require particular attention from police. Having reviewed this literature, the chapter discusses the implications of research on behavioral consistency and what it may mean for the successful application of investigative techniques (e.g., offender profiling and case linkage) to serial juvenile sexual crime. Finally, the offenses of a small sample of serial juvenile sex offenders are analyzed. The characteristics of the offenders, the victims, and the offenses are described; and the degree of behavioral consistency seen in the offending of this group is reported.

INTRODUCTION

Juveniles commit a sizable minority of sexual offenses each year. For example, Ayres and colleagues *(1)* analyzed the arrests for sexual offenses during 2000–2002 in England and Wales and found that male juveniles (aged under 18 years) were suspected and had been arrested for 7500 cases, approximately 16% of all sexual offenses for these two years. According to the

From: *Serial Murder and the Psychology of Violent Crimes*
Edited by: R. N. Kocsis © Humana Press, Totowa, NJ

FBI's National Incident-Based Reporting System, in the United States during 1991–1996, juveniles (7–17 years of age) were responsible for 23.2% of all sexual assaults committed *(2)*.

The investigation of juvenile sexual crime therefore requires considerable police resources. Some juvenile sex offenders are what can be called serial offenders in that they commit more than one sexual crime against different victims. The rationale behind the policy of intelligence-led policing is to focus limited police resources on the small number of offenders who commit most of the crimes *(3)*. Serial juvenile sex offenders would therefore be a policing priority.

Although serial juvenile sex offenders might be a policing priority, surprisingly little has been written about these young people. Instead, the literature has focused on juvenile sex offenders in general and recidivist juvenile sex offenders. A juvenile is a recidivist if he or she sexually re-offended after some form of official action (e.g., conviction, incarceration). At first glance, it might be assumed that juveniles who sexually re-offend could be considered the same group as serial juvenile sex offenders. However, there are some subtle differences between these two groups. A juvenile could be classed as a recidivist if he or she had committed a new sexual crime against the *same* victim, whereas to be labeled a serial juvenile sex offender the juvenile must commit a new sexual crime against a *different* victim.

Although these subtle differences exist between recidivists and serial sex offenders, in the absence of literature on serial juvenile sex offenders, some findings from the literature on recidivists may be relevant. This chapter attempts to address the dearth of literature on serial juvenile sex offenders by drawing together what is known about juvenile sex offenders in general, and what has been written about repeat juvenile sex offenders that would be of interest to police investigators of juvenile serial sexual crime. In addition, preliminary findings are reported of a study analyzing the characteristics and offending behavior of a small sample of serial juvenile sex offenders. Much of the research on juvenile sex offenders has sampled males only, and this is reflected in the content of this chapter.

JUVENILE SEX OFFENDERS

The victims of juvenile sex offenders are varied. Although they assault known and unknown victims ranging from small children to the elderly *(4)*, it is believed that typically juveniles sexually assault a known victim who is younger than themselves *(5,6)*. Whether this is the case generally or whether this conclusion results from much of the research literature focusing on apprehended juveniles is unclear.

Official statistics suggest that most juvenile sex offenders are older teenagers *(1,2)*. However, some juveniles begin their sex offending at a young age, with some as young as 6 years old being reported in research papers *(4)*. It is important to remember that official statistics can mask the real age of onset as juveniles are not captured by such statistics unless they are above the age of criminal responsibility.

With regard to the type of sexual assaults perpetrated, juvenile sex offenders do not seem to differ from their adult counterparts *(5)*. The types of sexual offense these young people commit include noncontact offenses, such as exhibitionism; and they range to more serious penetrative offenses, such as rape *(7)*. Typically, juvenile sex offenders are more likely to engage in digital penetration, whereas adult sex offenders engage in anal, oral, and vaginal penetration *(6)*. Adults' greater sexual knowledge and experience may explain such findings. What is concerning however, is the greater use of force by juvenile sex offenders in comparison to that used by adults *(6)*. Långström and Lindblad *(4)* reported that 71% of their juvenile sex offenders had used physical violence in their offense, and 14% had used a weapon. Although these figures for violence and weapon use are concerning, it is important to note that juvenile sex offenders are a heterogeneous group. This heterogeneity is not only in their choice of victim but in the way their offenses are committed. When investigating juvenile sex offending, this is an important point to bear in mind.

TYPES OF JUVENILE SEX OFFENDERS

Whether there are subtypes of juvenile sex offenders who behave in different ways has been the focus of some research attention. This attention has tended to focus on juveniles who assault children (termed child molesters) versus those who assault their peers or adults (termed sexual assaulters), and group offenders versus lone offenders. In addition, some research *(8,9)* has been conducted on a particular subgroup of juvenile sex offenders that is of particular interest to investigators—those who assault strangers.

Juvenile Child Molesters Versus Sexual Assaulters

Past studies have tended to treat juvenile sex offenders as a homogeneous population. However, more recent research is indicating that juvenile child molesters are in some ways different from juvenile sexual assaulters *(10,11)*. Although most of the findings are more relevant to the clinical task of the assessment and treatment of juvenile sex offenders, some findings are of interest to the police investigator, and they are the current focus.

There appears to be an association between victim age and the victim-offender relationship. Juveniles targeting younger children are more likely to be an acquaintance or family member *(12,13)*. In contrast, juveniles who target older females are more likely to be acquaintances or strangers to their victims *(10)*. Juvenile child abusers are reported as more likely to assault male victims, although they do not offend against males exclusively *(10)*.

As well as their victims differing, there appears to be variation in the way juvenile child abusers and juvenile sexual assaulters commit their crimes. Sexual assaulters are likely to commit their offenses outdoors or in a public place *(12,13)*, which is probably a product of the victim-offender relationship. Sexual assaulters more often physically assault their victims during the commission of the offense and use a weapon *(10,12–14)*. This pattern is likely, at least in part, to be a result of the level of victim resistance *(10)* and of the setting in which the crime occurs. Victims of attacks by sexual assaulters therefore potentially suffer greater injury. Because sexual assaulters are more likely to offend against strangers, this group requires greater investigative effort because their identity is more often unknown.

Group Offenders and Lone Offenders

Group sexual offending is predominantly a juvenile or adolescent crime *(15)*. Some research studies have suggested that two-thirds of juvenile sexual offenses are committed by groups (Boelrijk, 1997, as cited in *16*). Research has begun consistently to demonstrate differences in the way group sex offenders behave compared to lone sex offenders. This research relates to both adults and juveniles *(8,17,18)*. In general, group sexual offenders are more violent and commit more serious sexual assaults (e.g., penetrative) and so their offenses may therefore warrant investigative priority because of their greater severity.

As well as observing differences in behavior, researchers have observed differences in group versus lone offenders' characteristics. Bijleveld and Hendriks *(16)* reported lone offenders as significantly more neurotic, impulsive, and less sociable than group offenders. They were more likely to have experienced a history of sexual abuse themselves but, interestingly, had a more extensive sexual offending history than the group offenders. As a result of these differences, Bijleveld and Hendriks *(16)* considered group sex offenders to be less likely to continue re-offending. Therefore, it is difficult to recommend to the police which types of sexual offender should be prioritized. On the one hand, group sex offenses seem to hold greater potential for violence and more severe sexual assault; on the other hand, lone offenders appear more likely to re-offend, leaving the potential for a larger number of victims.

Juveniles Who Sexually Assault Strangers

The investigation of sexual assaults where the offender is unknown to the victim is a policing priority *(19)*. Research conducted in the United Kingdom found that juveniles were believed to be responsible for 14% of sexual offenses committed against unknown victims in a large metropolitan city during 1 year *(8)*. This is a notable proportion. In light of this finding, it is surprising that little has been written about this subgroup of juvenile sex offenders. One study conducted in the United Kingdom has investigated the offending behavior of this group *(8)*. This study sampled allegations of juvenile stranger sexual assault and therefore was not limited to apprehended offenders. The findings of this study are reported below.

In contrast to the assertion that juvenile sex offenders typically assault a victim younger than themselves *(5,6)*, this study found that most juvenile stranger sex offenders were believed by their victim to be younger than they were *(8)*. However, a similar offender age range was observed to those reported in studies of incarcerated offenders *(4)*—an age range of 6 to 17 years *(8)*. Most of the juvenile stranger sex offenders were older teenagers, as has been reported in official statistics of juvenile sex offending in general *(1,2)*. The sample committed contact and noncontact sexual offenses, with approximately 10% being penetrative attacks *(8)*. Violence was not as commonly used as has been suggested with apprehended samples *(4)*, with 14% of offenses involving the use of physical violence *(8)*.

The offenses committed by juvenile stranger sex offenders acting in groups were more serious than the offenses of those offenders acting alone. Group sexual offenses were more likely to be penetrative and were more likely to involve the use of physical violence against the victim *(8)*. Victim characteristics also were related to the seriousness of the offense, with younger victims being more likely to suffer penetrative attacks, although victim age did not relate to the level of violence used. Such findings again suggest that group stranger sex offenses could warrant becoming an investigative priority. With regard to crime prevention, interventions that better educate youngsters about the potential risk of sexual assault from strangers could be considered.

The heterogeneity of juvenile sex offenders has been recognized only relatively recently in the academic literature. This has implications for the assessment and treatment of offenders, but it also has implications for policing. The nature of the victim-offender relationship will undoubtedly influence the targeting of resources for investigation; however, the research also suggests that some types of juvenile sex offender pose a greater risk to the public than do others. The following section discusses what is known about juvenile sex offenders who have committed more than one sexual offense.

JUVENILE REPEAT SEX OFFENDERS

Although juvenile serial sex offenders have not been studied, research has investigated juveniles who continue their offending after official action, such as arrest or conviction. This group are termed recidivists or repeat offenders. Although they are not identical groups, the literature on repeat offenders is perhaps most comparable to serial sex offenders.

Not all juvenile sex offenders are repeat offenders. Rates of sexual re-offending range from 5% to 20% *(20–24)*, which are relatively low compared to rates of nonsexual re-offending, which can reach 47% *(23)*. The question should be raised as to how juvenile repeat sex offenders differ from juveniles that desist from sexual offending. Little has been written about the demographic characteristics of juvenile repeat sex offenders, their victims, or their offenses. However, some studies have been conducted that have had a more therapeutic focus and have sampled apprehended repeat juvenile sex offenders *(25–28)*. If it can be considered that these findings may have some application to serial offenders, some of the findings from these studies can be used to guide the investigator of serial juvenile sexual crime. Relevant findings are presented below from this perspective.

Prioritization of Offenses for Investigation

When faced with a number of sexual offenses that require investigation or crime analysis, there is currently little guidance available as to how these crimes should be prioritized. Some findings in the therapeutic literature suggest factors that could be helpful in this regard. A stranger victim-offender relationship has been consistently reported as a risk factor for juveniles sexually re-offending *(25–28)*. Offenders who use violence against their victims during the sexual assault are also reported to be more likely to re-offend *(26,28)*. Police investigators may therefore wish to prioritize stranger sexual assaults and violent sexual assaults for investigation because the literature suggests that a serial offender may be potentially responsible for these types of crime.

Crime analysts may also wish to prioritize violent sexual assaults for possible case linkage. This is a process that aims to identify crimes committed by the same offender through their behavioral similarity *(29)*. Case linkage is used for crimes where the offender's identity is unknown. If the analyst is faced with a violent sexual offense, he or she could surmise that it is likely that the offender has committed other sexual crimes and is a serial offender because violence within a sexual offense is associated with a propensity to re-offend. A number of police forces hold databases of solved and unsolved sexual crimes that can be searched by the analyst. If an offense includes violence toward the victim, the analyst can prioritize this crime for analysis on the basis that the database is likely to contain other crimes committed by the same offender.

Monitoring Known Juvenile Sex Offenders

A greater risk of sexual re-offending has been associated with a larger number of offenses *(28)*, suggesting that offenders with a longer history of sexual offending are more likely to continue offending. This finding has implications for the police's monitoring of juvenile sex offenders who are already known to them.

It is important to recognize that these implications are based on a small number of studies. It is also important to consider that the findings have been developed from samples of apprehended offenders. It is quite possible that apprehended repeat sex offenders differ from serial sex offenders who remain at large *(8)*; hence, these data should be examined with an appropriate level of caution. This issue is clearly an area for future research.

USE OF OFFENDER PROFILING AND CASE LINKAGE WITH JUVENILES

Police officers faced with investigating a series of sexually violent crimes may choose to request an offender profile or may request case linkage analysis. Offender profiling refers to the "Derivation of inferences about a criminal from aspects of the crime(s) he or she has committed" *(30, p. 23)*. In other words, the offender profiler reviews the way a criminal has behaved at the crime scene and based on this information makes predictions about the likely characteristics of that individual. The police investigator could use this information to narrow down his or her pool of suspects. As outlined above, case linkage involves "identifying behavioral similarities between offences that point to them being committed by the same perpetrator" *(29)*. In this way, crimes can be "linked" and investigated as a series rather than singularly, or evidence of similarity can be presented as similar fact evidence in legal proceedings *(31)*. Although offender profiling and case linkage have received academic attention and undergone investigation, neither appears to have been investigated from the perspective of their appropriateness for juvenile sexual crime.

The theoretical basis for both offender profiling and case linkage has its basis in personality psychology and research into behavioral consistency *(32)*. Offender profiling assumes a relation between offender characteristics and behavior, which has been termed the "homology assumption" *(33,34)*. To be able to make predictions about characteristics from behavior, the relation between the two must be stable over time. Both case linkage and offender profiling assume that criminals show consistency in the way they commit a type of crime (e.g., rape, robbery), which has been termed the "offender consistency hypothesis" *(35)*.

Several studies have investigated whether criminals commit their crimes in a consistent manner and the findings suggest a degree of consistency *(32)*. In relation to the consistency of sexual offending, three studies have investigated the consistency of adult sex offenders *(34,36,37)*. All three studies have shown that adult serial sex offenders commit their crimes in a relatively consistent manner. Grubin et al. *(36)* divided the offenders' behaviors into categories. Three of the categories were control behaviors (how the offender controlled the victim), escape behaviors (behaviors indicating the offenders' concerns about escaping), and sexual behaviors. Grubin et al. found that offenders showed greater consistency in control and escape behaviors than in sexual behaviors. It has been suggested that this greater consistency can be explained by the offender having more personal control over such behaviors, which are less dependent on the situation *(38)*. One study assessed the homology assumption of offender profiling with adult sexual crime *(34)*. This study found little support for this assumption.

Personality psychologists explain that when a situation is encountered features of the situation trigger a personality system, which consists of mental representations, goals, and expectations, which then determine the behavior that is produced *(39)*. For offender profilers to predict the characteristics of a criminal from their crime scene behavior and for crimes to be linked based on behavioral similarity, such internal systems would need to be relatively stable and fixed. However, researchers such as Mischel *(40)* have explained that these personality systems change during periods of personal development (e.g., childhood and adolescence) and that during such stages of development greater variation in behavior is therefore observed. This point raises the question as to whether case linkage and offender profiling would be successful with juveniles, who are likely to be going through a period of significant development. This possibility might be particularly the case for sexual crimes, where during adolescence knowledge of sexual acts and sexual maturation of the offender could well change offending behavior.

The authors of this chapter are not aware of any study that has assessed case linkage and offender profiling with juvenile offender populations; however, such research is underway at the University of Leicester, UK. In addition, some preliminary findings based on a small sample of serial juvenile sex offenders who assaulted other children are reported at the end of this chapter. Until more reliable findings are published, investigators of juvenile serial crime and practitioners of case linkage and offender profiling may wish to consider these preliminary findings in their work. Research is certainly needed in this field.

It is quite possible that case linkage and offender profiling will be successful with juvenile crime if we focus on only some types of crime scene behavior. For example, although not a study of criminal behavior, research by Shoda and colleagues *(41)* has demonstrated that children do show consistency in their aggressive behavior across situations that are psychologically similar. Based on such findings, it might be anticipated that the ways in which juvenile serial sex offenders control their victims would be a type of behavior in which they are relatively consistent.

PRELIMINARY FINDINGS ON SERIAL JUVENILE SEXUAL OFFENDING

Analyses have recently been conducted by the first author of this chapter on a small sample of serial juveniles who had sexually assaulted other children. The data presented below were obtained from Social Services records in the United Kingdom.

Offender Characteristics

Seven offenders were sampled who had committed a total of 16 offenses. All had committed their offenses on their own rather than as a group. Five offenders had committed two offenses, and two offenders had a series of three offenses. The offenders were all male and their ages at the time of the offense ($M = 11.81$, $SD = 2.43$) ranged from 6 to 15 years, an age range similar to those reported by Woodhams *(8)* and Långström and Lindblad *(4)*.

Victim Characteristics

The victims were of both sexes—half of the victims were male, and half were female. Within an individual offender's series, the sex of the victim varied for four offenders and was consistent for three offenders. The victims' ages ranged from 5 to 15 years ($M = 9.19$, $SD = 2.86$). In most cases ($n = 13$), the victim was younger than the offender by 1 to 8 years ($M = 3.25$, $SD = 2.14$). In one case the offender and victim were of the same age, and in two cases the offender was younger than the victim by 1 to 2 years. This sample clearly differs from other studies that have reported juveniles assaulting victims of a wider range of ages *(4)*. Rather than a preference for younger victims being a characteristic of serial juvenile sex offenders, it is possible that the findings presented here are an artifact of the data source being used (i.e., Social Services records). The female victims were younger (M = 8.13) than the male victims (M = 10.25), but this difference was not significant. Three of the victims could be considered vulnerable from the point of view that they had special educational needs.

The victims were all known to the offenders and therefore could be considered acquaintances, although the nature of the previous relationship varied. Some offenders knew their victim from school, or they were a family friend (n = 7). In relation to family relationships, victims were siblings (n = 5) or otherwise a member of the offender's extended family (n = 4).

Offense Characteristics

With regard to where the victim was approached, in four cases this could not be determined from the records. For the remainder, the victims were approached and assaulted in the same location. The most common location the offender approached the victim was either the victim's dwelling or a dwelling that the victim and offender shared (62.6%, n = 10). The types of offense location included outdoor locations (e.g., near a playground), the offender's dwelling, the victim's dwelling, or a shared dwelling, and also included indoor public places, such as public toilets. Typically, a con-type approach was used (87.5%, n = 14), where the offender "Gains access by winning the confidence of the victim and then betraying it" (42, p. 105). Within the current data set, a type of con approach emerged, one that would not generally be successful with adult victims. It involved the offender presenting the initial inappropriate behaviors to the naive child victim as a "game." Some offenders also showed their victims pornographic material prior to the offense. Both of these behaviors could be seen as an attempt by the offender to normalize the abusive behavior and desensitize the victim. In relation to offenses where the victims were children, the caretakers of the victim had been conned. In some cases, the offender gained access to their victims through babysitting. A surprise approach, which involved the offender ambushing the victim (43), was used in one offense (the offender hid in the victim's bedroom, overpowering the victim when the victim entered the room).

A range of sexual behaviors was recorded, ranging from relatively minor acts, such as kissing or fondling the victim, to digital or penile penetration of the victim. However, in relation to the seriousness of the offenses committed, all but one (93.7%) of the offenses involved penetration of some kind. This included both penetration of the victim by the offender and the victim being forced to penetrate the offender. This high incidence of penetration differs from the incidence reported in other studies (8) and may reflect the fact that the victims were children who could be easily overpowered. During 12 (75%) of the offenses only the victim was penetrated, whereas in 3 cases (18.8%), the victim was also forced to penetrate the offender. The latter offenses were committed by two different offenders and involved male victims. There were no significant differences in victim or offender age or in age gaps in relation to the occurrence on non-occurrence of penetration.

With regard to the use of physical violence, 25% ($n = 4$) of the cases did not involve violence at all. In 62.5% ($n = 10$) of offenses, physical violence was threatened but did not occur. Actual physical violence occurred in only 12.5% of offenses ($n = 2$). Victim or offender age was not significantly different in offenses when violence was used, threatened, or did not occur. When violence did occur, in one case it seemed to be related to increasing the offender's arousal. When threats of violence were made, they corresponded with the victims resisting the offender, or they occurred at the end of the offense and served the purpose of threatening the victim not to report what had occurred.

As well as using threats of or actual physical violence to control their victims, offenders used a range of other tactics. In one case the offender blocked the victim's exit from the room so that she could not escape him. Most victims were physically restrained by the offender, and some offenders used their hands to gag their victims. Some offenders also used bribery with their victims, offering them sweets to keep the "secret." One offender presented his behavior to his victim as normal in order to gain compliance. Several offenders ensured, before commencing the assault, that no adults were available to prevent the abuse. In another attempt to prevent abuse being reported, one offender reassured his victim that his behavior was normal. Alternative strategies to prevent reporting included threatening the victim's safety or using emotionally threats, for example, to "damage" the victim's reputation. Only one offender showed evidence of forensic awareness in using contraception when vaginally penetrating his victim; otherwise, no other forensic precautions were recorded.

Consistency of Sexual Offending Behavior

Even though this is a small sample, it is possible to investigate the degree of behavioral consistency shown by the offenders across their series. To determine this, a Jaccard's coefficient (used as a measure of behavioral consistency) was calculated for each pair of offenses in the sample committed by the same offender across 54 offense behaviors (identified from a content analysis of the offense accounts). Jaccard's coefficients can range from 0, indicating no consistency (similarity) to 1, indicating perfect consistency (similarity). A mean Jaccard's coefficient of 0.39 was calculated across all of the linked pairs. Thus, serial juvenile sex offenders do show a degree of behavioral consistency, although it is far from perfect. This figure is similar to the average Jaccard's coefficient reported by Mokros and Alison *(34)* for their sample of adult stranger rapists (0.41), although juveniles appear marginally less consistent than their adult counterparts. The Jaccard's coefficients for each of the pairs of offenses ranged from 0.05 to 0.83, indicating that some offenders were much more consistent than others. The relatively low overall degree of consistency may represent the development of the juveniles' personality systems, evolution of sexual fantasy, and sexual maturation. Alternatively, it could reflect the data source, as the information about each offense in the Social Services files was far less detailed than would typically be found in a victim police statement or interview. Thus, higher consistency rates might be found when victim accounts to the police are used, the usual source of information when conducting case linkage.

Albeit using different statistical methods, Grubin et al. *(36)* conducted research with adult stranger serial sex offenders and found that their sample showed greater consistency in control- and escape-type behaviors than in sexual behaviors. The 54 offense behaviors identified in the serial juvenile sex offender sample above were similarly categorized into control, escape, and sexual behaviors. The similarity scores for control, escape, and sexual behaviors were calculated separately using Jaccard's coefficients as above and compared to see which type of behavior showed the greatest consistency (similarity) across pairs of linked crimes. The mean Jaccard's coefficient for each behavioral domain can be seen in Table 1.

As shown in Table 1, the ordering of high to low similarity reported by Grubin et al. *(36)* is also reflected here. Control behaviors show greater consistency across linked crimes, followed by escape behaviors and then sexual behaviors. Great variation in the degree of consistency of offenders is clear in the ranges of Jaccard's coefficients between pairs in Table 1. Some offenders show perfect or near-perfect consistency whereas others exhibit no consistency at all.

Table 1
Descriptive Statistics for Jaccard's Coefficients for the Behavioral Domains of Control, Escape, and Sexual

Parameter	Control	Escape	Sexual
Mean*	0.51	0.36	0.31
SD	0.28	0.45	0.21
Range	0–1.00	0–1.00	0.07–0.80

*The distribution of Jaccard's coefficients was not significantly different from normal in all three cases as measured by a Kolmogorov-Smirnov test.

In relation to previous literature, the greater consistency observed in control behaviors is similar to that in the nonforensic study of children by Shoda et al. *(41)* and their finding of consistency in the use of aggression. With the current data set, aggressive behaviors such as threats and physical violence were located in the control domain. That sexual behaviors show least consistency is perhaps not surprising with this sample. Considering that adolescence is a period of sexual development and increasing sexual knowledge, it is perhaps not surprising that less consistency is seen in this domain; indeed, some linked offenses occurred 6 years apart.

Obviously, these findings relate to a small, select sample of serial juvenile sex offenders and hence cannot be generalized to other serial juvenile sex offenders. Research with larger, more representative samples of serial juvenile sex offenders is urgently needed. A research study is currently underway at the University of Leicester (UK) that is investigating victim, offender, and offense characteristics of a larger group of serial juvenile sex offenders who assaulted strangers. The data for this study are the victims' accounts to the police of the sexual crimes committed against them.

CONCLUSIONS

Serial juvenile sex offenders have received little research attention. This chapter has sought to draw together the literature on juvenile sex offenders in general and juvenile repeat sexual offenders with the aim of providing information that may be of use to investigators of serial juvenile sexual crime. The chapter has also reported some preliminary findings on a small sample of serial juvenile sex offenders who assaulted children known to them. In this sample, greater consistency in offending behavior was observed in the behaviors related to controlling the victim and escaping the scene than in other behaviors. Future studies are required to determine whether the degree of behavioral consistency shown by serial juvenile sex offenders is sufficient for their crimes to be accurately linked. That such a high proportion of juvenile sex offenses are committed by groups also suggests that researchers of case linkage must develop means of measuring similarity for group crimes.

Because juveniles show a propensity to commit serious sexual assaults— as seen by their penetrative nature and the use of physical violence and weapons—they certainly warrant investigative attention. Currently, there is little guidance that can be given to investigators of such crimes because of the relative dearth of literature on the subgroups of juvenile sex offenders who appear to warrant the greatest investigative effort. These groups are certainly research priorities for the future.

REFERENCES

1. Ayres, M., Perry, D., & Hayward, P. (2002). *Arrests for Notifiable Offenses and the Operation of Certain Police Powers Under PACE, England and Wales 2001/02.* London: Home Office.
2. Snyder, H. N. (2000). *Sexual Assault Of Young Children As Reported to Law Enforcement: Victim, Incident, and Offender Characteristics.* Washington, DC: Bureau of Justice Statistics, US Department of Justice.
3. Innes, M., Fielding, N., & Cope, N. (2005). The appliance of science? The theory and practice of criminal intelligence analysis. *British Journal of Criminology*, 45, 39–57.
4. Långström, N., & Lindblad, F. (2000). Young sex offenders: background, personality and crime characteristics in a Swedish forensic psychiatric sample. *Nordic Journal of Psychiatry*, 54, 113–120.
5. Barbaree, H. E., Hudson, S. M., & Seto, M. C. (1993). Sexual assault in society: the role of the juvenile sex offender. In: Barbaree, H. E., Marshall, W. L., & Hudson, S. M. (Eds.). *The Juvenile Sex Offender.* London: Guilford Press.
6. Miranda, A. O., & Corcoran, C. L. (2000). Comparison on perpetration characteristics between male juvenile and adult sexual offenders: preliminary results. *Sexual Abuse: A Journal of Research and Treatment*, 12, 179–188.
7. Becker, J. V., Johnson, B. R., & Hunter, J. A. (1996). Adolescent sex offenders. In: Hollin, C. R., & Howells, K. (Eds.). *Clinical Approaches to Working with Young Offenders* (pp. 183–196). Chichester: Wiley.
8. Woodhams, J. (2004). Characteristics of juvenile sex offending against strangers: findings from a non-clinical study. *Aggressive Behavior*, 30, 243–253.
9. Woodhams, J., Gillett, R., & Grant, T. (2007). Understanding the factors that affect the severity of juvenile stranger sex offenses: the effect of victim characteristics and number of suspects. *Journal of Interpersonal Violence*, 22, 218–237.
10. Hendriks, J., & Bijleveld, C. C. J. H. (2004). Juvenile sexual delinquents: contrasting child abusers with peer abusers. *Criminal Behavior and Mental Health*, 14, 238–250.
11. Van Wijk, A., van Horn, J., Bullens, R., Bijleveld, C., & Doreleijers, T. (2005). Juvenile sex offenders: a group on its own? *International Journal of Offender Therapy and Comparative Criminology*, 49, 25–36.
12. Hunter, J. A., Figueredo, A. J., Malamuth, N. M., & Becker, J. V. (2003). Juvenile sex offenders: toward the development of a typology. *Sexual Abuse: A Journal of Research and Treatment*, 15, 27–48.
13. Hunter, J. A., Hazelwood, R. R., & Slesinger, D. (2000). Juvenile-perpetrated sex crimes: patterns of offending and predictors of violence. *Journal of Family Violence*, 15, 81–93.
14. Zolondek, S. C., Abel, G. G., Northey, W. F., & Jordan, A. D. (2001). The self-reported behaviors of juvenile sex offenders. *Journal of Interpersonal Violence*, 16, 73–85.
15. Amir, M. (1971). Group rape. In: *Patterns in Forcible Rape* (pp. 182–226). Chicago: University of Chicago Press.

16. Bijleveld, C., & Hendriks, J. (2003). Juvenile sex offenders: differences between group and solo offenders. *Psychology, Crime, and Law*, 9, 237–245.

17. Cordner, S. M., Ainley, C. G., & Schneider, M. A. (1979). Rape and rapists in Victoria. *Australian and New Zealand Journal of Criminology*, 12, 41–50.

18. Gidycz, C. A., & Koss, M. P. (1990). A comparison of group and individual sexual assault victims. *Psychology of Women Quarterly*, 14, 325–342.

19. Hakkanen, H., Lindof, P., & Santilla, P. (2004). Crime scene actions and offender characteristics in a sample of Finnish stranger rapes. *Journal of Investigative Psychology and Offender Profiling*, 1, 17–32.

20. Hanson, R. K., & Bussieré, M. T. (1998). Predicting relapse: a meta analysis of sexual offender recidivism studies. *Journal of Consulting and Clinical Psychology*, 66, 348–362.

21. Långström, N., & Grann, M. (2002). Psychopathy and violent recidivism among young criminal offenders. *Acta Psychiatrica Scandivavica*, 106, 86–92

22. Rasmussen, L. A. (1999). Factors related to recidivism among juvenile sexual offenders. *Sexual Abuse: A Journal of Research and Treatment*, 11, 69–85.

23. Waite, D., Keller, A., McGarvey, E. L., Weickowski, E., Pinkerton, R., & Brown, G. L. (2005). Juvenile sex offender re-arrest rates for sexual, violent nonsexual and property crimes: a 10-year follow-up. *Sexual Abuse: A Journal of Research and Treatment*, 17, 313–331.

24. Worling, J. R. (2001). Personality-based typology of adolescent male sexual offenders: differences in recidivism rates, victim-selection characteristics, and personal victimization histories. *Sexual Abuse: A Journal of Research and Treatment*, 13, 149–166.

25. Långström, N. (2002). Long term follow up of criminal recidivism in young sex offenders: temporal patterns and risk factors. *Psychology, Crime, and Law*, 8, 41–58.

26. Ross, J., & Loss, P. (1991). Assessment of the juvenile sex offender. In: Ryan, G. D., & Lane, S. L. (Eds.). *Juvenile Sexual Offending: Causes, Consequences and Corrections* (pp. 199–251). Toronto: Lexington.

27. Smith, W. R., & Monastersky, C. (1986). Assessing juvenile sexual offenders' risk for reoffending. *Criminal Justice and Behavior*, 13, 115–140.

28. Worling, J. R. & Långström, N. (2003). Assessment of criminal recidivism risk with adolescents who have offended sexually: a review. *Trauma, Violence and Abuse: A Review Journal*, 4, 341–362.

29. Woodhams, J., & Grant, T. (2006). Developing a categorization system for rapists' speech. *Psychology, Crime and Law*, 12, 245–260.

30. Canter, D. (2000). Offender profiling and criminal differentiation. *Legal and Criminological Psychology*, 5, 23–46.

31. Hazelwood, R. R., & Warren, J. I. (2003). Linkage analysis: *modus operandi*, ritual, and signature in serial sexual crime. *Aggression and Violent Behavior*, 8, 587–598.

32. Bull, R., Cooke, C., Hatcher, R., Woodhams, J., Bilby, C., & Grant, T. (2006). *Criminal Psychology: A Beginner's Guide*. London: One World.

33. Alison, L., Bennell, C., Mokros, A., & Ormerod, D. (2002). The personality paradox in offender profiling: a theoretical review of the processes involved in deriving background characteristics from crime scene actions. *Psychology, Public Policy and Law*, 8, 115–135.
34. Mokros, A., & Alison, L. J. (2002). Is offender profiling possible? Testing the predicted homology of crime scene actions and background characteristics in a sample of rapists. *Legal and Criminological Psychology*, 7, 25–43.
35. Canter, D. (1995). Psychology of offender profiling. In: Bull, R., & Carson, D. (Eds.), *Handbook of Psychology in Legal Contexts* (pp. 343–355). Chichester: Wiley.
36. Grubin, D., Kelly, P., & Brunsdon, C. (2001). *Linking Serious Sexual Assaults Through Behavior* (No. HORS 215). London: Home Office Research Development and Statistics Directorate.
37. Santtila, P., Junkilla, J., & Sandnabba, N. K. (2005). Behavioral linking of stranger rapes. *Journal of Investigative Psychology and Offender Profiling*, 2, 87–103.
38. Woodhams, J., & Toye, K. (2007). An Empirical Test of the Assumptions of Case Linkage and Offender Profiling with Serial Commercial Robberies. *Psychology, Public Policy & Law*, 13, 59–85.
39. Mischel, W., & Shoda, Y. (1995). A cognitive-affective system theory of personality: reconceptualizing situations, dispositions, dynamics and invariance in personality structure. *Psychological Review*, 102, 246–268.
40. Mischel, W. (1999). Personality coherence and dispositions in a cognitive-affective personality system (CAPS) approach. In: Cervone, D., & Shoda, Y. (Eds.). *The Coherence of Personality: Social-Cognitive Bases of Consistency, Variability and Organization* (pp. 37–60). London: Guilford Press.
41. Shoda, Y., Mischel, W., & Wright, J. C. (1993). The role of situational demands and cognitive competencies in behavior organisation and personality coherence. *Journal of Personality and Social Psychology*, 65, 1023–1035.
42. Holmstrom, L. L., & Burgess, A. W. (1979). Rapists' talk: linguistic strategies to control the victim. *Deviant Behavior*, 1, 101–125.
43. Davies, A. (1992). Rapists' behavior: a three-aspect model as a basis for analysis and the identification of serial crime. *Forensic Science International*, 55, 173–194.

Chapter 4

A Study of Offense Patterns and Psychopathological Characteristics Among Recidivistic Finnish Homicide Offenders

Helinä Häkkänen

Abstract

This chapter is based on a number of research projects on offender profiling and homicidal crime scene behavior carried out at the Finnish National Bureau of Investigation. This specific study investigated homicidal recidivism in Finland and analyzed offense and offender characteristics in these cases. The results diverge in many respects from the previous research findings attributed to serial homicide and emphasize the need to identify possible culture-specific patterns and psychopathological offender characteristics of serial homicidal behavior.

INTRODUCTION

In Finland, the homicide rates have for decades been about double the rates in most other West European democracies and triple the rate of the other Nordic countries *(1,2)*. The rate of homicides per capita is approximately 3.4 per 100,000 citizens, which means approximately 140 homicides committed per year *(3)*. Homicidal recidivism is rare in Finland, although the general homicide

From: *Serial Murder and the Psychology of Violent Crimes*
Edited by: R. N. Kocsis © Humana Press, Totowa, NJ

rate is high. Eronen and colleagues *(4)* identified 36 homicide recidivists among the 1584 offenders who committed homicides in Finland during 1981–1993. In another study, 13 recidivists were found among the 414 Finnish offenders who committed homicide during 1988–1991 *(5)*. The studies further showed that the general risk of homicidal behavior is high among persons already convicted of homicide, especially if the person has committed several additional previous violent offenses *(5)*. Furthermore, the studies suggested that alcoholism and personality disorder are frequent among Finnish homicide recidivists and that nearly half of the recidivist commit their second homicide shortly after their release from prison *(4)*. Except for these studies, the incidence of homicide recidivism has received only limited research attention, probably partly due to the infrequency of cases. In countries such as Great Britain, Finland, and Sweden, research has identified only a few homicide recidivists *(6–9)*.

In contrast, research literature on serial homicide is substantial. Studies have focused on analyzing interview data *(10,11)*, official homicide databases *(12–16)*, and media accounts (e.g., *17,18*). Serial homicide is usually defined as an unlawful killing of three or more human beings over a period of time *(19)*. However, serious controversy exists regarding the defining criteria of a serial homicide *(20)*. There is disagreement regarding the number of victims needed, the required nature of the locations of the killings, the time span that has to elapse between the homicides, whether group killers qualify, and the types of motivational backgrounds that qualify.

Despite these dissents, research literature has emphasized some general offense characteristics of serial homicides. First, compared to single homicide offenders, serial homicide offenders more frequently kill women *(13,15,21–23)*, children *(12,13)*, and strangers *(12,13,15,22)*. Second, there has been a consensus that most serial homicides are sadistic and sexually stimulated *(12, 15,16,22,24–27)*, although there are also contradictory results *(12,28)*. Third, studies suggest that serial homicide offenders employ a high level of planning, control, and forensic awareness in their crime scene behavior *(14,29,30)*. Thus, they commit unplanned offenses only rarely *(10)*. However, the prevalence of substance abuse disorders among serial homicide offenders is high, and many report using drugs and alcohol before the homicide *(31,32)*.

Other studies have focused on creating typologies of serial homicide offenders or analyzing their sociodemographic characteristics (e.g., *10,11,32*). These studies suggest that the offenders have often experienced early environmental problems (e.g., parental alcohol abuse and crime) *(10)* and have been subject to psychiatric assessment during childhood *(33)*, but only about one in five have a history of psychiatric treatment *(34)*. Major mental disorder is not usually considered to have a noteworthy role in serial homicide *(28,30,35,36)*.

In fact, it has been suggested that serial homicide offenders are often employed *(15,30)* and usually have average or above average intelligence *(10)*. However, in line with the homicidal sexual motive, research has suggested that serial sexual homicide offenders particularly have a high incidence of paraphilia *(37)*.

Serial homicide has rarely been examined from a global perspective, and empirical studies of serial homicide offenders worldwide are sparse *(17,20, 38)*. There is some evidence, however, that German serial homicide offenders differ from the serial killers in the United States. It was shown in a study on German serial homicide offenders *(20)* that the offenders did not seem to have the same motive for each homicide, and robbery as a motive was as frequent as the sexual motive. Furthermore, the offenders had typically minimal to average intelligence, an emotionally abusive childhood, and a history of criminal behavior. The study also suggested that in Germany these offenders do not rearrange the crime scene, and they rarely leave behind a signature or take trophies *(20)*.

Owing to the lack of research on European homicidal recidivists, the purpose of the present study was to investigate offense and offender characteristics among Finnish recidivistic homicide offenders. Because of the dissent regarding the number of victims needed to define a case as a "serial homicide," this term is replaced here with "homicidal recidivists." Some basic questions about homicidal recidivism were explored: whether a set of empirically valid offense characteristics was typical for this group of offenders, and whether such characteristics are in line with previous literature and research on serial homicide.

PRESENT RESEARCH

The research was designed to address the following questions.

1. What are the sociodemographic and psychopathological characteristics of recidivistic homicide offenders?
2. What is the nature of the offender-victim relationship in these offenses?
3. Is homicidal recidivism in Finland associated with sexual and sadistic crime scene behavior?

The research is empirical and descriptive. Information available in existing police records and forensic psychiatric examination reports is used. Information concerning homicides was obtained from the Finnish National Authority for Medicolegal Affairs (NAMA), which is responsible for organizing the forensic psychiatric evaluations. More than 90% of homicides committed in Finland are solved by the police, and 70% to 85% of all homicide offenders undergo a forensic psychiatric examination *(39,40)*. According to Finnish law, courts decide if a forensic psychiatric examination should be conducted. Both the prosecutor and the defense are allowed to request the examination. After deciding that an examination is required, the court asks the NAMA to arrange it. Forensic psychiatric examinations include data gathered from various sources (family members, relatives, medical and criminal records, school and military records), psychiatric evaluation, standardized psychological tests, interviews by a social worker and a psychologist, evaluation of the offender's physical condition, and observation of the offender by the hospital staff for approximately 2 months. The overall quality and reliability of Finnish forensic psychiatric examinations is considered high by both courts and scientists *(41)*.

The data on homicidal recidivism were obtained retrospectively by examining the history of criminality among offenders who had been subjected to forensic psychiatric examination because of being accused of a homicide. The NAMA's archives were searched for all homicide cases for the period 1995–2003. Cases in which, according to the examination report, the offender had previously committed a homicide or an attempted homicide were identified and collected for data analysis. The computerized Criminal Index File of the Finnish Police was searched for additional information on the selected cases. The Criminal Index File includes both quantitative data (e.g., age and sex of the victim and the offender) and an open-ended narrative appendix. All cases were retrospectively analyzed for several variables regarding the offense and offender characteristics. The variables correspond to criminological, psychological, sociological, and medical issues that have been defined in accordance with accepted judicial, clinical, and diagnostic standards. The list of variables was the same that has been used and tested (e.g., for interrater agreement) on several earlier studies on Finnish homicides (e.g., *42,43*).

All data reported represent minimum estimates of the actual frequency of the variables studied; it should be noted that the data were collected from sources of information not designed specifically for research. The relation between the victim and the offender was divided into the following groups: (blood) related, (ex)intimate, acquaintance, stranger, and other. A case was referred to the "acquainted" group, if the parties knew each other at least by name or by sight and to the "stranger" group if they did not know each other at all. The ethics committee of the NAMA and the Ministry of Interior approved the study.

RESULTS

Altogether there were 45 offenders who had been subjected to forensic psychiatric examination during the 8-year period and who had been previously convicted of a homicide ($n = 29$) or an attempted homicide ($n = 16$). The national homicide data maintained by Statistics Finland showed that there were a total of 1359 persons suspected of homicide during 1995–2003. Thus, the 45 offenders represent 3.3% of this population. Most of the homicidal recidivists (84%) had previously been convicted of one (attempted) homicide. Two offenders had two previous convictions of a completed homicide; one offender had two previous convictions of attempted homicides; one had previous convictions of three attempted homicides and one of one homicide and two attempts; and finally, one offender had a previous convictions of three homicides and one attempted homicide.

Age and Sex

In eight cases (18%), there were multiple offenders, usually two. The age (mean ± SD) of the offenders was 40.7 ± 11.5 years (range 20–79 years). Altogether, 16% of the offenders were < 30 years of age, 27% were 30–40 years, 38% were 40–50 years, and 16% were > 50 years. Only one of the offenders was female. The age (mean ± SD) of the victims was 41.2 ± 9.2 years (range 22–57 years). In four cases, there were two victims. In five cases (11%), the victim was female. ·

Offender-Victim Relationship and Circumstances

One of the victims was a stranger, two were intimate partners, four were blood-related, and the rest (*n* = 38, 84%) were acquaintances. In nearly all of these latter cases, it was a question of a drinking group conflict among social outcasts; 90% of the offenders and 71% of the victims were intoxicated at the time of the offense, and 8% of the offenders were under the influence of drugs. An argument and a fight preceded the killing in 64% of the cases. There were several motives for the killings, most frequently "drunken quarrels" (72%) or revenge (18%). Only one case involved robbery as a partial motive. Two cases, according to the records, involved planning.

Crime Scene Behavior

In 89% of the cases the body was found at the crime scene, and in 39% of the cases the offender remained at the scene. The offender was arrested within 24 hours of the killing in slightly more than half of the cases (52%). In 73% of the cases the body was found in an apartment—in nearly half of these cases in the offender's apartment. In four cases the body was found in an uninhabited area, such as woods or water. None of the cases involved binding, gagging, or any symbolic writing at the scene. Furthermore, none of the cases involved sexual or sadistic elements, such as penetration, biting, urinating, or necrophilia. Three cases involved mutilation.

Stabbing was the most frequent method of violence (71%), followed by shooting (18%), hitting and kicking (17%) and hitting with a blunt instrument (14%). Two victims were drowned, two were killed by setting fire, and two were strangled. In total, 73% of the cases involved one form of violence, 20% involved two forms of violence (usually stabbing and hitting or kicking), and 7% involved three forms of violence.

Offender Early Environment

Nearly half (46 %) of the offenders had been raised (at some point before the age of 16) in a single-parent home. The number of children in the family was high, being on average (±SD) 4.5 ± 2.43 (range 1–11); 53% of the offenders came from families with at least four children. Furthermore, most of the offenders came from families with severe problems. Two of every three offenders (67%) were raised in a family involved in parental alcohol abuse. Also, 58% of the offenders had experienced physical abuse during their childhood. In nearly all of these cases, violence was directed (also) at the offender, usually by their fathers. Sexual abuse during childhood was present in one case. Altogether, 18% of the parents were known to have mental health problems. In all, there were no indications of parental alcohol abuse, physical or sexual abuse, or parents with mental health problems in only 21% of the offenders.

In all, 36% of the offenders had been placed in an institution before the age of 16, and half of the offenders had received special education. Altogether, 70% had experienced severe difficulties at school, and 19% had had mental health services contact before the age of 18. In total, 26% of the offenders did not to have any of these experiences.

Living Conditions and Crime History

A total of 34% of the offenders had an ongoing intimate relationship at the time of the homicide, and 50% had children. However, the offender had custody of his child in only two cases. Only 27% of the offenders had occupational or job training; and at the time of the homicide, one offender was employed and another was studying. In all, 32% of the offenders were retired, and the rest of the offenders (59%) were unemployed. Most of the offenders, however, had sufficient intellectual capability, although they had failed in education and employment. The average IQ of the subjects (data were missing for nine subjects) was 95.11 ± 11.5 (range 75–118). The level of intellectual functioning was average or above average for 49% of the offenders.

In all, the offenders had a history of multiple violent crimes: 88% of them had previously been convicted for an aggravated assault, 84% for theft, 44% for robbery, and 11% for arson. Only one of the offenders had a previous conviction for rape. More than half of the offenders came from families with criminal activity. A history of criminal activity of a parent, parents, or siblings was present in 52% of the cases. Seven offenders (16%) had a relative or family member who had previously been suspected of a homicide.

Psychiatric Diagnosis

Most of the offenders (73%) had been in contact with the mental health services during adulthood, and 32% had an ongoing mental health contact. Nearly half (41%) of the offenders were known by their mental health professionals or people close to them to have been suicidal prior to the homicide. Two offenders tried to kill themselves after the homicide. Altogether, 82% of the offenders were diagnosed as having alcohol dependence and 25% drug dependence. Five of the offenders (11%) were diagnosed as having schizophrenia or other psychosis. Nearly all (89%) offenders were diagnosed as having a personality disorder (antisocial personality disorder in 63% of these cases). According to a forensic psychologist, 41% of the offenders had paranoid thoughts or orientation. Six offenders were considered not to be criminally responsible for the homicide owing to their severe mental illness (four of these offenders were schizophrenics, and two had a personality disorder with severe substance abuse).

DISCUSSION

The present results suggest that signs of antisocial lifestyle, alienation, social maladjustment, and anomalism are very much present in the cases of Finnish homicide recidivists. Psychiatric diagnosis, criminal history, and early developmental problems were notable. These results differ in some respects from earlier studies on serial homicide offenders. For example, compared to the German sample *(20)*, the prevalence of childhood physical abuse, parental alcohol abuse and crime were slightly higher (11–22%) in the present sample. Furthermore, the prevalence of unemployment was substantially higher in the Finnish sample. Also, the offenders' IQ levels in the present study were close to those in the German results *(20)* but in contrast with previous results of serial homicide offenders in the United States *(44)*.

Thus, the subjects in the present study seemed to be severely marginalized from the society in terms of previous crime history, substance abuse, and psychiatric diagnosis. The proportion of offenders who had previous convictions on sex-related crimes was lower than previously found in the United States *(12)*, which seems reasonable due to the differences in the homicidal motivation. However, the proportion of offenders having a criminal history of thefts, robberies, and burglaries was markedly higher in the present study *(12)*. The prevalence of personality disorder and the high degree of suicidal tendency in this study were in accordance with those in the German study *(20)*. In conclusion, the present results strongly support the understanding that a large proportion of serial homicide offenders or homicide recidivists share a constellation of psychological and family system disturbances.

The phenomenon of crime scene behaviors in serial homicides has for decades been mythologized in popular culture, sensationalized by the media, and increasingly scrutinized by academia. The results have been confounding, with fiction blurring with the facts and speculation outweighing valid, reliable research. The present results are in sharp contrast with some of the classical crime scene characteristics attributed to serial homicide. First, contrary to previous studies in the United States (e.g., *14*), in most of the present cases the body recovery site was an apartment, not outdoors. Furthermore, there were no cases in which the murder scene and the body disposal scene were not the same *(15)*. Second, contrary to previous studies, none of the cases involved sexual assault, binding, or gagging; and only a few of the victims were female or a stranger (e.g. *12,15,21,30*). Also, there was only one case in which the victim was strangled. In previous literature, strangulation has been associated with serial and sexual homicide in particular *(15,24,30)*. Third, none of the victims was a prostitute or a child, as suggested by the earlier research *(12,13)*. Most of the victims in the present data were acquaintances, which is in contrast with the common finding and understanding that serial homicide offenders kill primarily strangers *(12,13,15,20,22)*. However, this result is in line with Hickey's conclusion that "foreign serial killers also appear to target acquaintances" *(12)*.

Like all research, the present study has its share of limitations, and therefore it should be considered only preliminary and descriptive. The figures regarding the proportion of recidivist offenders among the total number of homicide offenders may be a slight underestimate because the national homicide data maintained by Statistics Finland is based on police data in regard to the annual number of suspects in homicides. Whether these suspects are in fact prosecuted (and therefore the forensic evaluation is considered) is a separate issue. This evaluation is further hindered by the fact that the national crime statistics reported the number of offenders prior to 1996 as a gross value, so one offender was represented in terms of the number of victims. Also, some subjects may have been missed from the index population because of not screening prison inmates who had not been subject to forensic psychiatric examination. However, one previous study suggests that only a few recidivists can be identified by this method *(4)*. Furthermore, the sample does not include recidivists who committed suicide after their homicide. Despite these limitations, the proportion of homicide recidivists in the present sample corresponded to the results of earlier studies on Finnish recidivist homicide offenders *(4,5)*.

One of the fundamental questions regarding the present study is whether these cases qualify, by definition, as serial homicides. One remarkable difference from previous studies is the fact that in the present study attempted homicides were considered to indicate homicidal crime history. Therefore, the present sample consists of offenders who during 1995–2003 were accused of a completed homicide and had a homicidal crime history in terms of attempted or completed homicide. The focus of the present study was on homicidal recidivism, and attempted homicides were considered to qualify for homicidal history, as the lethal outcome is often determined by factors other than the single-minded intent of the assailant (e.g., speed of medical care).

Most of the offenders were accused of their second homicidal behavior. Only three cases in the present sample would meet serial homicide criteria if at least three completed homicides are considered criteria for the definition *(19)*. Since the 1980s researchers have debated over the number of victims needed to define serial homicide. It has been argued that the minimum number of killed victims should be three *(12,20)*, four *(45)*, or five *(32)*. Meanwhile, others have stated that two temporally unrelated homicides would qualify for a case to be classified as serial homicide *(15,22,46,47)*. In the present study, using the broad definition of two separate homicides and including homicidal attempt (with regard to crime history) allowed a reasonable sample size.

In addition to the debate over the number of victims, some argue that the definition of serial homicide requires a pattern in killing that could be associated with the type of victim, the method of killing, or the motive *(20)*. Also, some may exclude a case from the definition of serial killers if the primary objective of the offender was something other than killing (e.g., robbery). To the best of my knowledge, there were no such cases in the present data. However, unlike in most of the previous studies, the offenders in the present sample had in fact been apprehended and convicted of their previous (attempted) homicide(s). Usually, serial killers are described as individuals who are caught only after a series of homicides. Because of these anomalies, the concept of homicidal recidivists was used when defining the present sample.

Regardless of the study's limitations, the importance of the findings lies in the fact that they emphasize the need to acknowledge possible culture-specific patterns in serial homicidal behavior and offender characteristics. The previous research on serial homicide derives mostly from data collected in the United States, and as such it cannot be generalized to homicidal recidivists in Finland. In terms of homicidal behavior, Finland is most likely different from the United States, with much more emphasis on impulsive, nonfirearm and alcohol-related homicides between persons known to each other. In time, there will be sufficient information with a view to have a more global perspective of serial homicide, which will allow researchers, investigators, and other criminal justice practitioners to advance beyond conclusions based on data derived from another country. It will further prevent us from erroneously assuming and believing that the serial homicide phenomenon or homicidal recidivism is universally similar in nature.

REFERENCES

1. LaFree, G., & Drass, K. A. (1999). Homicide trends in Finland and 33 other nations since 1995: is Finland still exceptional? In: Lappi-Seppälä, T. (Ed.). *Homicide in Finland: Trends and Patterns In Historical and Comparative Perspective*. Publication No. 181. Helsinki: National Research Institute of Legal Policy.
2. Salfati, C. G. (2001). A European perspective on the study of homicide. *Homicide Studies*, 5, 286–291.
3. Kivivuori, J., & Aromaa, K. (2000). Väkivaltarikokset [Violent Crime]. In: *Rikollisuustilanne 2000: Rikollisuus ja Seurantajärjestelmät Tilastojen Valossa* (pp. 12–41). Helsinki: Oikeuspoliittinen Tutkimuskeskus.
4. Eronen, M., Hakola, P., & Tiihonen, J. (1996). Factors associated with homicide recidivism in a 13-year sample of homicide offenders in Finland. *Psychiatric Services*, 47, 403–406.
5. Tiihonen, J., Hakola, P., Nevalainen, A., & Eronen, M. (1995). Risk of homicidal behavior among persons convicted of homicide. *Forensic Science International*, 72, 43–48.
6. Bluglass, R., & Bowden, P. (Eds). (1990). *Principles and Practice of Forensic Psychiatry*. London: Churchill Livingstone.
7. Lindqvist, P. (1986). Criminal homicide in Northern Sweden 1970–81: alcohol intoxication, alcohol abuse, and mental disease. *International Journal of Law and and Psychiatry*, 8, 19–37.
8. Anttila, J., Törnudd, P., & Westling, A. (1964). *Lifetime Sentence. Studies of the Finnish Criminological Research Center*, series A, no. 39. Juva: Finnish Criminological Research Center.
9. Tiihonen, J., & Hakola, P. (1994). Psychiatric disorders and homicide recidivism. *American Journal of Psychiatry*, 151, 436–438.
10. Ressler, R. K., Burgess, A. W., & Douglas, J. E. (1988). *Sexual Homicide: Patterns and Motives*. Lexington, MA: Lexington Books.
11. Holmes, R. M., & DeBurger, J. E. (1985). Profiles in terror: the serial murderer. *Federal Probation*, 49, 29–34.

12. Hickey, E. W. (2002). *Serial Killers and Their Victims* (3rd ed.). Belmont, CA: Wadsworth.
13. Godwin, G. M. (2000). *Hunting Serial Predators: A Multivariate Classification Approach to Profiling Violent Behavior*. Boca Raton, FL: CRC Press.
14. Salfati, C. G., & Bateman, A. L. (2005). Serial homicide: an investigation of behavioural consistency. *Journal of Investigative Psychology and Offender Profiling*, 2, 121–144.
15. Kraemer, G. W., Lord, W. D., & Heilbrun, K. (2004). Comparing single and serial homicide offenses. *Behavioral Sciences & the Law*, 22, 325–343.
16. Geberth, V. J., & Turco, R. N. (1997). Antisocial personality disorder, sexual sadism, malignant narcissism, and serial murder. *Journal of Forensic Sciences*, 42, 49–60.
17. Jenkins, P. (1988). Serial murder in England 1940–1985. *Journal of Criminal Justice*, 16, 1–15.
18. Mckenzie, C. (1995). A study of serial murder. *International Journal of Offender Therapy and Comparative Criminology*, 39, 3–10.
19. Protection of Children from Sexual Predators Act of 1998, 28 U.S.C. §540B (2), 2000.
20. Harbort, S., & Mokros, A. (2001). Serial murders in Germany from 1945 to 1995. *Homicide Studies*, 5, 311–334.
21. Brittain, R. P. (1970). The sadistic murderer. *Medicine, Science and the Law*, 10, 198–207.
22. Egger, S. A. (1984). A working definition of serial murder and the reduction of linkage blindness. *Journal of Police Science and Administration*, 12, 348–57.
23. Langevin, R., Ben-Aron, M. H., Wright, P., Marchese, V., & Handy, L. (1988). The sex killer. *Annuals of Sex Research*, 1, 263–301.
24. Meloy, J. R. (2000). The nature and dynamics of sexual homicide: an integrative review. *Aggressive and Violent Behavior*, 5, 1–22.
25. Keppel, R. D., Walter, R. (1999). Profiling killers: a revised classification model for understanding sexual murder. *International Journal of Offender Therapy and Comparative Criminology*, 43, 417–437.
26. Ressler, R. K., Burgess, A. W., Douglas, J. E., Hartman, C. R., D'Agostino, & R. B. (1986). Serial killers and their victims: identifying patterns through crime scene analysis. *Journal of Interpersonal Violence*, 1, 288–308.
27. Dehart, D. D., & Mahoney, J. M. (1994). The serial murderer's motivations: an interdisciplinary review. *Omega—Journal of Death and Dying*, 29, 29–45.
28. Levin, J., & Fox, J. A. (1985). *Mass Murder: America's Growing Menace*. New York: Plenum Press.
29. Canter, D. V., & Wentink, N. (2004). An empirical test of Holmes and Holmes's serial murder typology. *Criminal Justice and Behavior*, 31, 489–515.
30. Warren, J., Hazelwood, R., & Dietz, P. (1996). The sexually sadistic serial killer. *Journal of Forensic Sciences*, 41, 470–474.
31. Sears, D. J. (1991). *To Kill Again: the Motivation and Development of Serial Murder*. Wilmington, DE: Scholarly Resources Books.

32. Dietz, P. E. (1986). Mass, serial and sensational homicides. *Bulletin of the New York Academy of Medicine*, 62, 477–491.
33. Burgess, A. W., Hartman, C. R., Ressler, R. K., Douglas, J. E., & McCormack, A. (1986). Sexual homicide: a motivational model. *Journal of Interpersonal Violence*, 1, 251–272.
34. Myers, W. C., Reccoppa, L., Burton, K., & McElroy, R. (1993). Malignant sex and aggression: an overview of serial sexual homicide. *Bulletin of the American Academy of Psychiatry and Law*, 21, 435–451.
35. Brown, J. S. (1991). The psychopathology of serial sexual homicide: a review of the possibilities. *American Journal of Forensic Psychiatry*, 12, 13–21.
36. Ritter, B. (1988). Multiple murderers: the characteristics of the persons and the nature of their crimes (dissertation). *Abstracts International*, 49, 1971A.
37. Prentky, R. A., Burgess, A. W., Rokous, F., Lee, A., Hartman, C., Ressler, R., & Douglas, J. (1989). The presumptive role of fantasy in serial sexual homicide. *American Journal of Psychiatry*, 147: 887–891.
38. Gorby, B. (2000). Serial murder: a cross-national descriptive study. Master's thesis, California State University Fresno. Fresno, CA.
39. Pajuoja, J. (1995). *Väkivalta ja Mielentila* (Violence and Mental Health). *Oikeussosiologinen Tutkimus Syyntakeisuussäännöksistä ja Mielentilatutkimuksista*. Jyväskylä Suomalainen Lakimiesyhdistys (Finnish Law Association).
40. Joyal, C. C., Putkonen, A., Paavola, P., & Tiihonen, J. (2004). Characteristics and circumstances of homicidal acts committed by offenders with schizophrenia. *Psychological Medicine*, 34, 433–442.
41. Eronen, M., Repo, E., Vartiainen, H., & Tiihonen, J. (2000). Forensic psychiatric organization in Finland. *International Journal of Law and Psychiatry*, 23, 541–546.
42. Häkkänen, H., Laajasalo, T. (2006). Homicide crime scene actions in a Finnish sample of mentally ill offenders. *Homicide Studies*, 10, 33–54.
43. Laajasalo, T., & Häkkänen, H. (2004). Background characteristics of mentally ill homicide offenders—a comparison of five diagnostic groups. *Journal of Forensic Psychiatry and Psychology*, 15, 451–474.
44. Canter, D. V., Missen, C., & Hodge, S. (1996). Are serial killers special? *Policing Today*, 2:1.
45. Fox, J. A., & Levin, J. (1998). Multiple homicide: patterns of serial and mass murder. In: Tonry, M. (Ed.). *Crime and Justice: A Review of Research* (p. 407). Chicago: Chicago Press.
46. Geberth, V. J. (1996). *Practical Homicide Investigation: Tactics, Procedures, and Forensic Technigues* (3rd ed.). Boca Raton, FL: CRC Press.
47. Myers, W. C. (2004). Serial murder by children and adolescents. *Behavioral Sciences and the Law*, 22, 357–374.

Chapter 5

Sensational and Extreme Interests in Adolescents

Kathy E. Charles[1] and Vincent Egan

Abstract

This chapter addresses sensational interests and offending behavior in adolescents and examines if such interests can be said to cause offending. The quantitative assessment of sensational interests is a relatively new area within forensic psychology. This chapter reviews the literature so far and presents the first findings in this area based on an adolescent sample. Several recent case studies of adolescents with sensational interests who have also murdered are presented. Intrasexual competition (or mating effort) emerges as an important individual difference affecting the criminogenic relevance of sensational interests. Suggestions for improvements in the measurement of sensational interests are discussed along with the relevance of the current findings for offender profiling.

INTRODUCTION

The curious and dramatic interests of dangerous criminals have been a feature of populist forensic profiles since 1970 when Brittain published his work on violent offenders and their pursuits. This qualitative work based on subjective analyses of extremely violent men became a foundation for the

---

[1] Please direct all correspondence concerning this chapter to the first author via email at: k.e.charles@gcal.ac.uk. The first author wishes to thank Alfred Schobert of the Duisburger Institut für Sprach- und Sozialforschung for his insights on gothic culture and far right political groups in Germany.

From: *Serial Murder and the Psychology of Violent Crimes*
Edited by: R. N. Kocsis © Humana Press, Totowa, NJ

assumption that interests are eventually mirrored in behavior. This assumption has been partly propagated by the media, who give intense coverage to any unusual interests associated with criminals. This reaction is often particularly evident when the perpetrator of the crime is an adolescent, and the interests may even be regarded as causal, producing a subsequent media and social furore. In the United Kingdom, a British youth convicted of mutilating and murdering his girlfriend was found to have a marked interest in the occult and knives *(1)*. In the United States, a Native-American teenager who shot nine people (and then himself) contributed to discussions on a neo-Nazi website and created animations depicting a masked gunman carrying out a spree shooting *(2)*. Such offenses are often presented as driven by the offender's interests in the bizarre and violent.

It is not until recently that quantitative research in this field has been carried out to assess the validity of these assumptions in both convicted offenders and the normal population. This chapter explores some recent high profile cases and the media reaction generated by them. The chapter also presents contemporary understanding of sensational interests in adults and suggests several factors that may be important when attempting to link these interests to criminal behavior. Preliminary results of ongoing research with a community sample of almost 600 adolescents in Scotland are also presented. The prevalence of sensational interests in this group is assessed along with the relation to delinquency, mating effort, psychopathology, and personality.

RECENT JUVENILE CASES AND MEDIA REACTION

On June 30, 2003, Luke Mitchell, then 14 years old, met his teenage girlfriend, Jodi Jones, in a wooded area between their homes in Midlothian, Scotland at around 5.00 p.m. and then proceeded to murder and mutilate her. Forensic evidence suggests that he punched her several times in the face and then tried to strangle her with his hands. When she fell to her knees he continued the attack with a knife, severing a major artery in her neck, which caused her death. He slashed her neck another 20 times and then stripped her. Using her trousers to bind her naked body, he continued the mutilation by stabbing her abdomen, breast, and mouth. He also slashed her right arm and slit her eyelids. This murder resulted in the longest single-accused trial in Scottish history *(3)* and the longest prison sentence (a minimum of 20 years) ever given to a youth *(4)*. The trial also provoked a heated debate about what may have motivated such a young person to commit such a crime.

Many issues in Mitchell's background were discussed by the media as possibly contributing factors to the murder. He had used significant amounts of cannabis for approximately a year preceding the murder; a fact the trial judge believed had affected his ability to distinguish fantasy from reality. He had also developed an intense interest in Satanism and the music and imagery of Marilyn Manson—interests that had permeated his school work according to teachers' testimony at his trial. He adopted the "Goth" style of dressing (e.g., wearing long black clothes, growing his hair long) and gravitated toward Goths for friendship. His girlfriend, Jodi, also adopted a Goth style and smoked cannabis with Mitchell and their friends on a regular basis. Mitchell is also described as having a surprisingly close, physical relationship with his mother. Media reports *(3)* describe the police finding Mitchell and his mother sharing a bedroom when they arrested him. At Mitchell's televised declaration of innocence his mother was constantly stroking his neck, and she embraced him for several minutes at Jodi's graveside. Just a year before he became absorbed by drugs and macabre interests he had been a well-mannered, smartly turned-out army cadet.

Of the many elements in Mitchell's life that could have contributed to his becoming a murderer, it was his interest in Marilyn Manson and the Goth scene that received the most intense media scrutiny. Throughout the trial, examples that revealed Mitchell's Satanic and Gothic interests were reported at length and often in a way that made it appear that these interests and crime routinely go together. This happened on other occasions with young criminals in the United Kingdom and elsewhere.

Another British example is the case of Matthew Hardman, a 17-year-old Welsh teenager who murdered a 90-year-old widow. Hardman broke into Mabel Leyshon's home and stabbed her 22 times before removing her heart and placing it in a saucepan. He then made several incisions in her leg and drained her blood into a pan before drinking it. Hardman left an unusual crime scene: Mabel was in a chair with her legs elevated on a stool with an inverted cross at her feet made from two pokers. There were also two candlesticks at her feet and a candle on her mantelpiece. Hardman had consumed Mabel's blood in the stated belief that it would make him immortal after claiming that he believed that he could become a vampire. He claimed to believe that the small village in Wales where he lived was perfect for vampires because of the number of elderly people who lived there. The police found numerous magazines, books, and Internet material in Hardman's bedroom relating to vampires. It is also alleged that he had asked a German exchange student and a police officer to bite his neck to make him a vampire *(5)*. Hardman was sentenced to a minimum of 12 years in prison after DNA evidence linked him to the murder. His application for the right to appeal against his conviction was turned down.

Almost a year after the murder of Mabel Leyshon, a newspaper report from October 2003 on another vampire-driven killing claimed there had been an explosion in vampire cults in recent times. The murder of Thomas McKendrick in a quiet Scottish village echoed the murder of Mabel Leyshon. Thomas was stabbed 42 times, hit by a hammer 10 times, and had blood let from his neck into a cup. This was then consumed, along with part of his head (though this was later disputed by the pathologist) by Allan Menzies who claimed to believe that it would make him an immortal vampire *(6)*. A link was quickly established in the newspapers between his viewing of vampire films and television series and committing murder. This link is apparently so plausible and intuitive to many people that it tends to persist virtually unchallenged. Although some newspapers report other background information on the perpetrators of these crimes, it is always the occult aspect that is given the headlines. Pertinent information that distinguishes these individuals from the many thousands of others who have the same interests but do not offend is often mentioned quite casually or is reduced to statements such as "he was a loner" or "he was bullied." Readers who do not study the entire article concerning this type of crime may be left with the memory of a headline that simply pairs unusual interests with violent crime. Allan Menzies committed suicide in prison in November 2004.

Perhaps one of the most striking examples of this type of coverage is the media reporting that surrounded the Columbine High School massacre in 1999 in the United States. Dylan Klebold and Eric Harris were responsible for the deaths of 12 students and a teacher at their high school before committing suicide. Within days of the shootings, the press had latched onto several themes concerning the boys' interests. They were, according to the media, fans of Marilyn Manson, Nazi sympathizers, anti-Christian, and Goths. This pattern of interests fitted the widely held stereotypical ideas that Marilyn Manson and the Goth scene were responsible for a collapse in morals and standards among teenagers leading to violence and murder.

Three years after the Columbine shootings, the fear and perceived threat of Goth culture reached such a level that $273,000 of federal money was awarded to the Blue Springs Outreach Unit in Missouri to combat "Goth culture" *(7)*. In Robelen's 2002 article, the Goth culture is described as fostering troubling behaviors such as drug abuse and self-mutilation. Also in 2002, an article by Hooper featured in the UK *Guardian* newspaper explored the growing concern that Goth culture is becoming entwined with neo-Nazism.

Among other things, Hooper mentioned the German case of Hendrick Möbus. This 16-year-old boy from Sonderhausen had been part of a trio who murdered a classmate in a black magic ritual in 1994. While in a juvenile detention center Möbus formed a band and produced a CD that contained tracks with titles such as "Zyklon B." Möbus viewed the murder he had committed as "rendering race vermin harmless" and tried to claim political asylum in the United States. He failed to obtain asylum and is now back in Germany, in jail, after continuing to contravene Germany's laws on using symbols associated with the Third Reich. But to what extent can Goth culture *per se* be linked reliably to crime generally, or even to the specific crimes discussed here?

The British cases concerning Matthew Hardman and Luke Mitchell are so recent that there is relatively little detailed background information or analysis available to the general public. Considerable information on Dylan Klebold and Eric Harris, however, has come into the public domain, including extracts from their journals and transcripts from the videos they made for their parents. This kind of data may allow a better understanding of their personalities than the generalizations of journalists and secondary reportage about Goths, Nazis, and Marilyn Manson. Eric Harris's journal charted his developing knowledge of bomb-making and firearm acquisitions and detailed the plans he was making for the day in April 1999 that would make him infamous. His attention to detail and deep contempt for authority figures has been described as bordering on mania. Harris was also preoccupied with the idea of natural selection and "survival of the fittest" as an explanation for why he should be able to get away with criminal conduct. An example from his journal reads, "How come if I'm free I can't deprive a stupid fucking dumbshit from his possessions if he leaves them sitting in the front seat of his fucking van ... Natural selection. Fucker should be shot" *(8)*. Videos made by the two boys contain footage of pipe bombs, shotgun shells, boxes of 9 mm bullets, home-made grenades, sawed-off shotguns, a combat knife with a swastika on it, and a 50-foot coil of green fuse. The videos also show both Harris and Klebold apologizing to their parents for the murderous rampage they had planned. This apology is quickly followed by expressions of venom for their classmates and teachers, and complete acceptance that they will die during their attack.

Evidence of this sort being available publicly allows a more thorough exploration of the boys' motives than the earlier media reports, which focused on the Gothic theme. A thorough article by journalist Dave Cullen pulls together publicly available information and comments from authors such as Robert Hare on the mental state of the two teenagers. The conclusion that Harris was a psychopath and Klebold a depressive points to a pathological symbiosis at the core of this crime and not simply an alleged love of Goth culture. Analysis of Harris and Klebold's videos and journals shows no real support on their part of the Goth scene at all. Their musical tastes were for "techno" and "industrial," and they had an active dislike of Marilyn Manson. Although there are occasional rantings from Harris on the subject of wars and race, and the killings were planned for Hitler's birthday, there is no explicit support for Nazi ideals or evidence of far-right political memberships. It seems that it was the idea of the large-scale mass killings of the Nazi era that appealed to the boys, not necessarily the core principles of Nazism. If they had known more about other murderous political regimes, they may have also made reference to them. Harris emerges as the grandiose, narcissistic, even psychopathic leader in the crime, with Klebold his willing accomplice. One of Klebold's creative writing essays describes a black-clad avenging killer armed to the teeth who he watches murder a group of students. His essay ends with, "I not only saw in his face, but also felt eminating [*sic*] from him power, complacence, closure, and godliness. The man smiled, and in that instant, thru [*sic*] no endeavor of my own, I understood his actions" *(9)*. It cannot be claimed for certain that Klebold is referring to Harris; but given Harris's penchant for dressing in black and fantasizing about revenge, it is not an unreasonable conclusion.

A further examination of the boys' psychopathology is beyond the scope of this chapter. Harris and Klebold have been mentioned here with the two British teenage killers because of the media response to their actions. That response tends to link teenage criminality with *chosen subcultures* in contrast to psychopathology or other unselected variables in the adolescent's life. The examples discussed here are extreme and relatively rare—but they make sensational news, and such topics are of perennial fascination *(10)*.

DEVELOPMENT OF SENSATIONAL INTERESTS RESEARCH

In the last 8 years there has been considerable development in the quantitative study of sensational interests. This was initiated by Egan and colleagues *(11)* in their study of sensational interests and general personality traits. This research developed from a widely cited study by Brittain *(12)* containing numerous anecdotes concerning violent criminals and their bizarre and sensational interests that had never received formal examination. Despite anecdotes there were few "systematic, methodologically rigorous studies of sensational interests" *(11,* p. 568). Brittain described the interests he found in sadistic murderers during his long career working with them in forensic psychiatric settings in Scotland. His descriptions are extensive and wide ranging, but he made no attempt to compare his theories and observations with the then current literature. However, many of the interests he described have face validity and persist in many people's minds as "typical" interests of sadists and murderers, perhaps not reflecting on their own interests in such topics. He focuses quite extensively on Nazism and its associated atrocities: "A feature very frequently to be found in sadistic murderers is a consuming interest in Nazism and, in particular, in Nazi concentration camps. A number have fantasises of working in concentration camps . . . some collect badges, daggers, uniforms or medals" (*12*, p. 203). He also comments on the possible book collections of these individuals, which may contain texts on Nazism and Nazi leaders, war generally, black magic, erotica, escapology, weapons, uniforms, sadism, and torture. Additional features of the sadistic murderer include interests in spiritualism, an interest in prehistoric creatures, fictional monsters, and vampires. On such grounds, most viewers of *Lord of the Rings* could be deemed suspect.

It was this diverse set of interests reported by Brittain that influenced Egan et al. *(11)* in the development of the Sensational Interests Questionnaire (SIQ). The original SIQ contained 60 items, 31 of which were removed following principal components analysis. The 31 removed items included items that, in light of Brittain's research, seem to have forensic relevance but were so commonly of interest as to not differentiate persons: Hitler and fascism, serial killers, dinosaurs, science fiction and fantasy, horror films, detective films and stories, and funerals and death. These topics seemed to be popular with many of the 301 participants used in the development of the questionnaire. The remaining five factors of Egan et al., made up of 29 items, are presented in Table 1.

It is the first and second factors of militarism and violent occultism that are of forensic interest as they cover several of the topics highlighted by Brittain, and their items feature in many journalistic anecdotes about offenders. Indeed, both of these factors have elements of power fantasy in them, which rely on the transformation or subjugation of others. Egan et al. found significant independent predictors of militaristic interests to be lower agreeableness, higher extraversion, lower verbal IQ, and lower age. Predictors for violent occultism were lower agreeableness, lower conscientiousness, and lower age. It was also found that forensic subjects were more willing to admit to having militaristic and violent occult interests than the control group.

This first study by Egan et al. *(11)* produced a questionnaire that could be used to assess sensational interests quantitatively in large groups of people. It also generated two clear forensic interest factors with associated personality predictors. Research on sensational interests continued with a study of mentally disordered offenders *(13)*. It was revealed that in this group of participants an interest in sensational topics was associated with sensation-seeking (notably the disinhibition and thrill- and adventure-seeking components of Zuckerman's scale). Significant, positive correlations were also found between the militarism factor and antisocial (0.3) and borderline (0.28) personality disorders; and between the violent occultism factor and avoidant (0.33) and borderline (0.41)

Table 1
Items and Scales Comprising the SIQ Scales

Militarism	Violent occultism	Intellectual recreation	Occult credulousness	Wholesome activities
Martial arts	Vampires and werewolves	Philosophy	Paranormal	Gardening
Motorbikes	Drugs	Psychology, psychiatry	Flying saucers	Country and hill walking
Crossbows, knives, swords	Tattoos, body piercing	Alternative medicine	Astrology	Camping
Bodybuilding	Black magic	Singing, making music		
Mercenaries and the SAS	Paganism	Foreign travel		
Guns and shooting	Home brewing	Environment		
Survivalism		Medicine		
Armed forces				
Sporting activities				
Fishing				

SIQ = Sensational Interests Questionnaire; SAS = Special Air Service (equivalent to Navy SEALS or other crack troops).

personality disorders. However, these associations broke down once sensation-seeking was controlled for.

Associations between sensational interests and personality traits and disorders were further investigated *(14)*. In this study, again using mentally disordered offenders, the authors found that personality traits and personality disorders overlapped considerably to produce four dimensions. These four dimensions derived from the big five personality traits and nine personality disorders from the International Personality Disorder Examination-Screening Questionnaire (IPDE-SQ) *(15)*. The four dimensions derived were asocial, anxious, antisocial, and anankastic (the four A's) *(16)*. Sensational interests were found to correlate with the antisocial dimension, which comprised low agreeableness, low conscientiousness, paranoid, antisocial, narcissistic, and histrionic personality disorders.

With sensational interests becoming established as a research area and firm associations being demonstrated with various personality traits and disorders, the focus shifted toward studies on more "normal" samples. Much of the initial research had centered on the role of interests in mentally disordered forensic samples, implicitly maintaining the view that sensational interests are prototypical of criminals and the mentally ill. The most recent studies on sensational interests have included American undergraduates *(17)* and cross-cultural comparisons using American, British, Chilean, and Mexican undergraduates and the general public *(18)*. After reviewing several studies showing that sensational interests were strongly linked with low agreeableness, low conscientious, younger age, and elements of antisocial personality disorder, a comparison was drawn with the typical offender *(17)*. Numerous researchers *(19–21)* have highlighted the link between age, sex, and crime—that is, young men commit most of the crimes. This relation has held across different cultures and different time periods. It has been suggested that the reason for these universal crime correlates is evolutionary *(21)*.

Quinsey suggests that "behaviors involved in delinquency are a manifestation of mating effort and inter-male competition" *(21, p. 3)*. Mating effort has been defined as "that portion of the total reproductive effort that is invested in the initial acquisition of mates as sexual partners" *(22, p. 106)*. At the opposite end of the reproductive continuum is parental effort, which centers on high levels of investment in a small number of offspring, rather than participating in a high number of sexual encounters. Quinsey and others before him *(23)* have suggested that young males have higher mating effort than any other group in society, and this places them in fierce competition with one another for access to females. During the process of competing with each other, they are driven to impress females directly; but they also perpetrate acts of victimful criminality *(24)* against other males to "handicap" them. The degree to which they become involved in crime to show their status may depend largely on the alternative avenues available to them display status. There is debate over whether high mating effort and criminality develop as a result of social disadvantage or exist as a genetic predisposition *(22)*.

Displays of status and power designed to impress females and subdue males, respectively, may not be related to criminal conduct exclusively but more broadly to sensational interests *(17)*. The hypothesis of Weiss et al. was rooted in the idea that the core factors of sensational interests center on power and symbolic dominance. Their results suggest that mating effort does indeed play a significant factor in the development of sensational interests in their sample of undergraduates. Males were found to have higher mating effort and a greater interest in sensational topics than females, and these differences were found between younger and older participants. "Mating effort caused sensational interests and moderated sex and age effects on sensational interests" *(17, p. 571)*. This study brings the research on sensational interests a step further in that it addresses, to some degree, what importance these interests may have for a normal individual. It establishes apparently robust links between interests and mating effort and thus offers some explanation of why certain characteristics (those of an antisocial nature) are found in individuals who show a strong interest in sensational topics.

A cross-cultural approach to assessing links between sensational interests, mating effort, and personality was adopted by Egan and others *(18)*. The aim of their research was to test empirically whether sensational interests were specific to: competitively disadvantaged males, mentally disordered offenders, particular cultural settings, or a particular individual difference. Egan et al. found that the relation between mating effort and sensational interests found previously *(17)* also existed cross-culturally. This supports the hypothesis that there is a universal relation between sensational interests and mating effort. The relation with personality is less clear-cut, suggesting that it may be more readily affected by cultural differences than by mating effort. These findings led Egan et al. to conclude that "mating effort appears to be a reliable predictor of sensational interests across cultures and differing socioeconomic strata within those societies ... [but] we predict that competitively disadvantaged individuals [will] adhere to sensational interests for longer" (*18*, p. 17–18).

SENSATIONAL INTERESTS IN ADOLESCENTS

With the relation between sensational interests, mating effort, and potential criminality established across various adult groups, cultures, and languages, the next research direction was to examine these relations in adolescents. One method of doing this was to investigate trait rebelliousness in adolescents and their preference for defiant music *(25)*. Subcultures that come under attack from the media are normally attached to a particular musical genre (e.g., "Death Metal" or "Industrial" music). Previous research has shown that young people who demonstrate a preference for music with defiant lyrics celebrating aggression and destruction tend to score higher on measures of rebellious tendencies than those who prefer nondefiant music. For example *(26)*, measures of recklessness in adolescents who liked "heavy metal" music were compared with those who did not. A positive relation between liking heavy metal music and reckless behavior was found in 5 of the 12 variables measured. However, in a review of the literature *(25)*, the relation between specific musical preferences and rebelliousness was not straightforward. Rebelliousness can be regarded as having two forms: proactive and reactive rebellion. Proactive rebellion comprises a tendency to break rules in the pursuit of excitement and engage in impulsive behaviors. It has also been found to correlate with trait psychoticism. In contrast, reactive rebellion is more of a "dispositional negativism arising from dissatisfactions with interpersonal encounters and manifesting itself as vindictive behavior" (*25*, p. 1645). The correlations found with rebellion and defiant music have been with *proactive* rebellion, which suggests a sensation-seeking motive for listening to the music.

The idea that liking heavy metal music (and other "hostile" music such as rap) is driven by arousal-seeking and not hostility was explored *(25)*, with the finding that high levels of trait rebelliousness were associated with increased exposure to defiant music. However, more specifically, it was revealed that "teen rebellion associated with defiant music consumption is more fun-seeking than hostility-inspired . . . only aspects of excitement-seeking corresponded with actual defiant music consumption" (*25*, p. 1653). These findings are relevant to the debate on sensational interests during adolescence because they go some way toward confirming that most young people are attracted to bizarre, macabre, and defiant things out of curiosity and excitement. This is not to dismiss the possibility that a small number of adolescents are attracted to heavy metal or rap as a means of expressing hostility toward society. Rather, it suggests that hostility should not be viewed as the driving factor in all cases.

Further evidence to support the idea that defiant music is not as dangerous as certain sections of society appear to believe is the mainstreaming of previously "shocking" material. Marilyn Manson, who is frequently mentioned as an example of the devil incarnate by shocked adults who have forgotten about the comparable Alice Cooper during the 1970s, is shunned by many metal fans as being *too* popular. One source that is possibly worth a proper investigation may be sales from Internet vendors such as Amazon. A visit to Amazon's website to examine the sales patterns around artists such as Marilyn Manson provides useful information. Manson's new album is on the Polydor label (hardly "underground"), which also produces a CD of Joseph and the Amazing Technicolour Dreamcoat. On examining what other Manson customers bought, it can be seen that they purchased work by artists such as Placebo, who appeared on the BBC music program "Top of the Pops." A simple exercise such as this quickly places Marilyn Manson and other "shocking" artists in their mainstream place. A more useful analysis of personality, hostility, and musical preference may come from researching customers of groups such as "Kirlian Camera," who produce only 500 CDs at a time and who occasionally perform wearing balaclavas. This particular group also include speeches on their CDs by Corneliu Codreanu, a Romanian fascist from the interwar period who led an anti-Semitic terrorist group and took his inspiration from Mussolini.

In addition to music as a badge of adolescent identity, there are also acquired "appearance anomalies" associated with this age group. How appearance anomalies relate to adolescent misbehavior was examined in a recent study *(27)*. Participants were asked to describe which subculture they belonged to as a teenager and concurrently measured self-report levels of misbehavior, self-esteem, and psychopathy. Some of the teen subcultures included were jocks/athletes, skaters, Goths, religious, nerds, and troublemakers. Appearance anomalies (e.g., tattoos, piercings, dark clothes, unusual makeup and hair color) were not associated with high levels of misbehavior. The best predictor for misbehavior was not a particular subculture but psychopathy. This led to the suggestion of three possibilities of why teenagers attach themselves to a subculture that produces particular anomalies in appearance *(27)*. First, there is the idea that those with low self-esteem embrace a subculture as a way of accepting social rejection and forging an identity. Second, there are those with high levels of openness for whom a modified appearance serves as an expression of creativity and personal aesthetics. Finally, there are those with high levels of psychopathy for whom subculture membership provides support for impulsive, reckless behavior and aggressive status display. Although these three ideas link appearance anomalies with personality, they do not present appearance as a guide for predicting personality. A tattoo on one body may mean something very different from the same tattoo on another.

TESTING THE LINKS BETWEEN SENSATIONAL INTERESTS, MATING EFFORT, AND PERSONALITY IN ADOLESCENTS

New research using Egan's SIQ to measure adolescent interests for the first time is ongoing. However, data are now available from phase I of a longitudinal study that examines the relation between sensational interests, personality, psychopathology, mating effort, and self-reported delinquency *(28)*. Intending to test the relations found in the adult population, this study used adolescent participants from two mainstream schools in East Dunbartonshire, Scotland. The schools were mixed-sex, nondenominational, and nonselective, providing the best cross section of pupils in the specified age range (12–16 years). A total of 564 participants were used in phase I of the study; 308 were male (54.7%), and 256 were female (45.3%). The age range of the pupils was 12.0 to 15.9 years (mean $\pm$ SD: 14.1 $\pm$ 0.92).

The responses to the SIQ were analyzed with a principal components analysis using varimax rotation to test if the same sensational interests factor structure that existed for adolescents is true of adults. The data showed a factor structure different from that generated in Egan's original research *(11)*. Instead of five factors, the adolescent data generated three (Table 2). The militarism factor was virtually the same as the original and had a good alpha (α) reliability (0.85). The second factor, labeled "intellectualism" ($\alpha = 0.78$),

Table 2
Items and Scales Following an Item-Factor Analysis in Adolescents (n = 695)

Militarism	Intellectualism	Occultism
Crossbows/knives/swords	Environment	Black magic
SAS	Psychology	Vampires/werewolves
Armed forces	Philosophy	Paranormal
Guns and shooting	Medicine	Paganism
Motorbikes	Alternative medicine	Flying saucers/UFOs
Fishing	Singing and music	
Bodybuilding	Country and hill walking	
Martial arts	Foreign travel	
Survivalism	Astrology	
Camping		
Sport		

was a combination of the original "intellectual recreation" and "wholesome activities" factors. The third and final factor, labeled "occultism" ($\alpha = 0.76$), was a combination of "occult credulousness" and "violent occultism" found in the original research *(11)*. For the analysis with the adolescent data, drugs and gardening failed to load on any of the factors so they were removed from the final factor structure.

One way to explain the different factor structure found with adolescents is to consider their degree of knowledge on certain topics. This could be particularly pertinent with regard to the merging of the original two occult factors *(11)* into one. Adolescents may not necessarily distinguish between topics such as paganism and the paranormal with the same degree of discrimination that adults did in the original SIQ study. They may view mystical topics as being similar to one another and not consider black magic to be any more unusual than flying saucers or astrology. Care was taken to try to avoid participants thinking like this by providing one-sentence descriptions of some of the less obvious interests. The collapsing of intellectual recreation and wholesome activities into one factor may represent interest patterns that have not yet crystallized into indoor and outdoor pursuits. The original "wholesome activities" factor contained outdoor items, whereas intellectual recreation reflected more sedentary interests. It is possible that adolescents have not yet associated different interests in this way, and the new intellectualism factor may represent general curiosity about a variety of topics. Despite the differences in the adolescent data, there are still important similarities with the adult findings; there is a clear militarism factor that is virtually identical in both groups, and there is an occult-based factor that clearly differentiates "dark" interests from other topics.

There are significant sex differences in the adolescent interest factors, with males showing significantly more interest in militarism than females and significantly less interest in intellectualism. There was no sex difference in occult interests. Given these differences the relations observed between delinquency and sensational interests may not be surprising. Delinquency was measured using the Self-Report Early Delinquency Instrument (SRED) *(29)*, which produced a general delinquency score from 58 items containing illegal and rule-breaking activities. The correlation between delinquency and militarism was $+0.251$ ($p < 0.001$), but between delinquency and intellectual interests it was -0.256 ($p < 0.001$).

In the light of existing theories based on adults, this relation between males, militarism, and delinquency could be ascribed to mating effort rather than to gender *per se*. Further correlations show that mating effort positively correlates with militarism (0.267, $p < 0.001$) and is negatively correlated with intellectualism (-0.209, $p < 0.001$). These findings raise the question of what exactly is the nature of the relation between sensational interests and delinquency, and how, if at all, is it mediated. It is clear from phase I of this longitudinal study that in a large sample of ostensibly normal adolescents occult interests are not related to self-reported delinquency. These occult interests are not particular to one sex and show no relation to mating effort, and their association with psychopathology only just reaches significance ($r = 0.085$, $p = 0.049$). Intellectual interests show a significant negative correlation with delinquency and mating effort and a small relation with psychopathology ($r = 0.095$, $p = 0.029$), indicating that they may act as a protective influence with regard to delinquency.

The candidate sensational interests construct to consider as an influence on delinquency is clearly militarism. Using structural equation modeling to analyze part of the phase I data, clear pathways to adolescent offending can be seen from mating effort through military interests and from the mating effort directly.

The SEM model (Fig. 1) also shows the relation between sex, mating effort, and militarism, highlighting being male as an important factor in the development of military interests and offending. Previous research *(30)* using a subset of these data has shown that although males have significantly higher mating effort and are more likely to commit crimes the strength of the correlation between mating effort and delinquency is the same for both males and females (~ 0.5). The sensational interests factor of militarism is clearly important in the development of offending. These findings and those of adults *(17)* suggest that military interests may develop as a result of high mating effort. These interests may be serving

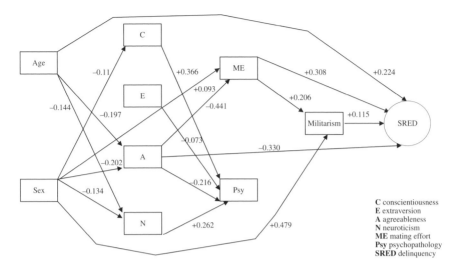

Fig. 1. Structural equation model showing pathways to delinquency. Comparative fit index $= 0.945$; Bentler-Bonett nonnormed fit index $= 0.911$; root mean squared error of approximation $= 0.058$.

as a type of status display to show dominance over other males and to impress females. In some cases, these interests escalate into delinquency. However, high mating effort does not always manifest in military interests and then crime; it can lead to delinquency without the perpetrator displaying sensational interests.

Interestingly, and possibly with good reason, an emerging concern in Europe is the "militarization" of Goth culture by far-right political groups. If the results from the phase I data can be generalized to other countries, a concern about militarization is a valid one. In British adolescents, occult interests do not relate to delinquency at all, but militarism does. There are modest, but significant, correlations between militarism and neuroticism (-0.19), agreeableness (-0.2), and extraversion ($+0.11$). The personality correlates of occult interests are quite different: neuroticism ($+0.15$) and openness ($+0.38$). Militarism tends to share some of the personality correlates typically found with delinquency; the occult interests factor shares none of them. Of course, the items in the occult factor do not necessarily represent the whole spectrum of Gothic interests.

DISCUSSION

Although the idea of occult/Gothic interests and militarism coming together may be a cause for concern, the extent to which it is happening as a broad social phenomena is debateable. There is plenty of evidence that branches of Goth culture and metal music are incorporating Nazi symbolism into their clothes, jewelery, and CD covers. An example of this is the British band Death in June, which is described as a "neofolk" band. However, some of their CDs contain renditions of the Nazi anthem, the Horst Wessel song, and references to the SA (brown shirts). Der Blutharsch, an Austrian group, is cited *(31)* as a similar example. The inside of their album cover contains a hologram of a sun rune that appears similar to the SS symbol, which was designed based on sun runes. Michael Moynihan is an American artist who has generated more attention than most over his book *Lords of Chaos* and music "Blood Axis." He is described variously as a "crypto-Nazi" or a "scholar" depending on the reader's perspective *(32)*. Ironically, Moynihan himself admits that most of the 20,000 copies of his book that have been purchased are in the hands of journalists and sociologists, rather than Nazi youths. Moynihan explored several high profile murders from Western Europe that were linked to Satanism and the black metal subculture *(33)*. He also interviewed convicted killers and arguably gave a platform to their extremist thinking.

The reality of Nazi infiltration of the Goth scene is thought to be modest *(34)*. Most Goths are opposed to Nazism and tend to be left-wing if they are political at all. In Germany, there is a movement called *Grufties gegen Rechts* [Goths Against the Right] that has been reasonably successful at keeping right-wing infiltration at bay. A small number of German Goths can be described as "flirting with Nazi or fascist images/symbols" *(34)*. That these Goths necessarily *believe* in the "ideals" of Nazism is unlikely. Moynihan has been interviewed on the subject of Nazism and his answers included, "I wouldn't want to meet any Nazis . . . I don't subscribe to the whole ideology . . . I don't have an interest in the 'wholesome goodness' ideas of Nazi morality" *(35*, p. 225). Moynihan goes on to describe how it is really only the symbolism of Nazism that appeals to him. Schobert *(34)* suggested that only a small number of those flirting with the symbols actually subscribe to Nazism. It is likely that the use of Nazi symbolism has been adopted for its guaranteed and instant shock value; and any spectacular and dramatic imagery is powerful when appropriated, whether by pop groups or politicians. It is important not to lose sight of the idea that adolescents like to shock and be noticed: Challenging established norms in society is vital for young people in many cultures.

The concept of the mating effort is also an important variable to consider—Nazi symbols are usually associated with brutality, dominance, and cruelty. The fact the some Nazi policies included teaching women how to cook vegetables, encouraging them to eat wholemeal bread, and discouraging them from smoking and using makeup *(36)* is probably the last thing with which a black metal enthusiast would want to be associated. In most cases, the symbols or clothes of extremism are sufficient to serve the needs of the wearer. They provoke shock, outrage, fear, and admiration, and they serve to increase record and book sales for the artists who use them. It is through the use of political imagery and the resulting condemnation it receives from society that many black metal artists have become famous. Dark, satanic imagery and a violent murder did nothing to diminish the appeal of Luke Mitchell, who now has a female fan base who regularly write to him quoting Marilyn Manson lyrics and suggesting sexual scenarios *(37)*.

CONCLUSIONS

Thorough research on sensational interests has made progress in recent years and has questioned generalizations and anecdotes about crime and interests. Research with adults has shown that sensational interests are related to antisocial personality characteristics and mating effort in offender populations and normal adults and undergraduates. The new and ongoing research with adolescents suggests that sensational interests have a different meaning for this age group. The sensational interests factor structure is more straightforward in an adolescent sample (containing three factors instead of five). The adolescent factors of militarism and occultism have quite different relations with measures of personality, mating effort, and delinquency. This suggests that in an adolescent sample it is an interest in militarism that may lead to delinquency, not an interest in occult topics. The relation of militarism to mating effort and delinquency implies that the militarization of occult/Gothic topics may result in individuals who become involved in this subculture getting involved in crime. Research and media reports suggest that violent crimes that appear to have been committed by regular Goths often have a military/Nazi element to them.

However, the "crossover" between Goth culture and militarism is quite small. In Germany, where it is considered more popular than in some other parts of Europe, the crossover is estimated to be about 9% of Goths incorporating military themes into their music, clothes, and ideas. Despite the moral panic about Goth culture and the quick attribution of blame by some sections of the media, research has demonstrated that an adolescent's interest in the occult is not related to delinquency. Being part of the Goth scene is widespread among teenagers, and it is related more to openness than something sinister.

Can adolescent sensational interests tell the onlooker anything about the likelihood of the adolescent becoming involved in delinquency? One of the limitations of current sensational interests research is the reliance on the participant honestly disclosing their interest patterns. Several researchers

(13,14,25,27) have suggested that research into interests and preferences would be improved if there was some kind of behavioral or observational assessment available to measure such things. It is relatively easy to suggest someone is a Goth because they have expressed an interest in Satanism and wear black clothes. What cannot be seen from a basic analysis is that there are many layers in subcultures, some of which are more concerning than others.

An interview with Varg Vikernes *(33)*, a Norwegian allegedly responsible for burning down churches and sentenced to 21 years in prison for a brutal murder, illustrates this point. Superficially, he could be labeled a Goth with his interest in the occult, Satanism, and mysticism. However, when interviewed he made the following statements, which are hardly typical of what regular Goths believe or do: "I was mostly socializing with weapon freaks. My hobby was shooting guns, militia training, and playing in the woods with a shotgun... we were into weapons, German weapons... our big hope was to be invaded by the Americans so we could shoot them. The hope of war was all we lived for" *(33*, p. 157).

Having general sensational factors is perhaps not the best way to approach potential adolescent extremists. The SIQ factor structure is based on the factors being orthogonal. Some of the most extreme individuals have interests in both militarism and occultism. Predicting violent offending from interest patterns should be possible, as the relations between militarism, mating effort, and delinquency are clear. However, the methods currently available for measuring these interests are not sensitive enough to detect the progression from curiosity about a large topic (e.g., mysticism) to participation in a specific niche of that topic (e.g., use weaponry). When the ongoing longitudinal study into adolescent interests is completed, it may be possible to assess the stability over time of sensational interests. The duration of the average adolescent's interest in a sensational topic is not known. It is probable that those who show only a passing fascination with macabre or militaristic interests are unlikely to become involved in dangerous or criminal behavior. The persistence of an unusual interest may be one way to predict the teenagers who may develop a problem.

Using evidence of occult interests in criminal profiling is not new. A U.S. Federal Bureau of Investigation (FBI) report from 1989 *(38)* discussed the usefulness of occult or satanic indicators in a variety of crimes. A significant problem highlighted in the report is the issue of deciding what should be regarded as an occult indicator. Body mutilation, amputation, eating of flesh, and drinking of blood have all been deemed occult indicators by virtue of their strangeness to the average person. However, it can be argued *(38)* that such desecration of a body is a reflection of psychosis, and it is the religious persuasion of those investigating that attaches a satanic interpretation to the event. There is no clear working definition for investigators of what is or is not satanic. Available information and personal beliefs vary greatly, and it is arguably unhelpful to try to attach a religious label to particular actions. Coupling these problems with the findings so far on adolescents suggests that occult interests (however they are defined) are not necessarily good predictors of criminal behavior. Satanic themes at a crime scene may have value in informing investigators of the personality of an adolescent offender in that they suggest psychopathological problems. In the cases discussed here, it has been demonstrated that the apparently "occult theme" of several adolescent murders has turned out to be superficial to deeper (often psychotic) issues.

It is also worth reiterating that the militarization of Gothic interests, and military interests generally, are tied much more closely to offending than Gothic or occult interests alone. If a murder occurred that displayed signs of occult or satanic practices (accepting problems of definition), a profiler should consider a militarized, high mating effort individual above the classic idea of a Goth. Such an individual may display Goth signals outwardly, but they would be superficial and are likely to have been adopted merely to legitimize disturbing behavior. Luke Mitchell is a good example of this. He superficially fitted into the "Goth scene" but with many anomalies; he smoked far more cannabis than his peers, he had a strong interest in weapons, and he had an unusual relationship with his mother—all things that set him apart from his peers despite fitting in on the surface.

The role of sensational and extreme interests in adolescents is complicated. Despite news coverage of exceptionally violent and destructive crime perpetrated by "satanic" or "Nazi" teenagers, to say that those interests *cause* the individual to commit crime is to grossly oversimplify the issues. There are many nuances in adolescent subcultures and many motivations for teenagers to become involved with them. There are individuals who actively seek out violent confrontations despite some of them having the social skills to avoid such situations *(39)*. "Fight-seeking" behavior is thought to be perpetrated for "neurobiological self-calming" (*39*, p. 953) by individuals who have a high basal state of agitation. There is a possibility that instead of teenagers being seduced by extreme branches of a subculture they actually seek out that cultural niche as a means of allowing them to express aggression. By expressing their aggression through a subculture, they may see it as a legitimization of violence for a cause or belief system. However, most teenagers pass into adulthood having experimented with many styles and interests and having been involved in a degree of delinquency. They mature into useful members of society and have children of their own. Being able to detect those who are not destined to follow this harmless path based on their unusual interests is still in its infancy.

REFERENCES

1. *Killer 'obsessed by the occult.'* Retrieved April 5, 2005, from http://news.bbc. co.uk/1/hi/scotland/4187007.stm.
2. *School killer 'made violent film.'* Retrieved April 5, 2005, from http://news.bbc.co. uk/1/hi/world/americas/4382087.stm.
3. McDougall, L. (2005). Silent and defiant to the end, Luke Mitchell denied the family of Jodi Jones the one answer they needed. *Sunday Herald*, January 23.
4. Robertson, J., & Gray, L. (2005). Cannabis blamed for 'wicked' Jodi murder. *The Scotsman*. February 12.
5. *'Vampire boy' asked officer to bite him.* Retrieved April 27, 2004, from http://news. bbc.co.uk/1/hi/wales/2134693.stm.
6. Khan, S. (2003). Celebrity cult of vampires can turn into real-life evil. *The Observer*, October 26.
7. Robelen, E. W. (2002). Spending plan for 2002 laden with 'earmarks.' *Education Week*, 21(20), 23–27.
8. Prendergast, A. (2001). I'm full of hate and I love it. *Denver Westword*. Retrieved April 27, 2004, from www.westword.com/issues/2001-12-06/news.html.
9. Cullen, D. (2004). The depressive and the psychopath. Retrieved April 23, 2004, from http://slate.msn.com/id/2099203.
10. Davis, H., & McLeod, S. L. (2003). Why humans value sensational news: an evolutionary perspective. *Evolution and Human Behavior*, 24, 208–216.
11. Egan, V., Auty, J., Miller, R., Ahmadi, S., Richardson, C., & Gargan, I. (1999). Sensational interests and general personality traits. *The Journal of Forensic Psychiatry*, 10, 567–581.
12. Brittain, R. P. (1970). The sadistic murderer. *Medicine, Science, and the Law*, 10, 198–207.
13. Egan, V., Charlesworth, P., Richardson, C., Blair, M., & McMurran, M. (2001). Sensational interests and sensation seeking in mentally disordered offenders. *Personality and Individual Differences*, 30, 995–1007.
14. Egan, V., Austin, E., Elliot, D., Patel, D., & Charlesworth, P. (2003). Personality traits, personality disorders and sensational interests in mentally disordered offenders. *Legal and Criminological Psychology*, 8, 51–62.
15. Loranger, A. W. (1999). *International Personality Disorder Examination*. Odessa, FL: Psychological Assessment Resources.
16. Austin, E. J., & Deary, I. J. (2000). The 'four As': a common framework for normal and abnormal personality? *Personality and Individual Differences*, 28, 977–995.
17. Weiss, A., Egan, V., & Figueredo, A. J. (2004). Sensational interests as a form of intrasexual competition. *Personality and Individual Differences*, 36, 563–573.
18. Egan, V., Figueredo, A. J., Wolf, P., McBride, K., Sefcek, J., Vasquez, G., & Charles, K. (2005). Sensational interests, mating effort, and personality: evidence for cross-cultural validity. *Journal of Individual Differences*, 26, 11–19.
19. Gottfredson, M. R., & Hirschi, T. (1990). *A General Theory of Crime*. Stanford, CA: Stanford University Press.

20. Moffitt, T. E. (1993). Adolescence-limited and life-course-persistent antisocial behavior: a developmental taxonomy. *Psychological Review*, 100, 674–701.
21. Quinsey, V. L. (2002). Evolutionary theory and criminal behaviour. *Legal and Criminological Psychology*, 7, 1–13.
22. Rowe, D. C., Vazsonyi, A. T., & Figueredo, A. J. (1997). Mating-effort in adolescence: a conditional or alternative strategy. *Personality and Individual Differences*, 23, 105–115.
23. Wilson, M., & Daly, M. (1985). Competitiveness, risk taking, and violence: the young male syndrome. *Ethology and Sociobiology*, 6, 59–73.
24. Ellis, L. (1988). Criminal behaviour and r/K selection: an extension of gene-based evolutionary theory. *Personality and Individual Differences*, 9, 697–708.
25. Carpentier, F. D., Knobloch, S., & Zillmann, D. (2003). Rock, rap, and rebellion: comparisons of traits predicting selective exposure to defiant music. *Personality and Individual Differences*, 35, 1643–1655.
26. Arnett, J. (1991). Heavy metal music and reckless behavior among adolescents. *Journal of Youth and Adolescence*, 20, 573–583.
27. Nathanson, C., Paulhus, D. L., & Williams, K. M. (2003). Marks of misbehavior: personality, predictors and behavioral correlates of appearance anomalies. Presented at the 4th Annual Meeting of the Society for Personality and Social Psychology, Los Angeles.
28. Charles, K. E. (2006). The effects of sensational interests, intrasexual competition, and psychopathology on juvenile delinquency. Doctoral dissertation, Glasgow Caledonian University.
29. Moffitt, T. E., & Silva, P. A. (1988). Self-reported delinquency: results from an instrument for New Zealand. *Australia and New Zealand Journal of Criminology*, 21, 227–240.
30. Charles, K. E., & Egan, V. (2005). Mating effort correlates with self-reported delinquency in a normal adolescent sample. *Personality and Individual Differences*, 38, 1035–1045.
31. Hooper, J. (2002). Flirting with Hitler. *The Guardian*, November 16.
32. Dundas, Z. (2005). The notorious Michael Moynihan. Mumblage International. Retrieved March 29, 2005, from www.mumblage.com/story.php?id=36.
33. Moynihan, M., & Søderlind, D. (2003). *Lords of Chaos*. Los Angeles: Feral House.
34. Shobert, A. (2005). Private communication, March 29, 2005.
35. Baddeley, G. (1999). *Lucifer Rising*. London: Plexus.
36. Haste, C. (2001). *Nazi Women*. London: Channel 4 Books.
37. Harris, G. (2005). Jodi killer attracts female 'fanclub.' *The Times*, February 12, 2005.
38. Lanning, K. (1989). Satanic, occult, ritualistic crime: a law enforcement perspective. *Police Chief Magazine*, October.
39. Swett, B., Marcus, R. F., & Reio Jr., T. G. (2005). An introduction to "fight-seeking," and its role in peer-to-peer violence on college campuses. *Personality and Individual Differences*, 38, 953–962.

Chapter 6

Narcissism, Sadism, and Loneliness

The Case of Serial Killer Jeffrey Dahmer

George B. Palermo

Abstract

Jeffrey Dahmer, the notorious Milwaukee, Wisconsin, serial killer, was charged with 15 counts of first-degree intentional homicide. The homicides took place between 1987 and 1990 and were discovered during the summer of 1991. Dahmer pleaded not guilty by reason of mental disease or defect. The author was the court-appointed forensic psychiatric expert in the case. This chapter reports historical and psychological features of Dahmer the man and Dahmer the killer.

INTRODUCTION

A society that stresses conformity, individualism, and hedonism may create confusion and frustration in its members and, at times, plunge them into a moral crisis. Such a type of society reduces reason to mere calculation. "Reason can [then] impose no limits on the pursuit of pleasure, [or] on the immediate gratification of every desire, no matter how perverse, insane, criminal, or merely immoral" *(1)*. The above social panorama easily brings about behaviors on the part of some individuals that are socially perturbing and unacceptable.

From: *Serial Murder and the Psychology of Violent Crimes*
Edited by: R. N. Kocsis © Humana Press, Totowa, NJ

Indeed, without minimizing personality factors, one could opine that such a social climate breeds psychopathic behaviors and, at times, serious criminal acting out.

Holmes and DeBurger, writing on serial murder, expressed their view that the social and cultural context in which the killer and victims live may be a cofactor in the genesis of serial murder. They stated that "socialization is unfortunately saturated with norms, values, beliefs and behavioral models that carry strong potential for normalizing violence in interpersonal relationships" *(2)*. They were referring to the excessive violence in mass media entertainment in the United States, to the anonymity and dehumanization of urban society, and to the great mobility of Americans as possible facilitators of criminal acting out. Undoubtedly, all of the above factors play a significant role in unleashing the antisocial homicidal fury of a psychopathic serial killer.

Antisocial behavior should be viewed as a continuum of increasing degrees of psychopathy. Such behaviors range from the simple antisocial personality disorder to the psychopathic personality disorder, with its severe antisocial conduct. The socially destructive hostility of a psychopath is often an unconscious means to overcome feelings of worthlessness. It gives persons who are filled with anger a spurious sense of pseudo-omnipotence that allows them to control and dispose of their innocent and unsuspecting fellow humans. Such psychopathic behaviors are strictly connected to the widespread phenomenon of serial killing. In its worst manifestations psychopathic behavior becomes malignant, similar to malignant narcissism *(3)*.

Psychopathy is a social construct that describes a combination of personality traits and socially deviant behaviors. Attention to this phenomenon has been given during the past centuries by numerous scholars, from Lombroso to Cleckley to Kernberg and Hare. The psychopath has been described by them all as a selfish, impulsive, aggressive, loveless, remorseless, callous, two-dimensional person—a person able to use emotions when it is to his advantage. A distinction, however, should be made between the ordinary psychopath (who acts antisocially, is frequently impulsive, and whose crimes are characterized by an affective reaction, consciously related to actively pursuing materialistic gains) and the malignant type of psychopath (a clearly predatory, violent individual whose goal is the gratification of vengeful or sexual sadistic fantasies).

With the malignant type of psychopath, the antisocial behavior is repetitively similar. Such a psychopath is akin to the malignant narcissistic individual described by Kernberg *(4)*. He displays a combination of narcissism, egosyntonic antisocial aggression, sadism, and paranoid features. He voices distrust and feelings of rejection and of not being accepted. Morally restless, he disregards society's values. Halleck *(5)* accurately described the psychopath as an extremely egocentric individual who wants to suit the world to his needs. Those traits are an integral part of a serial killer's personality. Generally, the serial killer is a lonely person, cold, distant, callous, and ruthless in his violence. He entices his victims with an apparently charming but deceitful and manipulative approach. His purpose is to achieve complete control over them.

Contrary to the common psychopath, the malignant psychopath/serial killer is able to control his impulsivity. Although able to control his impulses, he uses his sadistic fantasies in the construction of a murderous scenario, typical of a predator. He is able to organize, program, and direct his destructive impulses, unleashing them at the most opportune moment for achieving what he wants. The malignant psychopath/serial killer has difficulty forming lasting bonds with others, exhibiting a deficit in object relations. Psychoanalysts theorize that this is a consequence of his misperception of his mother's behavior during the infantile period. That could well explain this killer's lack of empathy, his ambivalence and noncaring attitude toward others. Also, he tends to misinterpret social cues. However, Blair and colleagues *(6)*, looking at psychopaths in relation to the Theory of Mind, or mentalizing, which tests an individual's capacity to appreciate the mental states of others (thoughts, desires, hopes, feelings), found that psychopaths do not have a deficit in mentalizing but appear to lack the emotional apparatus to feel empathy or guilt. This is typical of the malignant psychopath/serial killer who, even though aware of the feelings of his victims, disregards them. Indeed, it is through the reification of the victims that he is able to carry out the sadistic torture and killing.

The U.S. Federal Bureau of Investigation (FBI) summarized the personality traits of the serial killer as "a sense of social isolation, preference for autoerotic activities and fetishes, rebelliousness, aggression, chronic lying...lack of trust and commitment to a world of rules and regulations...[and a] personal affective life dependent on fantasies..." *(7)*. In fact, fantasies play a large role in the criminal conduct of narcissistic, lust serial killers, who often spend a great deal of time imagining how they will go about their criminal actions. Morally restless and often nonsocial, disregarding society's values and norms, they create fantasies that become the primary source of emotional arousal.

Typical of serial killers are sadism, narcissism, and loneliness. During the 18th century, the erotic and licentious writings of the libertine Marquis de Sade shocked the world with their descriptions of cruel sadistic violence and unbound perverted lust. De Sade believed that instincts are the motivating force in life and that pleasure is the most important goal for which one should aim. His books about debauchery and acts of sexual violence were written while he was in jail for crimes of poisoning and sodomy, and his life ended in a lunatic asylum *(8)*. Years later, in 1869, Richard von Krafft-Ebing coined the term sadism; the term acquired the meaning of a sexual perversion in which the pervert forced upon the subject of his sexual attraction physical or moral suffering, deriving sexual pleasure from his actions *(9)*. The infliction of pain seems to be part of the complete mastery of another person. As one killer stated, the most radical aim of a sadistic act is to make the person suffer because there is no greater power over another person than inflicting pain. Nevertheless, it has been hypothesized that rather than to express cruelty in and of itself, the object of sadism is to procure strong emotions *(10)*.

Brittain's seminal work in 1970 laid the foundation for a possible typology of a sexual sadist. His description is basically that which fits some present-day sadistic murderers. He described the sadist as a secretive male individual who is generally nonviolent in everyday life, but he is obsessive, insecure, and narcissistic, often suffering from hypochondriasis, a loner with a rich fantasy life. He believed that the sexual sadist creates sadistic scenes in his fantasies that he later acts out in his killings *(11)*. This type of killer is single and may hate his mother; his perversion starts early in life; and he exhibits an interest in pornography and is excited by cruelty. Brittain's description of the sexual sadistic murderer is remindful of Jeffrey Dahmer who, a typical charming psychopath, behaved well even on apprehension but hid behind his calm and socialized appearance destructive sexual fantasies.

FANTASY

Many of the fantasies found in the serial killer, as stated above, are sadistic sexual fantasies. Sexual fantasies, at times violent in type, are also present in juvenile offenders and, when frequent, may degenerate into sadistic sexual fantasies. In such cases, they are sometimes the forerunners of homicidal acting out. According to MacCulloch et al., the sadistic sexual fantasies have their origins at the time of traumatic episodes, such as sexual or physical abuse during early childhood *(12)*. It has been theorized that the sadist may suffer from an arrest of psychosexual development, possibly at the anal stage (the anal-sadistic stage), or from a neurotic regression to that level. Fantasies of rape or murder were found in 86% of the cases of adults in one study of serial sexual homicide conducted by Robert Prentky and colleagues *(13)*. Similarly, Janet Warren and colleagues found evidence of violent fantasies in 80% of their cases *(14)*.

The important role of sadistic fantasies, especially repetitive masturbatory fantasies, in these killers was emphasized by MacCulloch et al., and that of daydreaming and compulsive masturbation was reported by Prentky and colleagues and by others *(15,16)*. Although Sigmund Freud first viewed sadistic drives as primary instincts camouflaged by the drive to dominate, he later came to believe that sadism is the excessive outward manifestation of the death instinct *(17)*. The gratuitous cruelty of sadism is possible because of insufficient control by the basic mechanism of defense. It can be theorized that the behavior of the sadistic, power- and control-driven serial killer reflects the conduct of a curious child during the demolition of his toys.

MALIGNANT NARCISSISM

Various theories of behavior can be considered when trying to understand the serial killer's malignant narcissism. Kohut *(18)* hypothesized that a narcissistic trauma suffered by the child during the process of individuation does not enable him to tame the archaic, grandiose, and exhibitionistic self, which is necessary for wholesome development. Therefore, because of this inability to develop properly, the child—future adult—carries within himself not only a disappointing parental image but an image of his archaic grandiose self. This could explain the serial killer's deeply rooted destructive hostility and his feelings of omnipotence.

Mahler *(19)*, instead, posited that if hampered in his efforts while in the process of individuation and while attempting to distance himself from his mother the child may become frustrated and develop a neurosis. He then becomes extremely ambivalent toward his mother, whom he sees as a castrating person; a mounting rage takes root because of his difficulty in achieving a reasonable separation from her. He develops feelings of hostility, frustrated dependence, and a tendency to explosive behavior. These are all particular psychological characteristics of serial killers.

Klein *(20)* theorized that during infancy the child perceived his mother's breast in an ambivalent way, not only as a source of nourishment but as a frustrating object. This ambivalence may be translated into paranoid anxieties and fears, which lead to ambivalent relationships during adult life if not corrected. A tendency to paranoia is present as a feature of the personality disorder of the serial killer.

Narcissistic tendencies, part of the grandiose self described by Kohut, are often present in the serial killer. Originally described by Freud, narcissism was later subdivided by Kohut into primary and secondary narcissism. Primary narcissism is seen as the investment of libidinal energy in the achievement of object love, empathy, and possible creativity; secondary narcissism is the withdrawing of the original psychic libidinal energy from objects back to the ego. The latter mechanism seems to be present in the psychodynamics of serial killers. They are indeed not only pathologically narcissistic but unrealistically grandiose, and their exaggerated self-importance is fragile and sensitive to shame.

Walsh expressed his belief that when aggression is expressed sadistically, it leads to an increase in self-esteem and the confirmation of grandiosity *(21)*. Serial killers assume a detached stance that eventually erupts into destructive fury. Almost without exception they choose vulnerable victims who are easy to dominate. It is apparently indifference, not hatred, toward the victim that allows the killer to depersonalize him or her, and the experience of killing seems to increase the killer's willingness to kill again, even more brutally. In so doing, he asserts his pseudo-superiority, which covers up for his basic feelings of inadequacy.

LONELINESS

Serial killers generally are basically lonely persons. Loneliness appears as a feeling and a state of separation from others. Preconscious awareness of the immediacy and accessibility of others, as well as a memory of past togetherness, are prerequisite for loneliness. Infrequently loneliness involves some kind of choice and willful separation *(22)*.

Loneliness is an ancient nemesis. It can involve excruciating physical as well as mental suffering and is implicated in numerous somatic, psychosomatic, and psychiatric diseases *(23)*. It is a mundane yet arcane human affliction that is often hazardous to health and hostile to happiness. There are distinctive types of loneliness, such as emotional (Eros loneliness), social (friendship loneliness), cultural, ethical, ontological, existential, communicative, epistemological, and metaphysical *(24)*. Thus, extreme loneliness may lead to internal hardening, social and moral numbing, indifference, and anger.

Philosophically speaking, loneliness has been described as the defining feature of human awareness and the fundamental question of human existence *(25)*. Jaspers viewed it as a possible springboard to self-realization and as a presupposition of communication *(26)*. However, not every lonely human being is able to make the step from loneliness to communication. Long-lasting loneliness may lead to the painful belief in one's inability to be a part of humankind and to severe distortion of reality. One result of social isolation is an associated lack of the possibility to utilize the constructive psychosocial, emotional, and moral feedback of others.

In a retrospective study of a Dutch population of violent, forensic psychiatric patients ($n = 634$), Martens *(27,28)* found that a systematic distortion of reality, as well as too much contact with the harsh dimensions of reality (when these negative experiences concerning reality differ fundamentally from the reality experiences of other people), may result in pathological loneliness, social isolation, and devastating feelings of being cast out and thrown away. However, severe social isolation and correlated loneliness may also be the consequence of a lack of social support, neglect and/or emotional/physical abuse, mental disorders and associated cognitive impairments, and social-emotional and moral incapacities *(29)*.

A study by Seidman et al. found that sex offenders were both more lonely and more deficient in intimacy than other offenders and community controls *(30)*. Intimacy seemed to be the most important deficit among the sex offenders they studied. In another study indicating a link between loneliness and sexual offending, child sexual offenders reported significantly more emotional loneliness than did nonsexual offenders *(31)*.

People who are lonely are bound to focus on their inner conflicts; and because of their tendency to withdrawing from others, their ability to express love and warmth in a normal relationship is greatly diminished. Deviant sexual and nonsexual fantasies take the place of normal socialization, and at times they become destructive and fuel antisocial acting out.

Many psychopathic killers verbalize feelings of loneliness together with low self-esteem and feelings of shame for not being able to live up to family and societal expectations.

THE LUST KILLER

The description and dynamics of the lust killer or sexual sadistic killer are the same as those of the larger group of serial killers. In a study of serial killers by Stone, 71 of 77 male subjects met the criteria for SPD (sadistic personality disorder) *(32)*. The classification of the FBI subdivides the serial lust killer into the disorganized asocial murderer and the organized nonsocial murderer.

The disorganized asocial murderer frequently suffers from a serious mental disorder, is usually of below average intelligence, is socially inadequate, is an unskilled worker, is sexually incompetent, has a low birth order status, and was harshly disciplined as a child by a father who was an unstable provider. He claims to be rather anxious during the perpetration of his crimes, uses small amounts of alcohol, and reacts strongly to even minimal environmental stress. He usually lives alone and lives and works near the crime scene. He has little interest in the news media, and his behavior is often erratic.

The organized nonsocial, lust murderer, on the other hand, is of average to above-average intelligence, is socially competent, is often a skilled worker, is sexually competent, and usually displays a personality disorder. He has a high birth order status. His father held a stable job, and his childhood discipline was inconsistent. He is usually well controlled during the offense, even though he uses moderate amounts of alcohol before or during the crime.

A mixed form of organized/disorganized serial killer also may be encountered.

JEFFREY DAHMER: THE MAN AND THE KILLER[1]

Typical of the organized, nonsocial lust murderer, Jeffrey Dahmer made local, national, and international news at the time of his apprehension in 1991 following the discovery of his crimes. Dahmer, a white man, was 31 years old when examined by the author to ascertain his mental status and his criminal responsibility at the time of his killings. He was tall, well developed, and well nourished. He had a light complexion, his hair was brownish-blond, and his face was unshaven. His posture was erect and his ambulation normal; on observation, there was no evidence of neurological deficits, unusual facial mimicry, tics, or mannerisms. He sat up straight in his chair, a bit tense only during the first part of the many hours of interviews, and his attitude was one of cooperativeness and friendliness. Calm and free from any obvious emotional lability, his speech was clear and understandable. His answers and statements were coherent, relevant, and logical. He spoke without any circumstantiality or tangentiality, and his thinking did not show any disorganization or delusional or hallucinatory ideas. He generally provided direct and full answers to questions posed to him, and he appeared to have a high level of intelligence. He showed reflective capacity and unimpaired and rational thinking. He assumed complete responsibility for all of the murders with which he was charged. He was emotionally tranquil and at ease as he recounted the many memories pertinent to his offenses. He gave the impression of being happy to be able finally to unburden his conscience of his horrendous crimes.

Dahmer recounted a number of changes of residence for family reasons as he was growing up. He described himself as surrounded by arguing parents at home and "arrogant jerks" in school. He claimed that during adolescence he was prone to violent fits of anger and occasional rage and said that his deceitful behavior at home was frequently reprimanded. He became angry when he was found to be lying but eventually would admit his wrongdoing. He denied sibling rivalry with his younger brother, David. He said that his father's strict demands and his mother's unpredictable and argumentative behavior, toward both his father and himself, angered him; and he spoke of their frequent arguing during a long predivorce period. However, he also recalled that he and his father

---

[1] The author was the court-appointed forensic psychiatric expert in State of Wisconsin vs. Jeffrey Dahmer, case no. F-912542, 1992. Dahmer was charged with 15 counts of first-degree intentional homicide. The examinations were conducted over a period of several days for a total of 14 hours. His father, his mother, his stepmother, and his brother were interviewed at length, either in person or by telephone.

often used to massage each other's backs, almost as a routine; he voiced no sexual feelings about it. When he was not sulking, he would often express his resentment by destructive activity in his backyard.

As an adolescent Dahmer was interested in taxonomy and collected insects. He claimed that when he was 15 or 16 years old and attending biology dissection classes at school he developed an interest in dissecting animals, using formaldehyde to preserve them. They were mostly dogs and foxes but also smaller animals that he found dead on the road. His intention was to keep the bones and make a statue out of them, he said, but he never actually did so. He remembered taking home from school the head of a pig and keeping the skull. He graduated from high school at age 18 with a C grade average.

During his early adolescence Dahmer was involved in homosexual experimentation on a few occasions and also in streaking (running naked). At age 13 he began to drink alcohol, alone and with friends. However, most of his heavy drinking and marijuana smoking (three or four joints daily) started at age 17. He experienced some drunkenness and hangovers, and several times he passed out. He said that he did not think highly of himself during childhood and adolescence. That was probably the beginning of the low self-esteem that he later claimed. He described himself as a loner who frequently became upset with classmates and others who teased him, but said that he never got into fights. He was unable to express his anger openly for fear of retaliation. That inability may have been an expression of his deep feelings of inadequacy as well as aggression. He stated that he had never enjoyed sports, always thinking that the other guys were better than he. He was envious of them and stated that at times felt so angry that he had thoughts of killing them. He said that he masturbated daily while looking at pictures of good-looking men in magazines—trim with good muscle tone, youngish, not older than 30. He stated that he admired their physical appearance and when he imagined himself in bed with them it was always as a male practicing sodomy. He enjoyed sodomizing people but abhorred the thought of being sodomized himself. He stated that he had no racial preferences in his fantasies. He had never had any heterosexual experiences.

At one time while he was growing up, Dahmer was disturbed about his increased weight due to his continuous use of marijuana. He attended college in Florida, but while there he felt directionless and without clear ideas. At college his drinking (mostly beer) increased, and he felt isolated and lonely. He was shy and somewhat uncomfortable when having to start new relationships. He felt attracted to men and helpless and frustrated in his desire to change his sexual orientation and his social timidity; he was basically withdrawn and sad. After a semester at college, at his father's suggestion, he joined the army; and he seemed to be proud of having gone through basic training. He became a medic and after 2 weeks he was transferred overseas to Germany. He had been taught CPR (cardiopulmonary resuscitation) and basic first-aid, including how to set bones and stop bleeding. While overseas, he drank heavily—a six- or twelve-pack of beer a night—and at times other alcoholic drinks. At camp, he was involved in a few fights and yelling matches, for which he was punished. His sexual activity, he claimed, was limited to looking at pornographic magazines and masturbating himself. He disclaimed any romantic or nonromantic homosexual relations at that time, stating that he was afraid of engaging in any such relations while in the army. In reply to specific questioning, he stated that while stationed in Germany he never killed anybody. (Interpol had questioned him about several unsolved murders that had taken place at the time of his military service there.)

Honorably discharged from military service, Dahmer returned to the United States. After a brief period in Ohio with his father, at his father's suggestion he moved to Milwaukee to live with his paternal grandmother, hoping that by living with her his heavy drinking might diminish. At first, he limited his drinking mostly to weekends, but eventually he began to drink more. He went to local taverns and often got drunk, returning home at 2 to 3 a.m. or occasionally staying out all night. On three occasions he was arrested for drunkenness and jailed overnight. He was fired from his job at the city's blood plasma bank after 1 year because of poor performance. He had been ambivalent about the job; and, ironically, he stated that he did not like to stick people with needles. He did temporary odd jobs until he was hired by a local chocolate manufacturing company where he worked for 7 years.

Dahmer claimed that during the time he resided at his grandmother's he began to go to church with her, attempting to stop drinking, stop his homosexual behavior, and turn his life around. He claimed that he did not drink for 2 years until one day, while in a public library quietly reading a book, one of the library patrons handed him a note inviting him to have sex with him downstairs in the library bathroom. Even though he had dismissed the offer, he claimed that the episode changed his life for the worse.

While still living at his grandmother's house, again drinking heavily, Dahmer began going to porno bookstores, gay bars, and Chicago bathhouses. At the bathhouses he started his homosexual behavior again and, wanting to be in control of the relationship, began to give his occasional sexual partners drinks containing dissolved sleeping pills. He sodomized his partners and left the locale when they were still asleep for fear of being sodomized himself, to which he had previously agreed. The bath house patrons reported his behavior to the management, and he was denied further admittance.

In 1989, he moved to his own apartment in the inner city because, he stated, he wanted a place of his own that was close to work and had low rent. He stated that he did not want his drinking behavior to upset his grandmother any longer and, at the same time, wanted to be free of her supervision. Even more central to this move was the fact that by that time he had been turned out of the bathhouses and had no place to go to engage in homosexual relations. Shortly after his move, he was charged with and convicted of second degree sexual assault for enticing a child for immoral purposes and was placed on probation for 5 years, during which period he had to report to the state correctional service.

When specifically questioned about the offenses with which he was currently charged, Dahmer explained in a calm and spontaneous fashion that his 15 homicide charges did not include his killing a white male victim after a rendezvous in a hotel in Milwaukee and his taking the victim's body from the hotel in a large piece of luggage to dispose of him. Nor did it include that of a young man his own age whom he had killed after a brief encounter when he was 18, and whose dismembered body he had buried in the backyard of his family's home in Bath, Ohio. Asked whether he remembered how far back his mixture of homosexual and homicidal fantasies and behavior went, he said that when he had been about 15 years old and out for a walk a few miles from his home he saw a good-looking young man slightly older than he and he began to fantasize about hitting him on the back of the head with a baseball bat and then having sex with him. He admitted to frequent sadistic sexual fantasies after that, in which he eventually killed his victim.

While discussing each murder Dahmer was coherent, relevant, and logical. In a calm, controlled, perfunctory way he went into specific details about the enticement and sexual seductions of his victims, love-making, use of drugged drinks, the way in which he killed them by strangling or stabbing, and the trophy collection of some of their skulls. He also recounted his photographing the dead persons or parts of the dead bodies. He explained what he did with the dead bodies—dismembering them, disemboweling them, cutting them to pieces and then boiling the flesh in a large boiler he had purchased for that purpose to get rid of the stench of the many accumulated cadavers. He added that in some cases he attempted to preserve some body parts. He also defleshed six of his victim's skulls. It was evident that on each and every occasion his murderous actions were performed in a calm, calculated, prearranged plan. He described how he obtained all the necessary items for his heinous crimes and how he felt compelled to secure his apartment with a high quality security system.

CONCLUSIVE REFLECTIONS

Repressed hostility, frustrated acceptance, and intense fear of rejection by his peers were freely voiced by Dahmer when specifically questioned about them. He claimed to suffer from intense loneliness, and his remarks that he did not want to lose his victims but wanted to keep some mementos of them testify to that. He said that at times he lay next to the cadavers of his victims, kissing them. He attributed the motivation for his actions to lust. He described his maneuvering to keep some of the victims in a zombie-like state and how he intended to make fetishes out of some of their body parts. Parts of the victims' bodies, isolated bones, or entire skeletons and skulls found in his apartment testify to their symbolic fetishism for him. Sexual sadism seemed to be at the base of his desire to keep his victims sedated while sexually abusing them and drilling holes into their skulls. The latter was done in order to inject muriatic acid into their brains so he could dissolve the brain substance and obtain, as he wished, a perfect nonsectioned skull. He claimed that occasional anthropophagy climaxed some of the murderous scenes.

During the various examinations, Dahmer clearly stated that in his life and at the time of his homicides he always wanted to be in control. Asked about the main theme of his fantasies, he replied that they were more about lust than power and said that he believed that he had made them the most powerful thing in his life. He admitted to getting a thrill from the killing. He drank moderate amounts of alcoholic beverage while carrying out his criminal acts but said that he was always aware of what he was doing. He demonstrated only lip-service remorse for what he had done.

Sexual immaturity, perverse sexuality, frustration, passivity, loneliness, fear of nonacceptance by a hostile world, and a mixture of emotional detachment and aggressive hostile behavior are encountered in the psychopathology of the personality of serial killer Jeffrey Dahmer. Dahmer's ambivalence about his own confused sexuality and his feelings of anticipated rejection by others brought about compulsive, sadistic sexual behavior, destructive of the object of his pseudo-sexual attention.

Dahmer was a loner as a child, growing up in a dysfunctional family. Frequent quarrels between his mother and father lead to his hostile feelings toward them. A neurotic, depressed mother and a frequently absent father who was absorbed in his career did not allow Jeffrey Dahmer a complete masculine identification. Since adolescence, he had medicated his anger and frustration with alcohol. He was greatly ambivalent about his homosexual tendency, felt frequently frustrated by it, and eventually channeled his hostility into sadistic behavior against people who accepted his homosexual advances. Attraction and rejection exploded in his first murder at age 18 while he was alone in his parents' home in Ohio. After strangling, in a fit of rage, his first young victim by exercising pressure on his throat from behind with a weight-lifting bar (someone he had met casually who was not himself a homosexual), he destroyed the body by cutting it into pieces that he buried in his backyard.

Later, in Milwaukee, Dahmer actuated a methodical program of enticing to his home 15 young victims, mostly in their twenties, who were attracted by his promises of money for posing for photographs and an unspoken exchange of sexuality. He had sex with them, sodomizing them, frequently after having handcuffed them and offering them intoxicating drinks containing soporific substances. Afterward, while they were still under the effect of the soporific substance, he killed them and he later dismembered their bodies. The survivor of his last encounter stated that Dahmer had been charming, calm, and completely normal in his behavior when he invited him to his apartment. He described him as the opposite of the person who dismembered his victims' bodies, boiled the body parts to destroy the flesh and to keep the bones and skulls as fetishes, and/or photographed symbolic body parts and whole naked bodies in sexually suggestive positions—a typical signature for him—because, he later said, he wanted to keep them as mementos—to keep him company.

In the author's view, Dahmer's destructive behavior and his symbolic fetishes were the expression of his deep ambivalence about his own homosexual behavior and a love–hate relationship with his victims. He was clearly sadistic in his cruelty to his victims. His sexual involvement with his victims was paraphilic in nature. Even though his behavior was not due to psychosis, he showed ananchastic features; and it was of a programmed, meticulous, distorted sexual type. With his tendency to act on weekends, he showed calculated planning with risk avoidance. Because most of his victims were black, he told the author, the media interpretation that his behavior was racially oriented concerned and frightened him. He was afraid of possible retaliation by the Black prison community. In that, he seemed to have foreseen the future because he was eventually killed in prison by a Black inmate.

A possible explanation for Dahmer's abhorrent conduct is that he was driven by compulsive hostile aggressivity. His violence was so profound that he killed, cut, dismembered, and dissected in an obsessive, sadistic way, the body that attracted and repelled him at the same time—a body that he wanted to torture and destroy because he felt that by doing so he would be able to get rid of his inner, torturing homosexual drives and unwanted attraction to men—a body he really did not love, contrary to what he wanted to believe or wanted others to believe. The possible anthropophagy of his young victims may have been the expression of his desire to incorporate and make his own their attractive qualities, or perhaps it simply demonstrated a superstitious, atavistic tribal belief. His actions may have, in some way, saved him from committing suicide. Even his sadism was the exercising of power and violence upon another for the assertion and preservation of Self. He joined a long list of sexual murderers. He shared with them not only a deeply violent, destructive hostility but also boredom, loneliness, sadism, and narcissism.[2]

REFERENCES

1. Lasch, C. (1991). *The Culture of Narcissism: American Life in an Age of Diminishing Expectations.* New York: W.W. Norton.
2. Holmes, R. M., & DeBurger, S. T. (1988). *Serial Murder.* Newbury Park, CA: Sage.
3. Palermo, G. B. (2004). *The Faces of Violence*, (2nd ed). Springfield, IL: Charles C Thomas.
4. Kernberg, O. F. (1992). *Aggression in Personality Disorders and Perversions.* New Haven, CT: Yale University Press.
5. Halleck, S. L. (1967). *Psychiatry and the Dilemma of Crime.* New York: Harper & Row/Hoeber Medical Books.
6. Blair, J., Sellars, C., Strickland, I., & Clark J. (1996). Theory of mind in the psychopath. *Journal of Forensic Psychiatry*, 7(1), 15–25.
7. Federal Bureau of Investigation. (1990). *Criminal Investigative Analysis: Sexual Homicide.* Quantico, VA: National Center for the Analysis of Violent Crime.
8. Pauvert, J. J. (1965). *Vie du Marquis de Sade.* Paris: Édition Jean-Jacques Pauvert et Éditions Gallinard.
9. Von Krafft-Ebing, R. ([1869] 1965). *Psychopathis Sexualis: With Special Reference to the Antipathetic Sexual Instinct. A Medico-Forensic Study.* New York: Bell.
10. MacCulloch, M. J., Snowden, P. R., Wood, P. J. W., & Mills, H. E. (1983). Sadistic fantasy, sadistic behaviour, and offending. *British Journal of Psychiatry*, 143, 20–29.

---

[2] Jeffrey Dahmer, after being thoroughly examined and undergoing repeated psychological tests (including the MMPI-II and the Rorschach) and tests to rule out organic or genetic pathology (MRI of the brain, EEG, and chromosomal analysis) was diagnosed as suffering from a mixed personality disorder with sadistic, obsessive, fetishistic, antisocial, necrophilic features, typical of what has been called the organized nonsocial, lust murderer. He entered a plea of not guilty by reason of insanity, in part to avoid being placed in a correctional institution in the midst of Black inmates, from whom he feared retaliation for his crimes. The verdict of the jury found him legally sane on all 15 murder counts, and the Court sentenced him to 15 consecutive terms of life in prison, one for each count of murder with which he had been charged, without possibility for parole. In 1994, he was killed by another inmate in the correctional institution in which he was confined. I had examined Dahmer's killer in 1991 when he had entered a plea of not guilty by reason of insanity and found him to be legally responsible for his crime of murder committed during a robbery.

11. Brittain, R. P. (1970). The sadistic murderer. *Medicine, Science and the Law*, 10, 198–207.

12. MacCulloch et al. Op. cit. (1983).

13. Prentky, R. A., Burgess, A. W., Rokous, F., Lee, A., Hartman, C., Ressler, R., & Douglas, J. (1989). The presumptive role of fantasy in serial sexual homicide. *American Journal of Psychiatry*, 146, 887–891.

14. Warren, J. I., Hazelwood, R. R., & Dietz, P. E. (1996). The sexually sadistic serial killer. *Journal of Forensic Sciences*, 41, 970–974.

15. Prentky, et al. Op. cit. (1989).

16. Johnson, B. R., & Becker, J. V. (1997). Natural born killers? The development of the sexually sadistic serial killer. *Journal of the American Academy of Psychiatry and the Law*, 25(3), 335–348.

17. Freud, S. (1960). *The Ego and the Id*. Strachey, J. (Ed.),. Riviere, J. (Trans.). New York/London: W.W. Norton.

18. Kohut, H. (1971). The psychoanalytic study of the child. Monograph No. 4. In: *The Analysis of the Self*. New York: International University Press.

19. Mahler, M. (1972). A study of the separation-individuation process. *Psychoanalytic Study of the Child*, 26, 403–444.

20. Klein, M. (1935). A contribution to the psychogenesis of manic-depressive states. *International Journal of Psychoanalysis*, 16, 145–174.

21. Walsh, T. C. (1999). Psychopathic and nonpsychopathic violence among alcoholic offenders. *International Journal of Offender Therapy and Comparative Criminology*, 43(1), 34–48.

22. Gotz, I. L. (1974). Loneliness. *Humanitas*, 10, 289–299.

23. McGraw, J. G. (2000). The first of all evils. In: Wawrytko, S. A. (Ed.). *The Problem of Evil: An Intercultural Exploration* (pp. 145–158). Atlanta: Editions Rodopi PV.

24. McGraw, J. G. (1995). Loneliness, its nature and forms: an existential perspective. *Man and World*, 28(1), 43–64.

25. Art, B. (1992). Isolation, loneliness and falsification of reality. *International Journal of Applied Philosophy*, 7(1), 31–36.

26. Salamun, K. (1988). Moral implications of Karl Jaspers existentialism. *Philosophy and Phenomenological Research*, 49, 317–323.

27. Martens, W. H. J. (1997). *Psychopathy and remission*. Maastricht, The Netherlands: Shaker Publishing/Tilburg University.

28. Martens, W. H. K. (2002). The hidden suffering of the psychopath. *Psychiatric Times*, 19(1), 1–7.

29. Martens, W. H. J., & Palermo, G. B. (2005). Loneliness and associated violent antisocial behavior: analysis of the case reports of Jeffrey Dahmer and Dennis Nilsen. *International Journal of Offender Therapy and Comparative Criminology*, 49(3), 298–307.

30. Seidman, B. T., Marshall, W. L., Hudson, S. M., & Robertson, P. J. (1994). An examination of intimacy and loneliness in sex offenders. *Journal of Interpersonal Violence*, 9(4), 518–534.

31. Marsa, F., O'Reilly, G., Carr, A., Murphy, P., O'Sullivan, M., Cotter, A., & Hevey, D. (2004). Attachment styles and psychological profiles of child sex offenders in Ireland. *Journal of Interpersonal Violence*, 19(2), 228–251.

32. Stone, M. H. (1998). The personalities of murderers: the importance of psychopathy and sadism. In: Skodol, A. E. (Ed.). *Psychopathology and Violent Crime*, (pp. 29–52). Washington, DC: American Psychiatric Press.

Part II

New Dimensions to Violent Crime

Chapter 7

Sexual Homicide
An Overview of Contemporary Empirical Research[1]

Leonard I. Morgenbesser and Richard N. Kocsis

Abstract

This chapter provides an overview of studies conducted during the past two and a half decades on sexual homicide and its perpetrators. These studies are primarily considered in the context of their collated data sets and key findings. The final discussion centers on overall findings of the various research as well as suggested directions for the future.

INTRODUCTION

This chapter presents a brief overview of empirical research[2] conducted over the past two and a half decades pertaining to the topic of sexual homicide.

---

[1] Opinions expressed herein are solely those of the authors and do not represent those of the State of New York. The first author wishes to thank Distinguished Professor Hans H. Toch, PhD and Distinguished Professor Ann Wolbert Burgess, DNSc. RNCS, FAAN for their valuable mentoring.
[2] Most of which has been published and is thus available in the public domain.

From: *Serial Murder and the Psychology of Violent Crimes*
Edited by: R. N. Kocsis © Humana Press, Totowa, NJ

This overview canvasses the diverse range of studies and provides some brief commentary on notable aspects of the respective research endeavors.[3]

Integral to presenting this overview of sexual homicide is the adoption of a definition for this crime. Defining what is sexual homicide is not, however, as elementary an issue as one may initially anticipate owing to the often-synonymous conceptualization the term "sexual homicide" shares with the crime phenomenon of "serial homicide." As the objective of this chapter is to provide a succinct yet holistic anthology of contemporary literature, a broad conceptualization of what may constitute sexual homicide has been adopted. As a simple benchmark, we rely on the definition proposed by Douglas et al. *(1)*. Thus, any data pertaining to sexual homicide can be viewed as those crimes involving *(1,* p. 18):

> ...a sexual element (activity) as the basis for the sequence of acts leading to death. Performance and meaning of this sexual element vary with the offender. The act may range from the actual rape involving penetration (either pre- or postmortem) to a symbolic sexual assault, such as insertion of foreign objects into a victim's body orifices.

It must be clearly understood that the sequence of the literature canvassed in the following overview is based solely on the alphabetical order of the principal investigator's surnames in each of the research endeavors. As such, this overview is not intended to act as a critique of the merits of these various endeavors but, rather, to canvass research holistically and highlight key findings.

BEECH

The research of Beech and colleagues *(2,3)* gathered its data from prisoners incarcerated in the United Kingdom. The sample pool consisted of 28 subjects serving life terms for murder who had completed a treatment program for sexual offending. Twenty-four had murdered adult women, and three had killed young girls. One had murdered a 9-year-old boy. The work of Beech and colleagues makes an interesting contribution with the proposition of an "implicit theories" model, which considers various cognitive attributions of offenders in the perpetration of sexual murders. In particular, Beech et al. noted that sexual murderers

---

[3] The boundaries of this chapter do not allow sufficient space for coverage of every manuscript published related to the topic of sexual homicide. Accordingly, the present overview has endeavored to discuss research characterized by original, quantitatively orientated data sets and analysis of sexual homicides and/or their offenders.

could be clearly distinguished by three key attributes: grievances, sexual, and sadistic motivational attributes. With reference to these motivational tenets, a three-tier typology was proposed by Beech et al. *(2)* for the classification of sexual murderers. These categories were 1) grievance-motivated (catathymic homicide) sexual murderers; 2) sexually motivated[4] killers; and 3) sadistic sexual murderers.

BRIKEN

A group of psychiatrists based in Hamburg Germany, Briken and colleagues *(4–6)* have, over a 46-year time period (i.e., 1945–1991), amassed a substantial data set consisting of 166 offenders. Most of these cases involve single homicides, with, however, 22% (i.e., 36 offenders) having murdered more than one victim.

The work of Briken et al. *(4–6)* is particularly notable for its rare physiological examinations of sexual homicide offenders. In this regard 31% of the offenders were found to possess brain abnormalities.[5] Among those with brain abnormalities, histories of early behavioral problems were also found to be highly prevalent as were psychiatric diagnoses for paraphilia. Far more intriguing were the outcomes of chromosomal analyses,[6] which found evidence of XXY chromosomal abnormalities in the sampled offenders in a much higher ratio than what would be encountered in an unselected prisoner sample (i.e., nonsexual murder offenders) or in the general population.

FBI BEHAVIORAL SCIENCE UNIT

Published in various contexts *(1,7–11)*, the work of the FBI Behavioral Sciences Unit represents one of the earliest examinations of sexual homicide offenders from the perspective of law enforcement and is particularly synonymous with the development of criminal profiling techniques. This research is primarily derived from an examination of 36 sexual murderers who were incarcerated in various U.S. penitentiaries. This data set of 36 offenders consisted of 7 single sexual murderers, 4 offenders who each committed two sexual murders, and 25 offenders who each committed three or more sexual homicides *(9)*.

---

[4] The sexually motivated generally use instrumental violent force against the victim.
[5] Most offenders (69%) were found not to have brain abnormalities.
[6] Undertaken on a smaller pilot sample of the total sample presumably due to the cost of such analysis.

Outcomes from this research included the development of a motivational model for sexual homicide offenders *(7)* as well as a dichotomous typology on how offenders and crime scenes may be assessed. This dichotomy is premised on the level of behavioral sophistication exhibited in crime scenes. The categories to this dichotomy are labeled as either organized or disorganized. The organized category is reflective of crimes involving premeditation and planning with concomitant organizational features said to be evident in these offenders. Conversely, the disorganized category is proposed to be reflective of spontaneous, unplanned offense behaviors, with concomitant features of disorder said to be observable in the offenders.

FIRESTONE

The research by Firestone *(12)* comes from Ottawa, Ontario, Canada and involves phallometric measurements and psychological assessments of 48 homicidal sex offenders[7] between 1982 and 1992. Eight of the sampled offenders were convicted of homicide where the murder involved significant mutilation of the victim's corpse. Another 20 were convicted of homicide, and the final 20 featured charges of attempted homicide. Evidence of psychopathologies was explored via the use of the Psychopathy CheckList— Revised (PCL-R). Key findings of this research was that a large number of homicidal sex offenders were diagnosed as suffering from psychosis, antisocial personality disorder, paraphilia, sexual sadism with or without pedophilia, and substance abuse. Indeed, 75% of the sampled offenders earned three or more of these diagnoses.

GERARD

From the region of French-speaking Belgium, Gerard and colleagues *(13)* collected a data set involving 33 sexual homicide offenders who were responsible for the murder of 28 victims. The focus of this study was similar to other research endeavors in the area of criminal profiling in undertaking a combined examination of crime scene behavior patterns and typical offender demographics. The key findings of this analysis was the development of two broad offense templates that were labeled opportunistic-impulsive and sadist calculator. The opportunistic-impulsive template is characteristic of an impulsive, spontaneous offender who acts with little reflection. The sexual dimension to crimes representative of this pattern are said to be impulsive, and

---

[7] This data set also includes attempted sexual homicide cases.

the offender is merely seeking immediate gratification when an opportunity arises. In contrast, the sadistic-calculator template embodies an offense style wherein offenders plan and prepare for the murder and are far more sadistic in its perpetration.

GODWIN

Another study primarily undertaken from the perspective of criminal profiling, the research of Godwin *(14)* involved the analysis of 96 North American cases of serial murder. In combination with the development of various demographic statistics pertaining to these offenders, the research of Godwin *(14)* identified four behavioral themes—cognitive object, affective object, cognitive vehicle, affective vehicle—that are said to be discriminatory of behavioral patterns typically observable in these crimes. The cognitve object pattern is indicative of highly sadistic offenders who plan their offenses, and the affective object is characteristic of a crime pattern where the offender has some attachment to the victim as an object. In contrast, the cognitive vehicle pattern is suggestive of an offense style wherein there is said to be controlled, yet quite sadistic aggression, whereas the affective vehicle pattern is said to be a totally unplanned emotional attack.

HICKEY

In what appears to be an ongoing research endeavor with an ever increasing sample, Hickey *(15)* has been collating data pertaining to serial murderers for more than two decades. The analysis of this data set by Hickey is primarily focused on explicating broad statistical patterns pertaining to these offenders and their victims. Interestingly, Hickey appears to classify serial murders based on such factors as their choice of victims and *modus operandi*. Thus, offender categories are described as "men who kill men," "men who kill children," "men who kill the elderly," and "team killers" to name but a few. Beyond descriptive analysis, however, the research of Hickey also considers various broad psychological attributes of serial murderers in general. Akin to the work of Burgess et al. *(7)*, Hickey proposes a developmental model for the perpetration of serial murders.

KOCSIS

Another examination of sexual homicide from the perspective of developing criminal profiling techniques is the research by Kocsis and colleagues *(16)*. This study collated a data set of 85 sexual homicide cases from across Australia. Analysis of this data set primarily focused on crime scene behavior patterns during the perpetration of these murders. This study produced a graphical model allowing systematic matching and prediction of offender characteristics as determined by observable crimes scene behaviors *(17)*. Integral to this research was also some exploration of cohesive clusters of behavior. Four discriminatory clusters were identified—predator, rape, fury, and perversion. Crime scene behaviors evident in the predator pattern embodied a sadistic purpose to the murder, and the fury pattern was demonstrative of an unfocused outburst of violence by the offender. Central features to the rape pattern was sexual intercourse with the victim, and the perversion pattern was suggestive of extreme aberrant motivations within the offender.

LANGEVIN

The research by Langevin and colleagues originates from Toronto, Canada. It began with an original data set of 13 male sexual homicide offenders *(18)* that has since grown to a total of 38 offenders who have engaged in sex and killed or attempted to kill their victims *(19,20)*. Cases are reported as being drawn from a database of more than 2800 cases seen since 1973. Altogether, 23 cases involved adult victims, and 15 cases involved child victims.

Key findings to emerge from Langevin and colleagues' research *(18–20)* is that the sampled offenders exhibited an early onset of criminal careers. Thus, sexual homicide offenders start their criminal careers at a very young age and appear to have a highly disturbed childhood. Evaluations for evident psychopathologies indicated that these offenders often showed a history of sadism and/or voyeurism, fetishism, transvestism, and/or sexual identity disturbance prior to committing murder. Additionally, one-fourth (9/38) were diagnosed as psychotic, and almost all were diagnosed with antisocial personality disorder as well as engaging in substance abuse such as alcohol and especially drugs.

MACDONALD

In an early unpublished study by MacDonald and Morgenbesser *(21)*, a total sample pool of 50 rape-homicide offenders were examined from the New York State Department of Correctional Services. The study identified, under State of New York custody as of December 1983, a total of 34 inmates who had been committed for sexual homicide and an additional 16 inmates incarcerated for attempting to kill the victim of their sexual assault.

The researchers found that the violence committed in both the sex homicides and the attempted sexual homicides was generally the same. Regarding prior criminal records (with particular reference to crimes of a sexual nature), it was found that one-third of the 34 sex-homicide offenders and 44% of the 16 attempted sex-homicide offenders had prior criminal records related to sexual offenses.

Alcohol or drug abuse played a role in only 6 of the 23 sex-homicide cases where there was no history of sex crimes. Of the 23 sex-homicide cases without a sex crime history, nearly all ($n = 21$) had a criminal history of nonsex crimes, frequently violent crimes. Only 2 of the 50 offenders had a psychiatric history or exhibited psychotic symptoms at the time of examination. Of the 50 offenders, more than one-third ($n = 18$) had a history of sex crimes arrests.[8] The two-thirds of offenders who did not have a history of sex crimes nonetheless frequently had an extensive criminal record for other offenses. With respect to the age of these offenders, nearly one-third were reported as being under 21 years of age.

MELOY

Two key publications appear to have emerged from the work of Meloy on sexual homicide *(22,23)*. As of 2000, the data set amassed by Meloy consisted of 38 subjects who had been convicted of sexual homicide crimes and were incarcerated in prisons and forensic hospitals in the states of California, Florida, Illinois, Massachusetts, and the District of Columbia.

The research by Meloy and colleagues is an interesting hybridization of exploring psychological underpinnings of sexual homicide offenders coupled with behaviors evident in their crime scene patterns. Central to the findings of Meloy is the classification of sexual homicides as either being of a "compulsive" or "catathymic" nature. Thus, compulsive sexual murders are described by Meloy *(23*, p. 1) as demonstrating:

> …organized crime scenes and are usually diagnosed with sexual sadism and antisocial/narcissistic personality disorders. They are chronically emotionally detached, often primary psychopaths, are autonomically hyper-reactive, and the majority experience no early trauma.

In contrast, the catathymic-orientated sexual murderer is said to (*23*, p. 1):

> …leave behind disorganized crime scenes, and are usually diagnosed with a mood disorder and various personality disorders that may include schizoid and

---

[8] This appears consistent with the general belief that certain sex offenders progress to more violent crimes in the absence of effective therapeutic interventions.

avoidant traits. They are hungry for attachment, only moderately psychopathic, are autonomically hyper-reactive, and have a history of physical and/or sexual trauma.

Meloy also noted that two-thirds of his sample of 38 sexual homicide perpetrators "are psychopaths, suggesting autonomic hypo-reactivity, and chronic emotional detachment; while the remaining one-third are not psychopaths and are affectionately hungry for an attachment" (*23*, p. 16). Interestingly, an unexpected finding from Meloy's work was "evidence of an inordinate amount of non-volitional ideation or obsessions" (*23*, p. 19).

MYERS

The work of Myers *(24–26)* is, arguably, unique as it focuses on sexual homicides perpetrated by juvenile offenders. As what is most likely a consequence of this circumstance (i.e., apprehended juveniles), the data set relates exclusively to offenders who have committed only a single homicide. In total, the study examines 16 offenders, 9 of whom were identified as serving sentences in the Florida State Corrections Department; an additional 7 were serving sentences for sexual assault with attempted murder.

Myer's examination of these offenders is primarily undertaken with reference to the organized/disorganized dichotomy espoused by the FBI *(1)*. Thus, Myers *(24)* observed that among the 16 juvenile offenders, 6 were classified as primarily matching the organized category, another 5 similar to the disorganized category, and the remaining 5 described as "unmixed." Interestingly, Myers notes that virtually all 16 cases contained some elements of both the disorganized and organized categories. A notable aspect of these juvenile sexual murderers was that 75% of the offenders knew their victims prior to the murders. In this context, offenders and victims were often neighbors living in relatively close proximity to one another. Thus, only a relatively small proportion (i.e., 25%) of the cases could be described as occurring between complete strangers.

PORTER

The research by Porter and Woodworth *(27)* examined 125 incarcerated homicide offenders from two Canadian federal prisons. From this data set of homicide offenders, 30.4% had had sexual activity during the commission of the homicide. In examining evident psychopathologies inherent to these offenders it was found that just under half (i.e., 47.4%) were diagnosed as psychopathic and that the murders committed by these offenders featured a far greater degree of gratuitous and sadistic violence than those committed by the nonpsychopathic offenders.

PROULX

In an ongoing research program, Proulx and colleagues have been studying sexual murderers incarcerated in the French Province of Quebec, Canada. The first publication *(28)* reported on a data set consisting of 36 offenders who had each killed a woman 14 years of age or older. A subsequent publication *(29,30)* referred to a slightly larger sample pool of 40 offenders.

Central to the research by Proulx and colleagues has been the development of a dichotmous offender typology wherein offenders are classifiable as either following a "sadistic" or an "anger" pathway. In the sadistic pathway offenders tend to complete the homicide in more than 30 minutes. These offenders plan their offenses and mostly select victims who are strangers. They use physical restraints, humiliate and mutilate their victims, and are more likely to hide the bodies of their victims.

In contrast, offenders said to be in the anger pathway tend to complete the homicide in less than 30 minutes. Thus, these homicides are described as not typically involving premeditation, physical restraints, or humiliation or mutilation of the victim and are likely to leave the victim's body at the crime scene. In a breakdown of the data set of Proulx et al. *(29)* using this dichotomy, found that 55% of the offenders were classifiable via the anger pathway, and 45% of the offenders matched the characteristics of the sadistic pathway.

SAFARIK

Akin to Myers *(24)* the research undertaken by Safarik and colleagues *(31)* represents another specialized study of sexual homicide crimes. In this regard, Safarik et al.'s research examines the perpetration of sexual homicides upon elderly[9] women. A data set was collated from across the United States and consisted of 110 offenders who were responsible for the murder of 128 victims.

The ethnicity of the sampled offenders was split relatively evenly between white and African American offenders with a less significant contribution by Hispanic offenders. Almost all (94%) of these elderly sexual homicide victims were killed in their home. Just over half (56%) of the offenders lived within six blocks of the crime scene, whereas a larger percent (81%—higher for African Americans and Hispanics) began the assault by walking to the crime scene. In contrast to the overall homicide statistics on elderly victims, for sexual homicides the use of firearms is virtually negligible (1%); while strangulation accounts for 63% of the homicides. Relying on the dichotomous typology of

---

[9] All victims being ≥ 60 years of age.

organized or disorganized offenders espoused by the FBI *(1)* as a method of classification, it was determined that an overwhelming number of cases matched the characteristics of the disorganized category.

A final notable observation to emerge from this study was that offenders tended to come from the same neighborhood and knew of the victim. Thus, although the victim and offender may not have had a prior acquaintance, there was often evidence to suggest that the offender knew where the victim lived and if they lived alone. Interestingly, although many murders involve an element of theft (i.e., jewelry or other items being stolen), Safarik et al. *(31)* argue that the sexual murder was premeditated and supercedes any intent to steal. That is, theft appears to be an ancillary factor.[10]

SALFATI

The work by Salfati has focused on criminal profiling with particular reference to crimes of homicide (not always of a sexual nature). Akin to other research in the field of profiling, the analysis focused on behavioral patterns evident in crimes scenes. In this context, Salfati appears to have published two sets of analyses that relate to sexual homicide offenses. One study used state of Washington (USA) data related to 69 sexual homicides committed by 23 offenders. The key finding of this analysis appears to be the observation of a strong element of sexual behavior among these serial offenders, with 61% (42 cases) involving sexual assault of the victim *(32)*.

In another study, the analysis was carried out on a data set consisting of 37 sexual homicide cases and 37 solved rape cases *(33)*. Central to this study was the discernment of behavioral themes in how offenders interact with their victims. It was found that the distinguishing element between murder and rape offenses was the degree of exhibited violence that was said to exist on a single continuum.

SCHLESINGER

A number of data sets pertaining to sexual homicides have been examined by Schlesinger and colleagues over the years *(34–40)*. One data set is described in the study by Schlesinger and Revitch *(35)* and is comprised of a total of 52 sexual murderers evaluated by the authors. Most were referred for a forensic evaluation after their arrest for murder. The number of victims per offender in this sample ranged from one to six, but the sample of 52 offenders accounted for a total of

---

[10] Support for this conclusion comes from various obtained admissions/confessions to police, uninvolved third parties, etc.

106 victims. Thus, this study examined a combination of both single and serial sexual murderers. The second data set reported by Schlesinger *(39)* specifically excluded single sexual homicides. This study utilized data compiled by the FBI on 21 sexually motivated serial murderers responsible for the murder of 97 victims.[11]

In the earlier Schlesinger and Revitch *(35)* study 42% (*n* = 22) of the sampled offenders had a criminal history related to burglary offenses. This group included 15 who combined voyeurism with their burglaries and 7 who featured various fetish activities with their burglaries. However, in the later 2004 study of 21 serial sexual homicide perpetrators, an overall 38% (*n* = 8) of these 21 perpetrators had a burglary arrest in their criminal background.

Further analysis indicated that 61% (13/21) had killed victims in their own residence or had abducted victims from their own residences (and later killed them). Furthermore, 62% (*n* = 8) of these 13 perpetrators had a criminal history of burglary. These findings were viewed as supportive of the earlier 1999 study. Finally, Schlesinger's work is particularly notable for his exploration of issues regarding the ability to predict future sexual murderers *(38)*.

SHACKELFORD

In what may represent one of the largest data sets related to sexual homicide, Shackelford utilized the Supplementary Homicide Reports (SHR) of the FBI over an 18-year period (1975–1994) to amass a total pool of 564 rape-murders by male perpetrators unknown to the victim *(41,42)*.[12] Central to this research was the observation that young males commit most of the rape-murders and theft-murders. Additionally, young reproductive-age women are overrepresented among the victims of rape-murder while such sexual homicide victims are underrepresented among the victims of theft-murder. Shackelford further pursued this focus by finding that such young reproductive-age women are overrepresented among the victims of multiple offender rape-murder and underrepresented among the victims of multiple offender theft-murder.

CONCLUSIONS

Although it can be seen from the present overview of the literature that many advances have been made in understanding crimes of sexual homicide, it should also be apparent that the topic is still very much in its infancy with ample room for further development.

---

[11] Each offender responsible for the murder of two to eight victims, respectively.
[12] Shackelford did not report on the criminal histories of the perpetrators including whether there were prior rape-homicides.

In the context of law enforcement it is obvious that interest in sexual homicide, particularly with reference to criminal profiling, is rapidly growing since the original research undertaken by the FBI during the early 1980s. Admittedly, such studies seem to be focused on discerning cohesive behavioral patterns in sexual homicide crime scenes, but these research endeavors nonetheless offer some valuable insights into the typical demographic attributes of offenders.

In the context of more mainstream psychological and/or psychiatric analysis, advances in the clinically based classification and development of typologies for sexual homicide offenders can also be observed in such research endeavors as those by Langevin, Schlisinger, and Proulx to name only a few *(18,29,39)*. Also emerging in this clinical context are some innovative and rare biological factors concerning sexual homicide offenders that offer much food for thought with respect to the classic nature-versus-nurture debate, especially given the high proportion of physiological irregularities found.

At this time, perhaps the most unexplored issue is the specific treatment[13] and recidivism of sexual homicide offenders. In the context of a crime that typically attracts a life sentence (often without the possibility of parole) concern for such issues may, on initial consideration, seem redundant. However, the work of Myers *(24)* poignantly highlights that crimes of sexual homicide are not the exclusive province of adult offenders. Consequently, unless the crimes of such juvenile offenders are tried within an adult jurisdiction these perpetrators are more than likely to be released back into the community, thus necessitating the exploration of these issues in the future.

REFERENCES

1. Douglas, J., Burgess, A., Burgess, A., & Ressler, R. (2006). *Crime Classification Manual* (2nd Ed.). New York: Jossey Bass.
2. Beech, A., Fisher, D., & Ward, T. (2005). Sexual murderers' implicit theories. *Journal of Interpersonal Violence, 20,* 1–24.
3. Beech, A., Oliver, C., Fisher, D., & Beckett, R. (2005). *The SOTP (Sex Offender Treatment Programme) in Prison: Addressing The Offending Behaviour of Rapists and Sexual Murderers.* Prepared for HMPS (Her Majesty's Prison Service). London, UK.

---

[13] To the best of the authors' knowledge, the only dedicated treatment program for sexual homicide offenders was within Her Majesty's Prison—Brixton (UK). At the present time there does not appear to be any equivalent in North America.

4. Briken, P. (2005). Influence of brain abnormalities on psychosocial development, criminal history, and paraphilias in sexual murderers. *Journal of Forensic Sciences,* 50, 1204–1208.

5. Briken, P., Habermann, N., Berner, W., & Hill, A. (2006). XYY chromosome abnormality in sexual homicide perpetrators. *Amerian Journal of Medical Genetics: B. Neuropsychiatric Genetics,* 142, 198–200.

6. Briken, P., Habermann, N., Kafka, M., Berner, W., & Hill, A. (2006). The paraphilia-related disorders: an investigation of the relevance of the concept in sexual murderers. *Journal of Forensic Sciences,* 51, 683–688.

7. Burgess, A. (1986). Sexual homicide: a motivational model. *Journal of Interpersonal Violence,* 1, 251–272.

8. Hazelwood, R., & Douglas, J. (1980). The lust murderer. *FBI Law Enforcement Bulletin,* April, 11–14.

9. Prentky, R., Burgess, A., & Francis, L. (1989). The presumptive role of fantasy in serial, sexual homicide. *American Journal of Psychiatry,* 146, 887–891.

10. Ressler, R. (1983) Rape and rape-murder: one offender and twelve victims. *American Journal of Psychiatry,* 140, 36–40.

11. Ressler, R., Burgess, A., & Douglas, J. (1988). *Sexual Homicides: Patterns and Motives.* New York: Lexington.

12. Firestone, P. (1998). Homicidal and nonhomicidal child molesters: psychological, phallometric, and criminal features. *Sexual Abuse: A Journal of Research and Treatment,* 10, 305–323.

13. Gerard, F., Mormont, C., & Kocsis, R. N. (2007). Offender profiles and crime scene behaviors in Belgian sexual murders. In: Kocsis, R. N. (Ed.). *Criminal Profiling: International Perspectives In Theory, Practice and Research.* Totowa, NJ: Humana Press/Springer.

14. Godwin, G. M. (1999). *Hunting Serial Predators.* Boca Raton, FL: CRC Press.

15. Hickey, E. W. (2006). *Serial Murderers and Their Victims* (4th ed.). Fresno, CA: Thomson-Wadsworth.

16. Kocsis, R. N., Cooksey, R., & Irwin, H. (2002). Psychological profiling of sexual murderers: an empirical model. *International Journal of Offender Therapy and Comparative Criminology,* 46, 532–554.

17. Kocsis, R. N. (2006). *Criminal Profiling: Principles and Practice.* Totowa, NJ: Humana Press/Springer.

18. Langevin, R., Ben-Aron, M., Wright, P., & Marchese, W. (1988). The sex killer. *Annals of Sex Research,* 1, 263–302.

19. Langevin, R. (2003). A study of the psychosocial characteristics of sex killers: can we identify them before it is too late? *International Journal of Offender Therapy and Comparative Criminology,* 47, 366–387.

20. Langevin, R. (2006). An actuarial study of recidivism risk among sex killers of adults and children: could we have identified them before it was too late? *Journal of Forensic Psychology Practice,* 6, 29–49.

21. MacDonald, D., & Morgenbesser, L. (1984). Inmates Committed for Sex Homicides. New York State DOCS (Department of Correctional Services). Unpublished study.

22. Meloy, J., Gacono, C., & Kenney, L. (1994). A Rohrschach investigation of sexual homicide. *Journal of Personality Assessment*, 62, 58–67.
23. Meloy, J. (2000). The nature and dynamics of sexual homicide: an integrative review. *Aggression and Violent Behavior*, 5, 1–22.
24. Myers, W. (2002) *Juvenile Sexual Homicide*. San Diego: Academic Press.
25. Myers, W. (2003). A media violence-inspired juvenile sexual homicide offender 13 years later. *Journal of Forensic Sciences*, 55, 1–6.
26. Myers, W. (2004). Serial murder by children and adolescents. *Behavioral Sciences and The Law*, 16, 357–374.
27. Porter, S., & Woodworth, M. (2003). Characteristics of sexual homicides committed by psychopathic and nonpsychopathic offenders. *Law and Human Behavior*, 27, 459–470.
28. Proulx, J. (2002). Profiles in the offending process of non-serial sexual murderers. *International Journal of Offender Therapy and Comparative Criminology* 46, 386–399.
29. Proulx, J., Cusson, M., Beauregard, E., & Nicole, A. (2005). *Les Meurtriers Sexuels* [Sexual Murderers: Comparative Analysis and New Prospects] (published in French). Montreal: Presses of The University of Montreal.
30. Proulx, J., Blais, E., & Beauregard, E. (2006). Sadistic sexual aggressors. In: Marshall, W. (Ed.), *Sexual Offender Treatment: Controversial Issues* (pp. 61–77). New York: John Wiley.
31. Safarik, M., Jarvis, J., & Nussbaum, K. (2002). Sexual homicide of elderly females: linking offender characteristics and crime scene attributes. *Journal of Interpersonal Violence*, 17, 500–525.
32. Salfati, G., & Bateman, A. (2006) Serial homicide: an investigation of behavioural consistency. *Journal of Investigative Psychology and Offender Profiling*, 3, 121–144.
33. Salfati, G. (2006). Differentiating sexual violence: a comparison of sexual homicide and rape. *Psychology, Crime and Law*, 12, 107–125.
34. Schlesinger, L., & Revitch, E. (1990). Outpatient treatment of the sexually motivated murderer and potential murderer. *Journal of Offender Counseling, Services, and Rehabilitation*, 15, 163–178.
35. Schlesinger, L., & Revitch, E. (1999) Sexual burglaries and sexual homicide: clinical, forensic and investigative consideration. *Journal of American Academy of Psychiatry and the Law*, 27, 227–238.
36. Schlesinger, L. (1999) Adolescent sexual matricide following repetitive mother-son incest. *Journal of Forensic Sciences*, 44, 746–749.
37. Schlesinger, L. (1999). Murder and sex murder: psychopathology and psychodynamics. In: Hall, H. (Ed.). *Lethal Violence: A Sourcebook on Fatal Domestic, Acquaintance and Stranger Violence* (pp. 383–402). Boca Raton, FL: CRC Press.
38. Schlesinger, L. (2001). The potential sex murderer: ominous signs, risk assessment, *Journal of Threat Assessment*, 1, 47–72.
39. Schlesinger, L. (2004). *Sexual Murder: Catathymic and Compulsive Homicides*. Boca Raton, FL: CRC Press.
40. Schlesinger, L., Pinizzotto, A., & Pakhomou, S. (2004). Burglary and sexually motivated homicide. *Sex Offender Law Report*, 5, 21–22, 36.

41. Shackelford, T. (2002). Risk of multiple offender rape-murder varies with female age. *Journal of Criminal Justice*. 39, 135–141.
42. Shackelford, T. (2002). Are young women the special targets of rape murder? *Aggressive Behavior*, 28, 224–232.

Chapter 8

Serial Killers and Serial Rapists
Preliminary Comparison of Violence Typologies

Stacey L. Shipley[1] and Bruce A. Arrigo[2]

Abstract

This chapter reviews the typologies for serial murder and serial rape. The aim here is to showcase the principal conceptual models that have accounted for these two forms of criminal behavior in the extant literature. Additionally, however, the chapter considers where and how the typologies on serial rape and murder could be integrated, especially with respect to offender motivations, cognitions, biological predispositions, fantasies, impulses, and personality structures. Along these lines, several points of continuity and discontinuity are featured. The chapter concludes by speculating on the relevance of the proposed exploratory analysis, particularly in relation to future research efforts that seek to explain and prevent both forms of violence based on scientific model making, theory testing, and empirical validation.

[1] Acknowledgments: I appreciate the support of Greg Grasty and Courtney Cooner and their assistance on related projects. As always, I offer my gratitude to my parents, Robert and Carol Shipley.
[2] Please direct all correspondence to: Bruce A. Arrigo, Ph.D. Professor, Crime, Law, & Society, Department of Criminal Justice, University of North Carolina at Charlotte 9201 University City Blvd. Charlotte, NC 28223-0001 USA. 704-687-2686, barrigo@email.uncc.edu

From: *Serial Murder and the Psychology of Violent Crimes*
Edited by: R. N. Kocsis © Humana Press, Totowa, NJ

INTRODUCTION

Theory building efforts regarding the phenomena of serial homicide and serial rape remain mostly in their infancy. Although efforts to construct useful typologies, or models, over the past 30 years can be identified in the extant literature *(1–14)*, few attempts to integrate these two organizing schemas have been undertaken. This is surprising, especially as consolidation seems both plausible and logical when noting the various linkages among offender profiles, victim selection strategies, and crime scene variables *(15–18)*. In short, these acts are expressions of violence in which several biological, behavioral, cognitive, and psychodynamic properties appear assimilable.

Admittedly, relevant theory building and model development in the realm of serial rape and repetitive homicide is a complicated and cumbersome exercise. A host of factors ranging from, among others, *modus operandi*, criminal background of the assailant, the use of fantasy, paraphilias, psychiatric illness, psychopathy, and the role of sadism in the commission of the crime would have to be explored carefully and systematically *(19)*. As such, the proposed synthetic effort can be interpreted only as provisional at best. This notwithstanding, given the two forms of criminality in question, some commentary on the way in which motivational forces, crime scene behavior, offender personality characteristics, and strategies to thwart detection are complementary as well as distinct, is warranted. Indeed, such an initial foray could be quite suggestive for future theoretical and empirical work.

Accordingly, this chapter is divided into three substantive sections. First, the most commonly featured serial murderer typologies are summarized. Second, the serial rape typology that is the most frequently cited in the literature is delineated. This is the model developed by Groth and colleagues *(9)*. All other organizational frameworks represent a slight variation of their original schema. Third, several tentative observations on integration are enumerated, specifically, important differences among and similarities between the serial murder and rape typologies. Along these lines, a novel continuum between these two types of offenders is suggested.

Throughout the ensuing observations, readers are cautioned that all the typologies examined in this chapter are of a theoretical nature. Moreover, minimal to no empirical validation pertaining to any one of them has been undertaken. However, the sundry typologies provide a sensible structure that enables investigators to initiate much needed conceptual and synthetic work. Arguably, this is a task that can benefit psychologists and criminologists, especially as they endeavor to comprehend better the extreme and repetitive violence committed by these assailants.

SERIAL MURDERER TYPOLOGIES

Typologies generally classify offenders based on a combination of factors. Examples of these factors or elements include inferred motives, crime scene evidence, and the background characteristics of the aggressor *(20–22)*. For example, some serial killers sexually attack their victims as an integral part of the murder, both psychologically and physiologically *(10)*. However, in other homicides the sexual attack is used instrumentally. It is the best way to degrade, dominate, and subsequently annihilate the victim *(16)*. In this respect, then, the behavior is not directly related to the actual motive for the murder.

Special agents for the Federal Bureau of Investigation (FBI) Training Academy in Quantico, Virginia first introduced the most widely cited classification dichotomy of violent serial offenders. The organized/disorganized dichotomy examined lust and sexually sadistic serial murders *(13)*. This dichotomy has since been used to differentiate all types of sexual and serial homicides, as well as arson, as delineated in the *Crime Classification Manual (20)*.

Ressler et al. (1986) maintained that offenders could be distinguished and categorized based on crime scene variables, victim selection, life history factors, and forensic reports, as well as related evidence. Indeed, dimensions of the assailant's personality structure and behavioral patterns are discernible through the offense *(18)*. Thus, the crime scene can be used much like a fingerprint to help identify the murderer *(13,21,22)*. The body of evidence or the distinct characteristics left behind at the crime scene is classified as either organized or disorganized. The premise of this dichotomy is that "highly repetitive, planned, and well-thought-out offenses [can] be distinguishable from spontaneous, random, sloppy offenses" *(23,* p. 888). Various conceptual models on serial homicide have appropriated the organized/disorganized dichotomy *(10, 11,19)*. As such, some summary observations on the distinction between these two types of serial offender are warranted.

The organized offender is considered to be of average to above-average intelligence, male, and to lead an orderly existence *(20)*. Ressler et al. *(13)* noted that the organized offender is motivated by internal mechanisms consisting of a rich fantasy life that compels the criminality. Moreover, the organized offender is likely to have skilled employment and to be socially adept in contrast to his disorganized counterpart. Often the organized assailant owns a car that is in good running condition. He commits his crimes away from his residence, given his considerable mobility. Fantasy and ritual are highly important to this assailant. As such, he selects a victim that is the "right" type—usually a stranger *(24)*. The social capital of the organized offender enables him to approach and gain proximity to the victim verbally before escalating to physical violence.

Typically, the murders committed by the organized offender are precipitated by a stressful event *(10)*. Examples of these disturbances include a relationship conflict, financial hardship, or employment problems. These events can be so overwhelming that they preclude the use of restraint that would otherwise prevent the individual from actualizing his fantasies. Indeed, given the debilitating life event, feelings of profound inadequacy surface and a desperate need to restore emotional equilibrium materializes, thereby precipitating the murder. Finally, the organized killer is likely to be a psychopath or someone who could be diagnosed with antisocial personality disorder given the irresponsible, immoral, and callous nature of his crimes and his character (11,24; for discussion of psychopathy see *25,26*).

The crime scene is more organized with serial murderers than with one-time homicide offenders *(27)*. Indeed, for the organized assailant, it reflects considerable planning and control. Crime scene staging or manipulation is also noted, especially if the killer takes pride in the expertise he believes he has in the commission of his murders and his ability to avoid detection. The organized slayer methodically crafts his crimes: he brings his own weapon with him and carefully disposes of it when he leaves, rather than discarding it haphazardly at the location of the murder or elsewhere. This serial offender is also likely to use various restraints on his victim, arriving at the crime scene with a rape kit, or "death kit" *(11,15,22)*. Moreover, this offender is inclined to perform sexual acts with a live victim and take a "trophy" or souvenir from the place of the murder *(10)*.

By contrast, the disorganized offender is thought to be of below-average intelligence, male, and interpersonally incompetent *(13)*. He is socially isolated, mostly withdrawn, and likely to have significant feelings of inadequacy. According to Canter and colleagues *(28)*, "The lack of normal, healthy social relationships increases the likelihood of sexual ignorance as well as the potential for sexual perversions or dysfunctions as part of the homicidal acts" (p. 294). Sadistic fantasies, pornography, and compulsive masturbation are used to compensate for the lack of healthy interpersonal relationships *(14,19)*.

The disorganized slayer leads a chaotic existence, characterized by unsystematic behavior especially in the commission of his homicides *(13)*. The offender is opportunistic and usually resides in close proximity to the crime scene *(20)*. The murder is not planned away from the assailant's residence, and there is significant disarray at the crime scene. Indeed, typically there is a wealth of forensic evidence such as blood and semen samples, fingerprints, and the presence of the murder weapon *(28)*. Moreover, there is no effort to conceal the body, and it is often left in full view. The corpse is also more likely to be positioned by the disorganized offender than by his organized murder counterpart.

This disorganized slayer is impulsive and often commits his murders in a frenzied fashion, approaching victims in an all-out blitz-style method of attack *(24)*. Blunt force trauma may be used quickly to silence the victim and to obtain control. There is sudden violence followed immediately by death, leaving mutilation and sexual activity to occur postmortem *(10)*. The disorganized offender is more likely to perform sexual acts with the cadaver and depersonalize the body by massive assaults to the face *(29)*. His personal hygiene is usually poor and his acquaintances consider him odd. This is because he is strange in both appearance and behavior *(24,28)*. A psychotic killer would most likely be responsible for a disorganized crime scene. This type of offender may be delusional and have a diagnosable mental disorder.

In their *Crime Classification Manual*, Douglas et al. *(20)* introduced a third grouping of killers called the "mixed" offender. They maintained that there are some individuals who share characteristics of both the organized and disorganized types. As such, they could not be easily distinguishable.

To illustrate, the murder may involve more than one assailant or the offender may be young and/or under the influence of drugs or alcohol. Moreover, there might be unanticipated events such as victim resistance or escalating the offender into a different pattern during the course of the attack or over a series of homicides *(28)*. Additionally, there might be some evidence of planning, such as the absence of a murder weapon left at the location of the crime; however, the body might not be disposed of or otherwise concealed. Then, too, the topography of the crime scene might be chaotic, with severe manual violence inflicted against the victim. Interestingly, Myers et al. *(27)* indicated that the slayings by many organized killers are likely to become more disorganized over time. To substantiate their claim, they cited the pattern of murders committed by Ted Bundy. Near the end of Bundy's reign of terror, he began to drink heavily, used stolen credit cards, and experienced increasing paranoia and desperation. These pre-offense circumstances stood in stark contrast to his early pre-offense hypercontrolled persona.

Canter et al. *(28)* cautioned that if the majority of serial murder cases were mixed there would be little utility to the organized/disorganized dichotomy. They also suggested that this typology was widely disseminated in movies and among popular media outlets, giving it extra cultural credibility even though it remains an unsubstantiated theory without systematic study *(10)*. In addition, Canter et al. *(28)* cited methodological flaws in the exploratory investigation on which the Ressler et al. *(13)* typology was based. Instead, Canter and colleagues *(28)* proposed that human beings rarely fall into distinct offender types. Indeed, as they suggested, ". . . the concept of organized and disorganized offenders is not a genuine psychologically based distinction but, rather, is a commonsensical day-to-day speculation about differences between people. Clearly, this and all typologies are meant to begin to structure a framework in our understanding and identification of serial offenders and cannot be absolute" (*28*, p. 318).

The classification schema proposed by Ressler et al. *(13)* is useful in that it provides a framework out of which subsequent theoretical and empirical inquiries can be conducted. However, another, more frequently cited model that accounts for serial murder is the typology developed by Holmes and DeBurger *(30)*. They classified repetitive homicides into four subtypes based primarily on the motives and characteristics of the victims and offenders, as well as the *modus operandi* of the assailant. Moreover, Holmes and DeBurger *(30)* identified the differences between geographically transient murderers versus stable offenders. They based their typology on an analysis of case materials involving 110 serial murderers. Subsequent conceptualizations by Holmes and Holmes *(11)* refined the original model's formulations.

The theoretical underpinnings of the subtypes were based on specific assumptions about the authors' assessment of serial killers. The researchers observed that the offenders' motivations to commit serial homicide existed only in their minds and, thus, could not be fully appreciated by others. For example, Holmes and DeBurger *(30)* suggested that insanity or economic incentives were rarely responsible for the homicides. Instead, they noted that internal rewards or psychological reinforcers functioned as motivational factors that were intrinsically meaningful to the subjects of their study. Finally, the researchers indicated that serial offenders exhibited characteristics or displayed behaviors from more than one typology. Thus, they recognized that their four-fold classification system was not constituted by mutually exclusive categories. With these observations in mind, Holmes and DeBurger *(30)* identified the following types of serial killers.

1. *Visionary Type*—these murderers kill as a result of command hallucinations, delusions, or visions whose sources customarily include the forces of good or evil *(10)*. These offenders are typically psychotic, leaving the crime scene in utter disarray. The homicides occur quickly with no extensive acts of torture. Frequently, the assailant relies on weapons of opportunity to commit his crimes and discards or locates the death instrument(s) in the victim's body *(28)*.

2. *Mission-Oriented Type*—the goal for these slayers is to kill certain types of people or to rid society of particular types of individuals. These serial murderers target victims based on their ethnicity, occupation (e.g., prostitutes), and/or age *(15)*. Additionally, they determine whom to assail based on whether the person is deemed unworthy, undesirable, or somehow less than human. To illustrate, Jack the Ripper targeted prostitutes and viewed them as disposable. He dehumanized their bodies

through mutilation in the process of killing them. In a letter written to the press by Jack the Ripper, he stated, "I am down on whores and shan't quit ripping them (*31*, p. 213)." Typically, the murders occur quickly and they are often planned. The mission-oriented offender does not engage in postmortem activities such as necrophilia or dismemberment and the weapon employed is not disposed of at the crime scene *(28)*.

3. *Hedonistic Type*—these offenders murder as a result of sensation seeking or otherwise derive some sort of pleasure from their killings. Holmes and Holmes *(11)* divided this type of assailant into two subcategories: the lust killer and the thrill killer. Both are summarily described below.

The lust killer murders principally for sexual gratification even if this does not entail traditional intercourse. However, sex or multiple sadistically erotic acts with a live victim are common *(32)*. Orgasm or sexually arousing behavior (i.e., masturbation) is the driving force for this offender, even after the person has killed the victim *(28,29)*. Moreover, this attacker may also be sexually excited and/or satisfied from the murder itself. Ritualistic displays of sexual mutilation, facial disfigurement, cannibalism, body dismemberment, vampirism, and necrophilia are routinely featured in this type of homicidal act *(19)*. The body is often concealed and the murder weapon taken. Close contact murder; specifically, beating or manual strangulation, are noted as most common *(30)*.

The thrill killer murders for the visceral excitement the assailant experiences. However, once the victim is dead, the offender loses complete interest *(28)*. As a result, the process of killing is prolonged as long as possible through extended acts of torture *(22)*. The use of restraints and the presence of bite marks and burns on the victim's body are characteristic behaviors for this type of slayer. Sadistic acts whose frequency is prolonged as long as possible prior to death, a concealed corpse, manual or ligature strangulation, and an animated victim during multiple sexual acts all characterize the patterns and motives of this type of assailant.

4. *Power/Control Oriented Type* – these offenders harbor deep-seated feelings of inadequacy or attempt to compensate for a perceived lack of social or personal mastery over themselves by thoroughly dominating their victims *(3)*. Holmes and DeBurger *(30)* maintained that the primary motive for these offenders is not sexual in nature. Instead, these assailants desire complete and unfettered control over and subjugation of their powerless victims, including during the postmortem period. Consequently, torture, the use of restraints, strangulation, severed body parts, and decapitation are all routinely featured in these homicidal acts *(22,28)*. A profound sense omnipotence – having the ultimate power of life or death over one's victims as they cower and plead for their lives – fuels this type of serial killer *(10)*. The act of murder is extended in order to increase the felt sense of gratification. The offender's *modus operandi* is planned and organized, the body is concealed, and the weapon is absent *(30)*.

Canter et al. *(28)* indicated that one weakness of this subtype model is the lack of specific criteria by which to ascertain which category best suits an offender when characteristics from several subtypes are evident. Moreover, critics note that the overall model is of limited utility, given its lack of empirical validation and its generally unclear methodology *(7,10)*. Interestingly, Canter et al *(28)* suggested that Holmes and Holmes *(11)* employed the organized-disorganized typology in their model. As they explained, the subtype model incorporates the organized-disorganized framework as a continuum. The visionary murderer is located at one end of the spectrum reflecting the disorganized type of assailant. The power/control-oriented killer is positioned at the other end of the continuum, consistent with the organized type of offender. However, Canter et al. *(28)* asserted that the most ambiguity (and inconsistency) occurs in the middle of the field. Finally, they cautioned that the power/control variable was not discriminative as a motive. As they noted, "...power and control appear to be at the heart of these serial killings. They are not typical of any one type of serial killing but of serial killings in general" *(28* p. 508).

Dietz *(33)* also proposed a serial homicide typology. His framework included the following five categories: 1) psychopathic sexual sadists (e.g., Ted Bundy); 2) crime spree killers who kill repeatedly and are motivated by excitement and financial gain (e.g., Bonnie and Clyde); 3) functionaries of organized crime (i.e. hit men, gang members); 4) custodial asphyxiators (i.e. nurses and physicians, serial killings in nursing homes); and 5) "supposed psychotics" (e.g., David Berkowitz or the "Son of Sam").

According to Dietz *(33)*, the only true category for a prolific serial killer is the sexually sadistic offender. This person enjoys killing people. Moreover, Dietz *(33)* found that serial slayers frequently engaged in their murderous acts by strangulation, beating, or stabbing. These methods are much more intimate than the use of firearms or projectile weapons. In Dietz's typology, serial murderers are usually male and they can be diagnosed with antisocial personality disorder, narcissism, psychopathy, and sexual sadism. However, there are some female serial killers (i.e. Aileen Wuornos) *(26,34,35)*. Consistent with all other serial homicide typologies described in this chapter, Dietz's *(33)* model is theoretical in nature lacking significant empirical validation.

SERIAL RAPE TYPOLOGIES

According to Kocsis, Cooksey, and Irwin *(36)*, while there have been many typologies offered that are relevant to the psychological profiling of rape, fundamentally they have been elaborations of the original ideas developed by Groth, Burgess, and Holmstrom *(9)*. Their typologies identify the actual sexual assault as secondary to the motivational role of power and aggression. These investigators classified three main patterns of rape. These patterns include the following: 1) anger rapist, 2) power rapist, and 3) sadistic rapist.

The anger rapist uses more force than is necessary in order to control the victim. The individual is motivated by anger and rage toward the party harmed or who the victim symbolizes. This sexual offender employs considerable physical violence, subjects the victims to a variety of degrading sexual acts, and typically inflicts significant bodily injury *(36)*. The power rapist is motivated by a need to assert his potency and dominance over a victim *(8)*. The level of force this offender utilizes will likely depend on the degree of compliance proffered by the victim. The sadistic rapist experiences eroticized violence. Sexual and aggressive urges are fused and the offender is aroused by the degradation, pain, suffering, torture, and mutilation of the victim *(37)*. The pain and suffering of the victim is not incidental; it is central. This offender typically uses restraints and bondage; engages in paraphilias, torture, and mutilation; and inflicts significant physical injury on the victim, which, in some instances, can escalate to death *(36)*.

The three categories specified by Groth et al. *(9)* were situated into a fourfold typology. The typology consisted of the following: the power-reassurance, power-assertive, anger-retaliatory, and anger-excitation rapist. Again, as with the serial murder models, the essential criticism is that there is little empirical validation for these subtypes. This notwithstanding, the categories themselves are frequently cited and extremely well known, especially among those investigating sex crimes *(8,22,29)*.

In an effort to further define the three rapist categories identified by Groth et al. *(9)*, Hazelwood and Burgess *(38)* developed profiles corresponding with the four-fold typology. Each of these profiles is delineated below. Although far from exhaustive, these summary descriptions provide greater insight into the motivational, behavioral, and personality features of different serial rapists *(8)*.

1. *Power-reassurance rapist*—This individual harbors significant feelings of inadequacy and wants to restore his depleted sense of masculinity. Typically, this rapist is concerned with not injuring the victim, is generally apologetic, makes several efforts to reassure the person harmed, and uses less intrusive forms of sexually assaultive behavior *(39)*. Often identified as the "gentleman rapist," *(40)*, this individual looks for reassurance regarding his manliness. He is less aggressive than other rapists, and his objective is to have sexual intercourse. His attacks are premeditated and fueled by persistent rape fantasies. He likes to pretend that the rape is "consensual" and that the victim is actually enjoying the assault. It is not uncommon for him to experience some form of sexual dysfunction. Usually, this offender relies on the threat of a

weapon; however, he might not even possess one. It is likely that this attacker will spend a great deal of time with the victim, attempting to engage in "pillow talk," asking personal questions of the assaulted party, and offering comments about himself. He generally suffers from low self-esteem, is gentle and passive, has low social competence, and takes little pride in his personal appearance *(40)*.

2. *Power-assertive rapist*—This offender uses the rape as confirmation of his virility, his machismo, and his ability to dominate women. He does not need to be reassured; rather, he wants to dominate women and display his ability to control them *(38)*. His attacks may be impulsive and unplanned. His use of force is moderate and dependent upon victim resistance. This offender frequently uses his fists as weapons and the nature of the assault is short. This rapist may be described as arrogant, self-absorbed in his macho-like image, and hot headed. It is not uncommon for such assailants to have a history of conflict with women *(37)*. This sexual offender perceives himself as very socially competent; however, it is likely he has a series of failed marriages *(40)*.

3. *Anger-retaliatory rapist*—This person is motivated to sexually assault as an extension of anger and rage *(39)*. This retaliatory posture may or may not be focused exclusively on women. The offender overtly expresses anger by using excessive force, relying on lethal instruments (e.g., a knife), and projecting a macho facade to his victims *(41)*. The rage is not sexualized and the rapes do *not* appear to be motivated by compulsive, sadistic fantasies *(37)*. Women are viewed as whores, as dirty, and as individuals not to be trusted *(40)*. This rapist is likely to employ a blitz-style method of attack, severely injuring his victim. The attack usually results in a severe beating and can end in murder; however, this result is not typical of this offender type. Moreover, the victim's resistance can produce even more savage attacks because it fuels the anger. This type of offender can exhibit displaced anger after a fight with a girlfriend or wife. Under these conditions, the assailant may symbolically assault a female victim to equalize the perceived inequalities in his own relationship. In this way, the rape is used to punish or humiliate another and often represents a general disdain for women.

4. *Anger-excitation rapist*—This offender is also identified as a sadistic-ritualistic rapist *(40)*. He incorporates sadistic behavior into his sexual assaults because he enjoys the pain and suffering inflicted on his victim. This assailant is more likely to bind and transport victims, to withhold reassurance towards them, and to terrorize those whom he harms by telling them how he will hurt them *(37)*. In this way, the anger-excitation rapist maintains something of a detached interaction with his victims. Additionally, there is greater planning with the offense and the behavior itself is less impulsive *(39)*. The attacks are generally calculated and orchestrated, including the offender transporting weapons and other items to the crime scene for purposes of restraint and torture. Hazelwood and Burgess *(38)* noted that this type of rapist was sexually stimulated or gratified by the victim's response to and suffering from physical as well as emotional pain. The primary motivation is to inflict injury, to induce fear, and to insure total submission. Hazelwood and Burgess *(38)* further

described the offender relying on a "brutal" level of force that often resulted in death. This assailant typically employs verbal strategies or cues to gain confidence from and access to the victim.

This assailant's instructions to his victims are cold and detached. The offender is very ritualistic and habitual in his behavior. Mutilation is commonly featured in sexually significant areas of the woman's body (e.g., vagina, breasts). Bizarre acts of torture, dismemberment, necrophilia, and other forms of extremely violent conduct are routinely noted *(38,40)*. The assault is prolonged and the weapon of choice is a knife. Instruments used for restraint and torture are also regularly employed. Once again, the victims are strangers; however, they symbolize others in his compulsive, sadistic fantasies *(37)*. This offender may lack a criminal record. Drug or alcohol use during the offense is minimal so the attacker remains in control. The sadistic rapist is not likely to have a mental health history, possesses an average to an above average intelligence, and may work as a white-collar employee. It is not uncommon for him to be married; however, his wife is firmly under his control and, indeed, she may be a compliant victim herself *(40)*. Typically this offender is an outgoing white male, who is respected by his peers. His habitual and sadistic fantasies are probably concealed from most of those around him.

As previously specified, the Groth et al. *(9)* typology is perhaps the most well known and respected of the serial rape models in existence today *(42)*. The organizing framework or profiles developed by Hazelwood and Burgess *(38)* provide investigators with important demographic, offense characteristics, and lifestyle information that facilitates offender identification *(39,43)*. To date, researchers have found that there is no consistent escalation in the physical force used by the vast majority of serial rapists *(38,39)*. As such, this suggests that most repeat offenders of this sort are distinct in their *modus operandi* and, likely, in their motives as compared with their serial murder counterparts.

The categories of the Groth et al. *(9)* model were originally created and subsequently modified from clinical experience and an investigative perspective *(39)*. Prentky and Knight *(44)* are responsible for considerable empirical validation of this model and they named their assessment version the Massachusetts Treatment Center: Rape 3 (MTC:R3). This instrument is composed of four primary rapist types, differentiated based on inferred motives: *opportunistic* (high/low social competency), *pervasively angry, sexual* (sadistic-overt/muted or non-sadistic-high/low social competency), and *vindictive* (moderate/low social competency). Critics contend that although this typology is much more empirically anchored, it nonetheless appears to overlap behaviors, motives, and cognitions without clear distinctions concerning or explanation about how best to classify those that engender a combination of characteristics *(41)*.

SERIAL MURDER AND SERIAL RAPE: DICHOTOMY
AND CONTINUUM

In this final portion of the chapter, several important differences among the similarities between serial murder and serial rape are identified. The cataloging here is certainly not exhaustive. However, this effort is designed to encourage future theory construction, model building, and empirical examination, especially as necessary steps in furthering society's understanding of extreme violence. In what follows, criminal motives, victim and offender characteristics, crime scene behavior, and methods to avoid detection and apprehension are all principally (and very tentatively) explored.

Differences Between Serial Murder and Serial Rape

When the various subtypes of serial rapists are considered collectively, they have more characteristics that are distinct from their serial murderer counterparts than those that are similar. For example, most serial rapists use nondeadly force and many use just enough force to gain compliance from their victims *(44)*. For these serial rapists, the motivation is primarily sexual with a relative absence of violence and brutality *(45)*. Additionally, most serial rapists do not increase the amount of physical force used in their series of sexual assaults *(43)*. Overall, then, serial rapists are a much more heterogeneous group than serial murderers, especially with respect to motivations and backgrounds.

For example, the power-assertive serial rapist may want to exert his sexual prowess but may lack the need to feel omnipotent toward or in control of the life and death of his victims. This is something that is customary among serial murderers *(10)*. Additionally, although lust murderers and sadistic serial rapists appear quite similar, what distinguishes them is that the homicide is primary for serial killers and the sexual assault is secondary *(22)*. Indeed, in these instances, the act of murder itself is by far the most exhilarating, rather than the acts that led up to its commission. Under these circumstances, the assailant may fantasize exclusively about the murder without engaging in sexual assault or intercourse. The elaborate scenes of death erotically stimulate and satisfy this offender *(29)*. Still, for other serial murderers, the act of killing is a necessity. It is a natural and essential progression of the mutilation and torture that takes place as linked to the sexual assault. However, for the serial rapist, sexual assault and torture are the primary inducements that fuel one's criminality.

Almost all serial rape victims walk away from their injuries, albeit with lasting psychological and, sometimes, physical scars. Those persons harmed are critical to the development of rapist profiles *(8,17)*. In particular, they provide investigators with invaluable information about offender character-istics (e.g., attack styles, amount of force used, verbalizations, personality features, physical attributes, grooming patterns). Conversely, it is rare for potential victims of serial murder to escape their assailants *(15,16)*. Thus, the ability on the part of investigators to establish testable models regarding serial homicide offender typologies is considerably circumscribed *(18)*. In short, law enforcement personnel and behavioral scientists seldom get a first-hand glimpse into the predatory world of this offender at the time of the assailant's attack *(46)*.

Moreover, it is easier to investigate serial rapists (and serial rape typologies) as the incidents of these assaults are much more frequent than their serial homicide counterparts *(11,22)*. If an offender's goal is to rape rather than to murder, the living sexually assaulted victim typically provides a plethora of clues that enable investigators to apprehend the perpetrator *(29)*. Generally speaking, while one-time rapists frequently assault victims known to them, serial rapists usually harm strangers and do so by utilizing a blitz-style method of attack *(47)*. Conversely, serial homicide offenders almost always assail strangers but employ more of a manipulative approach in which to secure the confidence of and gain access to the injured party. For example, Ted Bundy, Jeffrey Dahmer, John Wayne Gacy, and Gary Ridgway all primarily used chicanery and pretense as the preferred method by which to interact with their respective victims *(15)*. This strategy was employed in order to guarantee the victim's trust and to establish a situation where the attack could occur *(19,22)*.

Methods to avoid detection also differ between these types of offenders. To illustrate, rapists may wear masks (e.g., Gilbert Escabedo) or cover the victim's face in order to conceal the assailant's identity or because the offender harbors feelings of shame over his sexual inadequacies *(37)*. However, in cases of sexual or lust murder, the victim's face may be covered in order to dehumanize or depersonalize the victim *(10,48)*. Consequently, despite the frequency with which the incidents of rape occur, there are likely to be many more unreported or undetected serial rape than serial murder victims *(8)*.

In instances of serial rape, there will likely be more identifiable rituals than in serial homicide cases *(17)*. This is because live victims are typically a product of the former type of offense and they can describe discrete offender behaviors. However, the vast majority of serial murderers engage in ritualistic forms of conduct, notwithstanding the absence of living victims *(10)*. Interestingly, though, an opportunistic killer who is less likely to be successful as a serial offender may not exhibit any rituals, especially since their primary objective is to obtain control over the victim with little forethought or calculation *(40)*. Still, the crime of rape tends to occur in areas characterized by construction, urban development, and temporary lodgings *(49)*. This reflects the more opportunistic, impulsive nature of a greater number of rapes than serial homicides. However, in the context of ritual and habituation, what this suggests is that serial rapists tend to "use repeatedly the same geographic and ecological space" (*49*, p. 40). Thus, the difference on the element of ritual may be a function of degree rather than kind for serial rapists versus serial murderers.

Similarities Between Serial Murder and Serial Rape

Geographic profiling is utilized in both serial rape and serial murder cases *(16,18)*. Commenting on this notion in relation to sexual assault, Warren et al. *(49)* noted that, "while rapists tended to vary in the distance that they traveled from home to rape, they consistently seemed to restrict their attacks to within one-half mile of their previous attacks" (p. 40). Moreover, it is also common for serial murderers to reuse the same locations or places that are in close proximity to one another for disposing of bodies *(15)*. Not surprisingly, this is often the first clue for law enforcement that they are searching for the same assailant.

However, serial killers are less inclined to worry about establishing a "buffer zone;" a locale that ensures that the murders are not committed too close to home. While the crime scene will often be different than the dump site, the assailant does not possess a living corpse that could lead police back to the offender's place of residence (e.g., Jeffrey Dahmer, John Wayne Gacy) *(10)*. Conversely, the serial rape offender's desire to avoid detection trumps the inclination to identify victims with the least amount of geographical and time restraints *(49)*. Indeed, Warren et al. *(49)* maintained that the assailant's travel patterns consist of movement away from the perpetrator's home, thereby creating a larger victim pool. The offender often moves toward other significant places in which to engage in criminality (e.g. places of work, red light districts). The locale is usually significant for the offender; however, its meaning typically does not manifest itself until after the offender's apprehension.

Serial murderers and anger excitation- sadistic/ritualistic serial rapists both have sexual motives that are closely fused with violence. These groups likely have a disproportionate number of male offenders who experience sexual dysfunctions *(14,17)*. For the serial murderer, particularly the hedonistic (lust killer), torture and homicide erotically excite him. Moreover, it is plausible to assume that as the serial sadistic rapist finds the degree of violence escalating, an increase in aggressiveness and sadism is needed in order to sustain the arousal state *(50)*.

The organized/disorganized serial murder typology as proposed by Ressler et al. *(13)* has also been utilized to describe the crime scenes of serial rapists;

however, victims' reports in serial rape cases have facilitated further understanding of offender characteristics *(37)*. The premise of this dichotomy is to analyze crime scenes and to formulate offender profiles based on the level of planning and behavioral sophistication of the assailant (i.e. methodical, premeditated, and calculated versus chaotic, impulsive, and opportunistic). This typology can be applied to both serial killers and repetitive rapists, regardless of the type. Indeed, as Kocsis et al. *(36)* observed, "... planning and perpetration of the offense on the part of the offender with an associated expression of sexual violence forms the basis of most serial rapes (p. 162)."

There are a large number of serial murder and serial rape victims created by a small number of offenders. Both types of attackers possess a dynamic *modus operandi* that changes based on criminal experience, education, situational needs, and relatively static rituals. The ritual is defined as "repeated patterns of behaviors which are unnecessary to the commission of the crime; provide psychosexual arousal and gratification; and compliment the motive" *(46)*. The ritual remains the same over time but the offender might make improvements. For example, a decision to bind someone with rope instead of tape signifies a change.

Victims of both serial sexual murders and sadistic/ritualistic serial rapes are typically strangers to the perpetrator interpersonally but are "known" to the assailant symbolically. Indeed, they can be easily integrated into the offender's fantasy system. This is an imaginary realm where constructions of oneself, others, and situations have been repeatedly rehearsed *(19)*. Thus, for the attacker, the victim is in some meaningful way incorporated into or is otherwise a part of the offender, securing for the assailant profound feelings of omnipotence *(10)*.

Moreover, both offender types are experts at intimidation and control. They harbor frequent, compulsive fantasies that fuel their criminal actions. Violent, sexualized imagery plays a critical role in the offense chain for these respective assailants. They are methodical with considerable ritualized behavior. Power and control are essential themes present in both offenses. For example, it is not uncommon for these offenders to have their acts of brutality audio-taped, videotaped, and/or recorded in journal format so they can relive the experience through fantasy *(29)*. Both offenders are almost never psychotic, nor do they suffer from delusions, hallucinations, or disorganized thinking. However, their behavior is abnormal and frightening *(51)*. Both plan to avoid detection and often bring death or rape and torture kits to the crime scene.

Some researchers have argued that rape murderers are distinct from lust murders in terms of motives and personality dynamics *(29,52,53)*. Indeed, according to Rada *(53)*,

The rapist who murders rarely reports any sexual satisfaction from the murder and does not perform sexual acts on the dead victim. Rape murder occurs subsequent to sexual assault and does not appear to have sexual connotations itself. The lust murderer, on the other hand, frequently needs the murder to arouse his sexual interest and desires. Often he does not perform intercourse with the victim, dead or alive. He may, however, experience intense sexual pleasure and orgasm at the time of the murder- some compulsively disembowel the victim and masturbate to orgasm... Rapists are capable of murder but typically for different reasons. In some rapists, however, there appears to be a progressive increase in aggressive fantasies toward women which over time may eventually lead to murder. (Cited in Liebert *(52)*, pp. 189–190).

However, notwithstanding these observations, we contend that there exists a subgroup of serial rapists that represent burgeoning lust murderers *(19,32)*. As such, serial murder and serial rape typologies suggestively create a distinct continuum when specifically examining the hedonistic (i.e., lust killers) and anger excitation- sadistic/ritualistic type serial rapists. There are several justifications that substantiate this position. Psychopathy and sadism are typically observed in both offenders. Moreover, there is a lack of empathy toward and remorse for the individual's actions (including deviant sexual behavior), which is motivated in part by thrill or sensation seeking conduct.

Still, there is an even darker side *(54)*; that is, a more brutal dimension to these crimes: sexual sadism that makes the assailant not only dismissive of the agonizing suffering of his victims, but also exhilarated, aroused, and motivated because of its presence *(29)*. Both types of offenders are quite effective as imposters. And, they can persuasively appear as "normal" or "healthy" to those around them. The manifestation of this pernicious and sinister persona is extremely destructive for others; however, it is thoroughly rewarding, indeed enticing, for the individual offender.

Ritualized and paraphilic behaviors are intertwined with sexual sadism *(32, 55,56)*. Sadistic rapists and serial murderers are always ritualistic because all paraphilic behavior is habitual *(22)*. The anger excitation- sadistic/ritualistic serial rapist has more in common with serial sexual murderers than other types of serial rapists. This is based on the nature of, motives for, and types of assaults committed against their victims. To illustrate, Dickey, Nussbaum, Chevolleau, and Davidson *(57)* conducted a study based on three sexual offender subject pools: rapists, pedophiles, and sadists. The researchers found that one third of the sexual sadists had committed first or second degree murder, whereas none from the other two groups had these crimes on their record.

What this suggests is that there are some obvious parallels between the ritualistic or sadistic serial rapist and several typologies available within the serial homicide literature *(1,13,36,48)*. While the murder has yet to occur, the motivations for and context of the attacks are strikingly similar to that of hedonistic (lust murderer) and the organized sadistic offender, based on the FBI's serial murder typology *(20,21)*. Indeed, given the circumstances, it is likely that some interruption prevented the murder and that the homicide will likely occur in the near future *(36)*.

These very speculative and certainly provisional observations support the position that a sadistic serial rapist can be located on the same continuum as the lust murderer. Indeed, with each successive rape, sadistic deviance and sexual violence will likely increase. This pattern will intensify until, eventually, one's progression along this continuum will result in murder. When these actions are repetitively and habitually sustained over time, the behavior becomes serial in nature.

IMPLICATIONS AND CONCLUSION

Future research is needed on the behavioral and personality characteristics that are distinct to specific categories of serial murderers and serial rapists. Moreover, future research is warranted with respect to etiological and motivational factors, as well as crime scene behavior and methods to avoid detection and apprehension that appear theoretically constant across various offender typologies and subgroups. The absence of controlled studies that could help empirically validate both serial murder and serial rape typologies is problematic. This matter is particularly complicated and thorny when considering possible expert forensic psychological testimony in a criminal court of law *(28)*. Arguably, additional interviews with offenders would also provide more detailed information. The data elicited here could improve our understanding of these serial offenders, including deeper insight into their motivations, cognitions, biological predispositions, fantasies, impulses, and personality structures.

This chapter represents one very provisional step in this critical direction. The primary models pertaining to serial murder were delineated. The principal typology regarding serial rape was enumerated. Several integrative comments were then supplied. Important differences between serial murder and serial rape were noted. However, commonalities were also described. As we suggested, there is considerable room to explore a useful assimilation between the sadistic/ritualistic serial rapist typology and the hedonistic (lust killer) model for serial homicide. Future investigators are encouraged to undertake this explanatory exercise, especially as a basis to promote model making, theory testing, and empirical validation. This is the scientific process by which violence is predicted, treated, prevented, and abated.

REFERENCES

1. Burgess, A. W., Hartman, C. R., Ressler, R. K., Douglas, J. E., & McCormack A. (1986). Sexual homicide: a motivational model. *Journal of Interpersonal Violence*, 1, 251–272.
2. Burgess, A. W., Hazelwood, R. R., Rokous, F. E., Hartman, C. R., & Burgess, A. G. (1988). Serial rapists and their victims: reenactment and repetition. *Annals of New York Academy of Sciences*, 528, 277–295.
3. DeHart, D. D., & Mahoney, J. M. (1994). The serial murderer's motivations: an interdisciplinary review. *Omega*, 29(1), 29–45.
4. Brittain, R. P. (1970). The sadistic murderer. *Medical Science Law*, 10, 198–207.
5. Davies, A. (1992). Rapists' behavior: a three aspect model as a basis for analysis and the identification of serial crime. *Forensic Science International*, 55, 173–194.
6. Hazelwood, R., & Warren, J. (1989). The serial rapist: his characteristics and victims. Part I. *FBI Law Enforcement Bulletin*, January, 11–17.
7. Giannangelo, S. J. (1996). *The Psychopathology of Serial Murder: A Theory of Violence*. Westport, CT: Praeger.
8. Graney, D. J., & Arrigo, B. A. (2002). *The Power Serial Rapist: A Criminology-Victimology Typology of Female Victim Selection*. Springfield, IL: Charles C Thomas.
9. Groth, A. N., Burgess, A., & Holmstrom, L. (1977). Rape, power, anger and sexuality. *American Journal of Psychiatry*, 134, 1239–1243.
10. Hickey, E. W. (2006). *Serial murderers and their victims* (4th ed.). United States: Wadsworth, Press, Belmont, California.
11. Holmes, R. M., & Holmes, S. (1999). *Serial murder* (2nd ed.). Thousand Oaks, CA: Sage.
12. Money, J. (1990). Forensic sexology: paraphilic serial rape (biastophilia) and lust murder. *American Journal of Psychotherapy*, 44, 26–36.
13. Ressler, R. K., Burgess, A. W., Douglas, J. E., Hartman, C. R., & D'Agostino, R. B. (1986). Sexual killers and their victims: identifying patterns through crime scene analysis. *Journal of Interpersonal Violence*, 1, 288–308.
14. Schlesinger, L. B. (2003). *Sexual Murder: Catathymic and Compulsive Homicides*. Boca Raton: CRC Press.
15. Egger, S. A. (2002). *The Killers Among Us: An Examination of Serial Murder and Its Investigation* (2nd ed.). Upper Saddle River, NJ: Prentice-Hall.
16. Holmes, R. M., & Holmes, S. T. (2003). *Profiling Violent Crimes: An Investigative Tool* (3rd ed.). Thousand Oaks, CA: Sage.
17. Palermo, G. B. (2004). *The Faces of Violence* (2nd ed.). Springfield, IL: Charles C Thomas.
18. Palermo, G. B., & Kocsis, R. N. (2005). *Offender Profiling: An Introduction to the Sociopsychological Analysis of Violent Crime*. Springfield, IL: Charles C Thomas.
19. Purcell, C. E., & Arrigo, B. A. (2006). *The Psychology of Lust Murder: On Paraphilia, Sexual Murder and Serial Killing*. San Diego, CA: Elsevier.

20. Douglas, J. E., Burgess, A. W., Burgess, A. G., & Ressler, R. K. (1992). *Crime Classification Manual: A Standard System for Investigating and Classifying Violent Crime*. New York: Simon & Schuster.
21. Douglas, J. E., Burgess, A. W., & Ressler, R. K. (1995). *Sexual Homicide: Patterns and Motives*. New York: Free Press.
22. Holmes, R. M., & Holmes, S. T. (2002). *Sex Crimes: Patterns and Behavior* (2nd ed.). Thousand Oaks, CA: Sage.
23. Prentky, R. A., Burgess, A. W., Rokous, F., Lee, A., Hartman, C., Ressler, R., & Douglas, J. (1989). The presumptive role of fantasy in serial sexual homicide. *American Journal of Psychiatry*, 146, 887–891.
24. Gerberth, V. J., & Turco, R. N. (1997). Antisocial personality disorder, sexual sadism, malignant narcissism, and serial murder. *Journal of Forensic Sciences*, 42(1), 49–60.
25. Arrigo, B. A., & Shipley, S. L. (2001). The confusion over psychopathy. I. Historical considerations. *International Journal of Offender Therapy and Comparative Criminology*, 45(3), 325–344.
26. Shipley, S. L., & Arrigo, B. A. (2001). The confusion over psychopathy. II. Implications for forensic (correctional) practice. *International Journal of Offender Therapy and Comparative Criminology*, 45(4), 407–420.
27. Myers, W. C., Reccoppa, L., Burton, K., & McElroy, R. (1993). Malignant sex and aggression: an overview of serial sexual homicide. *Bulletin of the American Academy of Psychiatry and Law*, 21, 435–451.
28. Canter, D. V., Alison, L. J., Alison, E., & Wentink, N. (2004). The organized/disorganized typology of serial murder: myth or model? *Psychology, Public Policy, and Law*, 10(3), 293–320.
29. Hickey, E. (2005). *Sex Crimes and Paraphilia*. Upper Saddle River, NJ: Prentice-Hall.
30. Holmes, R. M., & DeBurger, J. E. (1988). *Serial Murder*. Newbury Park, CA: Sage.
31. Schlesinger, L. B. (1998). Pathological narcissism and serial homicide: review and case study. *Current Psychology*, Fall, 17(2/3), 212–221.
32. Arrigo, B. A., & Purcell, C. E. (2001). Explaining paraphilias and lust murder: an integrated model. *International Journal of Offender Therapy and Comparative Criminology*, 45, 6–31.
33. Dietz, P. E. (1986). Mass, serial, and sensational homicides. *Bulletin of New York Academy Medicine*, 62, 477–491.
34. Arrigo, B. A., & Griffin, A. (2004). Serial murder and the case of Aileen Wuornos: attachment theory, psychopathy, and predatory aggression. *Behavioral Sciences and the Law*, 22, 375–393.
35. Shipley, S. L., & Arrigo, B. A. (2004). *The Female Homicide Offender: Serial Murder and the Case of Aileen Wuornos*. Upper Saddle River, NJ: Prentice Hall.
36. Kocsis, R. N., Cooksey, R. W., & Irwin, H. J. (2002). Psychological profiling of offender characteristics from crime behaviors in serial rape offences. *International Journal of Offender Therapy and Comparative Criminology*, 46(2), 144–169.

37. Groth, A. N., & Birnbaum, H. J. (2001). *Men Who Rape: The Psychology of the Offender.* New York: Perseus.
38. Hazelwood, R., & Burgess, A. (1987). An introduction to the serial rapist: research by the FBI. *FBI Law Enforcement Bulletin,* September, 16–24.
39. Warren, J. I., Reboussin, R., Hazelwood, R. R., & Wright, J. A. (1991). Prediction of rapist type and violence from verbal, physical, and sexual scales. *Journal of Interpersonal Violence,* 6(1), 55–67.
40. National Center for Women and Policing (2004). Suspect typology; profiling the sex offender. http://www.hawaii.edu/hivandaids/Suspect%20Typology%20%20%20%20Profiling%the%20Sex%20Offender.pdf.
41. McCabe, M. P., & Wauchope, M. (2005). Behavioral characteristics of men accused of rape: evidence from different types of rapists. *Archives of Sexual Behavior,* 34(2), 241–253.
42. Richards, H. J., Washburn, J. J., Craig, R., Taheri, A., & Yanisch D. (2004). Typing rape offenders from their offense narratives. *Individual Differences Research,* 2(2), 97–108.
43. Warren, J. I., Reboussin, R., Hazelwood, R. R., Gibbs, N. A., Trumbetta, S., & Cummings, A. (1999). Crime scene analysis and the escalation of violence in serial rape. *Forensic Science International,* 100, 37–56.
44. Prentky, R. A. & Knight, R. A. (1991). Identifying critical dimensions for discriminating among rapists. *Journal of Consulting Clinical Psychology,* 59, 643–661.
45. Prentky, R. A., Knight, R. A., & Rosenberg, R. (1988). Validation analyses on a taxonomic system for rapists: disconfirmation and reconceptualization. *Annals of the New York Academy of Sciences,* 528, 21–40.
46. Arrigo, B. A. (2006). *Criminal Behavior: A Systems Approach,* Upper Saddle River, NJ: Prentice Hall.
47. LeBeau, J. L. (1987). The journey to rape: geographic distance and the rapist's method of approaching the victim. *Journal of Police Science and Administration,* 15(2), 129–136.
48. Kocsis, R. N., Cooksey, R. W., & Irwin, H. J. (2002). Psychological profiling of sexual murders: an empirical model. *International Journal of Offender Therapy and Comparative Criminology,* 46(3), 532–553.
49. Warren, J. I., Reboussin, R., Hazelwood, R. R., Cummings, A., Gibbs, N., Trumbetta, S., & Cummings A. (1998). Crime scene and distance correlates of serial rape. *Journal of Quantitative Criminology,* 14(1), 35–59.
50. Kafka, M. P. (2003). Sexual offending and sexual appetite: the clinical and theoretical relevance of hypersexual desire. *International Journal of Offender Therapy and Comparative Criminology,* 47 (4), 439–451.
51. Drukteinis, A. M. (1992). Serial murder: the heart of darkness. *Annals,* 22 (10), 532–538.
52. Liebert, J. (1985). Contributions to psychiatric consultation in the investigation of serial murder. *International Journal of Offender Therapy and Comparative Criminology,* 28, 187–200.
53. Rada, R. (1978). *Clinical Aspects of the Rapists.* New York: Grune & Stratton.

54. Carlisle, A. L. (1993). The divided self: toward an understanding of the dark side of the serial killer. *American Journal of Criminal Justice*, 17(2), 23–36.
55. Blanchard, G. T. (1995). Sexually addicted lust murderers. *Sexual Addiction & Compulsivity*, 2(1), 62–71.
56. Johnson, B. R., & Becker, J. V. (1997). Natural born killers? The development of the sexually sadistic serial killer. *Journal of the American Academy of Psychiatry and the Law*, 25(3), 325–348.
57. Dickey, R., Nussbaum, D., Chevolleau, K., & Davidson, H. (2002). Age as a differential characteristics of rapists, pedophiles, and sexual sadists. *Journal of Sex & Marital Therapy*, 28, 211–218.

Chapter 9

Firesetting
A Burning Issue
Jeffrey L. Geller

Abstract

Firesetting or arson destroys property, extinguishes lives, costs individuals and governments huge sums of money, and remains one of the most underprosecuted felonies. Focusing on knowledge accrued during the past decade and a half, this chapter examines what is known about adult firesetting. Firesetting is approached by first elucidating its etiology, examining this from the perspectives of 1) motivation, 2) characteristics of firesetters, and 3) multifactorial factors. Particular populations of firesetters are described, including those with developmental disabilities, firefighter firesetters, those with communicative arson, self-mutilators, self-immolators, and serial arsonists. The assessment and treatment of adult firesetters is highlighted. The chapter concludes with a discussion of some troubling newer trends in arson, such as church fires and eco-terrorism, and calls for continuing the renewed interest in understanding and treating the adult firesetter.

INTRODUCTION

Despite thousands of years of criminalizing and 200 years of patholo-gizing arson *(1)*, pathological firesetting remains almost as enigmatic today as it was in 1833 when Marc, in France, labeled it *monomanie incendiare*, or "pyromania" *(1)*. Firesetting, like other potentially violent acts, can cause physical and psychological injuries, loss of earnings, and death. Unlike many other violent acts, firesetting can cause extensive property damage or loss, and its unintended victims far outnumber other forms of violence on a per-incident calculation. Firesetting is easy to do, requires neither special equipment nor special skills, and has a high rate of success in achieving the perpetrator's aim.

From: *Serial Murder and the Psychology of Violent Crimes*
Edited by: R. N. Kocsis © Humana Press, Totowa, NJ

Perhaps it is the nature of fire itself, or how difficult it is for us to understand acts of violence with apparently ill-defined motives that accounts for firesetters' and firesetting's continued fascination for the public. Rarely does a day go by without a fire story in the popular press. And these articles are often sensationalistic and misleading. A recent sampling:

There's a touch of pyromania in most guys *(2)*.

Five volunteer firefighters arrested for allegedly setting 11 fires in one county in West Virginia had a motto: 'We light 'em, we fight 'em' *(3)*.

One of six men charged with arsons... that are the biggest cases of residential arson in memory in Maryland... told investigators that the fires were intended to raise the profile of a local car club *(4)*.

Police allege [three former volunteer firefighters] set fire to the house so they could be the first on the scene and be viewed as heroes *(5)*.

A man who set himself afire yesterday just outside White House gate... was distraught over his inability to return to Yemin... *(6)*.

A 30-year-old man in Batavia, New York faces up to 20 years in prison after admitting he set fire to a woman's apartment while she and her three children slept there after the women rebuffed his advances *(7)*.

A 41-year-old man in Bellevue, Washington was arrested "after allegedly setting a fire to his home... to stop voices or get rid of people he thought were in the TV" *(8)*.

A 41-year-old New York City man "dressed up as a fireman on Halloween, set a couple of fires in a woman's West 24th Street building, knocked on her door, made his way in, and then drugged and molested her for about 13 hours" *(9)*.

Those who deliberately set fires are either incredibly stupid or in the grasp of pyromania, a dangerous psychosis *(10)*.

Although firesetting is often difficult to understand, even mysterious at times, it is not uncommon. Each year in the United States there are 250,000 to 500,000 arson fires that claim 475 to 700 lives, destroy 100,000 buildings, and cost $1.4 billion to $2 billion *(11,12)*. Arson accounts for about 25% of all U.S. fires and is the leading cause of dollar loss from fire *(11)*. In 2004 in the United States, there were 36,500 intentionally set structure fires and 36,000 intentionally set vehicle fires, accounting for $0.88 billion in damage or loss *(13)*. The problems caused by firesetting are compounded by the fact that it is one of the most underprosecuted felonies in the United States. According to the Center for Arson Research in Philadelphia, only 17% are successfully prosecuted *(14)*. Such a finding is not unique to the United States; Australia, for example, reports similar findings *(15)*. As the U.S. Fire Administrator said 10 years ago, "Arson is not a hidden crime. It's murder by fire, a violent crime against property and people" *(11)*.

During the early 1990s, there were a series of reviews of arson and pathological firesetting published that basically accounted for the state of knowledge up to 1990 *(16–20)*. This chapter focuses on what we have gleaned more recently about arson and pathological firesetting by examining the literature of the past decade and a half. The importance of this topic is highlighted by the simple observations that "arson is one of the easiest crimes to commit on the spur of the moment" *(21)* and that the "peculiar challenge presented by arson is that the very act of committing the crime obliterates much of the evidence" *(22)*.

ETIOLOGY

The long quest to understand the etiology of arson *(1)* continues with some significant recent progress. Understanding causation has fundamental implications for risk assessment and treatment. Explaining arson has been approached by three methodologies: 1) motivation; 2) characteristics of firesetters; and 3) multifactorial.

Motivation

Using motivation as a basis for classifying firesetting is challenging because motivations are not always easy to tease out and may be complex rather than unitary. Note, for example: A grand jury charged a former police officer, who denied any involvement, with setting his saloon on fire to collect insurance *(23)*; a 42-year-old man with a 10-year history of paranoid delusions, "believing that he was 'already under arrest' concluded that he 'may as well set the fire and get arrested openly'" *(24)*; a 42-year-old man "burned an automobile because his psychotherapist at the time objected to his dating another group therapy patient" *(25)*. One consideration, more clearly articulated in the recent literature than previously, is the concept that underlining all firesetting is an assertion of, or restoration of, power *(26,27)*.

Using motivation as the basis for the classification of firesetting has continued since 1990 in the medical/psychiatric literature *(28–31)* and in the arson literature *(32–35)*. Examining the literature of the past 15 years, and updating Geller's classification of arson by motive *(18)*, the resultant schema is shown in Table 1.

Table 1
Classification of Arson by Motive

Arson unassociated with psychobiological disorders
  Arson for profit
    Insurance fraud
    Welfare fraud
    Bankruptcy scam
    Property improvements
    Building strippers
    Burglary
    Business modifications
    Employment
  Assault/murder
  Crime concealment
  Revenge
  Vanity or recognition
    Hero syndrome
    Fire buff
  Vagrant
  Vandalism
  Political
    Riot
    Terrorism
    Protest

Arson associated with mental disorders
  Disorders of thought or perception
    Delusions
    Hallucinations
  Disorders of mood
    Depression
    Mania
  Disorders of judgment
    Developmental disorders
    Dementia
    Psychoactive substance-induced
  Disorders of impulse control
    Intermittent explosive disorder
    Pyromania
  Communicative arson

Arson associated with medical or neurological disorders
  Chromosomal disorders
    Klinefelter syndrome

XYY syndrome
Central nervous system disorders
  Epilepsy
  Head trauma
  Brain tumor
Infectious diseases
  Acquired immune deficiency syndrome (AIDS)
Endocrine and metabolic disorders
  Late luteal phase dysphoric disorder
  Hypoglycemia
Self-incineration
  Single episode, survives, no history of self-abuse
  Single episode, survives, history of "manipulative
  self-abuse"
  Single episode, survives, history of serious self-abuse
  Single episode, dies, diagnosis clear
  Single episode, dies, diagnosis unclear, question political motivation
  Multiple episodes of minor consequences
  Multiple episodes of major consequences, fires to self and other objects
  Multiple episodes of fire to self only

ARSON UNASSOCIATED WITH PSYCHOBIOLOGICAL DISORDERS

For arson unassociated with psychobiological disorders, there are a few updates to Geller's exposition *(18)* that are worth noting. Arson used for assault *(36)* or murder *(22–39)* has been added. Arson was responsible for the two largest cases of mass murder in New York City prior to September 11, 2001 *(22)*. Arson has been noted as one of the most frequently used means of filicide *(37,38)*.

It has been postulated that revenge, often cited as the most frequent motive for arson *(28–35)*, may have an identifiable biological basis—through striatal activation *(40)*.

ARSON ASSOCIATED WITH MENTAL DISORDERS

Firesetting that results from a disorder of thought, perception, or mood has not been better explicated than in the reviews of the early 1990s *(16–20)*. Better treatments for psychosis, depression and mania, introduced over the past 15 years, may be contributing to progressively lower rates of arson *(13)*, but there is no direct evidence to support this hypothesis.

Disorders of judgment due to psychoactive substance use continue to be reported *(41)*, with alcohol featured ever more prominently (see below). Firesetting associated with developmental disorders is receiving increasing attention and is discussed in the next section.

Pyromania, a residual 19th century monomania *(1)* from a list of monomanias as creative as to include drapetomania (the running away of slaves) *(42)*, continues to be misunderstood even by those who should be most knowledgeable *(43)*. Pyromania is no doubt rare *(1,28,44–48)*; some are even questioning its existence *(1,44–46)*. A recent line of inquiry relates pyromania to depression *(49)*. The one exception to the rarity of pyromania comes from a Finnish study, which reported using DSM-III-R criteria to make the diagnosis *(50)*. An unusual case of pyromania has been reported in which pyromania was the basis for a *folie a deux (51)*.

There have not been many efforts to determine the prevalence of firesetting behaviors in the psychiatric population, perhaps because "dehospitalization" *(52)* has made this population difficult to study. One group in Massachusetts *(53)* repeated a study at Worcester State Hospital that one of the authors had done 5 years earlier at Northampton State Hospital *(54)*. The results were remarkably similar: 27% of patients had lifetime histories of firesetting behavior (including, for example, setting off fire alarms, throwing lit matches), and 18% had actually set a fire *(53)*. Informal inquiries among psychiatrists, district attorneys, and police indicate this percentage is much higher than suspected.

Communicative arson *(55)* is discussed in the next section.

Arson Associated with Medical or Neurological Disorders

Firesetting has been reported in association with acquired immunodeficiency syndrome (AIDS) *(56)*, Klinefelter syndrome *(57–59)*, seizure disorders *(60,61)*, a cerebellar arachnoid cyst *(62)*, and even dyslexia *(63)*. Greater attempts are being made to examine causative links between organic pathology and arson, moving beyond simple associations. Recent investigations include space-occupying lesions *(62)*, kindling *(61)*, and dysfunction of the serotonergic system *(64)*.

Characteristics of Firesetters

Attempting to classify firesetters by their characteristics is really an attempt to differentiate firesetters from nonfiresetters. This has been generally done in correctional facilities, which does not differentiate the firesetter from the general population. Given this caveat, the results of a review of the literature that focused on characteristics of firesetters *(21,50,65–83)* and that looked at multifactorial explanations *(29,84,85)* are shown in Table 2, which presents characteristics of firesetters. There has been an increasing interest in, and a postulation for an increasing frequency of, firesetting by females (*65,66,70–72,79,80*); hence, the two sexes are presented separately. In Table 2, "Y" marks a positive indication and "N" a negative indication; a blank means there are insufficient data.

Table 2
Characteristics of Firesetters

Characteristic	Male	Female
Psychiatric		
Psychotic disorder	Y	Y
Mood disorder	Y	Y
Personality disorder	Y	Y
History of psychiatric treatment	Y	Y
Intellectual		
Borderline IQ or MR	Y	Y
Special education	Y	Y
Parental history		
Violence	Y	
Alcoholism	Y	
Separation during childhood	Y	Y
Maternal psychiatric history	Y	Y
Absent parent	Y	Y
Social status		
Unmarried	Y	Y
Ever institutionalized	Y	
Living alone	Y	Y
Living in parents' home	Y	
Unemployed	Y	N
Never had children		Y
Criminal history		
Prior firesetting	Y	Y
Other property crimes	Y	
Prior convictions	Y	Y
Self-injury		
Mutilation	Y	Y
Suicide attempt	Y	Y

(Continued)

Table 2
(Continued)

Characteristic	Male	Female
Alcohol		
History	Y	Y
At time of fire	Y	Y
Interest in fire		
Special interests	Y	Y
Compulsion	N	N
Abuse history		
Sex		Y
Physical		Y
Social skills		
Poor self-esteem	Y	Y
Feels unwanted/not understood	Y	
High level of dependence	Y	
Isolated	Y	N
Poor oral expression	Y	Y
Laboratory		
Low CSF-HIAA	Y	
Hypoglycemic at oral GTT	Y	

Y = positive; N = negative; IQ = intelligence quotient; MR = mental retardation; CSF-HIAA = cerebrospinal fluid hydroxyindoleacetic acid; GTT = glucose tolerance test

Multifactorial

Puri and colleagues *(85)* asserted that firesetting was best understood from a multifactorial perspective, indicating there were "predisposing factors" and "precipitating factors." Fineman *(84)* took the process one step further by creating a "dynamic-behavioral formulation" where firesetting (FS) = dynamic historical factors predisposing toward maladaptive and antisocial behaviors (G1) + historical and current environmental factors that taught and reinforced firesetting as acceptable behavior (G2) + the immediate environmental contingencies that encourage firesetting (E). Fineman indicated that E = crisis or trauma preceding firesetting (C) + characteristics of the firesetting act (CF) + distortion before firesetting (D1) + distortions during the firesetting (D2) + the feeling state before firesetting (F1) + the feeling state during the firesetting (F2) + external reinforcement (R_{ex}) + internal reinforcement for firesetting (R_{in}).

Other multifactorial explanations for firesetting are based on cluster analyses. Harris and Rice *(86)* did a cluster analysis to produce four subtypes of mentally disordered firesetters that were both internally homogeneous and clearly distinct from one another: "psychotics," "unassertives," "multifiresetters," and "criminals." The largest group was the first, although they had the lowest rate of firesetting.

Kocsis and colleagues *(87,88)* build a model for serial firesetting based on both firesetter characteristics and crime scene characteristics. They accounted for features common to all serial firesetting episodes and then developed four distinct clusters: 1) thrill pattern (older, socially competent, cognitively aware of their actions, take high degree of risk to commit arson, have outstanding physical features, live with others, employed, use alcohol and/or other drugs prior to firesetting, travel more than a mile to commit offense—which is in a visible location, and confess when apprehended); 2) anger pattern (targets are home or vehicles, arson is personalized harm, leave scene promptly after setting fire, fire holds no psychological meaning beyond harm infliction); 3) wanton pattern (targets are educational and business facilities, often have prior criminal histories, animosity toward a vague class of targets); and 4) sexual (sexual excitement/gratification with ignition, targets are easily accessible public locations, fires often of minor scale, low level of behavioral sophistication, do not travel far, remain at the crime scene). The authors conclude that their model is a "holistic depiction of all potential behavioral patterns" and is "not initially formulated on the inference of potential motives" (*87*, p. 650).

The most sophisticated multifactorial analysis of firesetting is that proposed by Canter and Fritzon in 1998 *(89)*. This model has been tested by them *(90)* and replicated by others *(29,91,92)*. The model rests on two fundamental principles: 1) an individual deliberately sets fire to a target assumed to be of some relevance to him or her, either directly or indirectly; and 2) persons who set fires according to a particular "mode" or action are distinct from others operating in a different mode. The modes were derived from the observation that a firesetter's target was either person-oriented or object-oriented, and the firesetter's motivation was either instrumental or expressive. Four modes result: expressive person; instrumental person; expressive object; and instrumental object. The modes were subsequently expressed as four distinct themes: 1) expressive acts realized within the firesetter's own feelings (e.g., suicide); 2) expressive acts on objects; 3) instrumental acts for personal indulgence (e.g., revenge); and 4) instrumental acts focused on objects (e.g., crime concealment). Four subtypes of arsonist—psychiatric history, younger offender, repeat arsonist, failed relationship—could be validly matched to the four themes *(89)*.

PARTICULAR POPULATIONS OF FIRESETTERS

In this section, five types of firesetting are examined: fires by persons with developmental disabilities, firefighter arson, communicative arson, self-immolation, and fires by persons with histories of self-mutilation.

Developmental Disabilities

Methodological problems in studying the relation between developmental disabilities and crime in general, and firesetting in particular, continue to hamper investigator and clinician alike *(16,18)*. It remains an open question as to whether persons with developmental disabilities commit more or less crime than persons without such disabilities, or whether criminal behaviors by individuals with developmental disabilities differ from the offender population overall *(93)*.

Lewis and Yarnell's seminal 1951 book on pathological firesetting *(94)* indicates a clear association between firesetting and mental retardation. Between 1951 and 1990 there was substantial support for this association *(8)* and some questioning of it *(54,95)*.

At this time the association between firesetting and developmental disabilities can be considered from two perspectives: 1) Is there a significant representation of persons with borderline IQ or mild to moderate mental retardation in populations of firesetters? 2) Is arson of significant frequency in intellectually impaired criminal offenders? As the characteristics of firesetters established above indicate, intellectual deficits are seen as a feature of firesetters, although with the exception of studies in forensic settings and two in Massachusetts' state hospitals *(53,54)*, this finding is more a clinical and law enforcement judgment than it is an evidenced-based finding *(65–83)*. Refutation of this association continues *(96)*.

The evidence for a significant representation of arson among the crimes of persons with intellectual disabilities is clearer. Barron and associates *(97)* found an "overrepresentation" of firesetters in a sample of 61 Londoners with intellectual disabilities. In this cohort, 13 (21.3%) had a history of firesetting; and of this group only two had not committed another offense. Crossland and colleagues *(98)* reported on 53 males, located through forensic case managers, who had an 11.3% rate of arson (six cases). In both of these studies, although it received no comment, there was a high rate of dually diagnosed individuals (i.e., mental retardation and mental disorder). Taylor and associates *(99)* reported that in a 159-bed facility in the United Kingdom that specializes in treating persons with developmental disability 51 (32%) had histories of firesetting. Of these subjects, 31 (19%) had convictions for arson and 20 (13%) had documented firesetting histories without arson convictions *(99)*.

Murphy and Clare *(100)* attempted to understand the function of firesetting for persons with developmental disabilities. They administered the Fire Assessment Scale (see below) and the Fire Interest Rating Scale to 10 individuals admitted to a Regional Health Authority service for people with mild learning disabilities and major behavior disorders. The findings did not differentiate this group from many other firesetters in terms of the functions of firesetting. Murphy and Clare found that fires were most frequently set at buildings of personal significance, were motivated by anger, and resulted in the dissipation of anger and the accrual of social attention *(100)*. Of the 10 firesetters, 3 had psychotic disorders and none met the criteria for pyromania *(100)*.

One inadequately studied aspect of firesetting by persons with developmental disabilities is the relation between the change in location of most of the individuals with mental retardation and arson. Persons who previously lived in large developmental disability facilities or state schools now reside in community residences. As of 2002, in the United States, 65% of persons with developmental disabilities/mental retardation lived in residences of one to six people, with only 24% living in residences/facilities of more than 16 inhabitants; public expenditures for the community setting was 3.5 times greater than the expenditures in institutions *(101)*. The transfer of those with developmental disabilities from large "institutions" to "community residences" has had complex medical *(102–104)* and psychiatric *(105)* sequela. Has it affected the incidence of firesetting? Early in the second generation of deinstitutionalized persons with mental illness *(106)*, Geller noted that the translocation of persons with mental illnesses from long-term hospital settings to community settings might well carry the risk of increased episodes of community-based firesetting *(106)*. This phenomenon is particularly worth studying given the association of firesetting and developmental disabilities and the utilization by this population of communicative arson *(55)*. The public is still waiting for the data. The general population is already fearful of persons with mental retardation and firesetters released from institutions into their communities *(107)*.

Firefighter Firesetting

No one who regularly reads newspapers is unfamiliar with headlines such as "Firefighter pleads guilty in arson cases" *(108)* or "Firefighter arrested on arson suspicions" *(109)*. Although the phenomenon of the firefighter firesetter is well known *(110)*, experts seem to agree that only a tiny fraction of firefighters set fires, and their numbers may be no different than a sex- and age-matched cohort from the general population *(111)*. Nonetheless, firefighter firesetting has been seen as a problem, particularly in volunteer fire departments *(112,113)*.

Because all-volunteer fire departments represent 71% of the fire departments in the United States and an additional 16% are mostly volunteer *(114)*, firefighter firesetting is a national problem.

Although fires set by firefighters are often unsophisticated *(113)*, a firefighter's knowledge of his fires and of how his department operates may make detection difficult. This may be especially true for wildland/forest fires, 10 to 20 of which are set per year in the United States by firefighters *(113)*, and particularly the case when the firesetter is a professional arson investigator *(113,115)*.

Efforts to profile the firefighter firesetter, especially those by the FBI, have resulted in this type of firesetter being characterized as a Caucasian male, 17 to 25 years old; the product of an unstable childhood with one or both parents missing; with a cold, distant, hostile or aggressive natural father and an overprotective mother; lacking in social and interpersonal skills; with poor marital adjustment or, if unmarried, living in the parental home; having poor occupational adjustment, with periods in low-paying jobs and unemployed; of average to above-average intelligence but poor school performance; having a history of alcoholism, suicidality, depression, and/or unusual stress; and being new to the fire department (less than 3 years) *(113)*.

The FBI has indicated that a series of nuisance fires (fires in dumpsters, trash piles, vegetation) in one company's fire response region is a good sign of firefighter firesetting *(113,116)*. Firefighter firesetters often escalate their fires over time.

The leading cause of firefighter firesetting is excitement *(113,116)*. A common theme in firefighter firesetter's case histories is the complaint of boredom and the use of fires to release that boredom *(113)*. Another motive for firesetting by firefighters is profit, either because the firefighter is only paid for hours actually spent fighting a fire or to accrue overtime pay *(113,116)*. A third motivation is revenge, sometimes for a grievance against the fire chief *(113,116)*. Some firefighters are motivated by putting themselves in the hero role; after setting the fire this firefighter is the first to call in the fire and the first on the scene *(113)*. Current research into firefighter firesetting is looking at what is referred to as RPM: The firesetter rationalizes the firesetting, projects blame, and minimizes the consequences *(113)*.

Not adequately studied, or much studied at all, is the relation between firefighter firesetting and the traumatic reaction of firefighters to their task *(117)*. Furthermore, do the qualities that may lead some to become a firefighter—fearlessness, low communion, low openness, low agreeableness *(118)*—increase the likelihood that a stress response will be behavioral (i.e., firesetting) rather than working through a problem by oral exchange with coworkers, superiors, or therapists?

Communicative Firesetting

In an editorial about fire, Prins quoted from Mary Shelly's novel *Franken-stein*, "I am malicious because I am miserable" *(119)*. This linkage of misery and "acting out" was used by Geller as an explanatory concept during the early 1980s when he noted a potential link between deinstitutionalization and firesetting *(106)*. Coining the term "communicative arson," Geller proposed that firesetting was used by persons with social skills/communication deficits to initiate a desire or need for some change (e.g., a change in residence, a desire for rehospitalization) *(55,106,120)*. This concept fit much of the psychiatric literature on pathological firesetting up through 1990 *(19)*.

The literature of the last 15 years continues to support this concept. In Leong's study of 29 court-referred individuals charged with arson, at least five demonstrated communicative arson. For example, three persons set fires to force a move from their board and care homes *(121)*. Steward, in a study of 28 female arsonists admitted to prison, states, "Many of the women of our sample reported that communication with partners or parents was difficult. For several women, arson became a dispute settling mechanism" *(81, p. 254)*. Rix, in a study of 153 forensic cases of arson, listed what is tantamount to communicative arson as the fourth leading cause of firesetting (preceded by revenge, excitement, and vandalism). Rix provided classic descriptions of a 44-year-old unmarried man unable to "express his worries to his doctor" and of a 30-year-old hygiene supervisor with "avoidant personality" who set fire to "rubbish sacks" *(79)*. Communicative arson is also compatible with the work of Canter and Fritzon in their multifactorial explanation of firesetting *(89)*, a fact these researchers point out themselves.

Communicative arson may be an explanatory concept for firesetting in the presence or absence of a diagnosed psychiatric disorder. A person with schizophrenia may demonstrate a behavior as a direct consequence of his psychosis or may exhibit a behavior unrelated to his psychosis. Firesetting is just such a behavior; and when the underlining psychopathology is not explanatory, communicative arson may well be.

Self-Mutilation

Given the information on the characteristics and motivations of firesetters and on communicative arson, one might expect an increased frequency of self-injurious behavior among firesetters as such behaviors seem to be exhibited by persons with similar histories, psychiatric disorders, and social skills deficits as firesetters. This supposition appears to be borne out.

Studies of self-mutilation in firesetters during the past 15 years have largely been conducted in forensic settings and predominantly in Great Britain and Finland. The work done by Geller and colleagues in two Massachusetts state hospitals during the 1980s, showing that persons with firesetting histories were statistically significantly more likely to have histories of nonlethal self-injurious behavior than nonfiresetter patients, still stands as the best examples of this relation documented in a psychiatric setting (53,54).

Self-mutilation by firesetters has been documented in case reports. One, from a secure unit in London, described a 21-year-old woman with a history of multiple arrests, arson, self-mutilation, and overdoses (66). Another, from Manchester, described a 31-year-old, mildly mentally retarded man with an arson conviction and a history of impulsively harming himself when confronted with stressful life events (122).

In a prison setting in Great Britain, 74 women remanded into custody had histories of self-mutilation. They were matched with 62 controls, women randomly selected from those remanded during the weeks immediately following the self-mutilation cohort. The current charges were arson in 7 (10%) of those who had self-mutilated and in 5 (8%) of those who had not. Although this difference is unimpressive, when one compares lifetime psychiatric histories, 25 (34%) of those with self-mutilation and 7 (11%) of those without had firesetting histories, a difference significant at the 0.001 level. Altogether, 19 (14%) of those who had self-mutilated had a diagnosis of pyromania, whereas there were no cases of pyromania among the non-self-mutilated women (123,124).

Repo and and colleagues investigated suicidal behavior among 304 male arsonists referred for pretrial psychiatric evaluation in Finland (77). They found that 153 (50.9%) firesetters had a history of suicide attempts, 62 (20%) had made serious suicide attempts, and 49 (16%) had slashed themselves. Furthermore, 25 of 62 (40%) of those with serious suicide attempts had slashed themselves. Extending this work (76), these investigators examined the outcomes for firesetters with a follow-up questionnaire 2 to 15 years after the pretrial evaluation. Of 127 respondents, 40 had died. Thirteen deaths were officially registered as suicides; four were of "unclear" origins. The suicide victims had a history of significantly more frequent slashing than the whole sample.

In another Finnish study, again done with a forensic population, Räsänen and colleagues compared arsonists ($n = 98$) with homicide offenders ($n = 55$).

They found that firesetters had statistically significantly higher rates of suicidal thoughts and suicide attempts *(125)*.

These data have important implications for risk assessment and treatment. Because firesetting, self-mutilation, and suicide seem to occur in the same cohort of individuals, persons with either frequent firesetting or self-mutilation should be screened for the other. Appropriate treatment for both might well decrease successful suicides in this population.

Self-Immolation

In 1997, Geller published a review of the psychopathology of setting oneself afire, largely concentrating on the literature from Western cultures *(126)*. He proposed a classification schema for self-incineration, shown in Table 1. In the study of Repo and colleagues described above *(77)*, these investigators found an association between a suicidal motive for arson and a history positive for both suicide attempts and slashing.

Self-immolation in Eastern societies is a complex matter, with deeply rooted cultural practices mixing with contemporary economic issues, the role of women, and psychopathology *(127)*. In a review of self-burning that drew on worldwide data published in English from 1983 through 2002, Laloe *(128)* was able to locate 3351 cases of self-burning that accounted for 2296 deaths. Laloe found distinct patterns of self-immolation when comparing Eastern and Western societies, the details of which are beyond the scope of this chapter. In summarizing the motives for self-burning, Laloe reported that psychiatric disorders were the common reason in Western countries and the Middle East; personal reasons in India, Sri Lanka, Papua-New Guinea, and Zimbabwe; and political reasons in India and South Korea *(128)*.

Does the more recent literature reveal any new findings? In a 1998 report from The Netherlands not included in Laloe's review, Van de Does and colleagues *(129)* reported a progressive increase in self-inflicted burns between 1981 and 1996 with an actual doubling of the rate between these years. Admission rates reached 16.2% of all burn center admissions during the 1991–1996 period. The authors indicated that neither the suicide rate in The Netherlands nor admission policies to the burn unit from which they collected their data changed during the study period *(129)*.

Between January 1996 and August 2001, a total of 1008 patients were admitted to the University of California Davis Regional Burn Center, of whom 32 (3.2%) had self-inflicted burns. This group had a larger burn size (34% ± 29% total body surface area, or TBSA) compared to all adult burn center admissions (15.9%) and had a higher mortality rate (25% vs. 9%). Most significantly, 91% had an active psychiatric disorder, 47% had prior suicide attempts, and

67% had a chronic stressor, such as a chronic medical illness and/or long-term disability *(130)*.

Between 1979 and 1998 there were 7139 individuals admitted to the Birmingham Burn Centre, with 184 (2.6%) having self-inflicted burns. As in other studies in Western countries, the number of males exceeded females; the average burn size (67% TBSA) of those who died exceeded that of those who did not die (21% TBSA). The preferred method was use of an accelerant. The mortality rate was 44%. At this burn center there was not a statistically significant increase in admissions for self-inflicted burns *(131)*.

Another report from Europe, this one of two cases from Germany, described complex suicide in which, in each instance, an individual shot himself and burned in a preset fire *(132)*. The gunshot was the actual cause of death, leading the authorities to label this sequence "postmortem self-immolation" *(132)*. Other incidents of complex suicide in which self-immolation is one component have been recently reported *(132–135)*.

In India, culture-based self-incineration remains a substantial problem. These days, dowries seem to be the major issue fueling self-immolation, replacing sati *(127,136)*. Most suicides by burning in India occur inside the house.

As one considers the subject of firesetting, certain aspects of self-immolation should be kept in mind. Leaving aside suicide for terrorist purposes, most successful suicides injure neither property nor others than the intended victim. Suicide by fire is an exception. Property is lost; others die in too many incidents of self-immolation. Suicide by fire may be the worst of all possible means of suicide, if for no other reason than if one fails the result is self-mutilation and the person has condemned himself or herself to a "hell on earth" *(137)*.

SERIAL ARSON

Newspaper headlines and articles about serial arsonists are not infrequent and are certainly inflammatory. Headlines read like: "Serial arson suspect arrested" *(138)*. "Man arrested in multiple arson case" *(139)*. "Suspect admitted 37 arsons, court told" *(140)*. "Louisiana police finally catch serial arsonist" *(141)*. The putative motives for these serial arsonists could not be more varied: "no motive other than the fact that at the spur of the moment he was having some personal issues in his life and if he was upset he would start a fire" *(138)*; a man set fire to 13 residences, 12 of which are owned by individuals of Indian descent and the Hindu faith and to a Hindu temple *(139)*; a 50-year-old fast-food restaurant manager who set fires in the 46 houses and apartments, including one that killed an elderly lady, complained of "demons and voices" *(140)*; and a 30-year-old man set 70 wood fires around New Orleans for "environmental" reasons, claiming that burning "downed and dying trees and brush from Hurricane Katrina... [would] help speed the progress of new growth" *(141)*.

One might expect that firesetting would be a behavior often repeated by the same individual because of the long reported association between firesetting and impulsivity *(1)*. However, personality disordered offender firesetters were found to be no more impulsive than comparable groups who were violent offenders or sex offenders *(142)*. Understanding recidivism in firesetters has been challenging, with recidivism rates reported between 4% and 60% *(143)*. Examining recidivism is one important step in comprehending serial arson.

Recidivism

In Canada, with the population of a maximum security forensic facility, Harris and Rice *(86,144,145)* found that predicting future firesetting was related to 1) age at the first fire (the younger, the more likely future firesetting); 2) history of firesetting (the greater the number of previous fires, the greater the likelihood of future fires); 3) intelligence (the less intelligent were more likely to set future fires); 4) confederates (those who acted alone were more likely to set fires); 5) other concurrent criminal charges (those without other charges were more likely to set fires); and 6) history of aggression (those without a history of aggression were more likely to set charges *(144,145)*. When developing a typology of firesetters, Harris and Rice found that multifiresetters and criminals were more likely to set future fires than were psychotic and unassertive firesetters *(86)*.

Virkkunen and colleagues *(50,67,75,82)*, studying convicted Finnish criminals, found that the lower the cerebrospinal fluid hydroxyindoleacetic acid (CSF5-HIAA) concentration, the lower the CSF methoxyhydroxyphenyl-glycol (MHPG) concentration *(82)*; and persons whose first criminal offense occurred shortly after 15 years of age *(50)*, the greater the likelihood of repeat firesetting. These findings, however, did not differentiate repeat firesetters from persons who repeated other violent acts. These researchers did find that prior suicide attempts reliably predict repeat firesetting episodes *(67)*. When looking at a subset of the study population with schizophrenia, Virkkunen's group found that the presence of schizophrenia did not predict recidivism; but among those with schizophrenia, the diagnosis of alcoholism predicted repeat firesetting *(75)*. The glucose tolerance test was not useful for predicting recidivism *(82)*.

With findings somewhat different from those in Finland, Barnett and colleagues *(146)* found in Germany that the presence of a mental disorder did make future firesetting more likely. However, like the Canadian sample, this group also had set more fires before the index fire, so perhaps this is the more important variable. Soothill and colleagues *(80)* reported a most interesting finding from Great Britain. They found that convictions for arson had increased between the 1950s and the 1980s, as had the rate of recidivism. It is not clear whether these data mean more fires and more repeat firesetters or improved arson investigation and conviction rates.

As in previous sections of this chapter, almost all the data on recidivist firesetting derive from forensic populations. In a rare study of a nonforensic psychiatric population, Geller and colleagues *(147)* attempted to determine the characteristics of repeat firesetters in a cohort of persons identified in a state hospital population with a history of firesetting. Matching firesetters and nonfiresetters in a state hospital and examining data 6.75 years later (during which time most persons spent most of their time outside of hospitals), these investigators could not distinguish who among the firesetters would set further fires because the firesetter group did not differ from the nonfiresetter group in terms of the rate of fires over the 6.75-year period—not because the firesetters did not set further fires but because the control group of nonfiresetters had set fires at a rate comparable to that of the firesetter group *(147)*.

Studies of recidivist firesetters do not provide solid data with which to work in ascertaining and evaluating serial arsonists. What do studies of serial arsonists reveal?

Serial Arsonists

It is not entirely clear when a repeat firesetter would be said to "graduate" to being a serial arsonist. What is clear is that "serial arsonists often create a climate of fear in entire communities" *(148)*. Serial arson is categorized by the United States' National Center for the Analysis of Violent Crime (NCAVC) as: 1) mass arson: three or more fires at the same location during a limited period of time; 2) spree arson: fires at three or more locations with no emotional cooling-off period between fires; and 3) serial arson: three or more fires with a characteristic cooling off period between fires *(148,149)*.

Based on the work of the NCAVC, the general profile of the serial arsonist is a young, Caucasian male with prior contact with law enforcement and prior misdemeanor and felony arrests. He is of average intelligence; had cold, distant, hostile relationships with parents; has poor interpersonal relationships and marital adjustment; and performed poorly in the military. Disfigurements and tattoos are not uncommon, as are medical and psychiatric histories. The first episode of arson is often during teenage years. Most fires are within 2 miles of the firesetter's residence and the site was reached by walking. Fires are set without sophisticated methods, and each fire is at a different location. Alcohol consumption may be a factor, and revenge is the most common motive. The frequency of firesetting does not increase over time, but the severity of the fires does *(149–151)*. Based on data developed from NCAVC investigations, the Center developed profiles of serial arsonists by motivation. These results are summarized in Table 3.

The Australians, much like the Americans, have been interested in profiling the serial arsonists. Kocsis has shown that profiling can be done successfully by professional profilers *(152)* and can be done by them for the crime of arson *(153)*. Police and fire investigators do not perform well at the task *(153)*.

Kocsis' efforts resulted in describing two patterns of serial arson: the commuter model (firesetter travels away from a base to another area to set a fire) and the marauder model (firesetters base acts as a spatial reference point for each individual act of firesetting) *(154)*. Several subtypes of arson by motivation were developed *(87)*: the thrill pattern, the anger pattern, the wanton pattern, and the sexual pattern. Profiles were developed for each subtype, with the anger pattern matching the revenge motivation in Table 1, the wanton pattern matching vandalism, and the sexual pattern and thrill pattern overlapping with the excitement motivation *(87)*. The Australian and American outcomes are quite similar.

ASSESSMENT AND TREATMENT

Profiling is well-and-good for the criminal justice sector, but clinicians require assessment tools that drive clinical interventions. Because so much of the work with firesetting has derived from forensic settings, the information on clinical assessment and treatment of adult firesetters is much less extensive than one would hope. The challenges are great. As one compulsive firesetter stated, "I picture everything burnable around me on fire... any fire set by someone else is one I wish I had set" *(155)*. A *New York Times* article read, "An Indiana drifter with a history of dabbling in satanic rituals was charged... with setting 10 church fires in Indiana and Georgia, including one last year in which a firefighter died" *(156)*.

Assessment

Assessing a firesetter requires a thorough psychiatric evaluation and complete assessment of the firesetting. Based on the literature *(28,31,113)* and my own experiences, the assessment of the firesetter should proceed as indicated in Table 4. Most of Table 4 is self-explanatory, but a few comments are worth

Table 3
Serial Arsonists by Motivation

Parameter	Revenge Motivated	Excitement Motivated	Vandalism	Crime Concealment	Profit
Sex	Male	Male	Male	Male	Male
Race	Caucasian	Caucasian	Caucasian	Caucasian	Caucasian
Markings	Tattoos Other disfigurement	Tattoos	Tattoo Scar	Tattoo	
Intelligence	Average	Average	Below to average	Average	Below to average
Education	10 Years	11 Years	11 Years	11 Years	9 Years
Work	Menial labor	Unskilled or skilled labor	Unskilled labor		Torch for hire
Institutionalizations					
Foster care	N	Y	N	Y	N
Juvenile detention	Y	Y	Y	Y	N
Jail	Y	Y	Y		N
State prison	Y	Y	Y		N
Mental hospital	Y	Y	Y		N
Psychiatric history	Y	Y	Y	Y	N
		Suicide attempts	Suicide attempts Depression	No chronic mental illness	
Family					
SES	Lower to middle	Middle	Middle	Middle	Lower
Parents in home	Both, unstable	One or both	Both	One, father	Both, stable
Atmosphere	Cold and distant	Warm mother Troubled father	Very religious, warm mother, distant father	Close	Warm mother, mixed father

Fire history					
Age at first fire (years)	12		8		18
Average no. of lifetime fires	40		12		11
Fire					
Target	Victim's vehicle, home, property	Nuisance fires; occupied apartment	School; abandoned structures		Building; property; forest
Distance	Walking	Walking	Familiar area	Walking	Distant travel
Accomplice	None	Available	None		None
Materials	Found at scene	Match or lighter	Available	Found at scene	Delay ignition devices
Ignition	Match		Match or lighter	Match or lighter	Delay ignition devices
Alcohol use	No change			Yes, usual usage	Delay ignition devices
					Sometimes usual usage
Following fire	Does not avoid getting caught; pleads guilty	Remains to watch; loses interest after fire out	Leaves and does not return	Returns in 1–2 days to view	Returns 1–2 days, following media reporting

SES = socioeconomic status.

Table 4
Assessment of Firesetter

Psychiatric history
  Detailed psychiatric history
  Detailed medical and surgical history
  Current mental status examination
  Psychological testing if indicated
  Laboratory, imaging, and other studies as indicated
Offending history
  History and outcome of all criminal charges excluding arson
  History of all potentially criminal acts never charged
Firesetting history
  Account of each firesetting episode
    Description of actually setting fire (e.g., methods, accomplices)
    Thoughts, fears, feelings before, during, and after firesetting
    Choice of target
    Transportation to target
    Stressors at time of fire
    Explanation for reason for setting fire (e.g., trigger, such as rejection)
    Expectation of outcome from fire
    Use of alcohol, drugs, medications at the time of firesetting
    Actions immediately following and for day or two after setting fire
  History of treatment for firesetting
Secondary sources
  Corroboration of psychiatric history
  Corroboration of offending history
  Corroboration of firesetting history
    Participants
    Witnesses
    Person firesetter told about fires

making. The firesetting history is best taken from the firesetter by having him describe each episode in reverse chronological order and in exquisite detail. Continue back through childhood until the first fire the firesetter can remember. Take into account periods when the individual may not have had his usual access to firesetting, such as periods of incarceration or hospitalization; even researchers have sometimes failed to account for this (e.g., *157*).

The use of assessment tools for firesetting may prove helpful. Murphy, Clare, and associates in the United Kingdom have developed the Functional Assessment of Fire-Setting (FAFS) and the Fire Interest Rating Scale (FIRS)

(*100,158*; personal communication, November 8, 2004). The FAFS has a "starting fires" section and a "fire and the consequences" section, each with 16 questions. Responses are "usually," "sometimes," or "never." Two questions per section are put together to get ratings on self-stimulation, anxiety, social attention, peer favor, auditory hallucinations, depression, anger, and demand escape/avoidance. The FIRS provides 14 situational statements to which the individual reports on "how would you feel" by indicating his response on a 7-point Likert scale from "absolutely horrible or most upsetting" to "lovely, very exciting, or very nice." The reliability and validity of these assessment tools is unclear, and they are not in general usage although they have been reported as used by Murphy's countrymen *(159)*.

Treatment

As in all other areas of medicine, assessment drives treatment. The first component of treatment is to address potentially remedial psychopathology that contributes to firesetting. Therefore, pharmacotherapy should be used to treat psychosis, mood disorders, or anxiety disorders *(19,55,160)*. If there appears to be a medical/neurological contribution, it should be treated *(19,160)*; and substance/alcohol abuse should be addressed *(19,160)*. The second component of treatment addresses the firesetting *per se*, which all firesetters should undergo unless it is clear that successfully treating the psychosis, for example, ends the risk of firesetting.

Treating firesetting is a veritable challenge of major proportions. So much so that a recent article on treating impulse control disorders simply left it out *(161)*. Treatment of firesetters needs to be multimodal, drawing on a wide range of interventions *(155,158,162,163)*. The approaches that can be included in the multimode approach are indicated in Table 5. The most fundamental aspects of treatment, given all the explanations of firesetting recounted in this chapter, are the social skills/assertiveness/alternative coping strategies. Assisting the firesetter to understand the before, during, and after events and feelings can be accomplished through graphing, a technique originally described by Bumpass et al. in its application for juvenile firesetters *(164)*. Psychotherapy of the insight-oriented type is occasionally still reported in the treatment of firesetters *(165)*, but there is little evidence that it should be the mainstay of treatment. Although medication has been recommended to try to address impulsive behaviors *(21)*, there is no evidence basis for this intervention to date. Clomipramine has been considered to treat the compulsive nature of some firesetting, but its use is mostly based on extrapolation from other compulsive and impulse disorders *(19)*. Surgery is a consideration when disfigurement appears to be a contributing factor *(158)* as is not infrequently the case (see

Table 5
Multimodal Treatment of Firesetting

Social skills training
Assertiveness training
Coping strategies
Relaxation
    Progressive muscle relaxation
    Biofeedback
Exposure
    Overt stimulation
        Recorded materials (video, DVD)
        Burn units
        Fire scenes
    Covert sensitization
Graphing
Psychotherapy
Psychopharmacology
Surgery
Fire safety and prevention education

previous discussion in this chapter). Education should make liberal use of resources of the local fire department, including appointments with the chief. The use of videos/DVDs can serve as both an exposure function and an educational function *(166)*.

Using some of the interventions from the multimodal approach, there is increasing use of group interventions *(159,167,168)*. These interventions are neither simple nor inexpensive; one calls for 62 sessions *(168)*, and another uses up to five facilitators *(167)*. Taylor and associates *(168)* used clearly measurable outcomes to demonstrate the effectiveness of their group intervention.

Therapeutic approaches in other populations may hold promise for firesetters and are worthy of consideration. They include relapse prevention used for substance-abusing populations *(169)*, dialectical behavior therapy originally designed for persons with borderline personality disorder *(170)*; and approaches used to treat self-injury *(171)*.

CONCLUSION

Fire is dangerous, destructive, and deadly. Fires are responsible for 1% of the global burden of disease and 300,000 deaths per year *(172)*. Although fire kills thousands, injures hundreds of thousands, and costs billions of dollars in the United States, government officials and the public fail to appreciate the magnitude of the problem *(173)*. This lack of appreciation for the negative potential of fire is surprising given the frequency with which fire is brought to the public's attention. In my local newspaper one Sunday, these articles were all in the first section: "5 Die in Early Morning Vermont Fire," "New Hampshire Death Is Ruled a Homicide [after a house fire]," "Phony Firefighter Faces Sex Charges," "Three Children Die in Arkansas House Fire," and "China Blames Electrician in Fire that Kills 39" (*Worcester Sunday Telegram*, December 18, 2005).

Arson fires were in the worldwide consciousness in 2005 with set fires being reported in the wake of hurricane Katrina *(174,175)* and in the Middle East war *(176)*. Arson fires have terrorized the modern world for hundreds of years. In a book covering the 100 most devastating fires, 12 are known cases of arson: 1) New York City—September 20–21, 1776: 500 buildings destroyed; 2) Moscow—September 14, 1812: fire to foil Napoleon destroyed 30,800 homes; 3) Ohio State Penitentiary, Columbus, Ohio—April 21, 1930: 318 prisoners die; 4) Berlin—February 2, 1933: Reichstag, a 430-foot long building with a 246-foot high dome destroyed; 5) Watts riots, Los Angeles—August 11–18, 1963: 43 dead and $50 million loss; 6) Riots in Newark, NJ—July 11–27, 1967: 23 dead and $10.2 million loss; 7) Dupont Plaza Hotel, Puerto Rico—New Year's Eve, December 31, 1986–January 1, 1987: 96 dead, 100 injured; 8) Happy Land Disco, Bronx, NY—March 25, 1990: 87 died in this illegal social club; 9) Scandinavian Star Ferry, North Sea—April 7, 1990: 158 dead; 10) Persian Gulf War oil well fires—February–March 1991: $1.5 billion loss in these fires set by Iraq's elite Republican Guard during their retreat; 11) Malibu/Laguna Beach Brush Fire, California—October 27–November 8, 2003: 3 dead, 200 injured (including 186 firefighters), 200,000 acres destroyed and $1 billion property loss; 12) Teatro la Feine, Venice, Italy—January 29, 1996: $100,000,000 loss *(177)*. To this list one could add the more recent fire at the Worcester Cold Storage building in Worcester, MA on December 3, 1999 in which six firefighters lost their lives *(178)*.

Although this chapter documents considerable progress in the assessment—psychiatric and criminal—of arson and even some gains in the treatment of firesetters, firesetters and firesetting continue to elude reliable comprehension. The lack of concern with which persons in contemporary society set fires may well be leading to an increase in arson. Recent examples that illustrate this point: A 19-year-old rookie firefighter committed arson "to fit in with his peers" *(179)*. A 57-year-old woman drove more than 3 hours to set fire to the home of a 65-year-old woman who was now the lover of her 72-year-old ex-boyfriend *(180)*. A 43-year-old intoxicated man randomly picked a home, broke in, and set it on fire for no apparent reason at all *(181)*. A 34-year-old man set fire to his girlfriend's house after they argued and he threatened to burn down the house with her inside *(182)*.

The FBI's figures on violent and property crime rates in the United States for the first 6 months of 2005 indicate that "reported arson offenses went down by 5.6%" *(183)*. It is unclear what this means in terms of the incidence of firesetting. Arson was the only crime designated with the adjective "reported" modifying it.

The last decade has witnessed the proliferation of some troubling forms of firesetting. One is church fires *(184)*. Arson is the leading cause of church fires, which averaged 1300 per year (1996–1998) in the United States *(184)*. Church fires are often hate crimes, as demonstrated by the fires at 30 churches in the southern United States between January 13, 1995 and June 6, 1996 that were attended predominantly by African American parishioners *(184,185,186)*. Most of these churches were of the Baptist faith *(185)*. Sometimes a church fire can be linked to diagnosed *(187)* or suspected *(184)* mental illness.

Perhaps most frightening of all is the recent trend of firesetting that falls under the category of "eco-terrorism" *(188)* or "protest incendiarism" *(189)*. As 2005 came to a close, individuals in the United States apparently associated with the Earth Liberation Front and/or the Animal Liberation Front were being arrested for conflagrations since 1998 that damaged or destroyed the University of Washington Center for Urban Horticulture, Vail ski resort ($12 million), U.S. Forest Industries, an Oregon meat plant, 36 vehicles at a car dealership ($1 million), a gasoline tank truck at a fuel company, and a wildlife laboratory *(190, 191)*. The fire at Vail Mountain is the worst act of eco-terrorism in United States' history *(191)*.

Finally, it is worth noting that fire is not an equal opportunity destroyer. The risk of death in a residential fire is greater for persons under 5 years of age or over 64 years old in the home, when the home is a mobile home, and when a home has no smoke detector or is in a rural area. Also at higher risk of death are residents who are male, disabled, poor, or members of minorities (controlling for all other factors) *(192)*. Alcohol is associated with residential fire fatalities *(192,193)*. In one study that examined 20 or more variables, the presence of an alcohol-impaired individual was the strongest independent risk factor for death *(192)*. These data make it clear that fire destroys those least able to take care of themselves.

As this chapter has shown, firesetting has been described as being used for myriad purposes by persons who are desperate and without other resources; unable to communicate needs, anger, desired changes, or other messages by less dramatic means; driven by symptoms of medical or mental illness; wishing to destroy others or themselves; wanting to be rebels or heroes; curious, bored, or impulsive; without judgment; or simply not caring.

What is hopeful is that there appears to be increasing interest in trying to understand adult firesetters after what can best be described as little attention through much of the 20th century. If we can generate as much interest in adult firesetting during the 21st century as there was during the 19th century, perhaps the serial arsonist will become extinct.

REFERENCES

1. Geller, J. L., Erlin, J., & Pinkus, R. L. (1986). A historical appraisal of America's experience with "pyromania"—a diagnosis in search of a disorder. *Int J Law Psychiatry*, 9:201–229.
2. Keenan, T., & Herald, C. (2005). Guys can't resist the allure of flames. *Real Life*, April 7, 2005, p. C3.
3. Firefighters arrested for alleged arson. Accessed November 25, 2005 at http://web.lexis-nexis.com/universe/document?_m=369.
4. Rich, E., & Horwitz, S. (2004, December). Were notoriety ploy, defendant says: man says car club leader wanted group to be 'famous.' *Washington Post*, p. B1.
5. Amato, A. M. (2005, January 7). Chief looks to stop firefighter arson. *Connecticut Post*.
6. Zongker, B. (2004, November 16). Man, 52, sets fire to himself. *Worcester Telegram & Gazette*, p. A3.
7. Man faces 20 years for torching woman's house. *Worcester Telegram & Gazette*, December 28, 2004, p. A6.
8. Bach, A. (2004, June 30). Suspect had past arrest. *Seattle Times*.
9. Elkies, L. (2005, November 17). 'Fake fireman' rape suspect is suicidal, his mother fears. *New York Sun*, p. 1.
10. A burning issue. *Leader-Post* (Regina-Saskatchewan), June 15, 2005, p. B6.
11. U.S. Fire Administrator combats nation's arson problem. Accessed December 1, 2005, at http://www.emergency.com/arsonrpt.htm.
12. *Arson in the United States*. U.S. fire administration topical fire research series, 2001. 1, 103.
13. USFA arson fire statistics. Accessed December 1, 2005, at http://www.usfa.fema.gov/statistics/arson/.
14. Gilmore, S. (2004, August 3). Arson experts say firebug is thrill seeker. *Seattle Times*.
15. Chappell, D. (1994). Opening address: focus on the arsonist and arson prevention national workshop. Australian Institute of Criminology.
16. Barker, A. F. (1994). *Arson: A Review of the Psychiatric Literature*. Oxford: Oxford University Press.
17. Barnett, W., & Spitzer, M. (1994). Pathological firesetting 1951–1991: a review. *Med Sci Law*, 34, 4–20.

18. Geller, J. L. (1992). Arson in review: from profit to pathology. *Psychiatric Clinics of North America* 15, 623–645.
19. Geller, J. L. (1992). Pathological firesetting in adults. *International Journal of Law Psychiatry* 15, 283–302.
20. Prins, H. (1994). *Fire-Raising: Its Motivation and Management.* London: Routledge.
21. Ritchie, E. C., Huff, T. G. (1999). Psychiatric aspects of arsonists. *Journal of Forensic Science*, 44, 733–740.
22. Micheels, P. A. (2004, December 12). A trail of ashes; who sets buildings on fire, and why. *Washington Post*, p. B1.
23. Former police officer charged with arson. Accessed October 19, 2004, at http://seattlepi.nwsource.com/local/193477_clubarson02.html.
24. Appelbaum, K. L. (1990). Criminal defendants who desire punishment. *Bulletin of the American Academy of Psychiatry and the Law*, 18, 385–391.
25. Leong, G. B., Eth, S., & Silva, J. A. (1991). The Tarasoff dilemma in criminal court. *Journal of Forensic Science* 36, 728–735.
26. Determining arson motives. Accessed November 21, 2005, at http://www.interfire.org/res_file/motives.asp.
27. Fras, I. (1997). Firesetting (pyromania) and its relationship to sexuality. In: Schlesinger, L. B., & Revitch, E. (Eds.). *Sexual Dynamics of Anti-Social Behavior* (2nd ed.). Springfield, IL: Charles C Thomas, pp. 188–196.
28. Jackson, H. F. (1994). Assessment of fire-setters. In: McMurran, M., & Hodge, J. E. (Eds.). *The Assessment of Criminal Behaviors of Clients in Secure Settings.* Bristol, PA: Jessica Kingsley, pp. 94–126.
29. Palermo, G. B., & Kocsis, R. N. (2005). *Offender Profiling.* Springfield, IL: Charles C Thomas.
30. Prins, H. (1995). *Offenders, Deviants or Patients* (2nd ed.). New York: Routledge.
31. Smith, J., & Short, J. (1995). Mentally disordered firesetters. *British Journal of Hospital Medicine*, 53, 136–140.
32. White, E. E. (1996). Profiling arsonists and their motives: an update. *Fire Engineering*, 149, 80–82.
33. Williams, D. (2005). *Understanding the Arsonist: From Assessment To Confession.* Tucson, AZ: Lawyers & Judges Publishing.
34. Woodward, C. D. (1994). The motives for arson. *Arson Control Bulletin*, 9, 4–8.
35. Woodward, C. D. (1994). The motives for arson. *Fire Prevention*, 273, 13–16.
36. Godwin, Y., Hudson, D. A. (1998). The burnt male—intentional assault on the male by his partner. *South African Journal of Surgery*, 36, 140–142.
37. Huff, T. G. (1999, July). Filicide by fire. *Fire Chief*, pp. 66–67.
38. Sapp, A. (1998, June). Gender differences in filicide: characteristics of victims and offenders. *National Fire & Arson Report*, pp. 3–7, 16–17.
39. Tsaroom, S. (1996). Investigation of a murder case involving arson. *Journal of Forensic Science* 41, 1064–1067.
40. Knutson, B. (2004). Sweet revenge? *Science* 305, 1246–1247.

41. Weller, M., & Somers, W. A. (1991). Differences in the medical and legal viewpoint illustrated by R v. Hardie [1984]. *Medicine, Science, and the Law* 31, 152–156.
42. Blackburn, R. (1994). *The Psychology of Criminal Conduct.* New York: John Wiley.
43. Geller, J. L., McDermeit, M., & Brown, J. M. (1997). Pyromania? What does it mean? *Journal of Forensic Science* 42, 1052–1057.
44. Doley, R. (2003). Pyromania: fact of fiction? *British Journal of Criminology* 43, 797–807.
45. Huff, T. G., Gary, G. P., & Icove, D. J. (1997). *The Myth of Pyromania.* Quantico, VA: National Center for the Analysis of Violent Crime, FBI Academy.
46. Huff, T. G., Gary, G. P., & Icove, D. J. (2001). The myth of pyromania. *Fire & Arson* 51, 28–29, 36–37.
47. Kocsis, R. N. (2002). *Arson: Exploring Motives and Possible Solutions.* Australian Institute of Criminology Trends & Issue, No. 236. Canberra ACT, Australia: Australian Institute of Criminology.
48. Shea, P. (2002). The lighting of fires in a bushland setting. *Judicial Officers Bulletin* 14(1), 1–5.
49. Michel, L., Arbaretaz, M., McLoughlin, M., & Ades, J. (2002). Impulse control disorder and depression. *Journal of Nervous and Mental Disease* 190, 310–314.
50. Repo, E., Virkkunen, M., Rawlings, R., & Linnoila, M. (1997). Criminal and psychiatric histories of Finnish arsonists. *Acta Psychiatrica Scandinavica* 95, 318–323.
51. Oberg, F. (ed) (1992). Couple share perverted thrills. *Minnesota Fire Chief*, January/February, pp. 8–9, 41–44, 59.
52. Geller, J. L. (2000). The last half-century of psychiatric services as reflected in *Psychiatric Services. Psychiatric Services* 51, 41–67.
53. Geller, J. L., Fisher, W. H., & Moynihan, K. (1992). Adult lifetime prevalence of fire-setting behaviors in a state hospital population. *Psychiatric Quarterly*, 63, 129–142.
54. Geller, J. L., & Bertsch, G. (1985). Firesetting behavior in the histories of a state hospital population. *American Journal of Psychiatry*, 142, 464–468.
55. Geller, J. L. (1992). Communicative arson. *Hospital and Community Psychiatry*, 43:76–77.
56. Cohen, M. A. A, Aladjem, A. D., Bremin, D., & Ghazi, M. (1990). Firesetting by patients with the acquired immunodeficiency syndrome (AIDS) (letter to the editor). *Annals of Internal Medicine*, 112, 386–387.
57. Eytan, A., Paoloni-Giacobino, A., Thorens, G., Eugster, N., & Graf, I. (2002). Fire-setting behavior associated with Klinefelter syndrome. *International Journal of Psychiatry in Medicine*, 32, 395–399.
58. Hecht, F., & Hecht, B. K. (1990). Behavior in Klinefelter syndrome, or where there is smoke there may be a fire (letter to the editor). *Pediatrics*, 86, 1001.
59. Miller, M. E., & Sulkes, S. (1990). Reply (letter to the editor). *Pediatrics*, 86, 1001–1002.

60. Brook, R., Dolan, M., & Coorey, P. (1996). Arson and epilepsy. *Medicine, Science, and the Law*, 36, 268–271.

61. Pontius, A. A. (1999). Motiveless firesetting: implicating partial limbic seizure kindling by revived memories of fires in "limbic psychotic trigger reaction." *Perceptual Motor Skills*, 88, 970–982.

62. Heidrich, A., Schmidtke, A., Lesch, K. P., Hofman, E., & Becker, T. (1996). Cerebellar arachnoid cyst in a firesetter: the weight of organic lesions in arson. *Journal of Psychiatry & Neuroscience*, 21, 202–206.

63. Cox, J. (2001). From inside prison. *Dyslexia*, 7, 97–102.

64. Brady, K. T., Myrick, H., & McElroy, S. (1998). The relationship between substance use disorders, impulse control disorders, and pathological aggression. *American Journal of Addictions*, 7, 221–230.

65. Balachandra, K. (2002). Fire fetishism in a female arsonist (letter to the editor)? *Canadian Journal of Psychiatry*, 47, 487–488.

66. Bruce-Jones, W., & Coid, J. (1992). Identity diffusion presenting as multiple personality disorder in a female psychopath. *British Journal of Psychiatry*, 160, 541–544.

67. DeJong, J., Virkkunen, M., & Linnoila, M. (1992). Factors associated with recidivism in a criminal population. *Journal of Nervous and Mental Disease*, 180, 543–550.

68. Law, D. K. (1991, January). The pyromaniac vs. the professional hired torch. *Fire Engineering*, pp. 50–51.

69. Leong, G. B., & Silva, J. A. (1999). Revisiting arson from an outpatient forensic perspective. *Journal of Forensic Science*, 44, 558–563.

70. Linaker, O. M. (2000). Dangerous female psychiatric patients: prevalence and characteristics. *Acta Psychiatrica Scandinavica*, 101, 67–72.

71. Morgan, N., Cook, D. A. G., Dorkins, C. E., & Doyle, M. E. (1995). An outbreak of copycat fire raising. *British Journal of Medicine and Psychology*, 68, 341–348.

72. Noblett, S., & Nelson, B. (2001). A psychosocial approach to arson—a case controlled study of female offenders. *Medicine, Science, and the Law*, 41, 325–330.

73. Rasanen, P., Hakko, H., & Vaisanen, E. (1995). Arson trend increasing—a real challenge for psychiatry. *Journal of Forensic Science*, 40, 976–979.

74. Rasanen, P., Paumalainen, T., Janhonen, S., & Vaisanen, E. (1996). Fire-setting from the viewpoint of an arsonist. *Journal of Psychosocial Nursing*, 34(3), 16–21.

75. Repo, E., & Virkkunen, M. (1997). Criminal recidivism and family histories of schizophrenic and nonschizophrenic fire setters: comorbid alcohol dependence in schizophrenic fire setters. *Journal of the American Academy of Psychiatry and the Law*, 25, 207–215.

76. Repo, E., & Virkkunen, M. (1997) Outcomes in a sample of Finnish fire-setters. *Journal of Forensic Psychiatry*, 8, 127–137.

77. Repo, E., Virkkunen, M., Rawlings, R., & Linnoila, M. (1997). Suicidal behavior among Finnish fire setters. *European Archives of Psychiatry and Clinical Neuroscience*, 247, 303–307.

78. Rice, M. E., & Harris, G. T. (1991). Firesetters admitted to a maximum security psychiatric institution. *Journal of Interpersonal Violence*, 6, 461–475.

79. Bix, K. J. B. (1994). A psychiatric study of adult arsonists. *Medicine, Science, and the Law*, 34, 21–34.

80. Soothill, K., Ackerley, E., & Francis, B. (2004). The criminal career of arsonists. *Medicine, Science, and the Law*, 44, 27–40.

81. Stewart, L. A. (1993). Profile of female firesetters: implication for treatment. *British Journal of Psychiatry*, 163, 248–256.

82. Virkkunen, M., Eggert, M., Rawling, R., & Linnoila, M. (1996). A prospective follow-up study of alcoholic violent offenders and fire setters. *Archives of General Psychiatry*, 53, 523–529.

83. Virkkunen, M., Rawlings, R., Tokola, R., Poland, R. E., Guidotti, A., Nemeroff, C., Bissette, G., Kalogeras, K., Karonen, S. L., & Linnoila, M. (1994). CSF biochemistries, glucose metabolism, and diurnal activity rhythms in alcoholic, violent offenders, fire setters, and healthy volunteers. *Archives of General Psychiatry*, 51, 20–27.

84. Fineman, K. R. (1995). A model for the qualitative analysis of child and adult fire deviant behavior. *American Journal of Forensic Psychology*, 13, 31–60.

85. Puri, B. K., Baxter, R., & Cordess, C. C. (1995). Characteristics of fire-setters. *British Journal of Psychiatry*, 166, 393–396.

86. Harris, G. T., & Rice, M. E. (1996). A typology of mentally disordered firesetters. *Journal of Interpersonal Violence*, 11, 351–363.

87. Kocsis, R. N., & Cooksey, R. W. (2002). Criminal psychological profiling of serial arson crimes. *International Journal of Offender Therapy and Comparative Criminology*, 46, 631–656.

88. Kocsis, R. N., Irwin, H. J., & Hayes, A. F. (1998). Organized and disorganized criminal behaviour syndromes in arsonists: a validation study of psychological profiling concept. *Psychiatry, Psychology, and the Law*, 5, 117–131.

89. Canter, D., & Fritzon, K. (1998). Differentiating arsonists: a model of firesetting actions and characteristics. *Legal Criminological Psychology*, 3, 73–96.

90. Fritzon, K., Canter, D., & Wilton, Z. (2001) The application of an action system model to destructive behavior: the examples of arson and terrorism. *Behavioral Sciences & the Law*, 19, 657–690.

91. Almond, L., Duggan, L., Shine, J., & Canter, D. (2005). Test of the arson action system model in an incarcerated population. *Psychology, Crime & Law*, 11, 1–15.

92. Santtila, P., Hakkanen, H., & Fritzon, K. (2003). Inferring the characteristics of an arsonist from crime scene actions: a case study in offender profiling. *International Journal of Police Science & Management*, 5, 1–15.

93. Sturmey, P., Taylor, J. L., & Lindsay, W. R. (2004). Research and development. In: Lindsay, W. R., Taylor, J. L., & Sturmey, P. (Eds.). *Offenders with Developmental Disabilities*. West Sussex, UK: John Wiley.

94. Lewis, N. D. C., & Yarnell, H. (1951). *Pathological Fire-Setting (Pyromania)*. Nervous and Mental Disease Monograph No. 82. New York: Coolidge Foundation.

95. Rice, M. E., & Harris, G. T. (1990). Firesetters admitted to a maximum security psychiatric institution: characteristics of offenders and offenses. *Penetanguishene Mental Health Center Research Report*, 7, 1–27.

96. Barron, P., Hassiotis, A., & Barnes, J. (2002). Offenders with intellectual disability: the size of the problem and therapeutic outcome. *Journal of Intellectual Disability Research*, 46, 454–463.

97. Barron, P., Hassiotis, A., & Barnes, J. (2004). Offenders with intellectual disability: a prospective comparative study. *Journal of Intellectual Disability Research*, 48, 69–76.

98. Crossland, S., Burns, M., Leach, C., & Quinn, P. (2005). Needs assessment in forensic learning disabilities. *Medicine, Science, and the Law*, 45, 147–153.

99. Taylor, J. L., Thorne, I., & Slavkin, M. L. (2004). Treatment of fire-setting behaviour. In: Lindsay, W. R., Taylor, J. L., & Sturmey, P. (Eds.). *Offenders with Developmental Disabilities*. West Sussex, UK: John Wiley.

100. Murphy, G. H., & Clare, I. C. H. (1996). Analysis of motivation in people with mild learning disabilities (mental handicap) who set fires. *Psychology, Crime & Law*, 2, 153–164.

101. Rizzolo, M. C., Hemp, R., Braddock, D., & Pomeranz-Essley, A (2005). The state of the states in developmental disabilities. Accessed December 10, 2005, at www.cu.edu/ColemanInstitute/stateofthestates/.

102. Lerman, P., Apgas, D. H., & Jordan, T. (2003). Deinstitutionalization and mortality: findings of a controlled research design in New Jersey. *Mental Retardation*, 41:225–236.

103. Read S. (2004). Mortality of people with learning disabilities following relocation from long-stay hospital to social care. *Journal of Learning Disabilities*, 8, 299–314.

104. Shavelle, R., Strauss, D., & Day, S. (2005). Deinstitutionalization in California: mortality of persons with developmental disabilities after transfer into community care, 1997–1999. *Journal of Data Science*, 3, 371–380.

105. Widrick, G. C., Bramley, J. A., & Frawley, P. J. (1997). Psychopathology in adults with mental retardation before and after deinstitutionalization. *Journal of Developmental Physical Disabilities*, 9, 223–242.

106. Geller, J. L. (1984). Arson: an unforeseen sequela of deinstitutionalization. *American Journal of Psychiatry*, 141, 504–508.

107. Kannapell, A. (1998, May 17) As an institution empties, community fears force nine men back. *New York Times*, p. 8NJ.

108. Firefighter pleads guilty in arson cases. *Boston Globe*, December 3, 2004, p. B2.

109. Firefighter arrested on arson suspicions. *Seattle Post-Intelligencer*, August 30, 2004. Accessed October 18, 2004, at http://seattlep1.nwsource.com/printer2/index.asp?ploc=b&refer.

110. Holt, F. X. (1994, June). The arsonist's profile. *Fire Engineering*, p. 127.

111. Goode, E. (2002, July 9). Do firefighters like to set fire? Just an urban legend, experts say. *New York Times*, p. F1.

112. Firefighter arson—an NVFC special report. Accessed December 3, 2005, at http://www.nvfc.org/news/hn_firefighter_arson.html.

113. *Firefighter Arson. Special Report.* FEMA: U.S. Fire Administration. USFA-TR-141, January 2003.
114. National fire department census summary data. Accessed October 6, 2004, at http://usfa.fema.gov/applications/fdonline/summary.cfm.
115. Dvorchak, R. (1995, February 26). Firefighter as arsonist: why some cross the line—states move to weed out troublemaker before he kills. *Seattle Times*, p. A4+.
116. Huff, T. G. (2004). Fire, filicide, and finding felons. In: Campbell, J. H., & DeNevi, D. (Eds.). *Profilers.* Amherst, NY: Prometheus.
117. Regehr, C., Hill, J., & Glancy, G. D. (2000). Individual predictors of traumatic reactions in firefighters. *Journal of Nervous and Mental Disease*, 188, 333–339.
118. Fannin, N., & Dobbs, J. M. (2003). Testosterone and the work of firefighters fighting fires and delivering medical care. *Journal of Personality Research*, 37, 107–115.
119. Prins, H. (1994). Fire—'good servant-bad master' (editorial). *Medicine, Science, and the Law*, 34, 2–3.
120. Geller, J. L. (1987). Firesetting in the adult psychiatric population. *Hospital and Community Psychiatry*, 38, 501–506.
121. Leong, G. B. (1992). A psychiatric study of persons charged with arson. *Journal of Forensic Science*, 37, 1319–1326.
122. Haddad, P. M. (1993). Ganser syndrome followed by major depression episode. *British Journal of Psychiatry*, 162, 251–253.
123. Wilkin, J., & Coid, J. (1991). Self-mutilation in female remanded prisoners. I. An indicator of severe psychopathology. *Criminal Behaviour and Mental Health*, 1, 247–267.
124. Coid, J., Wilkins, J., & Coid, B. (1999). Fire-setting, pyromania and self-mutilation in female remanded prisoners. *Journal of Forensic Psychiatry*, 10, 119–130.
125. Räsänen, P. (1995). The mental status of arsonists as determined by forensic psychiatric examinations. *Bulletin of the American Academy of Psychiatry & the Law*, 23, 547–555.
126. Geller, J. L. (1997). Self-incineration: a review of the psychopathology of setting oneself afire. *International Journal of Law and Psychiatry*, 20, 355–372.
127. Sen, M. (2001). *Death by Fire. Sati, Dowry Death, and Female Infanticide in Modern India.* New Brunswick, NJ: Rutgers University.
128. Laloe, V. (2004). Patterns of deliberate self-burning in various parts of the world. *Burns*, 30, 207–215.
129. Van de Does, A. J. W., Hinderink, E. M. C., & Vloemans, A. F. P. M. (1998). Increasing numbers of patients with self-inflicted burns at Dutch burn units (letter to the editor). *Burns*, 24, 584–586.
130. Tam, P., King, J., Palmieri, T. L., & Greenhalgh, D. G. (2003). Predisposing factors for self-inflicted burns. *Journal of Burn Care Research*, 24, 223–237.
131. Rashid, A., & Gowar, J. F. (2004). A review of the trends of self-inflicted burns. *Burns*, 30, 573–576.

132. Turk, E. E., Anders, S., & Tsokos, M. (2004). Planned complex suicide: report of two autopsy cases of suicidal shot injury and subsequent self-immolation. *Forensic Science International* 139, 35–38.
133. Cingolani, M., & Tsakri, D. (2000). Planned complex suicide: report of three cases. *American Journal of Forensic Medicine and Pathology*, 21, 255–260.
134. Bohnert, M., & Rothschild, M. A. (2003). Complex suicides by self-incineration. *Forensic Science International*, 131, 197–201.
135. Bohnert, M., Schmidt, U., GrobePerdekamp, M., & Pollak, S. (2002). Diagnosis of captive bolt injury in a skull extremely destroyed by fire. *Forensic Science International*, 127, 192–197.
136. Kumar, V. (2003). Burnt wives—a study of suicides. *Burns*, 29, 31–35.
137. Ravage, B. (2004). *Burn Unit*. Cambridge, MA: DeCapo.
138. Eldridge, K. (2004). Serial arson suspect arrested. Accessed October 19, 2004 at http://www.komotv.com/news/printstory.asp?id=33301).
139. Palkot, S. (2004). Man arrested in multiple arson cases. *Herald-Coaster*, September 3, 2004. Accessed October 18, 2004 at http://www.herald-coaster.com/articles/2004/09/03/news/top_story/topstory.txt.
140. Wilber, D. Q. (2005). Man arrested in D.C. area's arson wave. *Washington Post*, April 28, 2005, p. A1.
141. Boyd, R. (2005). Louisiana police finally catch serial arsonist. Accessed November 21, 2005, at http://cms.firehouse.com/content/article/printer.jsp? id=45395.
142. Dolan, M., Millington, J., & Park, I. (2002). Personality and neuropsychological function in violent, sexual and arson offenders. *Medicine, Science, and the Law*, 42, 34–43.
143. Brett, A. (2004). 'Kindling theory' in arson: how dangerous are firesetters? *Australian and New Zealand Journal of Psychiatry*, 38, 419–425.
144. Rice, M. E., & Harris, G. T. (1991). Firesetters admitted to a maximum security psychiatric institution. *Journal of Interpersonal Violence*, 6, 461–475.
145. Rice, M. E., & Harris, G. T. (1996). Predicting the recidivism of mentally disordered firesetters. *Journal of Interpersonal Violence*, 11, 364–375.
146. Barnett, W., Richter, P., Sigmund, D., & Spitzer, M. (1997). Recidivism and concomitant criminality in pathological firesetters. *Journal of Forensic Science*, 42, 879–883.
147. Geller, J. L., Fisher, W. H., & Bertsch, G. (1992). Who repeats? A follow-up study of state hospital patients' firesetting behavior. *Psychiatric Quarterly*, 63, 143–157.
148. Icove, D. J., & Horbert, P. R. (1990). Serial arsonists: an introduction. *Police Chief*, December, pp. 46–48.
149. Sapp, A. D., Huff, T. G., Gary, G. P., Icove, D. J., & Horbert, P. (1994). Serial arsonists: who are they? *National Fire Arson Report*, 12(3), 1–6, 14–15.
150. Sapp, A. D., Huff, T. G., Gary, G. P., & Icove, D. J. (1994) *A Motive-Based Offender Analysis of Serial Arsonists*. Washington, DC: National Center for the Analysis of Violent Crime, Federal Bureau of Investigation.
151. Sapp, A. D., Huff, T. G., Gary, G. P., & Icove, D. J. (1996). Serial arsonists: investigative considerations. *National Fire Arson Report*, 14(1), 10–12.

152. Kocsis, R. N. (2003). Criminal psychological profiles: validities and abilities. *International Journal of Offender Therapy and Comparative Criminology*, 47, 126–144.
153. Kocsis, R. N. (2004). Psychological profiling of serial arson offenses: an assessment of skills and accuracy. *Criminal Justice and Behavior*, 31, 341–361.
154. Kocsis, R. N., & Irwin, H. J. (1997). An analysis of spatial patterns in serial rape, arson, and burglary: the utility of the circle theory of environmental range for psychological profiling. *Psychiatry, Psychology, and the Law*, 4, 195–206.
155. Wheaton, S. (2001). Memoirs of a compulsive firesetter. *Psychiatric Services*, 52, 1035–1036.
156. MacFarquhar, N (2002). Man is indicted in 10 church fires in Indiana and Georgia, one in which a firefighter died. Accessed October 16, 2002, at http://query.nytimes.com/search/article-page.htm? res=9806E5DF143AF932A15757COA961.
157. Barnett, W., Richter, P., & Renneberg, B. (1999). Repeated arson: data from criminal records. *Forensic Science International*, 101, 49–54.
158. Clare, I. C. H., Murphy, G. H., Cox, D., & Chaplin, E. H. (1992). Assessment and treatment of fire-setting: a single-case investigation using a cognitive-behavioral model. *Criminal Behaviour and Mental Health*, 2, 253–268.
159. Swaffer, T., Haggert, M., & Oxley, T. (2001). Mentally disordered firesetters: a structured intervention programme. *Clinical Psychology and Psychotherapy*, 8, 468–475.
160. Geller, J. L. (1987). Firesetting in the adult psychiatric population. *Hospital and Community Psychiatry*, 38, 501–506.
161. Grant, J. E., & Potenza, M. N. (2004). Impulse control disorders: clinical characteristics and pharmacological management. *Annals of Clinical Psychiatry*, 16, 27–34.
162. Davidson, F. M., Clare, I. C. H., Georgiades, S., Divall, J., & Holland, A. J. (1994). Treatment of a man with a mild learning disability who was sexually assaulted whilst in prison. *Medicine, Science, and the Law*, 34, 346–353.
163. Soltys, S. M. (1992). Pyromania and firesetting behaviors. *Psychiatric Annals*, 22(2), 79–83.
164. Bumpass, E. R., Fagelman, F. D., & Brix, R. J. (1983). Interventions with children who set fires. *American Journal of Psychotherapy*, 37, 328–345.
165. Foy, C. (1997). The female arsonist. In: Welldon, E. V., & Van Velson, C. (Eds.). *A Practical Guide to Forensic Psychotherapy*. Bristol, PA: Jessica Kingsley.
166. Running the arson programme for prisoners. *Fire*, January 2000, p. 18.
167. Hall, G. (1995). Using group work to understand arsonists. *Nursing Standard*, 9(23), 25–28.
168. Taylor, J. L., Thorne, I., Robertson, A., & Avery, G. (2002). Evaluation of a group intervention for convicted arsonists with mild and borderline intellectual disabilities. *Criminal Behaviour and Mental Health*, 12, 282–293.
169. Marlatt, G. A., & Donovan, D. M. (2005) (Eds). *Relapse Prevention, Second Edition: Maintenance Strategies in the Treatment of Addictive Behaviors*. New York: Guilford Press.

170. Linehan, M. M. (1993). *Cognitive-Behavioral Treatment of Borderline Personality Disorder.* New York: Guilford Press.

171. Walsh BW. (2006). *Treating Self-Injury.* New York: Guilford Press.

172. Leistikow, B. N., Martin, D. C., & Milano, C. E. (2000). Fire injuries, disasters, and costs from cigarettes and cigarette lights: a global overview. *Preventive Medicine,* 31, 91–99.

173. About NFDC. Accessed October 6, 2004, at http://usfa.fema.gov/inside-usaf/nfdc-abt.shtm.

174. Hotel arson arrest. Accessed December 17, 2005, at http://www.fox8live.com/www/NewsItem.aspx?NewsID=932.

175. Hunter, M. (2005, November 10) Arson suspected in rash of fires. *Times-Picayune.* Accessed December 9, 2005, at http://www.nola.com/news/t-p/metro/index.ssf?/base/news-11/1131605687166260.xml.

176. Mosul captured without fight: Iraqi forces abandon city—looting, arson break out all over. Accessed November 13, 2005, at http://www.dawn.com/2003/04/12/topl.htm.

177. Goodman EC. (2001). *Fire! The 100 Most Devastating Fires and the Heroes Who Fought Them.* New York: Black Dog & Leventhal.

178. Flynn S. (2002). *3000 Degrees.* New York: Warner.

179. Rookie firefighter suspected of arson. Accessed December 17, 2005, at http://www.macon.com/mild/macon/news/politics/13349424.htm.

180. Love triangle may have sparked arson. Accessed December 17, 2005, at http://abcnews.go.com/US/Legal/Center/story?id=1368089&cmp=OTC-RSSFeeds0312.

181. Mason, J (2004). BF man charged with arson. Accessed October 17, 2004, at http://www.reformer.com/stories/0,1413,102~8862~2471811,00.html.

182. Agnew, S. (2005). Boyfriend is charged with arson. Accessed December 19, 2005, at http://www.columbiatribune.com/2005/Dec/20051219News001.asp.

183. FBI reports US murder rate increases. Accessed December 19, 2005, at http://today.reuters.com/news/newsArticle.aspx?type=topNews&storyID=2005-12-19T161027Z_01_SPI958203_RTRUKOC_0_US-Crime-FBI.xml&archived=False.

184. U.S. Fire Administration (2002). *Church Fires* 2(7).

185. List of black church fire investigations. Accessed December 19, 2005, at http://www.cnn.com/us/9606/08/arson.timeline/.

186. This was a set fire. Accessed December 19, 2005, at http://www.cn.com/us9606/07/church.fire.7pl.

187. Coen J. (2005). Firefighter-author sentenced for church arson. Accessed December 19, 2005, at http://www.chicagotribune.com/news/local/chi-051219arson,1,7852561.story?call=chi_news-bed.

188. Eagen, S. P. (1996). From spikes to bombs: the rise of eco-terrorism. *Studies in Conflict and Terrorism,* 19, 1–18.

189. Kuhlken R. (1999). Settin' the woods on fire: rural incendiarism as protest. *Geographical Record,* 89, 343–363.

190. Bernton, H., & Welch, C. (2005). Environmental-arson probe has Eugene activists on edge. Accessed December 19, 2005, at http://seattletimes. nwsource.com/html/local/news/2002688671_eugene17m.html.

191. Martin, R. (2005). Vail arson suspect nabbed? Accessed December 19, 2005, at http://www.newwest.net/index.php/main/article/4910/.

192. Runjan, C. W., Bangdiwala, S. I., Linzer, M. A., Sacks, J. J., & Butts, J. (1992). Risk factors for residential fires. *New England Journal of Medicine*, 327, 859–863.

193. Squires, T., & Busuttil, A. (1997). Alcohol and house fire fatalities in Scotland, 1980–1990. *Medicine, Science, and the Law*, 37, 321–325.

Chapter 10

The *"Gentler Sex"*
Patterns in Female Serial Murder[1]
Hannah Scott

Abstract

This chapter examines patterns of serial homicides committed by women from 1600 to 2004, which are estimated to comprise approximately 10% to 15% of all serial murder offenders. More specifically, this chapter seeks to lend understanding to those serial homicides committed specifically by women in dominant roles as murderer. Women who acted alone or in concert with another where the accomplice was in a subordinate role are also examined. Patterns suggest that women who commit serial murder and are dominant tend to have significantly different patterns of action when compared to those of men in the same role. Trends include, but are not limited to, the following: women are less likely to use physical violence, are more likely to use poison, are more likely to choose children and men as part of their victim pool, and have a higher estimated kill ratio than men. Implications of the lack of recognition of these killers' actions for both research and detection are discussed.

INTRODUCTION

It is well known that most serial murders are committed by men *(1–3)*. In fact, it was not long ago that it was a phenomenon thought to be solely committed by men *(4)*. Diverting the gaze from the acts of men, however, to

---

[1] This chapter is a partial summary of material initially outlined in Scott. H. (2005). *The Female Serial Murderer: A Sociological Study of Homicide and the 'Gentler Sex.'* Lewiston, NY: Mellen Press.

From: *Serial Murder and the Psychology of Violent Crimes*
Edited by: R. N. Kocsis © Humana Press, Totowa, NJ

the more rare acts of women might serve to highlight some of our sexual biases when we look at the criminal acts of women. The women outlined in this chapter have stepped out of the more traditional role and moved into another more dangerous social place: the offender class comprised of serial murderers. These women often cloaked themselves in their vulnerability, committing their atrocities in their own quiet way. What is ironic, as this chapter demonstrates, is that historically when a woman has made a habit of killing it does not attract attention. Her persona as the "gentler sex" comes in conflict with her actions, and other explanations are offered in an effort to rationalize the number of missing persons associated with a particular woman.

There has been considerable debate surrounding the definition of serial murder (5,6). For the purposes of this study, the serial murderer is defined as a person who has attempted to kill or successfully killed three or more victims. To be included in this class, intent to kill and acts of killing or attempted killing must be present. These killings, or attempted killings, take place over a prolonged period of time with a cooling down period between homicides. This killer class is more often male than female. The motives to these crimes are often intensely personal, giving the outward appearance of randomness. Finally, as is demonstrated in the pages that follow, whereas men have had motives that are more often associated with sexual fantasy (2,7–10) women often commit these crimes for more instrumental reasons, such as financial gain. Although these are predominant themes, it should be noted that the reasons for murdering, for both men and women of this class, are varied and sex does not ensure the motive type.

PERSPECTIVES OF WOMEN AND CRIME

Criminology has traditionally been a male-oriented social science. Until the very early 1990s, only three sources—Hickey (11), Holmes et al. (12), and Holmes and DeBerger (13)—addressed the issue of female serial killing. Before Hickey published his analysis, academics implicitly assumed, as Egger did in 1984 (4), that women did not commit serial murder. Holmes and DeBerger (13) were the only researchers who acknowledged women as serial murderers, citing three case studies. Ronald Holmes, since writing this study, has acknowledged that there are others (14).

To date, the largest comprehensive study on serial murder was conducted by Eric Hickey (2). His extensive work has captured characteristics of 367 male and 64 female serial murderers operating in the United States since 1800. In his study, women represent 14.85% of his offender pool. His analyses, for the most part, focus on only 61 of these women. Just over one-fourth (26.6%) of these women worked in teams. Hickey noted that a few of these teams were comprised of two women. It is not clear just how many in his sample were solely made up of female members. He does state that most of these pairings were with men and that the men took the dominant roles in the killing relationships. This chapter examines the actions of 102 female serial murderers from all over the world. The intent here is to identify patterns exhibited by women only or where women took dominant roles in team killings.

TRENDS IN SERIAL HOMICIDE COMMITTED BY WOMEN IN DOMINANT ROLES

Despite formal recognition, cases of serial homicide committed by women have been documented as early as the 17th century. Most (82.7%) of the women in this sample worked alone. Seven of the women had one accomplice, and fewer still had three or more accomplices. Working alone is common to serial murder in general. As with serial murders committed by men, murder is rarely palatable for more than one person. Hickey reported that 69% of the cases of serial murderers in his sample operated without another team member *(2)*. As illustrated in Figure 1, the number of female serial killers identified peaks during the first and last quartiles of the 20th century. As an overall trend, with each new century, the numbers of documented serial murderesses has increased in number. The 20th century has recorded the largest number of these killers to date.

Table 1 illustrates rates of known serial murder offending by women in the United States spanning over two centuries. What is revealing is that it provides evidence that argues against the statement that we are currently

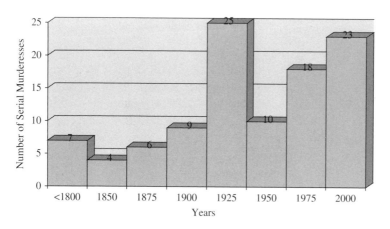

Fig. 1. Activity periods, by start date of female serial murderesses, 1600–2000.

Table 1
Rate of Female Serial Murderers in the United States' Population, 1790–1999

Year	Female killers caught or identified	U.S. population[a]	Rate per ten million
1790–1799	0	3, 929, 214	0
1800–1809	0	5, 308, 483	0
1810–1819	0	7, 239, 881	0
1820–1829	0	9, 633, 822	0
1830–1939	0	12, 866, 020	0
1840–1849	0	17, 069, 458	0
1850–1859	0	23, 191, 876	0
1860–1869	1	31, 443, 321	3.18
1870–1879	1	38, 558, 371	2.59
1880–1889	0	50, 155, 783	0
1890–1899	0	62, 979, 766	0
1900–1909	4	76, 303, 387	5.24
1910–1919	7	91, 972, 266	7.61
1920–1929	6	105, 710, 620	5.68
1930–1939	2	122, 775, 046	1.63
1940–1949	2	131, 669, 275	1.52
1950–1959	3	151, 325, 798	1.98
1960–1969	5	179, 323, 175	2.79
1970–1979	3	203, 302, 031	1.48
1980–1989	12	226, 542, 199	5.30
1990–1999	7	248, 718, 301	2.81

[a] U.S. Census Bureau (2002). Appendix A: United States' Population and Census Cost. *Measuring America: The Decennial Census from 1790–2000* Washington, DC: US Department of Commerce: Economics and Statistics Administration.

experiencing an upward trend in offending of this type. Even though we detected and apprehended more female serial murderesses in any given 10-year period during the 1980s, the highest rates of offending among women in this criminal class occurred around the turn of the 20th century. Therefore, although the public has been made aware of more serial killing women during the last 30 years, we are actually experiencing a downward trend of this crime type by women. The higher numbers are more reflective of the increases in population, not an actual increased risk of offending.

Newspaper reports analyzed from the United States, Canada, England, and France indicate that more than half (51%) of the women included in the sample operated in the United States. The United States has had a consistently higher

Table 2
Countries of Operation of Female Serial Murderesses, 1600–2003

Country of operation	No. of murderesses	%[a]
United States	52	51.0
Canada & Mexico	4	3.9
England	11	10.8
Europe, excluding England	25	24.5
Russia	1	1.0
Australia and New Zealand	4	3.9
Africa	1	1.0
More than one country	3	2.9
Unknown	1	1.0
Total	102	100

[a] Numbers may not add exactly to 100 due to rounding.

murder rate, on average, than other Western nations. Additionally, Table 2 demonstrates that just over one in ten serial killing women were found in England. The remaining murderous women, identified here, were located in various other countries. There were no cases found in Western sources of serial killing women in South America, Asia, or Indo-Asia. Interestingly, given the populations of Africa and Russia, it is odd that there is only one recorded case in each country where a woman has committed these crimes.

There may be several underlying factors driving these numbers. The curiosity of Western nations has historically been focused in the direction of other wealthy nations, rather than on the poorer cohabitants of this planet. Therefore, news generated in non-Western nations often does not catch the interest of First World nations, as illustrated by the lack of these stories in newspapers and other media. Second, recording these types of crime statistics may not be a priority for these countries. Third, some of these countries, such as China, Japan, and Russia, have historically had their doors closed to inspection by other nations. Therefore, serial murder cases may have been kept secret from Western media sources for various political reasons.

Looking to Table 3, just under half (46%) of these women preferred a victim pool of children exclusively or in combination with adults. Hickey noted that approximately one-fifth (20%) of American serial murderesses targeted children (excluding teens) only, and 38% of women in the American sample targeted at least one child. In this sample, roughly one in five women (17.6%) targeted children only. Fully 47% of women in Hickey's study targeted women

Table 3
Sex and Age Preference Grouping of Victims of Female Serial Murderesses,
1600–2003

Sex of target	All victims[a]	Child victims only[a]	Adult victims only[a]	Children and adult victims[a]	Victim age preference unclear
Males only	17.6	0	14.7	2.9	0
Females only	2.9	0	1.0	2.0	0
Male & females	79.4	17.6	37.3	23.5	1
Total of sample	100	17.6	52.9	28.4	1.0

[a] Numbers may not add exactly to column totals due to rounding.

and teens. Only 10% of men in his sample targeted children and teens only. When comparing these two studies, it appears that, at first glance, serial murderesses tend to target children much more often than do men. This trend seems to intensify if we look at American women only.

Women in this sample are also more likely to exclusively target men over women; only three women targeted a victim pool comprised only of women. Four of five (79.4%) women chose to kill both adults and teens. The remainder, almost one-fifth of the sample, chose to kill adult men exclusively. This number was similar for the American murderess sample, although Hickey reported a slightly lower proportion (17%) in his sample killed men exclusively. Again, this may be due to the fact that some of the women in Hickey's sample were paired with men and therefore were subjected to murdering the victim type preferred by the dominant male member.

Fifteen of the female offenders in this study, who targeted males only, also targeted male adults specifically. The three remaining women in this sample targeted male children and adults. No female serial murderess chose to kill male or female children exclusively. Women in this sample were most likely to target a victim pool that was comprised of adult men and women only. When women targeted children exclusively, there was also relatively little sex discrimination. Age, in contrast to sex, was more strongly associated with victim preference. Roughly one-fourth of these women chose the widest range of demographic possibilities, killing in all age groups and without sex discrimination.

American male serial murderers prefer female victims (2). Two of every five offenders (42%) chose to kill females exclusively. Just over one in five (21%) chose to kill victims of the same sex. The remainder of Hickey's sample did not have any sex preference. The results presented here and those of Hickey suggest that women may be less biased when it comes to the sex of their victim for the most part. Evidence suggests that a female serial murderer is more likely to prefer a mixed-sex victim pool, followed by men only. The women in this study are less likely to target their own sex than are men.

Like Hickey, this study also found that women were more likely to target family members over nonfamily members and strangers. In Hickey's sample, 31% women targeted at least one stranger. Table 4 demonstrates that only 12.7% of women targeted at least one stranger. Hickey also noted that 23% of women in his sample targeted strangers only. This increased number of strangers in the American sample may be due to differences in sample eligibility between these two studies. Again, sample differences may vary owing to the fact that Hickey chose to include women who worked with dominant men, thereby increasing the likelihood that strangers would be considered in the victim pool.

More than half (53.9%) of the serial killing women in this study targeted those with whom they were sexually intimate. Fully 41.2% of women in this sample targeted a husband as part of their victim pool. Fewer (8.8%) chose to kill at least one lover, and fewer still (3.9%) went after potential suitors. Almost as popular as husbands were other women in the family of the female serial murderer. Just under half (44.1%) targeted other women in their family, excluding children. Three in ten (30.4%) targeted their own children as part

Table 4
Relationships of Female Serial Murderers to Victims, 1600–2003

Relationship	No. of women who killed within particular group
Familial	
Husbands, lovers, potential suitors	55
Other women	45
Own children, foster or stepchild	40
Mother, mother-in-law, stepmother	10
Siblings, cousins	6
Nonfamilial	
Friends, neighbors	10
Employers	3
Tenants or borders	2
Elderly under care (nonpatient)	17
Patients	20
Slaves or devotees	3
Strangers	13

of their victim pool. Another 8.8% of women targeted at least one foster or step child. Roughly four of five of the women (80.4%) in his sample killed at least one family member. Comparatively, only 48% of women in the American study were found to target at least one family member.

When women turned outside the family to commit these acts, they tended to target those who were dependent on them in some way. Altogether, 20 of the women in this sample killed at least one patient in their care, and another 17 women sought to murder people who they cared for, but not within the medical sphere. In other words, these women killed their clients. Only 10 women went out of this more traditional care-giving murderous role and killed friends and neighbors who were not in a dependent role.

Table 5 illustrates that almost two-thirds (62.7%) of the women in this sample used poison as the sole method of dispatching their victims. Approximately one-third (34%) of the American sample were dedicated specifically to this method *(2)*. In this study, suffocation, drowning, and strangulation were methods predominantly used on smaller victims such as infants and small children. The few women who did use firearms did so with adults only. Five women in the sample used torture as a method of killing. Again, in almost all cases the victims of torture were adults or young adults. Women who used torture operated in some sort of leading capacity, killing devotees, slaves, or servants under their care. Not only is torture unusual, it is reflective of a more rare, more complex social killing structure available to these women.

Table 5
Female Serial Murderers, 1600–2003: Method of Killing Victim

Modus operandi	No.	%[a]
Poisoned	64	62.7
Suffocation	9	8.8
Firearm	7	6.9
Torture/beatings	5	4.9
Strangled	2	2.0
Starvation	2	2.0
Other	3	2.9
Various methods	7	6.9
Unknown method	3	2.9
Total	102	100%

[a] Numbers may not add exactly to 100 due to rounding.

Table 6
Type of Poison Used, Female Serial Murderers,
1600–2003

Poison	No.	%[a]
Arsenic	29	28.4
Morphine	8	7.8
Thallium	2	2.0
Insulin overdose	2	2.0
Chorodyne	2	2.0
Other	10	9.8
More than one type	5	4.9
Unknown type of poison	9	8.8
Did not use poison	35	34.3
Total	102	100

[a] Numbers may not add exactly to 100 due to rounding.

Table 6 looks specifically at the methods of poisoning used by these women. Although most early poisoners found arsenic efficient and readily available, arsenic is now more easily detected with modern medicine. Before the 20th century, arsenic (usually found in ant and rat poison) was a product that was easily secured and brought little suspicion to the purchaser. Arsenic is no longer used in many household pest control systems because it was found to be so toxic. Additionally, with advances in technology, arsenic is now more easily detected as a heavy metal in the bloodstream. Finding arsenic in the bloodstream is highly unusual and instantly arouses suspicion. Ironically, medications have become more readily available as household items than arsenic and have replaced arsenic as a poisoning method of choice. The 20th century poisoners are more likely to be in the nursing and care-giving professions. The medications they have used to dispatch their victims were largely obtained while at work. Furthermore, the presence of these medications in the body does not necessarily arouse suspicion.

Table 7 notes that, in addition to being charged with various murders, more than one-fourth (26.5%) of this sample were charged with attempted murder. In another 15 cases, the public reports were not clear as to whether the women were charged with these lesser crimes. In these cases, the documents reveal strong suspicions or actual investigative evidence that such crimes were committed. Only one in ten of these women was known to have previous arrests. Most of these women, therefore, did not have a criminal history before embarking on their criminal career. This implies that these women were not

Table 7
**Female Serial Murderers, 1600–2003: Percentage of Previous Arrests
and Attempted Murder Charges**

Parameter	Previous arrests[a] (%)	Charges of attempted murder[a] (%)
Yes	9.8	26.5
No	81.4	4.9
Possibly	1.0	14.7
Not stated	7.8	53.9
Total	100	100

[a] Numbers may not add exactly to 100 due to rounding.

coming to the attention of authorities, for the most part, until it was established that they were responsible for at least one murder.

Table 8 documents the various motivations of these women for their murders. The most common motive for getting rid of someone was to gain from that death financially. Just over two in five women received insurance money or property, or they kept stolen money as a result of their murderous acts. In 11.8% of these cases there was strong evidence for mental illness as a motivating factor. These women suffered from Munchausen's Syndrome by Proxy or had other mental illness histories that motivated them to kill. Just over one in ten killed to exert control or power over their victims, and another 2.9% killed

Table 8
**Principal Motive for Killing, Female Serial
Murderers, 1600–2003**

Motive for killing	No.	%[a]
Money	42	41.2
Mental illness	12	11.8
Control or power	11	10.8
Thrill	3	2.9
Anger	2	2.0
Fear of abandonment	2	2.0
Other	10	9.8
Many motives	10	9.8
Unknown motives	10	9.8
Total	102	100

[a] Numbers may not add exactly to 100 due to rounding.

Table 9
Female Serial Murderers, 1600–2003, Type
of Sentence for Homicides Committed

Type of sentence	No.	%[a]
Life in prison	39	38.2
Death	29	28.4
Prison, not life sentence	15	14.7
Insane asylum	5	4.9
Acquitted	5	4.9
Never charged	4	3.9
Never caught	3	2.9
Unknown	2	2.0
Total	102	100

[a] Numbers may not add exactly to 100 due to rounding.

for the thrill of killing. Just fewer than one in ten killed for various motives. In these cases, the motives changed depending on the individual circumstance. Some killed for more altruistic reasons, such as the desire to free other women from the oppression of their husbands or to have their children in heaven with them; or they simply felt that killing people was a form of higher calling. Some killed those who interfered with their desire to marry, and another killed to get more attention from a partner. One simply hated seeing others being happy.

In Hickey's study, it is reported that 66% of women received some sort of prison time for their crimes *(2)*. He did not distinguish those who were sentenced to life from those who received a lesser sentence. Table 9 demonstrates that fewer women in this study received a prison term (52.9%). Almost two in five women (38.2%) received a life sentence for their crimes. Many more women received the death penalty in this study (28.4%) than were reported in the Hickey study (19%). Seven women in this study avoided capture and therefore were never held accountable for their crimes. These figures are similar to those of Hickey *(2)*. Five women were acquitted of all charges in this sample. No women were acquitted in the American sample *(2)*. Both studies found that roughly one in twenty women who had committed these crimes was confined to an asylum or other psychiatric facility.

DISCUSSION

This chapter is dedicated to the investigation of the role of women who have committed the crime of serial murder. More specifically, this work seeks to identify patterns of the women who play lead roles in this offender class by working alone, working with other women, or as a dominant partner. Unlike men, these women do not elicit the fear that men in this offender class command. Also unlike men, the public perception holds that these women are not a threat, nor are they lurking around every corner waiting to prey on some hapless victim. Criminological theories have emerged out of the need to explain the acts of dangerous men. Criminology has long had a history of contorting to explain the actions of women *(15,16)*. Women were either not the subjects of these studies, or their actions and participation in crime were dismissed. Work on serial murder has fallen under this same pedagogy. Initially, acts of extreme violence were identified as solely the responsibility of men.

The profiles that were created around this offender class grew out of this social experience. They are backed by the typologies and theoretical explanations of male violent behavior. Women, as a subset of this offender class are poorly explained by these ideas. These ideas must contort to meet the needs of women. For example, Hickey pointed out that the U.S. Federal Bureau of Investigation (FBI) has had problems categorizing women who killed with men. In 2004, women were allotted the category of "compliant victim," with the assumption that the women who participated in team killings were coerced *(2)*.

Contributing to this process is the social impact of the assumptions encompassing traditional gender roles. People are being both encouraged and discouraged from accepting traditional roles *(17)*. This paradox is mimicked in criminology. Crime has occurred traditionally in the male domain. Crime is still largely committed by men. Women are presently responsible for approximately 10% of all crime *(18)*, but the types of crime in which women are participating are changing. They are altering because women's access to opportunities is changing *(16,19)*. It is interesting that, on one hand, women are inhibited from entering into traditionally male roles and on the other hand are treated, in many cases, like men.

Sally Simpson addressed just this question. She attempted to answer the age-old question, "Why can't a woman be more like a man?" Her answer is that in criminology a woman is like a man *(20)*. This should not be confused with men being like women. Currently, women as offenders have often suffered from the tyranny of the majority. Women are categorized using definitions of behavior and attitudes constructed in a male-dominated social sphere; they are subject to court procedures that have traditionally dealt with men and have been issued sentences equal to those of men. When sex disparity emerges, it is often called preferential treatment. Equality within the criminal justice system means treating a woman like a man, which in fact is not equality. If it were, we would find the reverse to be equally palatable: Why not treat men like women? It has been my experience that most practitioners and criminologists would feel uncomfortable with this proposition, clearly and poignantly illustrating the very point of sex preference in criminology and criminal justice. More importantly, to simply assume that we can "add women and stir" and that our andocentric bias will not affect identification and detection of offenders is a dangerous presumption.

Much of how we perceive men and women has to do with palatability. Women are rarely offenders; they are more often victims. This is easier for us to accept. It does not negate that female offenders not only exist but also need and demand explanation. By not considering gendered behavior forms, the ontological assumption is being made that there is little value added to our understanding of the dominant form of criminal behavior by examining nondominant forms. The assumption is also being made that the dominant form of an offender class has been correctly identified and that we have the appropriate understanding of the phenomenon. For example, before 1990 few books, anthologies, and encyclopedias on serial murder discussed the criminal act of serial murder by women. Occasionally, a few cases were carefully placed in the annals. Studies that used these books to aid in their calculations of prevalence of this problem ultimately must have underestimated its occurrence. It is also important to remember that profiles that overlook an estimated one-sixth of a population may be cause for concern.

The female serial murderer tends to be less violent and more discreet than her male counterpart. Therefore, her crimes are less likely to be noticed in the community, whereas the male serial murderer's activities are high profile. The death of his victims rarely escapes public attention. The most common weapon of the female multiple murderer is poison. Male serial murderers often use more violent methods of killing, including bludgeoning, stabbing, strangulation, and mutilation (2). Women rarely overpower their victim to kill them. The female serial murderer gains the victim's trust in an effort to find vulnerability, in contrast to the male serial murderer, who uses the victim's lack of physical strength as the primary weakness.

Another difference between the male and female serial murderer is the need to relocate. As illustrated here, women do not need to change residence as much as men do in this offender class. This is because the female serial murderer draws less attention to herself and to the death of the victim. The murders she commits are considerably less obvious. She often can effectively explain the sudden disappearance of an individual from the trusted perspective of someone who was usually in close contact. The male serial murderer, on the other hand, is more likely to kill people in different communities, towns, cities, or states/provinces if he wishes to avoid detection. He usually kills strangers and therefore is not in a position whereby he can deflect attention away from the sudden disappearance of the victim.

Serial murders by women are often accompanied by the secondary crime of theft and ultimately fraud. Those by men are most often accompanied by sexual assault. However, it has been also noted that neither the male nor female serial murderers kill in order to commit these secondary offenses. These other crimes are perpetrated because there is an opportunity to do so. To take another's life seems to be the primary motivating force behind the murder. There are also other similarities between male and female serial murderers. Both plan "traps" whereby the murderer could take advantage of the victim. Men more often stalk their victims at various locations *(2)*, whereas women are more likely to lure the victim to a single location. In either situation, the murderer rarely has control of who falls into this trap. Each victim is chosen as the opportunity for the murderer presents itself. The motives behind setting the traps, by the male or female murderer, are personal and therefore undetectable to the public.

The research presented in this chapter supports findings of a smaller study conducted by Keeney and Heide *(21)*. Although they looked at the cases of only 14 women, they found that most used some form of poison, rather than more aggressive methods of killing. Women were more likely to lure their victims rather than stalk them, and the reasons for killing differed markedly from those of men. These researchers found that women were less likely to use torture, and therefore their victims were less likely to be physically damaged than the victims of male killers. Women killed largely for instrumental reasons (e.g., monetary gain) or affective reasons (e.g., achieving some sort of emotional satisfaction from the killings). Absent was the presence of sexual fantasy as a motivating force when committing the homicide.

Finally, it was noted that these particular sex divisions for serial murders are not to be considered descriptive models for these offenses. It is likely that the changing trends in the larger society will affect trends presently existing with regard to serial murder. It is predicted that as the roles of men and women begin to assimilate, moving away from the traditional models, so too will the identifying markers of the male and female serial killers. The murders committed by Aileen Wuornos Pralle, who killed seven men after promising and/or having sexual relations with them, may be foreshadowing this change. This is not to say that the number of female serial killers will eventually equal that of males, but the way and manner in which they murder may become less sex distinctive.

In essence, the patterns identified here, although associated with women, are acknowledged to not be solely in the domain of women. For example,

Dr. Harold Shipman is estimated to have killed 215 patients between 1978 and 1998 *(22)*. More recently, Dr. Sampath Kumar Reddy, a physician operating in Calcutta, killed five members of his family using lethal overdoses of medication to obtain property *(23)*. Although these men were not able to use their sex to their advantage, they were able to use their role as doctors to hide their activities. Doctors are ascribed many of the role characteristics of women—caring, nurturing—in addition to taking an oath to do no harm. Like the murderer's sex, these assumed attributes can be a powerful cloak that has the potential to mask illicit activity.

Perhaps the strongest observation throughout this work is that the study of crime, in general, has failed to anticipate the role of these women. In its rudimentary form, it has failed to conceptualize female criminal activity in its basic definitional and operational understanding of these phenomena. Initial definitions of this criminal phenomenon give understanding to the predominant and most obvious form. It is not until a crystallizing event occurs that we are forced to shift our gaze in another direction. Such was the service performed by the murders carried out by Aileen Wuornos, who in 1991 the FBI labeled the first female serial murderer. Through her manifestation of hate, she forced those who study serial murder to open their eyes to the serial murdering acts of women before and after her.

CONCLUDING REMARKS AND DIRECTIONS FOR FUTURE RESEARCH

A primary theme that has been emphasized in this chapter is the need for research to be continued in the area of the violent female offender, including acts of serial murder. As previously mentioned, there is a paucity of research in the area of serial murder and women. This is ironic given the amount of research into the area of the serial murdering male offender. Researchers who study female serial murderers, as with those who study other violent female offenders, are often asked about the significance of their research. The argument has been posed that serial murderesses, even more so than the violent female offender, represent a very small proportion of homicide offenses. It is assumed that, because of their small numbers, they are not worthy of study and that any differences found can be handled within the confines of what is currently known about offending men. In the case of serial murder, men also represent a small proportion of overall criminal activity. Why should we spend money on these few men when others could be served more effectively with our attention? Serial murder, given its andocentric definition, has been labeled a potential epidemic that is in need of curbing. Male serial murderers have also been deemed an important subject of study as their crimes represent an extreme form of violence; hence, we can potentially gain insight into less violent forms of serial offending such as rape. Perhaps the study of women who engage in this crime type can illuminate for us other serial offending acts of women.

Detection, and therefore the definition of serial murder, is critical to the apprehension of these dangerous people. It is the apparent random nature of the crime that makes the ability to identify a homicide as the work of a serial murderer very difficult. Part of the difficulty lies in the recognition that there indeed is a larger problem of definition. Although serial murderesses have existed for centuries, as argued throughout this chapter, they have been overlooked or placed in some other category of homicide. Many of these women have been categorized with monikers such as "Black Widow" or "Angel of Death" but have not been considered part of the larger problem of serial murder. Therefore, in the future, an emphasis on incorporating women into the serial murder equation should be implemented.

Although Hickey and Egger have moved in this direction, this was not always the case (2,8). Earlier editions of their books on this subject demonstrate a history of male dominance in this area. The acts of women in this offender class are only now being included, almost gratuitously. These books still predominantly focus on the male form of this crime, not offering clear integration of the actions of women into this offender class. This may be a costly mistake. What this study reveals is that there is a considerable continuity and breadth in the way people kill other people. Those who kill often take advantage of what is available to avoid detection. Sex bias, as a tool used to avoid detection, has been used fairly successfully by many of the women in this study.

By not picking up the challenge to incorporate the murderer's sex more effectively into our detection and explanation of criminal behavior we run a serious disservice to the victims of such perpetrators. Because we have a gendered profile of the serial murderer, we may overlook the most obvious suspect. Belle Gunness, who is estimated to have killed between 13 and 23 victims predominantly in her own family, was accidentally given extra time for her getaway when the investigation automatically turned to the male farmhand she had hired instead of Belle. Marybeth Tinning, who suffocated eight of her nine children, was permitted to kill one after the other because investigating personnel preferred to accept that these deaths were a phenomenal coincidence rather than the acts of a mother who simply got irritated with her children. Vera Renzci, who killed 35 men, including two husbands and eventually her own son to avoid detection, was able to purchase locally 35 personally engraved zinc boxes about the size of a coffin in which to place her victims. She rationalized the purchases to the public by telling them she was using them to collect a dowry for each new suitor. No one looked for the men she killed because assumptions about her sex and her ability to simply "not get a man" masked her actions. Orphanages where most of the children were murdered after they were abandoned by family members, such as those run by Lila Young in Canada and by Amelia Dyer in the United States, were allowed to continue to operate. The regulatory forces that watched such facilities refused to see that the children were being killed, not adopted *(24)*.

Although I have only mentioned a few cases here, all 102 women in this study had in common that they were seen as women first, and as such were considered incapable of committing violent crime. Because of this, their victim count is much higher than estimated by others. As Kim Rossmo so keenly pointed out *(25)*, the average kill ratio for these women was estimated at one offender for every 20 victims. In his study looking at FBI data, he found that male serial killers, on average, killed 13 victims *(24)*. Understanding that these are only approximations, and that data in this area are somewhat problematic, it still appears that for those who come to the public's attention women historically appear to have been able to get away with more murder largely because of their ability to artfully hide behind presumptions of the "gentler sex."

REFERENCES

1. Leyton, E. (1986). *Hunting Humans: The Rise of the Modern Multiple Murderer.* Toronto: McClelland-Bantam.
2. Hickey, E. W. (2006). *Serial Murderers and Their Victims.* (4th ed.). Belmont, CA: Wadsworth.
3. Wilson, C., & Seaman, D. (1990). *The Sexual Killers: A Study in the Psychology of Violence.* London: W. H. Allen.
4. Egger, S. A. (1984). A working definition of serial murder and the reduction of linkage blindness. *Journal of Police Science and Administration,* 12, 348–357.
5. Keeney, B. T., & Heide, K. M. (1995). Serial murder: A more accurate and inclusive definition. *International Journal of Offender Therapy and Comparative Criminology,* 39, 299–306.
6. Hinch, R. A., & Hepburn, C. (2006). Researching serial murder: Methodological and definitional problems. *Electronic Journal of Sociology,* 3, ISSN: 1198–3655. Retrieved May 1, 2006, from http://www.sociology.org/content/vol003.002/hinch.html.
7. Egger, S. A. (1990). Serial murder: An elusive phenomenon. *Encyclopaedia of Murder* (p. 1984). London: Pan Books.
8. Egger, S. A. (2002). *Killers Among Us: The Examination of Serial Murder and Its Investigations.* Upper Saddle River, NJ: Prentice Hall.

9. Hazelwood, R. (1992, April). Sadistic sexual serial murder. Presented at the First International Conference on Serial and Mass Murder, University of Windsor, Windsor, Ontario, Canada.

10. Warren, J. I., Hazelwood, R. R., & Dietz, P. E. (1996). The sexually sadistic killer. *Journal of Forensic Sciences*, 41, 970–974.

11. Hickey, E. W. (1991). *Serial Murderers and Their Victims*. Pacific Grove, CA: Brooks/Cole.

12. Holmes, S. T., Hickey, E. W., & Holmes, R. (1991). Female serial murderesses: Constructing differentiating typologies. *Journal of Contemporary Criminal Justice*, 7, 246–256.

13. Holmes, R., & DeBurger, J. (1988). *Serial Murder*. Newbury Park, CA: Sage.

14. Holmes, S. T., Hickey, E. W., & Holmes, R. (1992, April). Theoretical construction of a typology of female serial killers and its implication for homicide investigation. Presented at the First International Conference on Serial and Mass Murder, University of Windsor. Windsor, Ontario, Canada.

15. Naffine, N. (1985). The masculinity-femininity hypothesis: A consideration of the gender-based personality theories of female crime. *British Journal of Criminology*, 25, 365–381.

16. Naffine, N. (1987) *Female Crime: The Construction of Women in Criminology*. Sydney: Allen & Unwin.

17. Smart, C. (1979). The new female criminal: Reality or myth? *British Journal of Criminology*, 19, 50–59.

18. Hatch, A., & Faith, K. (1990). The female offender in Canada: A statistical profile. *Canadian Journal of Women and the Law*, 3, 432–456.

19. Box, S., & Hale, C. (1984). Liberation/emancipation, economic marginalization, or less chivalry: The relevance of three theoretical arguments to female crime patterns in England and Wales, 1951–1980. *Criminology*, 2, 473–497.

20. Simpson, S. S. (1989). Feminist theory, crime, and justice. *Criminology*, 7, 605–631.

21. Keeney, B. T., & Heide, K. M. (1994). Gender differences in serial murderers: A preliminary analysis. *Journal of Interpersonal Violence*, 9, 383–398.

22. Serial killer 'Dr. Death' murdered 215, inquiry finds (2002, July 19). Canadian Broadcasting Corporation. Retrieved May 1, 2006 from http://www.cbc.ca/story/news/national/2002/07/19/drdeath_020719.html.

23. Venkataraman, R. (2005, September 16) Life term for killer doctor. *The Telegraph: Calcutta India*. Retrieved May 1, 2006 from http://www.telegraphindia.com/1050916/asp/nation/story_5245774.asp.

24. Scott, H. (2005). *The Female Serial Murderer: A Sociological Study of Homicide and the 'Gentler Sex.'* Lewiston, NY: Mellen Press.

25. Rossmo, D. K., & Davies, A. (2001). Stealth predator patterns. *Crime Mapping News*, 3, 6–7.

Chapter 11

Anatomy of a Mass Murder
Psychological Profile of Martin Bryant and the Port Arthur Massacre

Ian Sale

Abstract

The Port Arthur Massacre represents one of the most notorious mass murder incidents wherein a single offender killed 35 persons and injured numerous others. Mass murderers predominantly either commit suicide or are slain by law enforcement officers during their attempted arrest. In an exceptional circumstance the perpetrator of the Port Arthur Massacre was apprehended alive. The following chapter provides rare insight into the circumstance of the Port Arthur Massacre as well as the characteristics of Martin Bryant by the forensic psychiatrist involved in his apprehension by police and then later charged to undertake psychiatric evaluation of Bryant for court proceedings.

INTRODUCTION: ANATOMY OF A MASSACRE

The island state of Tasmania (Australia) was previously known as Van Diemen's Land, a British colony established in 1803 primarily as a remote and forbidding place to send convicts sentenced to transport. Within this feared destination, colonial administrators established a further penal settlement at Port Arthur on Tasman Peninsula, a prison for convicts who further offended

From: *Serial Murder and the Psychology of Violent Crimes*
Edited by: R. N. Kocsis © Humana Press, Totowa, NJ

after transport. Port Arthur was also used to detain political prisoners such as Irish nationalists and the Tolpuddle Martyrs.

The prison at Port Arthur closed in 1877. A sinister collection of ruins in an exceptionally scenic setting, Port Arthur soon became a tourist attraction and remains a major drawcard to the present. On Sunday April 28th, 1996, Martin Bryant, a 29-year-old unemployed single man living alone in the northern suburbs of Hobart, traveled to Tasman Peninsula, a 90-minute drive to the east. He traveled alone. His car contained three firearms, a quantity of ammunition, a knife, a jerry can of petrol, rope and handcuffs, and a video camera.

He had spent the previous night with his girlfriend Petra. She was several years younger and had grown up in a rural area. Her life had been "sheltered." Bryant was her first boyfriend. Bryant sent her home early in the morning, telling her that there was something he had to do. She noticed nothing unusual in his behavior prior to her departure.

After interrupting his journey to have a cup of coffee and buy a cigarette lighter (he was a nonsmoker), he arrived at Seascape, a bed and breakfast facility, a short distance north of Port Arthur. There he murdered the couple who owned and operated Seascape. He then continued his journey, traveling to a small farm at Palmer's Lookout south of Port Arthur where he inquired after a local woman. Luckily for her, she was away.

Bryant then drove to the Port Arthur historic site, paid for an entry ticket, and drove to a car park area. He purchased a meal at the Broad Arrow Café, which he consumed on an outside deck. There was some conversation with other visitors. He made remarks about wasps and Japanese that puzzled the other visitors. A short time later he reentered the café, removed a semiautomatic firearm from a sports bag, and started shooting at visitors and staff.

The café and associated souvenir shop were crowded with tourists. Nineteen died, and several others were wounded. The shooting continued in the car park outside the café. He then returned to his car and drove away from historic site area. On the exit road, he shot and killed a woman and two young children fleeing the scene. He then shot four elderly tourists at the historic site entrance. He abandoned his car but commandeered another. He then held up a young couple at a nearby service station. The man was forced into the boot of the car. His companion was shot and killed. Bryant then drove away from Port Arthur, firing at oncoming cars. He returned to the Seascape bed and breakfast, where he took shelter after setting fire to the commandeered escape car.

During a homicidal spree that ended where it started, the Seascape bed and breakfast, 35 people died. The final fatality was the young man taken captive at the service station. A siege developed at the Seascape. Police were held at bay by Bryant's powerful weaponry and by their uncertainty about whether hostages remained alive. There had been some telephone conversations with police, but these soon came to an end when the cordless phone battery failed. He gave his name as "Jamie." Other than a demand for a helicopter, his conversations were inane and child-like. His high-pitched voice and fatuous conversation were a source of perplexity to police personnel who had determined that they were dealing with a 29-year-old man who, according to his family, suffered from schizophrenia.

Shortly after sunrise on the following day Bryant set fire to the building. The fire spread quickly in the timber dwelling. Bryant was forced out by the heat and overpowered by special operations police. He suffered extensive burns and required hospital care. Several months later Bryant was put on trial. He faced a number of charges including 35 counts of murder. He was convicted and sentenced to life imprisonment.

STUDY OF MASS MURDERERS

Although there have been far worse atrocities in areas of civil or ethnic conflict, such as Bosnia or East Timor, Bryant's actions on that day constituted the worst mass murder incident that Australia has seen. It was one of several civilian mass murder incidents in a number of countries and occurred only a few weeks after a horrifying incident in Scotland when Thomas Hamilton entered a kindergarten where he shot and killed 16 children and a teacher before killing himself.

Most perpetrators of mass killings are either killed by law enforcement personnel or commit suicide. Bryant is one of the few survivors. Unfortunately, Bryant has for the most part given misleading information about his activities and intentions on that day or has refused interviews altogether.

Although most mass homicide incidents have occurred in the United States, almost all Western nations have been affected by what appears to be an accelerating trend *(1)*. Attempts have been made to classify these horrific events and their perpetrators. These classifications have been based on chronology (mass killing, spree killing, serial killing), setting (family, cult, workplace, school), or presumed motive (criminal expediency, family annihilation, sociopolitical).

Many of these incidents are highly personal and idiosyncratic in motivation, described by Mullen *(2)* as autogenic or self-generating. One subtype of the autogenic killer is a so-called pseudo-commando, a male (almost always) who is preoccupied with weaponry and militaria *(3)*.

It might be questioned whether there is utility in developing a typology for a statistically rare event. Typologies tend to emphasize areas of similarity between different phenomena. Sometimes careful study of a single case is more instructive. With this in mind, this chapter endeavors to provide a detailed account of Bryant and his background. This information was derived from access to material assembled during the police investigation and from interviews of Bryant, family members, and associates. Bryant was interviewed by the writer on two occasions during 1996. He has refused further interviews.

Martin Bryant: An Offender Profile

Martin Bryant was the older of two children. The pregnancy, birth, and neonatal period were unremarkable; and, other than language, most developmental milestones were acquired at age-appropriate times. Although his father later suffered a depressive disorder, there is no other family history of psychiatric disorder. Speech acquisition was delayed, prompting his family to seek professional assistance. He was prone to nocturnal enuresis until late childhood.

His father was an English immigrant, by all accounts an industrious and reliable man, a good provider for his household. The household was conventional and middle class, although perhaps a little insular. From the outset, Bryant's behavior at school was a cause of concern. He was described as restless, disruptive, and attention seeking. He struggled to keep up. His relationships with other children were a particular source of difficulty. He was often aggressive and seemed to lack the capacity to form friendships. Assessment by educational psychologists identified problems with language and numeracy skills, working memory, and impulse control. His behavioral problems were beyond the capacity of some school environments, and he was eventually moved to an "opportunity class."

Bryant's behavioral problems caused increasing difficulties in the household, particularly his conduct toward his younger sister. In an attempt to manage a deteriorating situation, Bryant's father ceased work to care for his son; and for a period the family split into two households, father and son residing in a holiday home on Tasman Peninsula.

Bryant senior attempted to occupy his son's time by developing a role in the local community—gardening, selling vegetables, home maintenance. Through these activities they came to know a wealthy, eccentric, and never-married woman named Helen Harvey. This woman was a beneficiary of the founder of a lottery company and had never worked. She had sufficient funds to be able to follow various eccentric whims, notably keeping a large number of domestic dogs and cats, a cause of concern to local residents and municipal authorities.

Following her mother's death, Helen Harvey invited Bryant to board with her. He became her companion. It was a strategy that reduced the pressure on the Bryant family, and it was a source of support to Helen Harvey, who feared living alone. The relationship was, as far as is known, asexual, akin to that between a maiden aunt and a favored nephew. Ms. Harvey's wish to keep a range of animals led to her spending increasing amounts of time at a small farm, accompanied by Martin Bryant. A menagerie of animals including horses, dogs, poultry, and even a pig became part of this unusual household.

In October 1992 Helen Harvey and Martin Bryant were involved in a serious motor vehicle accident near her farm. Helen Harvey was killed, and Bryant suffered a fractured cervical spine. He made a full recovery, although hospital staff had regarded his behavior as odd. His family told them that he suffered from schizophrenia, an opinion that was likely derived from the family doctor. His odd manner was not further investigated, and he was discharged after making a full recovery.

A psychiatrist once examined Bryant during adolescence. Unfortunately records of this assessment no longer exist, and the psychiatrist no longer recalled the contact. It is suspected that the psychiatrist may have warned the family that Bryant's behavioral problems could represent nonspecific prodromal features of schizophrenia. However, no formal diagnosis of schizophrenia was made, and there were no aspects of Bryant's conduct that suggested the presence of psychotic illness. Nonetheless, the family believed him to be schizophrenic and later informed police that this was the case.

Bryant was distressed by the death of Helen Harvey. He became subject to sleep disturbance and nightmares and was briefly prescribed medication by the family doctor. His behavior became disruptive again. There was increasing friction with neighbors. His disinhibited remarks to women and children caused particular concern.

The death of Helen Harvey led Bryant's father to become involved again. Once again he became his son's "carer." He coped poorly with this and became increasingly depressed. Despite treatment from his doctor, his situation worsened, and he committed suicide by drowning during August 1993. As a result, the two individuals who had some capacity to exert a restraining influence upon Bryant's conduct were now dead.

Martin Bryant was the major beneficiary of Harvey's estate. Although his affairs were managed by a trustee, he received substantial amounts of money on a regular basis. He also inherited Harvey's house, vehicles, and chattels. Bryant was now free of economic restraints. Previously he had been reliant on welfare payments or Harvey's generosity. He was able to pursue a number of whims.

He traveled extensively. His wardrobe expanded. He paid for prostitutes. He bought a boat.

Martin Bryant also started to buy firearms. Although there had been occasions during his adolescence when he had caused problems with an air rifle, there appears to be no particular interest in firearms or militaria until after Harvey's death.

A factor that may have prompted Bryant's interest in firearms was the location of a gun dealer only a few blocks from his residence. At that time, the regulation of firearm ownership in Tasmania was somewhat laissez-faire. Bryant quietly acquired several powerful firearms and ammunition. Three of these weapons were later to be taken to Tasman Peninsula.

Despite his affluence, traveling, and a series of girlfriends, Bryant remained troubled about his father's death. There is no indication that these concerns were disclosed to others, but later behavior and conversations indicate that he developed a particular and mistaken belief about the cause of his father's distress and subsequent suicide. Some years previously, Bryant senior had wished to acquire two particular properties on Tasman Peninsula. However, in both instances the owners declined to sell. They were the Martins, the proprietors of Seascape, who became the first victims, and the woman who was absent when Martin Bryant came to call at her farm.

Bryant appears to have become convinced that these early real estate setbacks were the reason for his father's depression and suicide. This suggests that the massacre at Port Arthur is likely to have started as an act of vengeance for the loss of a father.

No one other than Bryant knows whether he planned also to visit the Port Arthur historic site or the idea evolved as the day progressed. It is believed that he expected to die at Port Arthur, to be shot down by police or security staff. However, there was no opposition. The site had only one security officer, but his main task was to regulate parking. In fact, he challenged Bryant about parking incorrectly but was ignored. In any event, he was unarmed. The nearest police were some distance away. Had they been present, the firepower brought by Bryant would have overwhelmed them—two semiautomatic rifles and a semiautomatic shotgun.

Bryant may have been surprised to have "survived" and may have had no formed intention beyond going to the historic site for a final shoot-out. It is likely that Bryant again expected to die during the subsequent siege at the Seascape. Frustrated when police maintained a safe perimeter, Bryant set fire to the premises, perhaps as a suicide attempt or perhaps an attempt to force police intervention and provoke a shoot-out. If so, this plan also failed. He was forced to flee after incurring significant burns to his back, leading to his capture and arrest.

Clinical assessment of Bryant was hindered by his limited cooperation. No major mental disorder was evident. He was considered to be of borderline intelligence. His personality was marked by a degree of obsessionality and rigidity. Social skills were poor. There were aspects of his development and behavior that raised the question of a pervasive developmental disorder of Asperger type. He was examined by a number of psychiatrists and psychologists. There was never any question of an insanity defense.

CONCLUSIONS

Dr. Paul Mullen, a psychiatrist from the neighboring state of Victoria, who had also examined Bryant, has remarked how, following a mass killing, mental health services are inundated by referrals of angry men who have threatened to behave in a similar manner. He described them for the most part as self-dramatizers, avid for attention. The writer's experience is similar. The phrase "Do a Bryant" crept into the local vocabulary. Even more striking was the frequency with which concerned schools, families, and welfare authorities sought guidance about children and adolescents they perceived as having similar characteristics to those of Bryant.

For the most part, their perceptions were reasonably accurate. Bryant, although undoubtedly unusual, was not exceptional. There are any number of young boys with social and learning difficulties who could, in certain circumstances, present a risk. Bryant clearly shared some features of other mass killers *(4)*. He was a loner, was obsessive, harbored a grudge, and developed an interest in firearms. However, what made the Port Arthur massacre possible was not so much Bryant's personality and developmental problems but other almost unique circumstances. These led to a situation where Bryant, who had few internal restraints, was now free of external restraints such as his family, his finances, or social agencies.

Bryant had no prior police convictions. Although qualifying for a disability pension during adolescence, he was unknown to disability or mental health services. Remarkably, he was known to intelligence services. He had once traveled alone to the United Kingdom. He stayed only briefly but visited Hereford where there were sensitive military facilities. His presence in Hereford and his unusual demeanor were a cause of curiosity and concern.

In ordinary circumstances, an individual as disabled and unemployable as Bryant, with limited social skills and exhausted family resources, would be known to, if not reliant on, community services. Furthermore, it is unlikely that such an individual would have been able to acquire assault weapons, even in a lax regulatory environment such as pre-1996 Tasmania without others becoming aware and presumably alarmed. However, other than the gun dealer who supplied him with weapons and ammunition, no one was aware that he was quietly acquiring an arsenal.

Weapons were concealed. Police later found another firearm hidden inside a piano. Although the Port Arthur massacre appears to have started as an act of revenge, an intersection of exceptional circumstances appear to be more of greater importance than the psychopathology and malice of a particular individual. Of these circumstances, only one factor was remediable—regulation of firearm ownership *(5)*. As a result of the Port Arthur shootings, the state and federal governments passed gun control laws that were among the strictest in the world. There have been no further mass killings in Australia since 1996.

REFERENCES

1. Linquist, O., & Lidberg, L. (1998). Violent mass shootings in Sweden from 1960 to 1995: profiles, patterns and motives. *American Journal of Forensic Medicine and Pathology*, 19(1), 34–45.
2. Mullen, P. E. (2004). The autogenic (self-generated) massacre. *Behavorial Sciences & the Law*, 22(3), 311–323.
3. Dietz, P. E. (1986). Mass, serial and sensational homicides. *Bulletin of the New York Academy of Medicine*, 62(5), 477–491.
4. Meloy, J. R., Hempel, A. G., Gray, B. T., Mohandie, K., Shiva, A., & Richards, T. C. (2004). A comparative analysis of North American adolescent and adult mass murderers. *Behavioral Sciences & the Law*, 22(3), 291–309.
5. Ozanne-Smith, J., Ashby, K., Newstead, S., Stathakis, V. Z., & Chapperton, A. (2004). Firearm related deaths: the impact of regulatory reform. *Injury Prevention*, 10(5), 280–286.

PART III

INVESTIGATIVE CONSIDERATIONS TO SERIAL VIOLENT CRIMES

Chapter 12

Blundering Justice
The Schiedam Park Murder
Peter J. van Koppen

Abstract

The murder of a young girl in 2000 in a park in the Dutch town Schiedam and the attempted murder of her friend resulted in a miscarriage of justice that shook Dutch society. After a description of the case, an attempt is made to analyze the factors that caused this miscarriage of justice and other dubious convictions in The Netherlands. Many factors that have been described in Anglo-Saxon legal systems that contribute to miscarriages of justice apply likewise to the Dutch legal system. Some do not, such as jury decision making and plea bargaining. Some factors are typical for an inquisitorial system as The Netherlands. Notably, the compromising nature of Dutch society that has too much trust in the work of the police and the prosecution contributed to the wrongful conviction in the Schiedam Park Murder. This is a problem because it can be argued that the quality of the police and the prosecution has decreased in recent decades. It is concluded that because of the growing role of the European Court of Human Rights that causes a mixture of accusatorial and inquisitorial elements to be introduced in the legal systems of its member states, comparative research is needed into factors that promote miscarriages of justice in different legal systems.

INTRODUCTION

On June 22, 2000, two children were in the Beatrixpark in Schiedam, a town adjacent to Rotterdam in The Netherlands. Nienke, 10 years old, and her 11-year-old friend Maikel were playing in a typical Dutch setting—a playing apparatus mimicking a dyke. After they had done this for some 20 minutes,

From: *Serial Murder and the Psychology of Violent Crimes*
Edited by: R. N. Kocsis © Humana Press, Totowa, NJ

they guessed it was time to go home for dinner and so asked an old gentleman the time; it was 5:15 pm. On the way to their bicycles a young man grabbed them from their necks and walked them some 90 meters to bushes. There he strangled both Maikel and Nienke. Maikel survived by acting dead; Nienke, however, was killed. The killer first tried to undress the children but was unsuccessful in doing so. He ordered the children to undress themselves and stabbed Maikel several times in the area around his neck. Finally, he strangled both children using the 100 cm long shoelaces of the army boots Maikel was wearing.

After the killer left, Maikel stepped out of the bushes, naked with the shoelace and dangling boot still around his neck. He walked to a man who was standing on the bridge near the bushes. That man stopped a passing cyclist, Kees Borsboom, who then called the police using his cell phone.

During the 2 days following the murder Maikel was interviewed twice by the police in hospital, where he stayed for a few days because of his stab wounds. In two interviews he told police what happened and gave a description of the killer: a man between 20 and 35 years, 1.80 meters tall, extremely pale, with a very spotty and unkempt face, the pustules on the attacker's face were scratched open with blood and pus coming out. As it later turned out, the statements by Maikel were extremely accurate. The offender description was right to the point of even describing the man's rather special face *(1)*. Apart from Maikel, there were no direct eyewitnesses of the man taking two children to the bushes or seeking to murder the two.

Some weeks before the murder Kees Borsboom, the man who called the police, asked a boy in the same park whether he wanted to earn 25 guilders. Although the boy said "no," Borsboom said: "If you jerk me off, I'll give you 25 guilders." The boy ran home. After the murder the boy saw Borsboom again, went home, and collected his father. His father, a police officer, identified himself to Borsboom and asked him what he had done to his son. Borsboom said sorry immediately and told the police officer that he was in therapy for his behavior and that he would never do this again. Nevertheless, the men agreed to meet at the police station a few days later. Before that meeting, the police officer typed in Borsboom's name in the police computer and saw he was a witness in the Schiedam Park murder case. From that moment on, Borsboom was the prime suspect for the murder. He was prosecuted for the murder and convicted both by the District Court and the Court of Appeals. He was sentenced to 18 years in prison, followed by compulsory assignment to a forensic mental hospital, which in this case is effectively a life sentence. Borsboom did not fit the offender's description given by Maikel at all because he was, in fact, innocent.

ABSENCE OF MISCARRIAGES OF JUSTICE IN THE NETHERLANDS

Dutch lawyers typically think that miscarriages of justice only happen abroad, especially in the United Kingdom and the United States. Cases such as the Birmingham Six (2–5) also have a familiar ring in The Netherlands. Indeed, the number of described miscarriages of justice in Anglo-Saxon countries suggests that such incidents considerably outnumber Dutch cases (e.g., 6–33). Until the Schiedam Park murder the history of known Dutch miscarriages of justice ended somewhere around 1930. Miscarriages of justice were believed to occur in systems with juries and elected legal officials.

My colleagues and I during the early 1990s frequently contested this opinion *(34,35)*, but we could not be sure that all the cases of wrongful convictions we found and described were certain miscarriages of justice. To stay on the safe side, we called them dubious convictions—convictions based on too little evidence. To identify a miscarriage of justice one must know for sure that someone else other than the original convict committed the crime or that the crime never occurred (or at least more sure than the fact finder in the original conviction).

As a consequence, we always had to rely on detailed analyses of the causes of miscarriages of justice in the English-speaking world to discuss Dutch cases (good examples are *6,18,19,36–38*). An interesting question arose about what special features of an inquisitorial system might promote miscarriages of justice (see, for a comparison *39,40*)?

The Schiedam Park Murder provided an opportunity for such detailed analysis. It is just a singular case study, but it is also one with much more opportunity for analysis than one normally gets. During the course of the trial at the Appellate Court, several professional individuals who were in some way or another involved in the case—I promised them anonymity—asked me to write a letter to the Appellate Court to explain that an innocent man might have been convicted. The problem was that all of these individuals, including me, had been involved in only a small part of the case. I asked the attorney of the accused to give me a full copy of the rather lengthy case dossier, containing some 750 documents. With the assistance of students, I undertook an analysis of the same material on which Borsboom had been convicted by the District Court and by the Appellate Court (and nothing more than that) *(41)*. We concluded that the probability that Borsboom was innocent was higher that the probability of him being guilty. Half a year before the publication of the book—by then Borsboom's appeal to the Dutch Supreme Court had been turned down—I sent an earlier draft to the Chief Prosecutor-General, the head of all prosecutors in The Netherlands, to no avail.

During the summer of 2004, however, the real killer confessed. He had been arrested for two violent rapes in other towns and while being interviewed spontaneously admitted to the Schiedam Park murder. It soon became clear, through DNA matches and his intimate knowledge of the case, that this was indeed a true confession.

Although it took the prosecution another 5 months to free Borsboom, it caused such a big row in the country that the new Chief Prosecutor-General ordered a thorough investigation of the conduct of the police and the prosecution in this case by Appellate Court prosecutor Frits Posthumus with the aid of a police squad headed by Theo Vermeulen. This resulted in an extremely candid and, for the police and prosecution, damaging report *(42)*. Although Posthumus in his reports sticks very much to what happened in this particular case, much can be learned about how more general factors influenced the generation of this miscarriage of justice *(43,44)*. Indeed, this case caused such a big shock and demonstrated so much failure on the part of the police and prosecution that the Minister of Justice proposed an improvement program for the police and the prosecution of an unprecedented scale *(45)*. Also, he set up a special investigation committee to look into all other cases that my colleagues and I, but also others, proposed as potential miscarriages of justice.

After describing some special features of the Dutch criminal legal system, I shall explain the mishandling of evidence in the Schiedam Park Murder and proceed to discuss the factors that may have caused or contributed to this miscarriage of justice.

DUTCH LEGAL SYSTEM

Lay participation in decision making in criminal cases is unknown in the Dutch legal system. All cases in The Netherlands are tried by professional judges, with minor cases by judges sitting alone; the more major cases are heard by a bench court consisting of three judges. Plea bargaining is also unknown: All cases are tried in full. District court decisions can be appealed to the Appellate Court—without leave to appeal—where the case is tried de novo (for descriptions in English on Dutch criminal procedure see *46–49*).

Dutch criminal procedure is dominated by written records. All officials involved—the police, the prosecution, the judge-commissioner (*rechter-commissaris*, or judge of instruction), the courts, and the defense—produce written records and documents that become part of the official case dossier. Dossiers include all important sources of evidence and information. In court, interactions between judges, prosecutor, accused, and counsel focus on evaluating the documents in the dossier.

In general, the parties make little use of their right to summon witnesses or experts at a trial *(49)*. Instead, experts write reports, and witness statements come to the courts in written form. Witness statements are written down by police officers; this document is formally a sworn statement taken by the police officers of what they saw and heard the witness do and say. The same applies to the suspect's statements. The police reports are almost never a full literal record of what the witness or suspect said; instead, it is a summary, usually with much police lingo and often full of grammatical and spelling errors. The witness statements are almost always written down as a monologue of the witness, in which the questions are either left out or are represented as something the witness said. "You show me a picture of a male individual on which I can see on the reverse the identification number.... On this picture I recognize the man who sold me the stolen vehicle."

This is a practice that originates from the French occupation of The Netherlands and nicely fits into the Dutch habit of doing things as efficiently as possible. In cases with clear-cut evidence this gives the attorneys, the prosecution, and the courts a lot less to read. In less clear-cut cases, however, it may become important what questions have been asked exactly and how the witness replied. It may make a big difference whether the police officer asked: "What brand was the getaway car?" and the witness answered: "I am sure it was a Volkswagen Rabbit." or that the exchange went as follows: "Was the getaway car a Volkswagen Rabbit?" "Yes." Both result in the sentence in the report: "I saw the getaway car was a Volkswagen Rabbit."

In more recent years the police sometimes tape important witness and suspect statements. Exceptions are interviews of children, usually in sexual abuse cases. These are always recorded on videotape in a special child-friendly studio to minimize the need for a second or third interview of the child.

In the Schiedam Park murder, the interviews with suspect Borsboom were not recorded until *after* the weekend he made his confessions. All interviews of the young victim Maikel were recorded, the first two in the hospital on audiotape and the rest in a child-friendly interview studio. None of the other statements of witnesses were recorded on tape.

The role of the prosecutor in Dutch criminal procedure is important. In Dutch legal doctrine, the prosecutor is a magistrate. For that reason, he is named *officer van Justitie* (officer of justice). He serves several roles in the proceedings. First, the prosecutor is formally responsible for the investigation by the police. Second, a prosecutor should bring a case to court only if he himself is convinced that the accused is indeed guilty. Therefore, it is not uncommon in The Netherlands that the prosecutor demands an acquittal at trial. That happens at the District Court level for a practical reason. The summons to court are served by the prosecution administration well before the prosecutor starts preparing the case. If he then concludes that there is, unlike the opinion of the police, too little evidence for a conviction, the case cannot be redrawn any more and an acquittal must be demanded. At the appellate level, a demand for an acquittal by the prosecution reflects a difference of opinion between the lower level prosecutor, who appealed the District Court's verdict, and the prosecutor, who handles the case at the Appellate Court.

The prosecutor is also responsible for the completeness of the dossier. This function, which in practice is served by the police, is central to Dutch criminal procedure. If a prosecutor says in court that the dossier is complete, it is considered complete without further ado *(50)*.

Not everything the police gather goes into the dossier. The Code of Criminal Procedure specifies that the dossier has to encompass all "relevant" documents. What is considered relevant appears to differ from prosecutor to prosecutor. Sometimes relevant is interpreted as "just all incriminating evidence." In the Schiedam Park murder, for instance, it became clear from some loose remarks contained in the dossier that there had been an unknown number of other suspects. Why these men came under suspicion at one point in time, what investigations had been conducted on them, whether they had been in custody, and why they were not considered a suspect any more remained completely hidden from the court and the defense. In a weak evidence case such as the one against Borsboom, this information, of course, can be highly relevant. Maybe there were more serious suspects among them.

Dutch judges enjoy wide discretionary powers in choosing the type and severity of punishment *(51)*. The penal code specifies minimum terms for punishments in general (e.g., 1-day imprisonment) and specific maximum terms for each offense in the penal code. Bench courts confer in chambers about the guilt and the sentence in one session. Dissenting opinions are forbidden, and the secret of the chamber is very strict. That is the reason there has been no public review of the conduct of the Rotterdam District Court and The Hague Appellate Court who convicted Borsboom on such slim evidence. There have been internal reviews, but presidents of these two courts only publicly described how these reviews were done, not what the results were *(52,53)*.

CONVICTION IN THE SCHIEDAM PARK MURDER

Borsboom was convicted by the Rotterdam District Court and the The Hague Appellate Court on virtually the same evidence. Please note that Dutch courts have to report the evidence on which they base their decisions in a written decision. The strongest evidence against Borsboom consisted of the confession he made to the police.

In fact, Borsboom was innocent, and the courts could have known it. In his first statements, Maikel gave an offender description that was very different from how Borsboom looked. Moreover, Maikel described in detail the expression of the face of the killer while he was strangling him. So, we may assume that Maikel had a good look at the killer. Right after he came out of the bushes he saw Borsboom while he was phoning the police alarm number. In his statements, Maikel also described this man. At no point in time did he ever say that the man phoning was the same man as the killer.

The time frame of that afternoon prevented Borsboom from committing the murder. He was employed by a firm in a nearby industrial park. There the working day ended when the packages had been loaded into the trucks. That day two trucks arrived to collect packages. The tachographs of the trucks indicate that one left at 5:18 p.m. and the other at 5:21 p.m. For a strong biker it takes 11 minutes to ride from the industrial park to the park where the children were attacked. So, Borsboom could have arrived there at 5:29 p.m. at the earliest. By then, however, two men who were walking their dogs were standing next to an adult bicycle near the bushes where the children were attacked, right on the route the killer walked with them. We only know this not because the two men told the police but also because a third witness described these two men to the police and was very sure about the time he saw them there: He punched a time-clock when leaving his work and rode straight home, where he arrived at 5:35 p.m. Soon after that, the men with the two dogs passed the bushes where the killer was attacking Maikel and Nienke. Maikel by then was pretending to be dead but looked out of the bushes with his head turned away from Nienke and the killer. Later he described the black and white dog of one of the men he saw passing. In short, Borsboom just did not have the time to commit the murder.

There was no technical evidence presented at trial that pointed to Borsboom. DNA was found under the nails and on the rubber boot of Nienke that belonged to someone other than Nienke or Maikel, an unknown male person. Note that the children had been playing with water for some 20 minutes; and because Nienke was biting her nails, she must have had clean fingernails. Thus, this DNA must have been collected after the children played in the park. Nevertheless, the expert of the Nederlands Forensisch Instituut (NFI; The Dutch Forensic Laboratory) told the court at trial that this DNA might very well come from a boy at school. It did not, as will become clear soon.

During a weekend in September Borsboom made confessions. His interrogations were not recorded, nor was his attorney present, although the attorney asked for that and the prosecutor refused. Borsboom later contended that the interrogations were made under extreme duress. Of course, the opposite was reported by the two interrogating police officers. At the time, there were indications that Borsboom may have been right. The report by the police officers of the first confession allegedly made on a Saturday night was written only some weeks later. That is very strange behavior for police officers, because in such a major case the first thing a police squad chief asks for after a confession is the police report, preferably also with the signature of the suspect. On Sunday morning Borsboom was interviewed again but now withdrew his confession. There was no report made of that interview, the police officers admitted later. That afternoon, Borsboom confessed again. From Monday morning onward Borsboom has maintained his innocence.

His confessions should have been suspect at that time. Not because Borsboom said they were false—a lot of suspects say so afterward—but because he told a story the details of which so differed from that of Maikel's account that the police should never have trusted his confessions. Instead, they did not trust Maikel. The police hired educationalist Ruud Bullens to give guidance with the interviewing of Maikel and to serve the interests of Maikel during the interviews. Almost from the beginning, they did not trust Maikel very much, even long before Borsboom had been arrested. The major reason for that seems to be that as Maikel's intelligence appeared high they considered him a very odd boy. Maikel had displayed behavior that was considered odd as well: He did not yell at any time during the attack, even though a lot of people were passing the bushes. More important, Bullens told the police that Maikel had "a big secret," without specifying what that secret was and without explaining how he knew. The police suspected that he killed Nienke, stabbed and strangled himself, and then made the knife disappear. The knife has never been found.

After the arrest of Borsboom, the police tried to explain away the big differences between the confessions and the statements by Maikel by strongly interviewing Maikel. The child did not give an inch, so the explaining away had to be done otherwise. It was done, again, using the statements of Bullens and a psychologist who reviewed the tapes of Maikel's interviews. Following their expert reports it was concluded that the perception of Maikel has been so blurred by the high emotional tone of the situation that his statements could not be trusted. Therefore, the police, prosecution, and courts did not trust the offender description given by Maikel and all the parts of his statements that contradicted the confession.

All of this allowed the prosecution to build a case not based on the guilt of Borsboom but on making him look suspicious enough. He still was a pedophile, wasn't he? The impossible time line was masked by an analysis by the prosecution that turned vague on essential points. Because the courts did not appear to read the *dossier*[1] – and as society often has the habit of trusting the prosecution, Borsboom was convicted.

WHAT REALLY HAPPENED IN THE SCHIEDAM PARK MURDER

We had to wait for the real killer to confess and the Posthumus investigation to be published before it became clear that errors had been made and that prosecutors and experts had not accurately assisted the court. The most important diversion of the truth was in fact revealed by the television program *Netwerk* on public television on September 5, 2005. The NFI not only discovered strange male DNA under Nienke's nails and on her boots, it found strange DNA on her bare stomach, her bare shoulder, and, most telling, on the ends of the shoelaces used to strangle Nienke.[2] These were not complete DNA profiles, but the same peaks returned in each of the samples. The experts at the NFI did not agree on what this meant and called in the prosecutors to discuss the matter. The prosecution instructed the NFI experts to leave these profiles outside their report. They acted accordingly. The prosecutor at the Appellate Court even inaccurately represented the situation to the court, saying: "DNA analyses of the shoelace used to kill Nienke did not give any result" [my translation]. Furthermore, the NFI expert told the court that the DNA that was reported—on Nienke's boot and her fingernails—could have come from a boy at school.

The way the prosecution handled the DNA evidence is an example of the compromised nature of the whole investigation and prosecution in this case. The Posthumus report *(42)*, published hastily after the *Netwerk* broadcast on the case, reported a long line of errors that cannot be effectively summarized here. Almost every conceivable error was made. I give only a few examples. The clock of the police incident room was not running on time so there is great confusion about what happened at what time at the crime scene, what police officers arrived at the scene of the crime in what sequence, etc. Three technical forensic detectives were active at the scene, but just one of them was

---

[1] We know that at least the District Court did not read the *dossier* because in the written decision they had a vital and not to be missed point wrong: They were talking about the shoelaces of Nienke as the strangulation means, rather than the shoelaces of Maikel. Whoever had only superficial knowledge of the dossier must have known this difference. Nienke was wearing rubber boots, without laces.

[2] The shoelace used to strangle Maikel had been too tainted with blood from Maikel to allow any useful analysis.

experienced. They employed a video team that never had taken pictures of a crime scene. Far too few photographs were made, usually from the wrong angle and with too much flash light. As a result, much of the crime scene was not photographed or filmed. This was enhanced because the pictures taken from a helicopter got lost.

The police cordon around the crime scene was much too narrow; too many people were roaming around. The police feared that it might start to rain, so they should have set up a tent. Instead, the search was done in great haste. Nienke's body was put in the body bag within the hour, without sampling it. This caused all kinds of traces to mix on her body.

It was not recorded where most things collected at the crime scene were found. If numbered identification shields were used, they had not been disinfected, creating the possibility of contamination. The search went on during the night, without enough light. No search dog was employed in the park.

Several objects got lost, among them the two bicycles of Nienke and Maikel. They had been driven over by a police officer to make room for the ambulance. There was no search for tire tracks, no record of the work of the forensic detectives and unclear drawings were made. Also, there was often an unclear or unknown chain of custody of the objects collected. Most importantly, Maikel's body was not sampled for traces.

The rest of the police investigation continued in the same vein as the work of the forensic detectives. For example, the offender description by Maikel was so special that only a few days after the murder the police released it to the press. A female police officer immediately recognized a friend of her brother from the description *(44)*. She knew he had a history of sexual violence. She delivered this information, including the man's criminal record and a picture of him to the chief of the police squad. Two other tips came in with the same information about the same man—the man who later turned out to be the real killer. By that time, however, the police team was of the opinion that Maikel might be the perpetrator. It took some months before the police started to address these and other tips, but dropped this immediately after Borsboom made his confessions. A professional police team could have solved the case within the week.

THE GENERATION OF MISCARRIAGES OF JUSTICE

Miscarriages of justice are committed by the fact finder, be it judge or jury. The wrong person can be convicted only after the prosecution prosecutes the wrong man. Similarly, the prosecution prosecutes the wrong man only after the police come up with the wrong suspect. Although the judge may be responsible in the end, all miscarriages of justice start at the police investigation level.

Gross *(36)* has described the typical high profile cases that are, he contends, prone to producing miscarriages of justice. These are cases where the pressure on the police and prosecution is high. That pressure may come from the media and the general public but not necessarily. A case such as the Schiedam Park murder is the type of horrible case where police officers do not need outside pressure to be heavily involved in the case. Such cases aided by large police squads, more money, and more time than the average case may amount to more cases being solved. These factors often however, also serve as a handicap to the police: If the victim died, there is no victim statement that can be highly valuable. Often these cases must be solved using indirect evidence, witnesses who were not actual eyewitnesses, and forensic evidence. Such evidence lacks the advantage that actual eyewitnesses give the police, as such witnesses can tell the full story of what happened, often even with the name of the offender *(54)*. This is the difference between *obvious cases* [called self-solvers by Innes, *(55,* pp. 198 ff.)] and *search cases.* Obvious cases are cases in which, for instance, someone is caught in the act, cases in which the perpetrator turns himself in, and cases in which the offender is arrested near the crime scene. In obvious cases, the evidence simply falls into the police's lap. In obvious cases there is a story, a suspect, and evidence that the story is true. Mostly it does not take much trouble to turn this initial situation into the desired situation—into a believable story that is proved by evidence. In contrast, on the other end of the continuum of case complexity are so-called s*earch cases* [called whodunits by Innes *(55,* pp. 198 ff.)] that do not come to the police in the form of a story about what has happened. That story has to be built up through investigation. These cases occur when there is no contact between the offender and the victim or when the victim cannot give a statement, for instance because the victim is missing or has been killed. In search cases the police are faced with only some consequences of the event. From these consequences they have to reason backward about the events that might have caused them. When investigated, these cases are characterized by a broad search for information that can possibly be connected to the crime.

Most of the time, eyewitnesses give a complete story of, for instance, a robbery or an assault. In those cases, the testimony of the witness provides evidence for all aspects of the story. Correspondence between two independent stories offers an even stronger indication of its truth. Unlike witness evidence, physical evidence can never prove an entire story. At most, physical evidence can support or weaken certain aspects of a story. In general, crimes produce few identifiable traces (see also *56*). Moreover, it is seldom possible to reconstruct one specific event solely on the basis of its physical consequences because in principle, physical evidence can be created by many different events. If, for instance, fingerprints of the suspect are found at the scene of the crime, it proves only that he was there sometime in the past, not that he committed the crime. This means that witness testimonies can, in principle, yield far more unique and far more complete support for the story under investigation than the physical evidence found at the crime scene. Complex search cases are typically dominated by the latter type of evidence. The Schiedam Park murder is an extreme example of this type of case. There was only one witness, Maikel (who was not trusted by the police), some indirect witnesses, and no useful forensic traces.

These cases have an additional characteristic. Usually a police squad turns up a large amount of information—an unknown mixture of irrelevant, partly relevant, and relevant information. This information soon creates an overload through which only highly skilled police detectives can find their way. The information overload can cause police detectives to miss important information or misjudge it. If some viable suspect is identified, the advantage is attained that all that information can be put aside and one can focus on what is considered relevant for proving that the suspect is indeed guilty. Then the investigation changes from an offense-driven investigation into a suspect-driven investigation (35, Chapter 5). The distinction between offense-driven and suspect-driven searches is related to the starting point of the investigation. In an offense-driven search the starting point is the crime and the facts related to the crime. The identity of the suspect then is inferred from the facts. In a suspect-driven search someone becomes a suspect, sometimes for no clear reason at all or at least no reason that is explained by the known facts of the crime. Only then is an attempt made to find evidence that links this particular suspect to the crime. Thus, the search is limited right from the start. The relevance of the distinction between offense-driven and suspect-driven investigations lies in the diagnostic value of the resulting evidence. For an offense-driven search, the narrative is the product of an inferential process based on information. For a suspect-driven search, the narrative is the starting point, and the information is its product. During an offense-driven search one collects so much information that the search logically excludes all possible alternative suspects. With a suspect-driven search, one needs only enough information to make the suspect look bad.

A suspect-driven investigation often involves long and frequent interrogations of the suspect, especially if he refuses to confess readily (57,58). That alone raises the probability that the suspect will make a false confession (59–61). The Schiedam Park murder is a good example of a suspect-driven investigation. As soon as Borsboom was identified as a suspect through a "happy" coincidence, the investigation was nothing but suspect-driven. Everything else the police were undertaking at that time, such as following through on tips, was dropped immediately after his confession.

DUTCH FORM OF JUSTICE

The factors involved in generating miscarriages of justice discussed above are common to many jurisdictions. The Schiedam Park murder, however, demonstrated that some may be typical for inquisitorial systems or at least for an inquisitorial system similar to that in The Netherlands. For this discussion, I must delve a little deeper into the Dutch legal culture.

Especially during the first half of the 20th century, Dutch society was strongly divided in so-called *zuilen* (pillars), parts of society that are divided according to religious and political denominations *(62)*. The most important pillars in which Dutch society was divided were Catholics, Protestants, Socialists, and Humanists [an extensive discussion is given by Kossmann *(63,* pp. 567–574)]. None of the pillars constituted a political majority at any point in time. Although these pillars were in some sense incompatible, the country had to be run and thus political and social coalitions between these pillars were always necessary. Thus, to ensure a stable society, the government system was built on negotiation and compromise among the denominations, rather than antagonism among the pillars. This compromising nature—nowadays called the Polder Model—permeated every part of Dutch society, including the legal system *(64)*. The most telling characteristics of the Dutch criminal justice system is the role of the prosecutor and the dominance of the documents in the dossier that I described above. However, there are more typical Dutch inquisitorial characteristics.

Dutch criminal trials are anything but a battle common in accusatory systems. Not so long ago, the Dutch trial was a polite conversation between gentlemen who, although each departing from his own point of view, together were searching for the truth. Involvement of the accused was more formal than practical. The search for truth instead of equality of arms dominated criminal cases. Equality of arms or anything accusatory would ruin the compromising nature of the criminal trial. In recent years this picture has changed somewhat. Especially in high profile cases—usually major drug cases—both the prosecution and the defense attorneys take a harder stance. This kind of behavior is called, by the way, an American form of trial. These changes occurred, although the basic setup of Dutch trials did not change very much.

There are a number of causes for this change. Courts put less trust in the police than they used to. This is the product of the Van Traa parliamentary investigation on police behavior at the beginning of the 1990s *(65)*, which uncovered illegal or semi-illegal police behavior when investigating major drug cases. The same distrust of the police can be seen in the Dutch prosecution arena. For that reason, the prosecution nowadays is much more actively involved in the police investigation in large cases, also as a consequence of the Van Traa Report. Extensive cooperation with the police however, makes the prosecutor less a magistrate in these cases and more a crime fighter. Added to these changes are defense attorneys. During the last decade a specialized criminal bar has developed. These specialized attorneys more often than in the past follow their client's strategy, rather than pursuing their own, their *domus litis*.

The manner of operation of prosecutors also changed because their organization changed. Until some 10 years ago, being magistrates, the Dutch prosecution was an organization that formally fell under the Minister of Justice but in fact was a loose group of more or less independent professionals. Because the Van Traa Report also demonstrated misconduct of prosecutors, tighter organization was demanded. During the mid-1990s the Dutch prosecution was transformed into a strictly hierarchically organized civil service type of organization. The chief prosecutor in each district became much more important, and a College of Prosecutors-General was formed that runs the prosecution service with directives and rules from the government seat, The Hague. In such an organization it is much more important to follow the rules than it is to follow one's own professional judgment, especially in complicated cases where that professional judgment is appropriate.

Police detectives also became less professional. That development in the police was steered by developments in society but also by the police themselves. Until the report *Politie in Verandering* by the Projectgroep Organisatiestructuren (Taskforce Organization Structures) *(66)* Dutch police formed a technocratic organization strongly directed to perform a government task. The report caused, at least within the police, a fundamental change in the traditional manner of thinking about police work and tasks.

During the first decades after World War II the Dutch police could stick to their classic manner of behavior: dutiful enforcement of law conformity. The rapid successions of social changes during and after the 1960s however, necessitated organizational and structural changes in the police. With the traditional police approach, the exercise of authority was justified by legal rules that in turn were seen as the highest norms supporting government behavior and thus also police behavior. The formal goals of police activity were maintaining the law and related to that, maintaining public order. More socially oriented assistance was of lesser importance than maintaining law and order. The dominant police attitudes were detached and reactive. Preventive work by the police was limited to mere public presence.

The absolute and oversimplified application of legal norms before the 1970s left little room for social developments. Police behavior showed a painful lack of flexibility and thus was seen as serving to maintain the social status quo. This really had to change when rapid changes in society took place during the mid-1960s. For the government in general, the society went from a stable, well divided society (compare *62,63*) to an unstable, heterogeneous one that showed uncertainty in many respects. As with many parts of the Dutch government, the police had not anticipated these changes. Instead, the police reacted with an abundance of sanctions and an even stricter application of law and order. Soon however, it was realized that this large scale force demonstrated only that the police were defeated and were not "up to" present day society any more. The course was therefore changed, first only by introducing better technical means and methods.

Social problems started to receive police attention but were still mainly assessed from the point of view of public order. Police assistance became a task for furthering welfare and maintaining law and order was the means. However, assistance took place in a detached and impersonal fashion, based on a technical instrumental concept of police work. Because social elements of police work were missing in this manner, special police squads were created for social police tasks.

In the report *Politie in Verandering (66)*, an attempt was made to change this sorry state of affairs. The report argued that the police should contribute to society in the form of social control, not just to protect but also to create conditions for social development aimed at realizing essential values in the Dutch democracy. The gap between the police and the citizenry had to be closed. Under the motto "know and be known," authority needed to be based less on the law and more on personal relations. The police had to be integrated into society but not to an extent that it would prevent intervention when needed. Policing would then be not just fighting the symptoms but removing the causes.

This new form of policing required the police to decentralize into small districts in which the police would assume all necessary policing tasks. Police officers were going to work in teams with strong internal coherence. Responsibility was to be decentralized to each team. The number of hierarchical levels needed to be brought down, and all police officers were going to participate in development of policy. One important and sorry consequence developed: each police officer was expected to be able to do everything, from writing parking tickets to solving complicated murder cases. Combined with inadequate police salaries, this caused detective squads to be filled with lowly trained, not too bright, underpaid police officers. A marker is that specialized murder squads disappeared everywhere, and specialized vice and youth squads remained in only some police forces.

So, through two venues both the police and the prosecution became increasingly less professional. At the same time courts maintained their trust within the inquisitorial framework that the prosecution delivered sound and complete dossiers without bias against the accused. However, by the beginning of the 1990s it was clear, at least to some, that this was no longer true (35, 67). Cases such as the Schiedam Park murder are the consequences of these developments. An additional example is the following. Dutch defense attorneys almost never engage in their own investigation of the case. They depend on what the police uncover. They can ask the prosecutor to have the police do additional investigations or ask the investigating judge (rechter-commissaris) to give an order to that effect. In the Schiedam Park murder case the defense attorney proposed long lists of additional inquiries and long lists of important documents that were missing from the dossier. Almost all of these requests were turned down and again at trial at the District Court and the Court of Appeals. The trust built in the past in police and prosecution apparently still holds.

The same form of trust is given to experts in the Dutch criminal legal system. The cross-examination or grilling of expert witnesses in the United States (for some fine examples see 68) is unknown in The Netherlands. Experts usually deliver a written report that goes into the dossier, are almost never asked about their background, and are never asked difficult questions about their report (69). This is strikingly different from the manner in which experts are treated in the United States. As a result, the statements made by educationalist Ruud Bullens and the psychologist went uncontested in the Schiedam Park murder trial (for a discussion of this problem see 70,71).

CONCLUSION

In light of the points discussed above, it is hoped that the reader has gained an appreciation of the prevailing environment of a Dutch trial. Foreign colleagues who attend Dutch trials always remark on the rather informal and cordial behavior of all the participants. It still is gentlemanly—although nowadays most professional participants are women[3].

---

[3] For instance, in 2000 a little more that 50% of the District Court judges and prosecutors in The Netherlands were female (72).

Courtroom behavior—the bedside manner of Dutch judges *(73)*—blurs what is really going on in a Dutch trial. The dossier is central to everything that happens there. The prosecutor is responsible for the integrity of the dossier and its completeness. If the prosecutor and his or her work cannot be trusted, the whole inquisitorial systems collapses. The major miscarriage of justice in the Schiedam Park murder case is an illustration of this. Through the prosecutor, the defense and the court can check the police investigation and check the scenario presented at trial by the prosecutor. This vital role in an inquisitorial system does not allow for any unprofessional behavior.

Indeed, the Minister of Justice oversaw an extensive program to improve the police and the prosecution, so lessons have been learned from the Schiedam Park murder case. At the same time, all police officers who worked on the case, all forensic detectives and all prosecutors still hold their position. Nobody it appears has been fired or transferred.[4]

Based on the changes in the police and prosecution over the last decades. it could be hypothesized that the number of miscarriages of justice has grown in The Netherlands. Indeed, some 20 cases could be identified as likely miscarriages of justice. For our project at Maastricht University on Reasonable Doubt Cases (*Project Gerede Twijfel*), some 175 convicts appealed. We have no data from earlier times however, so there is no way we can make a meaningful comparison.

The Schiedam Park murder case demonstrates that the inquisitorial system can increase the incidence of justice miscarried—but does it increase it more than an accusatory system? We do not know. We lack some of the factors that promote miscarriages of justice, such as a jury, plea bargaining, and capital cases *(75–77)* but seem to have others that do. A thoughtful comparison between different legal systems however is important, not just for speculation but also because of the work of the European Court of Human Rights in Strasbourg. That court has rapidly growing influence in the countries of the Council of Europe (not to be confused with the European Union—the Council has 45 member states, the Union 25). This is a court with judges coming from different

---

[4] Note that the prosecutors at both the District Court and the Court of Appeals presented inaccurate information to the Court. Also, two detectives coerced Kees Borsboom into false confessions and, according to the Posthumus report *(42)*, manufactured fraudulent documents. What happened to the officers in the Schiedam Park murder is in sharp contrast to a comparable case in Wales. In the case of the murder of Lynette White, three suspects, who became known as the Cardiff Three, were innocently convicted *(74)*. A special team squad under the heading of the Independent Police Complaint Commission is looking into unlawful behavior of the police and the prosecution in that case.

legal systems. Their judgments mean that elements from differing systems are entered into the legal systems of all member states. This blending of legal systems warrants a thorough analysis of what may result in best practice.

REFERENCES

1. Van Koppen, P. J., & Lochun, S. K. (1997). Portraying perpetrators: the validity of offender descriptions by witnesses. *Law and Human Behavior, 21*, 663–687.
2. Gilligan, O., Schneider, J., & Sotscheck, R. (Eds.). (1990). *The Birmingham Six: An Appalling Vista.* Dublin: Literéire.
3. Hill, P. J., & Hunt, G. (1995). *Forever Lost, Forever Gone.* London: Bloomsbury.
4. Blom-Cooper, L., & Brickell, S. J. (1998). *The Un-fixing of the Birmingham Bombing Cover-up.* Canterbury: Brickell.
5. Blom-Cooper, L. (1997). *The Birmingham Six and Other Cases: Victims of Circumstance.* London: Duckworth.
6. Bedau, H. A., & Radelet, M. L. (1987). Miscarriages of justice in potential capital cases. *Stanford Law Review, 40*, 21–179.
7. Borchard, E. M. (1970). *Convicting the Innocent: Errors of Criminal Justice.* New York: Da Capo.
8. Carrington, K., Dever, M., Hogg, R., Bargen, J., & Lohrey, A. (Eds.). (1991). *Travesty! Miscarriages of Justice.* Sydney: Pluto Press.
9. Frank, J. N., & Frank, B. (1971). *Not Guilty.* New York: Da Capo.
10. Frieswijk, J., & Sleurink, H. (1984). *De Zaak Hogerhuis: "Een Gerechtelijke Misdaad"* [The Hogerhuis Case: 'A court crime']. Leeuwarden, The Netherlands: Friese Pers Boekerij.
11. Gross, S. R. (1987). Loss of innocence: eyewitness identification and proof of guilt. *Journal of Legal Studies, 16*, 395–453.
12. Hale, L. (1961). *Hanged in Error.* Harmondsworth: Penguin.
13. Hannema, U. D. (1964). *De Hogerhuis-zaak* [The Hogerhuis Case]. Drachten, The Netherlands: Laverman (dissertation, Amsterdam University).
14. Hill, P., Young, M., & Sergeant, T. (1985). *More Rough Justice.* Harmondsworth: Penguin.
15. Huff, C. R., Rattner, A., & Sagarin, E. (1986). Guilty until proven innocent: wrongful conviction and public policy. *Crime and Delinquency, 32*, 518–544.
16. Huff, C. R., Rattner, A., & Sagarin, E. (1996). *Convicted But Innocent: Wrongful Conviction and Public Policy.* Thousand Oaks, CA: Sage.
17. Kee, R. (1986). *Trial and Error: The Maguires, the Guildford Pub Bombings, and British Justice.* London: Hamilton.
18. Radelet, M. L., Bedau, H. A., & Putnam, C. E. (1992). *In Spite of Innocence: Erroneous Convictions in Capital Cases.* Boston: Northeastern University Press.
19. Rattner, A. (1988). Convicted but innocent: wrongful conviction and the criminal justice system. *Law and Human Behavior, 12*, 283–293.
20. Walker, C., & Starmer, K. (Eds.). (1993). *Justice in Error.* London: Blackstone.
21. Waller, G. (1989). *Miscarriages of Justice.* London: Justice.
22. Woffinden, B. (1987). *Miscarriages of Justice.* London: Hodder & Stoughton.

23. Young, M., & Hill, P. (1983). *Rough Justice.* London: British Broadcasting Corporation.
24. Belloni, F., & Hodgson, J. (2000). *Criminal Injustice: An Evaluation of the Criminal Justice Process in Britain.* New York: St. Martin.
25. Dwyer, J., Neufeld, P., & Scheck, B. (2000). *Actual Innocence: Five Days to Execution and Other Dispatches from the Wrongly Convicted.* New York: Doubleday.
26. Westervelt, S. D. (Ed.). (2001). *Wrongly Convicted: Perspectives on Failed Justice.* New Brunswick, NJ: Rutgers University Press.
27. Walker, C., & Starmer, K. (Eds.). (1999). *Miscarriages of Justice: A Review of Justice in Error.* London: Blackstone.
28. Blaauw, J. A. (2002). *De Puttense Moordzaak: Reconstructie van een Dubieus Moordonderzoek* (3e ed.) [The Putten Murder Case: Reconstruction of a Dubious Murder Inquiry]. Baarn, The Netherlands: Fontein.
29. Israëls, H. (2004). *De Bekentenissen van Ina Post* [The confessions by Ina Post]. Alphen aan den Rijn, The Netherlands: Kluwer.
30. Governor's Commission on Capital Punishment. (2002). *Report of the Governor's Commission on Capital Punishment.* Springfield, IL: State of Illinois.
31. Forst, B. (2004). *Errors of Justice: Nature, Sources and Remedies.* New York: Cambridge University Press.
32. Wagenaar, W. A. (2002). False confessions after repeated interrogation: the Putten Murder Case. *European Review, 10,* 519–537.
33. Scheck, B., Neufeld, P., & Dwyer, J. (2000). *Actual Innocence.* Garden City, NY: Doubleday.
34. Crombag, H. F. M., van Koppen, P. J., & Wagenaar, W. A. (1994). *Dubieuze Zaken: De Psychologie van Strafrechtelijk Bewijs* [Dubious Cases: The Psychology of Criminal Evidence] (2nd ed.). Amsterdam: Contact.
35. Wagenaar, W. A., van Koppen, P. J., & Crombag, H. F. M. (1993). *Anchored Narratives: The Psychology of Criminal Evidence.* London: Harvester Wheatsheaf.
36. Gross, S. R. (1996). The risks of death: why erroneous convictions are common in capital cases. *Buffalo Law Review, 44,* 469–500.
37. Gross, S. R. (1998). Lost lives: miscarriages of justice in capital cases. *Law and Contemporary Problems, 61,* 125–149.
38. Huff, C. R., & Rattner, A. (1988). Convicted but innocent: false positives and the criminal justice process. In: Scott, J. E., & Hirschi, T. (Eds.), *Controversial Issues in Crime and Justice* (pp. 130–144). Newbury Park, CA: Sage.
39. Damaška, M. R. (1986). *The Faces of Justice and State Authority: A Comparative Approach to The Legal Process.* New Haven: Yale University Press.
40. Damaška, M. R. (1997). *Evidence Law Adrift.* New Haven: Yale University Press.
41. Van Koppen, P. J. (2003). *De Schiedammer Parkmoord: Een Rechtspsychologische Reconstructie* [The Schiedam Park Murder: A Legal Psychological Reconstruction]. Nijmegen: Ars Aequi Libri (with the cooperation of C. Dudink, M. van der Graaf, M. de Haas, J. van Luik, and V. Wijsman).
42. Posthumus, F. (2005). *Evaluatieonderzoek in de Schiedammer Parkmoord: Rapportage in Opdracht van het College van Procureurs-Generaal* [Evaluation

inquiry of the Schiedam Park Murder: A Report Commissioned by the College of Prosecutors-General]. The Hague: Openbaar Ministerie (zie www.om.nl).

43. Van Koppen, P. J. (2006). Lering uit de Schiedammer Parkmoord [Learning from the Schiedam Park Murder]. *Trema*, 29, 111–113.

44. Van Koppen, P. J. (2006). De fluwelen handschoen van Posthumus: over hetgeen ontbreekt in het rapport over de Schiedammer Parkmoord [The velvet glove of Posthumus: what is missing is his report on the Schiedam Park murder]. *Trema*, 29, 57–66.

45. Openbaar Ministerie, Politie, & NFI. (2005). *Versterking Opsporing en Vervolging: Naar Aanleiding van het Evaluatierapport van de Schiedammer Parkmoord* [Strengthening Investigation and Persecution: As a Result of the Evaluation of the Schiedam Park Murder]. The Hague: Ministerie van Justitie.

46. Van Koppen, P. J. (2002). The Netherlands. In: Kritzer, H. M. (Ed.), *Legal Systems of the World: A Political, Social, and Cultural Encyclopedia* (Vol. III, pp. 1114–1121). Santa Barbara, CA: ABC-CLIO.

47. Taekema, S. (Ed.). (2004). *Understanding Dutch Law*. The Hague: Boom.

48. Tak, P. J. P. (2003). *The Dutch Criminal Justice System: Organization and Operation* (2nd ed.). The Hague: Wetenschappelijk Onderzoek- en Documentatiecentrum.

49. Nijboer, J. F. (1999). Criminal justice system. In: Chorus, J. M. J., Gerver, P. H. M., Hondius, E. H., & Koekkoek, A. K. (Eds.). *Introduction to Dutch Law* (pp. 383–433). The Hague: Kluwer.

50. Anderson, T. J. (1999). The Netherlands criminal justice system: an audit model of decision-making. In: Malsch, M., & Nijboer, J. F. (Eds.). *Complex Cases: Perspectives on The Netherlands Criminal Justice System* (pp. 47–68). Amsterdam: Thela Thesis.

51. Tak, P. J. (1997). Sentencing and punishment in The Netherlands. In: Tonry, M., & Hatlestad, K. (Eds.). *Sentencing Reform in Overcrowded Times: A Comparative Perspective* (pp. 194–200). New York: Oxford University Press.

52. Verburg, J. J. I. (2005). Kantelende werkelijkheid [Tilting reality]. *Trema*, 28, 296–297.

53. Van den Emster, F. W. H. (2005). Reflectie op een rechterlijke dwaling [Reflections on a miscarriage of justice]. *Trema*, 28, 294–295.

54. De Poot, C. J., Bokhorst, R. J., van Koppen, P. J., & Muller, E. R. (2004). *Rechercheportret: Over Dilemma's in de Opsporing* [Detectives' Portrait: On Dilemma's in Police Investigations]. Alphen aan den Rijn, The Netherlands: Kluwer.

55. Innes, M. (2003). *Investigating Murder: Detective Work and the Police Response to Criminal Homicide*. Oxford: Clarendon.

56. Horvath, F., & Meesig, R. T. (1996). The criminal investigation process and the role of forensic evidence: a review of empirical findings. *Journal of Forensic Sciences*, 41, 963–969.

57. Inbau, F. E., Reid, J. E., Buckley, J. P., & Jayne, B. C. (2001). *Criminal Interrogation and Confessions* (4th ed.). Gaithersburg, MD: Aspen.

58. Vrij, A. (1998). Interviewing suspects. In: Memon, A., Vrij, A., & Bull, R. H. C. (Eds.), *Psychology and Law: Truthfulness, Accuracy and Credibility* (pp. 124–147). London: McGraw-Hill.

59. Gudjonsson, G. H. (2003). *The Psychology of Interrogations and Confessions: A Handbook*. Chichester: Wiley.

60. Kassin, S. M., & Gudjonsson, G. H. (2005). The psychology of confessions: a review of the literature and issues. *Psychological Science in the Public Interest*, 5, 35–67.

61. Kassin, S. M. (2005). True or false: 'I'd know a false confession if I saw one.' In: Granhag, P. A., & Strömwall, L. A. (Eds.). *The Detection of Deception in Forensic Contexts* (pp. 172–94). Cambridge: Cambridge University Press.

62. Lijphart, A. (1975). *The Politics of Accommodation: Pluralism and Democracy in The Netherlands* (2nd ed.). Berkeley, CA: University of California Press.

63. Kossmann, E. H. (1978). *The Low Countries, 1780–1940*. Oxford: Clarendon.

64. Van Koppen, P. J., & Penrod, S. D. (2003). The John Wayne and Judge Dee versions of justice. In: van Koppen, P. J., & Penrod, S. D. (Eds.). *Adversarial Versus Inquisitorial Justice: Psychological Perspectives on Criminal Justice Systems* (pp. 347–368). New York: Plenum.

65. Parlementaire Enquêtecommissie Opsporingsmethoden. (1996). *Inzake Opsporing* [Concerning Investigation]. The Hague: SDU (11 volumes; Tweede Kamer [1995–1996] 24072; M. van Traa, chair).

66. Projectgroep Organisatiestructuren. (1977). *Politie in Verandering: Een Voorlopig Theoretisch Model* [Changing Police: A Tentative Theoretical Model]. The Hague: Staatsuitgeverij.

67. Crombag, H. F. M., van Koppen, P. J., & Wagenaar, W. A. (1992). *Dubieuze Zaken: De Psychologie van Strafrechtelijk Bewijs* [Dubious Cases: The Psychology of Criminal Evidence]. Amsterdam: Contact.

68. Loftus, E. F., & Ketcham, K. (1991). *Witness for the Defense: The Accused, the Eyewitness, and the Expert Who Puts Memory on Trial*. New York: St. Martin.

69. Broeders, A. P. A. (2003). The role of the forensic expert in an inquisitorial system. In: van Koppen, P. J., & Penrod, S. D. (Eds.), *Adversarial Versus Inquisitorial Justice: Psychological Perspectives on Criminal Justice Systems* (pp. 215–254). New York: Plenum.

70. Van Koppen, P. J. (2004). *Paradoxen van Deskundigen: Over de Rol van Experts in Strafzaken* [Paradoxes of Experts: On the Role of Expert Witnesses in Criminal Cases]. Deventer, The Netherlands: Kluwer (inaugural lecture, Maastricht University).

71. Van Kampen, P. T. C. (1999). Expert evidence compared. In: Malsch, M., & Nijboer, J. F. (Eds.). *Complex Cases: Perspective on The Netherlands Criminal Justice System*. Amsterdam: Thela Thesis.

72. Bruinsma, F. (2001). Rechters in Nederland: een NJB-enquête [Judges in The Netherlands: an NJB survey]. *Nederlands Juristenblad*, 76, 1925–1934.

73. Crombag, H. F. M. (1997). 'Bedside manners' van rechters [Bedside manners of judges]. *Trema*, 20, 87–90.

74. Sekar, S., Soutter, A., & Bailey, M. (1998). *Fitted in: Cardiff 3 and the Lynette White Inquiry.* Greenford, Middlesex: Fitted in Project.
75. Turow, S. (2003). *Ultimate Punishment: A Lawyer's Reflections on Dealing with the Death Penalty.* New York: Farrar, Straus & Giraux.
76. Lynch, T. (2003). The case against plea bargaining: government should not retaliate against individuals who exercise their right to trial by jury. *Regulation*, 24(Fall), 24–27.
77. Sandefur, T. (2003). In defense of plea bargaining: the practice is flawed, but not unconstitutional. *Regulation*, 26(Fall), 28–31.

Chapter 13

Sexual (Lust) Homicide
Definitional Constructs, Dynamics, and Investigative Considerations

Janet McClellan[1]

Abstract

This chapter discusses the historical definitional origins of sexual homicide (lust murder), the dynamics of sexual homicide injury, offense definition constructs and their limitations, and key presumptions of injuries associated with sexual homicide offense models. The chapter concludes by arguing for the clarification of concepts, characterizations, linkages, and research into the offense dynamics and offender motivations of sexual (lust) homicides.

INTRODUCTION

Violent interactions in which people are engaged are based on experiences and expectations of reality. For that reason, an understanding of violence and its extremes must consider the offender's construct of reality. As Skrapec noted, "behavior is the product of one's own sense of reality regardless of the degree

---

[1] The author acknowledges with gratitude the assistance of Ms. Victoria Esposito-Shea, J.D. for her proof reading and copyediting of this manuscript.

From: *Serial Murder and the Psychology of Violent Crimes*
Edited by: R. N. Kocsis © Humana Press, Totowa, NJ

to which that reality matches the objective facts of that person's life" (*1*, p. 51–52). The mental representations of an offender's realities are acted upon and acted out, and they may be presumed to be detectable and specifiable in the processes of crime scene analysis.

The noted anthropologist James (*2*) stated that the rationale behind scientific inquiries is that there is an attempt to understand the causes and outcomes of human actions in order to determine or formulate sets of "relatively simple explanatory principles laying beneath immediate appearances, and behind what people say [or do]...[in defining] the reasons for their actions" (*2*, p. 18). Because humans engage in a constant state of "building and sustaining mental models of reality...[those realities perform as the]...regulator and arbitrator" of those behaviors. Therefore, violent offenders normalize their psychologically constructed violent propensities, realities, and motivations so as to normalize for themselves and within their life the violence they commit against others (*3*, p. 75–76). Those regulators and arbitrators of behavior for sexualized homicides are presented through the preparation, targeting, and violent assault processes toward the acquired victim(s). The current trend in the characterization and classification of sexual/lust homicides attempts to use and evaluate the violent character of those homicides to determine the psychological predispositions of the offender by analyzing the patterns, controls, wounding techniques, wounding focus, and injuries suffered by the victim(s).

Some critics find objectionable the interest in sexual homicide and discount as frivolous the examination of sexual homicide, as it is believed that such events account for less than 5% of serial homicides and single-event homicides annually in the United States. However, the official data are misleading, as flaws and inaccuracies in the identification and collection of homicide data are masked in the Uniform Crime Report (UCR) because "sexual homicide is generally indexed under Unknown Motive...[because]...law enforcement agents are largely unaware of the underlying sexual dynamics of criminal conduct" (*4*, p. 6). Regardless of the reporting inaccuracies, sexual homicide researchers believe that sexual (lust) murder is a researchable and important category of homicide (*5–8*) and as valid a research focus as any other motivationally construed murder (e.g., infanticide, patricide, matricide). Therefore, whether ascribed to a single incident or a series, the contemporary research distinguishes offenders various *modus operandi*, signature, and wounding as based on the totality of violence committed against the victim, victim targeting, and the offender's psychosexual predisposition(s).

It should be noted that much of the literature regarding sexual homicide does not employ the term "lust." Rather, it alludes to it in instances where the violence is presumed to be the result of the offender's motivations (*9–16*) being based on the actions of that offender, which include controlling the victim, location or concentration of injuries, and the tools or techniques used to inflict violence on the victim.

Five fundamental assumptions permeate the current literature on sexual (lust) homicide: 1) the sexual nature of the offense; 2) agreement on the features and definitions of the activities associated with sexual (lust) homicides; 3) the significance of offense activities as articulated by the offender's violence; 4) the validity of the offense/offender motivational models; and 5) the functionality of the models in the detection and identification of sexual (lust) homicide offenders.

This chapter discusses the historical definitional origins of sexual homicide (lust murder), the dynamics of sexual homicide injury, offense definition constructs and their limitations, and key presumptions of injuries associated with sexual homicide offense models. The chapter concludes by arguing the need for the clarification of concepts, characterizations, linkages, and research on the offense dynamics and offender motivations of sexual (lust) homicides.

ORIGINS OF SEXUAL (LUST) HOMICIDE

In 1886, Krafft-Ebing *(17)* presented his *Psychopathia Sexualis: With Especial Reference to the Antipathic Sexual Instinct, a Medico-Forensic Study.* He defined paraesthesia, or the perversion of the sexual instinct, and placed lust murder at its deadly apex. He further illustrated the definitions of lust and lust murder using case study examples, describing the generalities of acted upon impulses of violence, sadism, and torture as illustrative of "the perverse acts" of the perpetrators who used those means to pursue their sexual gratification. Krafft-Ebing *(17)* specified that the violent and murderous behavior found its origins in the otherwise normal sexual instincts and biological impetus of procreation.

Krafft-Ebing *(17,* p. 52) explained abnormality of the normal sexual instinct by stating,

> . . .there is perverse emotional colouring of the sexual ideas. Ideas physiologically and psychologically accompanied by feelings of disgust, give rise to pleasurable sexual feelings; and the abnormal association finds expression in passionate, uncontrollable emotion . . . this is . . . the case if the pleasurable feelings, increased to passionate intensity, inhibit any opposing ideas . . . the absence or loss of all ideas of morality, aesthetics and law.

Krafft-Ebing *(17)* elaborated a set of qualifications for behaviors associated with morally, legally, and socially sanctioned customs of human sexual behavior. The qualifications constructed provided a set of gradations and degrees, moving from the sublime through to ever-increasing levels of ferociousness to violent behavior, that occur during sexual excitement. The gradations of lust that exceed mutual gratification provide a primary analysis of violent hostile behavior as an instrument of violent sexualized activities. Key to the descriptions of the gradations and degrees of sexualized behavior illustrated by Krafft-Ebing *(17)* is the presentation and description of sexual encounters on a "continuum of sexuality" ranging from simple acts of playfulness, to passionate arousals and its response, to aggressive physical and psychological performances, to the extreme of murderous attacks against the object of attraction. As such, regardless of whether it was his intent, Krafft-Ebing *(17)* provided a definition and a rudimentary analysis of a continuum of sexualized violence.

Krafft-Ebing offered a basic profile of those romantic contests and motivations for male sexual aggression(*17*, p. 54).

...sadistic force is developed... the natural shyness and modesty of woman toward the... aggressive manners of males....Woman...derives pleasure from her innate coyness and the final victory of man affords her intense and refined gratification. Hence the frequent recurrence of these little love comedies.

Krafft-Ebing *(17)* considered those "little comedies" as the "rudimentary manifestations" of sadism expressed as the "innate desire to humiliate, hurt, wound or even destroy others in order... to create sexual pleasure" (*17*, p. 53). On the continuum of lust and assault sexual behavior, he noted that, "sadistic traces may be found in men who show superiority over a woman, to provoke her defense and delight in her subsequent confusion and abashment" (*17*, p. 54). Thus, Krafft-Ebing defined and described a continuum of sexual violence for a range of human sexual behavior and the rationale of that behavior spanning the course of contact from mutual gratification to lust murder. His discussion provides not only descriptive information on the psychosocial and psychosexual raison d'être for the escalation of violence against the victim-target by the offender but also (*17*, p. 52):

...perverse emotional coloring of the sexual ideas... give rise to pleasurable sexual feelings... and the abnormal associations finds expression in passionate, uncontrollable emotion...resulting in perverse acts.

Krafft-Ebing *(17)* presented a continuum of lust and its extreme actualization in the form of lust murder that is still an appropriate model of the continuum of sexualized violence. The continuum of lust is a primary model of examination in the contemporary analysis of violent sexualized murder (lust) typologies, which attempt to provide classification systems in the conduct of murderous behavior.

Activities and Characteristics of Sexual (Lust) Homicides

A homicide is generally classified as sex-related or sexualized when there is evidence or acknowledgment of sexual activity in the offense. Evidence of sexual activity characteristic of sexual or lust murder includes but is not limited to: 1) the condition of the clothing or lack thereof on the victim; 2) evidence of ejaculation or seminal fluid on, near, or in the body; 3) sexual injury and/or sexual mutilation; 4) extreme wounding (frenzied) or mutilation; 5) substitutive sexual activity indicating fantasy, ritualism, and symbolism; 6) removal of the victim's personal belongings for keepsakes, including the taking of personal property, portions, or substances from the body; and, 7) evidence of postmortem insertions into the body of the victim (whether in body orifices or wound areas).

Therefore, during the investigation of lust murder the collection of evidentiary materials is important. It is the understanding, and reconstruction, of the offender's actions and activities that comprise the complete collection of evidence and presentation of evidentiary significance. The characteristics of lust murder behavior include but are not limited to access to the victim through such activities as stalking, breaking and entering, work, socialization, location, travel, and acquisitional planning associated with the routine activities of the victim or perpetrator. Lust murder behavior at the crime scenes associated with the violence is also apparent in the generalized forensic awareness of the offender demonstrated by the removal of evidentiary significant items or artifacts. Specific indications of offender behaviors associated with victim targeting, predator preparations, and violence are further described in detail in numerous publications (5,6,9–11,16,18,19).

No two sexual/lust murderers are exactly alike. Motivations differ, target preferences differ, and hunting grounds vary. Crime scene behaviors, victim targeting, acquisition techniques, and mobility influence the classification and typologies of offenders. Various typologies and classifications have been developed via the use of empirical and qualitative research, noting such behaviors that are frequently inconsistent and rival one another. Moreover, such typologies are, in the author's opinion, often of limited use to investigators beyond providing some conceptual understanding of the offender.

Significance of Offense Activities in the Offender Violence

Lust murder is herein defined as the acting out of aggressive ideologies by various forms of cruelty, torture, and sexualized actions that ultimately culminate in the death of the victim. As has been observed, "for some serial killers the acts of killing are primary and sexualized; for other serial killers the killings are secondary to sexual gratification. Sexual motivation is implicated in each case but at a different level" (*1*, p. 164). Unlike Hazelwood and Dietz (*20*, p. 18), who defined the suffering of cruelties and injuries as significant to the investigation only if the victim was conscious and alive during the violence, the current definition does not require consciousness or life and is more broadly inclusive of the performance of sexualized torture. The rationale for a more inclusive definition arises from the discussion provided by Hazelwood and Dietz (*20*), who asserted that fantasy is a central feature and as such exists in the mind of the offender. It does not require the active presence of anyone other than the one who fantasizes. Therefore, the victim's presence or absence of consciousness or life is not an essential prerequisite for the offender's fantasy-driven conduct consisting of generalized violence, torture, or sexualization of those activities.

Lust murder (in Latin, *erotophonophilia*), also known as sexual homicide, is the commission of murder where the acting out of violence is exhibited by the presence of sexualized brutality that results in the death of the victim. Moreover, sexualized brutality is the means by which the offender commits the actions against a targeted victim and the violence is not its end. In sexualized brutality the victim is plainly an instrument for the offender to use to fulfill his needs as dictated by his psychopathological and paraphilic predilections.

Expressive Versus Instrumental of Lust Homicide

The definition of instrumentality, according to Talcott Parsons, is the "means of getting something done ... means that have one important factor in common—the absence of ... limitations ... imposed by ethical consideration" (*21*, p. 173). Most significantly, the later development and discussion of offender typologies hinge upon Parsons and Shils' definition of expressive and instrumental acts (*21*). An examination of expressive and instrumental violence helps clarify the differences between the triggering of violent behaviors.

Block and Block (*22*) defined expressive homicide as violence committed when the ultimate and primary goal is harm of a specifically identified or targeted type of person. As such, the expressive homicide occurs when a person is identified by the offender as a real or perceived threat to the offender's sense of personal integrity, their sense of self-worth, or has otherwise unwittingly provoked or triggered the offender's purposively violent response. During the violent interaction the victim is perceived as refusing to acquiesce to coercion, domination, or control by the offender; that refusal, or target-triggering response, renders the victim subject to the offender's violent intentions. Most commonly, expressive homicides are violent interactions that take place between spouses, other family members, strangers or acquaintances in contests of will, and machismo threat-related confrontations. Expressive violence, and therefore expressive homicide, occurs when the offender physically expresses specifically focused revenge or anger toward the known or familiar victim.

Instrumental violence, in contrast, is not prompted by the immediacy of revenge or specific anger. Instead, it is the expression of goal directedness and is not based on emotional prompting. Rather, instrumental violence does not find its primary targets among the offender's familiars. Instrumental violence and instrumental homicide occurs when the offender identifies a victim (individual or group) as appropriate or preferred type. Instrumental violence offenders exhibit planning and are intentionally directed at gaining their target and attaining satisfaction of their preexistent psychopathologies through the victim. Instrumental homicide is not a response to external motivations or actionable prompting by the victim. Therefore, with instrumental violence the victim is a vehicle or device for the offender to attain the psychological fulfillment of his or her paraphilic or psychosexual predisposition. The victim is unfortunately simply the means to an end.

In a study of 125 Canadian offenders, Woodworth and Porter *(23)* found that homicides committed by psychopathic offenders were more likely (93.3%) to be instrumental, or cold-blooded in nature, premeditated, and not requiring external motivation. They also found that the homicides committed by nonpsychopaths (48.4%) were more likely to be expressive in nature or "crimes of passion," resulting from external motivations and frequently associated with high levels of impulsivity/reactivity and emotionality *(23)*. Therefore, homicides committed by psychopathic offenders were significantly more instrumental in their nature than those committed by nonpsychopaths. Most significantly, the study demonstrated that psychopaths, long believed to be prone to impulsivity and expressive offenses, were in fact capable of modifying their behavior and planning; and they were much less likely to be reactive under provocation than nonpsychopaths.

Psychopathic homicide offenders have been found to be capable of controlling their impulsiveness, focusing on their targeted victim, planning and preparing the assault, and executing the violence in such a way as to elude detection. Psychopaths were found to be significantly less prone to respond under emotional provocation, engage in conscious decision-making, consider means of eluding capture, and carry out murders in a "cold blooded" fashion. They are able to gauge risk and modify or delay their response to ensure the availability and acquisition of a target and to choose their victim, time, location, and conduct to commit the offense.

Mott *(24)* examined the structures and crime scene behaviors of 399 unsolved serial homicides from 1800 to 1995. The 75 serial murders in the data highlighted factors frequently resulting in the offenses remaining unsolved. They included 1) highly vulnerable victims, such as prostitutes, homosexuals, and females; 2) bodies dumped outdoors; 3) longer periods of time between victims; and 4) offenders exhibiting distinct familiarity with the geographic area constituting their "hunting grounds." Mott's *(24)* findings supported the assertions that instrumental or serial murderers operate by means of targeting, calculating, and controlling the offense circumstances; and they have the ability to assess environmental risks associated with apprehension as previously noted by Woodworth and Porter *(23)*. It appears from Mott's *(24)* study that offenders who evade apprehension target highly vulnerable victims, have acquisition and secondary crime scene sites, display greater lengths of time between victimizations, practically demonstrate a conspicuous familiarity with the geographic "hunting grounds," and live near, travel through, or frequent the vicinity.

Gains and Value in Instrumental Lust Murder

Instrumental homicide, particularly instrumental lust murder, occurs when the offender attempts to obtain something of value. The thing of value sought by the perpetrator is the target's relationship or connection with the offender's predetermined presence type and/or what that type represents to the offender. More specifically, the offender targets the victim based on internal pathology and emotional drives. The motive of the offender is not about gain, money, or other artifact of real property as with traditional murder offenses. Instrumental lust murder is the commutation of the offender's psychopathology in the acts of acquisition, injury, and death of the victim.

Any removal of property or other belongings of the victim by the offender is important in its intrinsic nature, not the monetary value of the item. It is the violence and death of the victim that reflect the essential goals significant to the offender, and these are reflected in the items taken. Any item of property taken after a lust murder is merely a memento for remembrance and fantasy in which the offender indulges between offenses.

In summary, the serial instrumental offender does not act impulsively and is capable of planning, executing the offense, concealing their identity, and waiting for the next opportunity. Lust murderers respond to their environment from a psychological wellspring that contains the constructs of the target and offense significance. They have a propensity to choose victims for whom they have a particular preference and acquisitional opportunity. Additionally, they engage in victim target hunting from a position of geographic familiarity and comfort, target familiarity, and where they can acquire their target through a ruse or blitz. They commit the offense frequently and act out their offenses through means designed to reduce the likelihood of apprehension.

KEY PRESUMPTIONS OF SEXUAL (LUST) HOMICIDE: MODELS

Validity of Offense/Offender Motivational Models

Much of the criminological research during the last century has focused on attempts to discover the motivation and behaviors of persons who commit criminal offenses. Therefore, the investigator, through observation of the offense, crime scenes, and evidentiary artifacts, seeks to identify the planning, preparation, and style of execution of a sexual homicide offender and their psychosexual predispositions. The tools and methods used by the offender reveal their *modus operandi*, signature, and ritual significance. Within the sexual homicide, according to Keppel and Birnes (*15*, p. 7), the offender's action and activities amount to:

> [A] psychological calling card...an expression of the mindset of the offender made apparent by the actions of the offender toward the victim (plan, hunt, acquisition, violence and associated actions, and murder)...[containing]...plot, dialogue, character types and conclusion [of the criminal event]. It is...an evolving psychodrama that is the focus of the acting out of desire...or...fantasy.

A significant factor regarding the relationships and connections signifying the offender's "calling card" are opportunity, means, victim availability/vulnerability, and the setting of the offense. The victim in terms of being a target of opportunity, the symbolism inherent in the violence, and the geographic availability for predation are important considerations when identifying the offender. Consequently, a detailed examination of the victim's identity, life, lifestyle, and habits is vital (*5,9,10,15,16,25*). Key issues inherent to such a consideration should include:

1. Routine(s)—work, relations, hobbies, habits, frequency of contacts
2. Habits—indicated by residence, friends, and information from intimates
3. Risk-lifestyle—social, financial, living environment, economic, age, associations, etc.
4. Databases and criminal activities—criminal and civil histories, associates
5. Links to scene—what routine or activity associated, if any, to scene(s)
6. Physical appearance and demographics
7. How controlled by offender—weapon, ruse, bindings, other

8. Personality—psychological, physiological, emotional predispositions
9. Precursor incidents—including historic or previous assaults, threats, burglaries, robberies, etc.
10. Relationships—intimates, friends, associates, coworkers, interpersonal social and sexual lifestyles
11. Preference-selection—based on victimology, what would have made this person an "attractive target"
12. Last known 48 to 72 hours of victim's activities—related to known routines
13. Relevant national research data—re-risk assessment: likelihood that the person would have been a victim and classification of victimizer indicated.

The combination of the information obtainable regarding the victim and the crime scene comprise a substantial and frequently characteristic set of variables available for a homicide investigation that are of particular importance in the investigation of a sexualized homicide.

MODEL FUNCTIONALITY: DETECTION AND IDENTIFICATION OF THE OFFENDER

Sex-related offenses and sex-related homicide are low incidence offenses and as such do not represent the opportunity for experiential learning by investigators that high incidence offenses such as theft, robbery, and burglary provide. Investigator familiarity with, and practice at, investigating types of offenses provides a learning curve of offense associations, offender behaviors, and characteristics and identification techniques. Although academic inquiry to support investigative necessities of sex-related offenses may seem a responsive practical tactic, its reliability to an investigator has yet to be clearly determined. Indeed, the role of criminal profiling in violent crime investigation is complicated by a lack of agreement among researchers. Until greater coherence emerges in the literature, criminal profiling will continue to be more a matter of art than science.

Contemporary research regarding sex-related and serial murders indicate that the offender's criminal activity is premeditated and repetitive. Indeed, with serial predation the offender gains sophistication in tactics and demonstrates increased levels of violence to achieve greater control of the victim. Extremely violent, mutilating, and sexualized murder offenders' behaviors (single or serial) are planned and not necessarily the project of psychologically unsound persons. The offenders do not wish to be apprehended; they are forensically aware or forensically sophisticated; and they commit violence upon the victim (perimortem or postmortem) as part of their psychological predispositions (9–11,16). Sex-related murder is not a random act. It is not symptomatic of a disorganized mind or indicative of a diagnosable psychological malady; rather, it is a behavior that satisfies the needs of the offender who acts with premeditation and purpose (*9–11,16,26,27*).

Six issues appear to be highlighted in the literature. First, violent offenders demonstrate in their actions signature indicators denoting motivation and personality traits. There are, however, both conflicting and congruent classifications of those motivations and traits in the literature. Second, the subclassification of sex-related murder has not been a specific focus until the last decade. Third, there is agreement that determining the offender rationale (motivation) is an important tool for the investigator. Fourth, sex-related and sexual violence-murder motivation and personality traits inherent in crime scene analyses appear in instances of single homicide activity and serial offenses. Fifth, valid criminal profiling techniques require study of the perpetrator's actions. Lastly, there is some precedence for the use of case studies in the examination of violent offender classification systems. Although research has developed various forms of classifications for violent homicide and sex-related homicide, none of these classification systems, in the opinion of the author, has yielded a practical typological construct or tool for the criminal investigator.

The most persistent and controversial theoretical model used to explain lust murder that is often presented as a tool for investigators is a dichotomous classification of offender types developed from interviews of 36 sexual murderers incarcerated during the 1980s *(6)*. Douglas et al. *(28)* further elaborated on this dichotomized explanation of sexual homicide behavior from the assumed personality traits of offense behaviors, but this simple dichotomy has since been rejected by many researchers.

Hickey *(27)* tended to distinguish three types of serial killer as travelers, local, and place-specific. Travelers are defined as murderers who are geographically mobile (i.e., those with a transient lifestyle or occupational travel opportunities). "Local" refers ring to individuals who commit their offenses within a particular geographic area (urban zone or other community), and "place-specific" offenders are those who murder in their residence, work place, or other comfortable environment (pp. 153, 218).

Douglas et al. *(28)* identified four factors that define organized or disorganized sexual homicide: the victim, the crime scene, forensic evaluation, and assessment of the sexual/homicide acts. Additionally, these researchers distinguished the term "disorganized" and used it in reference to some sexual homicide offenders. Disorganized sexual homicide offenders was the label coined to describe the commission of acts "unplanned, spontaneous (perhaps reflecting the offender's) . . . youthfulness . . . lack of criminal sophistication, use of drugs and alcohol, and/or mental deficiency" (*28*, p. 128). After modifying their original dichotomy to include "mixed" as a category, combining parts of organized/disorganized typologies, the categories suffered from a lack of rigor in terms of distinguishing definitions.

Keppel and Walter *(16)* called attention to the need to record data and the analysis of observable facts available at the crime scene, victimology, and forensic evidence to discern the system of offender actions and motivations. Others *(9,10,11)* have stated that descriptive analysis of crime scene actions and behavior of offenders must be reducible to practical significance to discover rules-of-action relations, the rationale for criminal activity, motivation, and behavior are all important tools for an investigator. Over the years researchers have recognized the value of observing and interpreting crime scene activities.

In 1996, Holmes and Holmes *(19)* presented a four-part classification that categorized visionary killers, mission killers, hedonistic killers, and power/control killers. Holmes and Holmes' *(19)* structural concepts of serial killers and victims applied the theoretical construct of instrumentality and expressive motivations. Instrumental violence is used to express the observed fact that offenders act violently toward their victims because they wish to *(29,* p. 783). Unfortunately, as with their 1996 study, Holmes and Holmes *(19),* continued to use the dichotomy of the organized/disorganized typology that has largely been abandoned by many researchers as overly simplistic.

Keppel and Walter *(16)* introduced a set of refinements to the classification of sexual murder by using the subcategory called "descriptive," which takes into account crime scene classifications, offender behaviors, motivation of offenders, and the effects of offender learning over the series of murderous events. Keppel and Walter's *(16)* study ultimately developed a four-part classification system for serial murder that included power assertive rape-murder, power-reassurance rape-murder, anger-retaliation rape-murder, and anger-excitation rape-murder.

Hazelwood and Burgess *(30)* presented categories of rapists and used a slightly modified version of the types developed by Groth et al., *(31)* to categorize their sexual murder (lust) classification scheme. The significance of the revised classification model previously developed by Keppel and Walter *(16)* was that it claimed to include data from 2476 convicted sex-murder (lust) offenders who had committed single and/or serial homicide. The research examined case histories and data about offense dynamics, psychosocial characteristics, homicidal patterns, and victimology to develop a classification of sexual murder. Theirs is a richly supported classification analysis of sexual (lust murderers).

Kocsis et al. *(9,10,32)* used quantitative techniques to investigate and analyze the criminal behaviors of serial rape and serial/sexual homicide offenses. The research conducted by Kocsis et al. *(9,10,32)* provides a rigorous quantitative analysis of offender motivation, scene motivation displays at the crime scene, and the use of evidentiary artifacts indicating victim predation-risk assessment. The creation of typologies and classifications of offenders provided a means of developing a greater understanding of offender signature, ritual behaviors, and interactional typologies with victims and of demonstrating unique and categorical activities of the offenders. Ultimately, the research generated provides insight for the application of those variables to the development of an offender profile.

Although each of the classification systems provides a refinement of sexual (lust) homicide offenses, problems remain. First, typologies available in the current literature appear to agree on the need for classification and offender behavior analysis but do not agree on the associated elements—that is, the variables and classification definitions associated with either serial or sexual (lust) murder. Second, the violent offender characterizations have been largely reserved for a broad range of serial violent sexual homicidal perpetrators and infrequently to single-event sexual homicides. Third, the results are presented without congruent descriptive arrangements or classification systems that field investigators can utilize as an investigative tool. The availability of an investigative strategic decision-making tool would be of significant value when conducting an investigation of violent sexualized (lust) homicide. This, however, awaits the development of a more comprehensive or complimentary classification system of sexual homicide offense analysis.

CONCLUSION

For the continued evolution of lust murder analysis, classifications, and typological constructs, a critical information template is necessary rather than mere generalities or popularization of psychological motivations. Such a critical information template would utilize valid typologies, violence data generalities/summaries, and a continuum of decision-making supported by best practices in investigative procedure—thus providing a reliable classification synopsis for the field investigator.

In summary, four significant issues emerge.

1. Violent offenders signal nonverbal symbolic communication through their violent interactions that inform the investigator of the offense signature, motivation, and character traits.
2. The research that exists strongly supports offender behavior analysis as a means of identifying the offender and an important tool for the investigator.
3. Lust murder motivation and personality traits inherent in the crime scene occur during offenses involving both single homicides and serial offenses.

4. Although prior research has developed classifications of violent sexual homicide, none of the classifications systems to date has, in the author's opinion, yielded a reliable tool for the homicide investigator.

Criminal profiling, in its simplest terms, is the application of scientific investigation that fashions descriptive principles and perspectives about what lies beneath the immediate appearance of the crime scene evidence and offending activities and reveals the psychological and psychosexual identity of the perpetrator. In sexualized/lust murder homicide investigation, current typologies of offender behavior should develop an understanding of an offender's "social reality by identifying homogeneous groups of crime behaviors that are different from other clusters of crime behavior" (33, p. 1); more simply, typologies should distinguish one offender and pattern of behavior from another. In the definitional constructs of sexualized/lust murder the interpersonal goals characterized by behaviors and actions equate to ritual and/or ritualized activities that constitute deliberate performances, controlled use of space, and timing (2). The acts and actions are framed by the actor through ceremonial constructs and have meaning for both the actor and the informed observer. Those acts are the "demonstration of means of power as strategies" (2, p. 17) and the structure that provides the development of offender profiles, although the means of developing coherent profiles are currently inconsistent and rudimentary. Therefore, criminal profiling must move from its more artful constructs to the formalization of analytically derived analyses of offender actions, violence, victim interactions, offender tools and techniques, and "hunting" preferences. The classifications and typologies of various researchers are a beginning, but much work remains if the classifications are to be a means of formulating profiles that result in apprehension of the offender.

REFERENCES

1. Skrapec, C. A. (2001). Phenomenology and serial murder: asking different questions. *Homicide Studies*, 5(1), 46–63.
2. James, W. (2003). *The Ceremonial Animal: A New Portrait of Anthropology*. New York: Oxford University Press.
3. Donald, M. (2001). *A Mind So Rare: The Evolution of Human Consciousness*. New York: W.W. Norton.
4. Arrigo, B. A., & Purcell, C. E. (2001). Explaining paraphilia and lust murder: toward an integrated model. *International Journal of Offender Therapy and Comparative Criminology*, 45(1), 6–31.
5. Gerberth, V. J., & Turco, R. N. (1997). Antisocial personality disorder, sexual sadism, malignant narcissism and serial murder, *Journal of Forensic Sciences*, 42, 49–60.

6. Ressler, R. K., Burgess, A., & Douglas, J. E. (1988). *Sexual Homicide: Patterns and Motives.* New York: Lexington Books.
7. Revitch, E., & Schlesinger, L. B. (1989). *Sex Murder and Sex Aggression.* Springfield, IL: Charles C Thomas.
8. Warren, J. I., Hazelwood, R. R., & Dietz, P. E. (1996). The sexually sadistic serial killer. *Journal of Forensic Sciences,* 41, 267–277.
9. Kocsis, R. N., Cooksey, R. W., & Irwin, H. J. (2002). Psychological profiling of sexual murderers: an empirical model. *International Journal of Offender Therapy and Comparative Criminology,* 46(5), 532–554.
10. Kocsis, R.N. (2006). *Criminal Profiling: Principles and Practice.* Totowa, NJ: Humana Press.
11. Godwin, G. M. (1999) *Hunting Serial Predators.* Boca Raton, FL: CRC Press.
12. Schlesinger, L. B. (1998). Pathological narcissism and serial homicide: review and case study. *Current Psychology,* 17, 212–221.
13. Schlesinger, L. B., & Revitch, E. (1999) Sexual burglaries and sexual homicide: clinical, forensic, and investigative considerations. *Journal of the American Academy of Psychiatry and Law,* 27(2), 227–238.
14. Schlesinger, L. B. (2002). Stalking, homicide, and catathymic process: a case study. *International Journal of Offender Therapy and Comparative Criminology,* 46(1), 64–74.
15. Keppel, R. D., & Birnes, W. J. (1997). *Signature Killers: Interpreting the Calling Cards of the Serial Murderer.* New York: Pocket Books.
16. Keppel, R. D., & Walter R. (1999). Profiling killers: a revised classification model for understanding sexual murder. *International Journal of Offender Therapy and Comparative Criminology,* 43, 119–133.
17. Krafft-Ebing, R. (1965) *Psychopathia Sexualis: With Especial Reference to the Antipathic Sexual Instinct, a Medico-Forensic Study.* New York: Stein & Day.
18. Holmes, R. M., & Holmes, S. T. (2002). *Profiling Violent Crimes: An Investigative Tool* (3rd ed.). Thousand Oaks, CA: Sage.
19. Holmes, R. M., & Holmes, S. T. (2004). *Serial Murder* (2nd ed.). Thousand Oaks, CA: Sage.
20. Hazelwood, R. R., & Dietz, P. E. (1992). The criminal sexual sadist. *FBI Law Enforcement Bulletin,* 44, 13–17.
21. Parsons, T., & Shils, E. A. (Eds.). (1951). *Toward a General Theory of Action.* Cambridge, MA: Harvard University Press.
22. Block, C. R., & Block, R. L. (Eds.). (1992). Questions and answers in lethal and non-lethal violence. In: *Proceedings of the First Annual Workshop of the Homicide Research Working Group.* Washington, DC: National Institute of Justice.
23. Woodworth, M., & Porter, S. (2002). In cold blood: characteristics of criminal homicides as a function of psychopathy. *Journal of Abnormal Psychology,* 11(3), 436–445.
24. Mott, N. L. (1999) Serial murder: patterns in unsolved cases. *Homicide Studies,* 3(3), 241–255.
25. Eliopulos, L. N. (2003). *Death Investigator's Handbook.* Boulder, CO: Paladin Press.

26. Meloy, J. R. (2000). The nature and dynamics of sexual homicide: an integrative review. *Aggression and Violent Behavior*, 5(1), 1–22.
27. Hickey, E. W. (2002). *Serial Murderers and Their Victims*. Belmont, CA: Wadsworth/Thompson.
28. Douglas, J. E., Burgess, A. W., Burgess, A. G., & Ressler, R. K. (1992). *Crime Classification Manual*. New York: Simon & Schuster.
29. Cornell, D. G. Warren, J., Hawk, G., Stafford, E., Oram, G., & Pine, D. (1996) Psychopathy of instrumental and reactive violent offenders. *Journal of Consulting and Clinical Psychology*, 64, 783–790.
30. Hazelwood, R. R., & Burgess, A. W. (1995). *Practical Rape Investigation: A Multidisciplinary Approach* (2nd ed.). Boca Raton, FL: CRC Press.
31. Groth, N. A., Burgess, A. W., & Holmstrom, L. L. (1977). Rape: power, anger and sexuality. *American Journal of Psychiatry*, 134(11), 1239–1242.
32. Kocsis, R. N., Irwin, H. J., & Cooksey, R. W. (2002). Psychological profiling of offender characteristics from crime behaviors in serial rapists. *International Journal of Offender Therapy and Comparative Criminology*, 46(2), 144–169.
33. Miethe, T. D., McCorkle, R. C., & Listwan, S. J. (2006). *Crime Profiles: The Anatomy of Dangerous Persons, Places, and Situations* (3rd ed.). New York: Pergamon.

Chapter 14

Criminal Profile Construction and Investigative Procedures

Study of the Westley Dodd Serial Sexual Murders

Ronald Turco

Abstract

This chapter deals with the development and construction of a criminal profile. The integration of a psychological profile with an ongoing investigation is discussed in the context of a multiple child serial murder investigation. The importance of teamwork involving various members of a homicide task force and the independent skills they bring to an investigation is emphasized. Psychodynamic factors are reviewed on a theoretical basis, but emphasis is placed on practical investigative techniques and factual information. The material integrates forensic science, psychological issues, and detective work. The purpose is to provide an adjunct to an overall homicide investigation.

INTRODUCTION

Murder though it hath no tongue will speak—William Shakespeare

A psychological profile may focus on issues involving political (historical), artistic, or criminal behavior (*1–5*). For the purpose of this chapter the focus is limited to psychological criminal profiling (*6–12*). The psychological profile

From: *Serial Murder and the Psychology of Violent Crimes*
Edited by: R. N. Kocsis © Humana Press, Totowa, NJ

might be considered a "paper tiger." It can be powerfully aggressive in helping forensic scientists focus on an investigation, or it can be destructive in leading investigators astray. At best it is an adjunctive guide to a complete forensic and criminal investigation and a team effort. It should encompass the integration of material from the crime scene (i.e., blood stain evidence), witness statements, autopsy findings, photographs, related materials such as cameras seized at the crime scene, weapons, items used for torture, and a host of suggestions derived from "brainstorming sessions" with forensic experts and police detectives.

Added to this accumulation of knowledge is the psychodynamic experience of the behavioral scientist. This encompasses a psychological explanation and understanding of a given behavior based on conscious and unconscious motivations. The psychological criminal profile thus encompasses forensic evidence and known psychodynamic theory. The profiler attempts to understand the motivations and actions of the perpetrator. A biographical sketch is produced to help direct the investigation. It is important that this "profile" not be followed slavishly and in the face of contrary evidential material. To all of this is added the profile of the victim, including personal habits and relationships. The profile encompasses the victim, the crime scene, the perpetrator, and even the profiler himself or herself. One must consider the personality type and experience of the assigned profiler in any given case. The profile has the purpose of a psychological assessment of the crime scene as well as the victim or victims.

In this respect, the homicide scene is a sign of the "acting out" of the perpetrator in the context of a specific victim. The profiler utilizes working theories and specific crime scene evidence to prepare a biographical sketch-profile of a criminal whom we do not know. This is exactly the opposite of preparing a profile of a known artist or political figure. We are working backward, so to speak, in attempting to create a composite of an unknown person or persons. With regard to the psychological understanding of a crime scene, especially a serial murder crime scene, the most common diagnostic entity we consider is that of malignant narcissism and narcissistic personality disorder (13). These are sadistic individuals with paranoid tendencies but who are in good contact with reality. These individuals lack empathy and conscience. They utilize the defense mechanisms of projection, isolation, and dehumanization. In other instances, the perpetrator is sociopathic, psychopathic, or psychotic; and the evidence available may point in these directions (6).

The FBI utilizes a system of organized and disorganized individuals and differentiates the crime scene accordingly (12). The patterns and motives vary according to personality type and circumstances (14).

PREPARING A PSYCHOLOGICAL PROFILE

In my own work of forensic detection, I start by considering the first 3 years of life, the *separation-individuation phase* of development. These 36 months have a major lifelong impact on adjustment, personal happiness, and ultimate behavioral characteristics *(15)*. Psychological structure forms in the child largely through his interaction with parents, influenced by biological events in the environment and genetic patterns. There is a combination of nature–nurture in effect. An understanding of these theoretical concepts provides the profiler with a theoretical structure to begin work and understand the target. It is important for a profiler to have a basic knowledge of psychology. The most important factor in my profile work is a thorough understanding of developmental psychology from a psychoanalytic perspective. For example, in one instance of searching for a serial killer I hypothesized that he likely would contact a woman while at the crime scene. This related to the concept of *splitting* in psychoanalysis. When the suspect was apprehended, there was evidence that a telephone call had been made to a woman who, from my perspective, represented the "good mother" in contrast to the projected "bad mother" that he had just killed. This did not prove the theory but did allow a working hypothesis that provided some structure to the investigation. It was just one more concept with which to work. Had these data not been found, the investigation would still have proceeded in an objective scientific fashion. Demographic (statistical) data are helpful but are only a small part of the puzzle.

My preparation begins with a review of basic material relating to lust murder including the psychodynamics based on ego psychology and pathological malignant narcissism and borderline states *(10,16)*. These ideas encompass the field that psychiatrists refer to as object-relations theory. A review of all known data follows, including autopsy reports, crime scene observations, photographs, and interviews with potential witnesses, detectives, and members of the victim's social circle and family. I spend time alone allowing the data to distill in my mind. My own personal philosophy and, for lack of a better phrase, moral and religious direction are part of this approach. When I am comfortable with the material available, "brainstorming" sessions with detectives and forensic scientists can begin. Moral judgement and concepts of right and wrong, blame, and hostility must be set aside as much as possible. Our unconscious thinking must be freed up from conventional restraints. Some police detectives refer to this as developing a "hunch." I believe we have stored information available that must be freed up and allowed to surface. Sometimes it happens in a dream while sleeping. Many great scientific advances have developed from the scientist's dream state. The same is true of investigative work.

When creating the profile, the crime scene may be considered as a symptom of behavior and a projection of the perpetrator's personality, lifestyle, and development. Neurological aspects of behavior should also be considered, such as the dyscontrol syndrome and associated abnormalities of the limbic system. As many violent offenders have neurological deficits that reflect the nature of the crime scene, a neurologist might be consulted. When to do so is a matter of judgment and experience, as there is no easy formula for calling in consultants. Many defects are not detected until autopsy, and some killers have a predatory drive to stalk and kill based on underlying neurological issues—how the person is "wired," so to speak. Most important, however, is the attempt to understand, in psychological terms, what the killer is actually doing with his own psychological drives. With serial killers, there is an attempt to reduce tension, followed by a quiescent period, a buildup of tension, and another murder. The more the profiler knows about early developmental frustration and development the better position he/she is in to "get inside the head" of the perpetrator. At the same time conceptual opinions must be left open. The Zen masters refer to this as "beginner's mind." This "empty" mind is ready to receive insight from external as well as internal sources.

Demographic data include such information as the ages of the victims, style of dress, type of weapon, make of car of the perpetrator, and possible known psychiatric histories. Such data have been compiled statistically on national and local law enforcement levels (6). "Getting into the mind" of the suspect follows, utilizing the psychological information, insight (hunch), known behavioral characteristics, demographic data, available scientific evidence from the crime scene, and investigative information. Thus, the development of a psychological profile is truly a team effort. We consider a reconstruction of the crime scene, characteristics of the crime itself, motivational issues of the perpetrator, crime scene dynamics (in a psychological sense), antecedent behavior (the fantasies of the perpetrator, including the plan for committing a crime), selection of the victim, a profile of the victim, the manner of killing, disposal and/or display of the body, and postoffense behavior (17). The fantasy has become a reality. The fantasy may be maintained by continual killing, attending the victim's funeral, visiting the victim's gravesite, following the police investigation, teasing the police or news media people, and maintaining a fetish (usually a body part or article of the victim's clothing), among others. Sadomasochistic killers sometimes videotape their activities in a compulsive manner, and this becomes part of "reliving" the fantasy.

WESTLY ALLAN DODD INVESTIGATION: CLOSELY WATCHED SHADOWS

On September 4, 1989, the bodies of two young children were found in a park in Vancouver, Washington. On October 24, the police in Portland, Oregon responded to the disappearance of a young child from a public park. On November 1, Vancouver detectives were called to investigate the nude body of a white 5-year-old boy. The child had been dumped in the woods, and police determined that he was the child missing from the park in Portland. A multidimensional task force that included U.S. Federal Bureau of Investigation (FBI) agents and detectives from Washington and Oregon was assembled to investigate the murders, a standard procedure in suspected serial murder cases. I joined the task force on November 7 and was asked to develop a psychological "profile" of the perpetrator or perpetrators. Detectives and I examined crime scene photographs, autopsy reports, and photographs; and we consulted information that we had compiled regarding similar murders. That latter included the "demographic data" that some police agencies and forensic examiners maintain. We also considered the psychodynamic aspects of the perpetrator as well as the crime scene itself. After visiting the initial crime scene in the Vancouver park we considered the scene and location of the bodies as a symptom of psychopathology, much as a physician might consider a tremor a symptom of neurological disease. We pondered the character structure of the perpetrator. What kind of person would commit these kinds of crimes? What would his personality be like? His face to the world? His relationships? His community involvement and accomplishments?

This type of aggression, characteristic of Kernberg's description of "malignant narcissism," should not be viewed as a disease but as an aspect of personality structure and function *(18,19)*. Harry Stack Sullivan has used the term "malevolent transformation" to describe a similar process. "Soul death" is another term used to describe serial killers.

The rewards of serial murder are psychological and the motivations for the killer highly meaningful. An understanding of the integration of aggression in the personality is essential for comprehending the motivation of serial killers. Liebert and I have previously noted that even in the presence of severe psychopathology the actual reasons for committing serial murders is not obvious; and thus an understanding of the underlying psychopathology and personality dynamics of the murderer is essential for understanding the repetitive drive to kill—a drive that some investigators have termed "predatory murder" *(7,10)*.

Liebert and I proposed that narcissistic and borderline conditions provide the clinical foundation for understanding the offender's personality and behavior. My focus has been to build a "profile" based on the psychopathology of borderline and severe narcissistic disorders. Narcissistic pathology in the personalities of serial murderers is an intrinsic aspect when generating the motivation to murder. At least 10 prominent theorists working on the problem of serial murder have highlighted the sadism, malignant narcissism, fantasies of power, and experience with narcissistic insults, along with the underlying sense of inferiority, present in serial killers. Fantasies of power and control over others and a history of animal cruelty are also prominent characteristics of such individuals (7,10,18,20–26). Holmes and DeBurger characterized serial murderers as individuals with a motivation to exert total control and power over their victim. (26). They stated that the motivations are appreciated only by the murderer himself or herself, and my view is that they may be appreciated by the killer at an emotional level but without emotional and serious intellectual insight.

The task force assembled in the Vancouver-Portland child murders made 42 predictions regarding the suspect whom we termed a "typical offender" of such crimes: The killer would be a white man between 25 and 35 years of age, a nonaffiliated loner (a "cardboard person") who, if he had served in the military, would have been discharged under less than full honorable conditions or administratively without serving his full tour of duty. We predicted that he would be carefully assessing the investigation and its progress and might try to "assist" the police with the investigation, perhaps by providing information to the news media or directly to investigators. Such individuals keep records of their crimes, including a diary and newspaper clippings. More recently we have noticed the tendency to videotape the victim, crime scene, and perpetrator. The perpetrator in such videos is the center of attention—the protagonist, so to speak. These individuals maintain substantial amounts of pornography and also take still photographs of the victims alive and in the postmortem state. The have sexual activity with the victims while alive and, depending on the organization of the perpetrator, in the postmortem state—necrophilia. The exception to the sexual acting out involves the "spree" type of serial murder, a subgroup of serial killers.[1]

---

[1] Spree killings involve four or more victims in a short time frame, with no sexual assault or ritualism (i.e., sexual fantasies are minimal or absent) and a high degree of randomness in the selection of the victims. The underlying process of malignant narcissism, however, is still present.

In the case of the Vancouver-Portland murders we hypothesized that the suspect would have a late model car and would be employed at a job with limited responsibility, consistent with data derived from past experience and stored in our files. We predicted that the killer would keep a fetish, frequently a body part, a lock of hair, underclothing, or jewelry. These "souvenirs" are later used by the perpetrator to masturbate to his fantasy reenactment of the murder, a form of eroticism that continues long after the apprehension and incarceration of the perpetrator. We predicted that the murders would continue and that sexual molestation would be accompanied by sexual mutilation as is the pattern in such cases. The perpetrator would likely select only male victims, possibly viewing females as being "defective," a reference to castration fears. *Control* of the victim is always the primary motivator. During the investigation we discovered ligature marks on the neck and wrists of the 5-year-old child, who had also been sodomized postmortem.

Interviews with several hundred known child molesters and child murderers failed to convince the task force that we had a viable suspect in this group, and we began directing our attention to transients. To some extent this also included individuals who had recently moved to the area. Issues of prior mental health counseling, especially for violent or sexual crimes as well as a criminal history of sexual offenses were considered during the investigative process. We also hypothesized that the killer was not psychotic and would fit into the FBI classification of an "organized" serial murderer *(6,27,28,29)*. On a theoretical basis we continued to consider issues of projective identification and unresolved sadism *(30)*.

On November 13, 1989, a suspect was arrested by police officer in Camus, Washington and charged with kidnapping in the first degree. He had tried to abduct a 6-year-old white boy from a movie theater. Shortly thereafter, I performed a videotaped interview of the suspect,[2] during which time he confessed to murdering the three children, describing in specific detail the sexual assault, mutilation, murder, and postmortem sexual activity with the victims.

The psychological profile we had developed prior to his arrest was consistent with the behavior, description, and background of the apprehended suspect and was used as evidentiary material for the procurement of a search warrant, thus setting a precedent in Washington State. The warrant was issued contemporaneously with my videotaped interview. Although he was confessing to the murders (unbeknownst to the forensic examiners at his apartment),

---

[2] I began the interview by videotaping the reading of his Miranda rights and his signing them.

the suspect still had a right to refuse access to his apartment and car. In this instance, the judge ruled the "profile" sufficiently accurate to apply to the suspect in custody and granted the search warrant. In the apartment we found the underclothing of the 5-year-old murdered child neatly folded in the perpetrator's briefcase, numerous Polaroid photographs of the child tied to the bedposts, and an array of child pornography. As predicted, a diary highlighting the specifics of the three murders, including comments on the investigation and plans for the future abduction and dissection of the next child, was located in the clothes dresser. Ten years prior to this situation, I participated in the largest criminal investigation in Oregon's history, which resulted in the apprehension and conviction of the I-5 killer. The psychological profile developed in that case was similar to the child serial murder case with the exception that the victims of the I-5 killer were adult women who were sexually assaulted. Additionally, with the I-5 killer we considered the mechanism of "splitting," hypothesizing that the killer would make a telephone call to a woman friend each time he murdered another woman, thus perpetuating the "good mother"-"bad mother" experience (introject) *(19)*. Telephone logs seized at the time of his arrest confirmed this behavior.

CHRONOLOGY AND DETAILS OF THE INVESTIGATION

September 4, 1989—Two children's bodies were discovered in David Douglas Park. Attempts were made to protect the crime scene, which was understandably contaminated by rescue personnel. Bodies were identified as brothers Billie and Cole Neer. Shoestring and blood spatter evidence were photographed and collected.

October 29, 1989—Iseli child disappeared. Jean Boylan, a police artist, did a composite drawing of a possible suspect *(31)*.

November 1, 1989—Pheasant hunter discovered the body of Lee Iseli in Clark County, Washington. The homicide task force was assembled consisting of members from four police departments and two FBI agents. The body had been tossed like "garbage" and ligature marks were noted on the left ankle and neck of the child. Blue fibers were also located on the body and were later matched to a blanket in Westley Allan Dodd's closet. The child had been hung by his left ankle as well as his neck.

November 14, 1989—Camus Police arrested Westley Allan Dodd following an aborted kidnap attempt. Dodd was videotaped and confessed to the murders of three children. A simultaneous search of his apartment and automobile was conducted. A plant physiologist was consulted regarding foliage and plant debris found in the apartment. Satanic materials, an extensive diary, and pornographic materials were discovered.

Previous to his apprehension many suspects were interviewed. Composite drawings were done with the assistance of a witness with some resemblance to Dodd noted after his apprehension.

ORGANIZATIONAL ISSUES

A multiagency task force consists of members from different departments who often have different areas of expertise. Their involvement facilitates communication with different agencies in the area, thereby allowing information that would otherwise be compartmentalized to be shared. A special telephone line was set up for calls ("tips") to the department, and a "trap" was set as well in the event the perpetrator called. A hostage negotiator is also helpful in such instances, as he has experience in maintaining conversation. In many instances the killer returns to the crime scene, possibly to relive the incident, so appropriate surveillance is useful. A computerized system to keep track of license plates and other information is essential, and display hangings (chalkboard or paper) are a helpful visual reference. Suspects are prioritized and classified according to "tips" and other available information. Of the 160 suspects we considered in the Neer-Iseli murders, 30 met the priority one description as perpetrators. All 160 had raped boys, and 30 had murdered children. Westley Allan Dodd was not on the list, but he did have a history of prior sexual assault of children and had been released by at least one judge. As we studied photographs of the crime scene, autopsy, and "mug shots," someone also attended the funerals of the children to discreetly photograph and videotape bystanders. We also examined ATM photographs in the area.

Working in a single area facilitated the communication and camaraderie so necessary with such work. Daily meetings and "brainstorming" sessions facilitated the work product. One secretary was assigned the task of providing funds necessary for investigative progress, including "bribes" to informants and expense money. A single source also handled press information to minimize confusion and contradiction of information given to the public. A clerk was assigned to file and organize material objects such as match covers, soda pop bottles found at the crime scene, and so on.

Investigative Interview

The Camus police department, an agency in Washington State near Vancouver notified the homicide task force that a 28-year-old white male adult had been apprehended attempting to kidnap a 6-year-old child from a movie theater. He was not on the list of suspects. We videotaped his interrogation after reading him his Miranda rights and having him sign them while on video camera. The approach we took was one of "You might as well tell us what is going on as it is only a matter of time before we find out." The suspect spoke freely and discussed his history of "indecent liberties" by exposing himself to children.

He discussed the "fishing expeditions" he went on to find children, the techniques of "baby talk" and "child play," and his specific interactions with his victims. He had been given a general discharge from the Navy and moved to the area 1 month before the Neer boys were murdered. He said he was shocked when he saw a composite picture that had been circulated and that the likeness to him was so good. Initially he was reluctant to allow a search of his car and apartment, but the search warrant had already been issued and the search was underway while the interrogation was in progress. Photographs of the park where the Neer boys were murdered were found in his room along with a fishing fillet knife, the murder tool, and pornographic photographs of children. Dodd mentioned that one of the Neer boys ran, and he did not want surviving witnesses so he killed him on the run. The Iseli boy was murdered for the same reason. He told me, "He was a cute little kid but I knew I had to kill him." He said he went to Portland to kidnap a child because Vancouver had become "too hot" and he did not wish to arouse suspicion. He admitted to postmortem anal intercourse with the Iseli boy, and photographs in his apartment supported this version of his story. He used his hands to strangle the child and then used a rope to hang him in the closet. Later, before going to work in the morning, he put his body on a shelf in the closet. The boy's underwear was found in his briefcase neatly folded along with news clippings of the kidnappings and a diary. A low key sympathetic approach was used during the interrogation, rather than a tough "in your face" interview. In the meantime, along with a search of obvious objects in Dodd's apartment the floors and bed were vacuumed, and all evidence was under the control of one person for accountability purposes. A wooden framed rack for binding victims was fingerprinted. A reference in the diary indicated that this would be used to dissect the next child. The notes in the diary were neatly written, and the last notation read: " Third murder. Going to move for the next victim" *(32)*.

CONCLUSION

A psychological profile was developed during the course of a murder investigation utilizing a variety of information including profiling the victims. This profile was used as an aid in the investigative process as well as a source of obtaining a search warrant of the suspect's vehicle and apartment. Approximately 40 areas of information were included in the final profile in addition to some hypothetical material associated with malignant narcissism and malignant transformation. A view of the murders as having "restorative" value was examined as well as the issue of "unmetabolized" psychological elements of aggression and sadism. Dehumanization and "recycling" of aggressive elements were taken into consideration along with the concepts of "cardboard people" as postulated by Turco *(32)*. This includes the "nonaffiliates" in society. The idea of "soul death" was discussed in the context of Kernberg's use of the term "unambitious hedonism" as a stimulus hunger to replace the missing "internal world" of the perpetrator *(13,19)*.

We viewed this situation as one encompassing a malignant transformation in object relations resulting in identification with an omnipotent and cruel internal object resulting in identity transformation. The presence of pathological narcissism and psychopathic tendencies are of diagnostic significance in understanding the murderer's personality, functioning, and motivation to kill. Meloy considered the degree of sadism and aggression combined with narcissistic qualities to reflect the "malignancy" of the psychopathic disturbance where gratification (of aggression) occurs in the service of narcissistic functioning (i.e., cruelty toward others in the form of a triumphant victory over a rejecting object) *(33)*. Meloy also believed that dissociation is ubiquitous in the psychopath. The initial murder of the serial murderer may reflect a "new identity." The pathological object-relations of narcissism and malignant narcissism are important diagnostic indicators in the personality functioning of serial killers, and the occurrence of these phenomena are significant factors in the formation of the personalities of serial killers, their inner motivations, and the pattern of commission.

The practical points of importance in the profile included such factors as a Caucasian man between the ages of 25 and 35, a loner, military experience less than honorable, and a job with limited responsibility. We believed he would access the progress of the investigation through the news media and might even try to "assist" the police, thus generating a greater feeling of importance. We believed he would keep records of his crimes with a diary and news clippings. We expected to find child pornography in his residence as well as photographs of the victims alive and/or dead. We hypothesized he would be driving a late model car in poor condition and that he would keep a fetish of possibly a body part, hair, or underclothing. This would be his "souvenir." This article would later be used to masturbate and "re-live" the fantasy of erotic criminal behavior. Our expectation was that the perpetrator would continue to murder and molest male victims and may even have viewed females as being defective. The issue of control of the victims would be important and led us to search for ropes and ligatures. We did find a "torture rack" with ropes tied to it. The use of restraints was a "given." Our concern was that the perpetrator was a transient with a history of sexual indiscretions and possible mental health treatment. We hypothesized that he would be nonpsychotic and fit into the category of "organized" serial murderers.

The psychological profile the task force produced was consistent with the actual description, background, and behavior of a suspect who was apprehended by a local police agency. This profile set a precedent in Washington State for the procurement of a search warrant. A judge ruled that the profile was accurate enough to apply to the suspect in custody. This individual was later found guilty of murder and hung. The hanging was a choice he made.

REFERENCES

1. Wedge, B. (1968, October). Khrushchev at a distance—a study of public personality. *Transaction*, 3, 24–28.
2. Post J. (1984). Notes on a psychodynamic theory of terrorist behavior. *Terrorism: An International Journal*, 7(3), 241–256.
3. Bromberg, N. (1974). Hitler's childhood. *International Review of Psycho-Analysis*, 1, 227, 227–244.
4. Turco, R. (1998). *The Architecture of Creativity: Profiles Behind the Mask*. Yachats, OR: Dancing Moon Press.
5. Turco, R. (2005). *Kim Jong Il and the Korean Dilemma*. Portland, OR: Imago Books.
6. Geberth V. (1996). *Practical Homicide Investigation* (3rd ed). Boca Raton, FL: CRC Press.
7. Turco, R. (1998). *Closely Watched Shadows—A Profile of the Hunter and the Hunted*. Portland, OR: Imago Books.
8. Hazelwood, R., & Douglas, J. (1986) The lust murderer. *FBI Law Enforcement Bulletin*, 18–22.
9. Ault, R., & Reese, J. (1980). A psychological assessment of crime profiling *FBI Law Enforcement Bulletin*, 22–25.
10. Liebert, J. (1983). Contributions of psychiatric consultation in the investigation of serial murder. *International Journal of Offender Therapy and Comparative Criminology*, 187–199.
11. Geberth, V., & Turco, R. (1996). Antisocial personality disorder, sexual sadism, malignant narcissism, and serial murder. *Journal of Forensic Sciences*, 49–60.
12. Ressler, R., Burgess, A., & Douglas, J. (1988). *Sexual Homicide: Patterns and Motives*. Lexington, MA: D. C. Heath.
13. Kernberg, O. (1990). *Malignant Narcissism Continuing Education Tapes*, Tapes 1-3. Irvine, CA: CME.

14. Ressler R, Burgess A, Douglas J, Hartman C, D'Augostino R. (1986). Sexual killers and their victims: identifying patterns through crime scene analysis. *Journal of Interpersonal Violence*, 1(3), 288–308
15. Mahler, M. (1979). *The Selected Papers of Margaret S. Mahler* (Vols. 1 & 2). New York: Jason Aronson.
16. Geberth, V. (2003). *Sex Related Homicide Death Investigation—Practical and Clinical Perspectives*. Boca Raton, FL: CRC Press.
17. Turco, R. (1986). Psychological profiling. *International. Journal of Offender Therapy and Comparative Criminology*, 1, 147–154.
18. Fromm, E. (1964). *The Heart of Man: Its Genius for Good and Evil*. New York: Harper & Row.
19. Kernberg, O. (1982). *An Ego Psychology and Objects Relations Approach to Narcissistic Personality*. Washington, DC: American Psychiatric Association Press.
20. McCarthy, J. (1978). Narcissism and the self in homicidal adolescent. *American Journal of Psychoanalysis*, 38, 19–29.
21. Marohn, R. (1987). John Wesley Hardin, adolescent killer: the emergence of a narcissistic behavior disorder. *Adolescent Psychiatry*, 14, 271–296.
22. Hickey, E. (1991). *Serial Murderers and Their Victims*. Brooks, CA: Brooks/Cole.
23. Gacono, C. B. (1992). Sexual homicide and the Rorschach: a Rorschach case study of sexual homicide. *British Journal of Projective Psychology*, 37, 1–21.
24. Lowenstein, L. (1992). The psychology of the obsessed compulsive killer. *Criminologist*, 38, 26–38.
25. Palermo, G. B., & Knudten, R. D. (1994). The insanity plea in the case of a serial killer. *International Journal of Offender Therapy and Comparative Criminology*, 38, 3–16.
26. Holmes, E. M., & DeBurger, J. E. (1985). Profiles in terror: the serial murderer. *Federal Probation*, 49, 29–34.
27. Burgess, A., Groth, A., Ressler, R., & Douglas, J. (1980). Offender profiles. *FBI Law Enforcement Bulletin*, 49(3), 16–20.
28. Burgess, A., Groth, A., Ressler, R., & Douglas, J. (1985). The split reality of murder. *FBI Law Enforcement Bulletin*, 54(8), 7–11.
29. Ressler, R. (1985). Crime scene and profile characteristics of organized and disorganized murders. *FBI Law Enforcement Bulletin*, 54(8), 18–25.
30. Beljan, P. (1994). The vicissitudes of projective identification in serial murder: a primitive aspect of the antisocial personality. Dissertation, Doctor of Psychology degree, Wright State University.
31. Boylan, J. (2000). *Portraits of Guilt*. New York: Simon & Schuster.
32. Turco, R. (1993). Child serial murder. *Academy Forum—The American Academy of Psychoanalysis*, 37(3), 11–14.
33. Meloy, J. R. (1998). *The Psychopathic Mind: Origins, Dynamics and Treatment*. London: Jason Aronson.

Chapter 15

Psychological Skills
and Criminal Profile Accuracy

Erica P. Hodges and Kristine M. Jacquin

Abstract

The influence of psychological knowledge and education on profiling accuracy of sexual homicides was examined in this research. Participants included 269 university students (70.3% female, 29.7% male) whose ages ranged from 17 to 39 years (M = 19.3, SD = 2.6). The sample included 17.5% psychology majors; the other 82.5% were undeclared or had other majors. Participants completed two packets incorporating a demographic questionnaire, psychology test, murder case, and profiling offender characteristics questionnaire. A series of multivariate analyses of variance were conducted on the data; the between-subjects analyses found sex, psychology major, and psychology test to influence accuracy significantly. For females, psychological knowledge and education enhanced accuracy for profiling physical and cognitive characteristics of the offender, whereas the males' accuracy was not enhanced.

INTRODUCTION

According to the U.S. Federal Bureau of Investigation (FBI) 2002 Uniform Crime Report, only 64% of murders were solved, leaving approximately 3767 murders unsolved *(1)*. Some proportion of these unsolved homicides were likely committed by the 100 or so serial killers in the United States who have not been caught *(2)*. These facts alone emphasize the need for quick and concise methods for determining suspect characteristics to aid police investigations. Psychological profiling by competent and knowledgeable professionals can provide

From: *Serial Murder and the Psychology of Violent Crimes*
Edited by: R. N. Kocsis © Humana Press, Totowa, NJ

259

valuable assistance in identifying potential suspects. Timely identification aided by a profiler's offender characteristic report would facilitate suspect apprehension and prevent further damage by the offender *(3)*. Less than 15% of police work is dedicated to investigations *(4)*. Because so little time is available for police investigations, accurate profiles are vital, especially in such horrid crimes as serial murders.

Serial crimes are not limited to murder but can involve rape or sexual assault. A serial rapist may have two to more than 100 victims. An unsolved sex crime can lead to marked societal stress and fear; the manpower to resolve a mystery of such heinousness can be massive. For example, Hazelwood and Burgess described an unsolved investigation for a serial rapist that included more than 20 investigators and another that involved 50 officers *(5)*. Serial rape can lead to serial sexual homicide when the offender begins to murder his victims. These statistics also show the need for accurate profiling methods.

Although researchers are beginning to pinpoint the specific characteristics of the sexual murderer, there is little research on the accuracy of the application of this information by various types of profilers. Only a few studies compare profiling accuracy across professionals, and there are no known prospective studies. Pinizzotto and Finkel are pioneers in profiling accuracy research *(6)*. Their research compared 28 participants who were classified into five groups based on their profiling experience and knowledge. The researchers asked participants to write a profile of a sexual homicide and a sexual assault case. Closed cases were used, so the profiles could be compared to the actual offenders' characteristics. Four subjects were in the first group, which consisted of expert profilers who taught at the FBI Academy and had a range of 4 to 17 years of profiling experience. The second group consisted of six non-FBI professional profilers with 7 to 15 years in law enforcement and 1 to 6 years of profiling work. The third group consisted of six police detectives without psychological training or profiling experience but 6 to 15 years of investigative experience. The fourth group consisted of six clinical psychologists with no criminal profiling or investigative experience. The final group was composed of six university undergraduates with no profiling or police experience.

Each group was given photographs of the crime scene, victim information, autopsy and toxicology reports, and a crime scene description. The participants provided a suspect profile and answered a multiple-choice questionnaire about the suspect's characteristics. For the homicide, there was no difference between the groups on accuracy. However, there were several significant differences for the sex offense. The two groups of expert profilers combined had the most correct responses on the questionnaire, specifically on the characteristics of offender's age, offender's education, offender's vehicle's age and condition, and the relationship between victim and offender. The three groups of law enforcement combined had more accurate profiles than the combination of the psychologists and students. All the nonstudent groups combined were more accurate than the students alone. The small sample size is a limitation to this study as well as how the groups were compared to each other. The way in which the data were collapsed for analysis does not seem appropriate. For example, it does not seem logical that psychologists and students would be considered as one group. Perhaps if there were a larger and equal sample size across groups, it would not be necessary to find significance from collapsed data.

More recent research has examined how investigative experience influences profiling accuracy. Counter to Pinizzotto and Finkel's findings, police officers were not effective profilers in studies by Kocsis *(7–10)*. Kocsis and colleagues *(7)* compared 162 police officers divided into five groups. The groups were based on years of police experience, which ranged from little or no experience to many years of experience. A sixth group of 31 sophomore chemistry students was added as a non-law-enforcement comparison group. Surprisingly, the chemistry students outperformed all of the police groups on accuracy, including the senior detectives with the most experience and the homicide detectives with a lot of experience. In fact, performance was found to decrease with more years of experience. Overall, it was determined that the number of years of experience in police investigations does not seem to enhance a police officer's ability to determine offender characteristics accurately.

Other profiling accuracy research compared 35 police officers, 5 professional profilers who were consultants to law enforcement agencies, 30 psychologists with no prior forensic or criminal training, 20 psychics, and 31 sophomore science and economics students *(8)*. The overall accuracy score did not vary significantly across groups. There were, however, significant differences across the groups regarding the accuracy of physical characteristics and offense behaviors. Specifically, the psychologists were significantly more accurate than the police group for offense behaviors. Psychologists were more accurate than both the police and psychics on physical characteristics. When comparing the professional profilers to all the other groups collapsed as one "nonprofiling" group, the profilers were significantly more accurate overall. There was a difference found across the groups on profiling psychological characteristics. Specifically, the psychologists were found to be significantly more accurate than the police officers (no other comparisons were reported).

Kocsis thoroughly analyzed the current available profiling accuracy research and highlighted the importance of continued exploration *(9)*. Clearly, the scientific validity of profiling has yet to be strongly established. Profiles could potentially vary depending on profiler individual differences or even cultural differences surrounding the offense. Sample sizes of the previous research have failed to account fully for such variables. Interestingly, unexpected findings across the previous research does not entirely support that those more involved in the legal system (i.e., professional profilers or police) were accurate profilers. Kocsis suggested that the science majors and psychologists were more accurate due to critical and objective thinking, which is exercised more often in university settings than in law enforcement training. Therefore, intuitive thinking may not be as valuable. Distinguishing the precise attributes that lead to proficient profiles is the next step in profiling accuracy research.

In the current study, profiling accuracy was examined in individuals with different levels of psychological knowledge. The past research does not provide a clear answer about whether psychological knowledge or other professional knowledge or experience would lead to more accurate profiles. In one study, professional profilers were more accurate overall than a combination of various professionals and nonprofessionals *(9)*. Another study found psychologists to excel in profiling psychological, physical, and offense behavior character-istics *(8)*. A third set of studies suggest that investigative experience does not seem to enhance profiling abilities *(7–10)*. The current study expanded on the existing research by examining the influence of psychological knowledge on accuracy in profiling the offender of two sexual homicides. Accuracy was defined as choosing the correct responses on the profiling offender question-naire used by Kocsis and colleagues *(7–10)*. A total accuracy score was obtained from this questionnaire for each participant along with accuracy scores in the areas of physical characteristics, cognitive processes, offense behaviors, history and habits, and additional questions added by Kocsis et al. from Pinizzotto and Finkel *(6)*. Based on past research, it was hypothesized that students with more knowledge and more education in the field of psychology would provide more accurate profiles, especially with respect to psychological, physical, and offense behavior characteristics.

METHOD

Participants

The participants were 269 university students (70.3% female, 29.7% male). The participants' ages ranged from 17 to 39 years with an average age of 19.3 years (SD = 2.6). The ethnic sample was representative of the university as a whole; specifically, most of the participants (71.0%) were Caucasian, 25.3% were African American, 1.9% were other/mixed ethnicity, 1.5% were Asian American, and 0.4% were Native American. The educational levels of the participants were not representative of the university. Most of the participants were freshmen (62.8%), 11.9% were sophomores, 11.9% were seniors, 10.8% were juniors, and 1.9% were graduate students. Two participants did not report class rank.

Participants were recruited from university lower division (i.e., general psychology) and upper division (e.g., abnormal psychology) psychology classes. The general psychology classes have a diversity of majors because this course fulfills a social science requirement. The upper division psychology courses are more likely to have only psychology majors and minors enrolled. Although an attempt was made to recruit an equal number of psychology majors and nonmajors, most participants (82.5%) were nonmajors.

Materials

DEMOGRAPHICS QUESTIONNAIRE

The demographic questionnaire (DQ) assesses general demographic information, such as age, sex, and ethnicity. The DQ further attempts to assess the participants' level of expertise in basic psychology. Participants were asked to provide their grade point average (GPA) on a four-point scale, their major, and the number of psychology, criminology, and sociology courses they had completed. The participants were asked to list all psychology courses completed and their final grade in each class so a psychology GPA could be calculated.

PSYCHOLOGY TESTS

To further assess knowledge of psychology, participants completed a 30-question test created from general psychology and abnormal psychology test pools prepared by a professor of psychology *(11)*. Of the 30 items chosen from the test pools, half relate to abnormal psychology, and the remaining questions cover all areas of psychology. All test items in the test bank have been proven to distinguish high and low test scorers. Therefore, questions that are either too difficult or too easy were excluded from the bank. The abnormal and general psychology questions were scored separately, yielding two scores that consist of the percentage of correct questions in each area. The exact validity of this test is unknown, but it can be assumed to be as valid as any typical test in the respective courses.

MURDER CASE

As part of the profiling task, participants were given a murder case to read. All the information for the murder case was obtained from 1983 archived articles of *The Meridian Star*, a local newspaper of Meridian, Mississippi. The murder case is a compilation of information surrounding the disappearance and death of two sexually assaulted murder victims. The participants were asked to assume the cases were committed by the same offender because in a realistic scenario the police would generally ask for a profiler's assistance when there is a presumed connection between multiple murders. The written case provides evidence, *modus operandi*, and a timetable of events that a profiler would be given in an actual profiling situation. All names, dates, location, and identifying information of the case were modified. These changes were made to prevent participants from recognizing the case and therefore knowing the offender characteristics. The participants were told that the crimes were unsolved (even though they were solved).

PROFILING OFFENDER CHARACTERISTICS QUESTIONNAIRE

The profiling offender characteristics questionnaire used in this study is an adaptation of a measure created by Kocsis and colleagues *(8)*. The questionnaire also includes three questions created by Pinizzotto and Finkel *(6)*. This 33-item questionnaire yields a total accuracy score along with accuracy scores related to various aspects of the offender, including physical characteristics, cognitive processes, offense behaviors, and social history and habits. The additional questions from Pinizzotto and Finkel included profiling work habits, juvenile record, and prior assaults. Correct answers yielded one point each.

Based on the information that is known about the suspect, accurate profiles yield 6 points for physical characteristics, 5 points for cognitive processes, 7 points for offense behaviors, 5 points for social history and habits, and 1 point for adult convictions from the Pinizzotto and Finkel questions for a total accuracy score of 24 points. This score is lower than the total possible accuracy score of the original questionnaire because, for this case, information could not be obtained about the suspect for nine questions. Two of the unanswerable questions are on motive and fantasies of the suspect in the cognitive processes category. Five of ten questions from the social history and habits category are unanswerable. These questions include religious beliefs, romantic relationships, nonromantic friendships, service in the armed forces, and alcohol consumption. The work habits and juvenile record questions from Pinizzotto and Finkel are also unanswerable.

For three questions, more than one answer choice was considered correct; this occurred when the offender information was known but not at the level of detail necessary to distinguish between two answer choices. For example, it was evident that the offense was planned but the amount of planning is unknown. Therefore, for the question, "the offense was…," the answer was considered correct if the participant chose, "some planning" or "carefully planned." Also, it is known that the offender was a mechanic. Because this work could either be classified as semi-skilled or working as a laborer, both of these choices were regarded as correct. The age and condition of the offender's car was not obvious. If participants chose an answer between 3 to 10 years it was considered correct, and if they chose a conservative model in good or poor condition it was scored as a correct response.

For the current study, the profiling offender characteristics questionnaire was adapted into language that is common to this region. For the question related to the suspect's ethnicity, the options "Anglo-Saxon, Mediterranean, Eastern European, Middle Eastern, Asian, Aboriginal, Afro-American, or Other" were changed to "African American, Asian American, Caucasian, Hispanic/Latino(a), Native American, or Other." Similarly, "five kilometers" was changed to "five miles," and "de facto relationship" was changed to "common law relationship." In addition, additional answer choices were added to two questions. Specifically, "hatred toward a certain type of person" and "pleasure (sexual or other)" were added to the answer options of the primary motive question to include choices applicable to sexual homicides. "Completed some college but no degree" was added to the education question.

The first question of the offender characteristics questionnaire asks the sex of the offender. This question was used as a validity question to ensure that participants paid attention to the murder case. Six participants reported the offender to be female, so their data were excluded. It is clear in the case presented that the offender is male, and therefore this response was considered to be invalid.

DESIGN AND PROCEDURE

After signing the consent form, participants were given the demographic questionnaire and the psychology test. When participants completed them, they received the murder case and the profiling offender characteristics questionnaire. When they completed and turned in these documents, they were handed a debriefing form, thanked for their participation, and walked to the door.

RESULTS

Participants

The mean grade point average (GPA) reported by the participants was 3.37 on a 4-point scale (SD = 0.84, range = 1.30 − 4.00). There were 47 (17.5%) psychology majors, and the remaining participants (82.5%) were either majors in another area or had not declared a major. The average number of psychology classes that the participants reported completing was 1.35 (SD = 3.27, range =0–16). The mean calculated GPA for completed psychology classes was 3.14 on a 4-point scale (SD = 0.84, range = 0.00 – 4.00). There were 7 (2.6%) sociology majors. The average number of sociology classes that the participants reported completing was 0.59 (SD = 1.53, range = 0–20), and the average number of criminal justice classes was 0.11 (SD = 0.73, range = 0–10).

The average percentage of correct answers on the abnormal psychology test was 36.7% (SD = 12.0%, range = 7–73%) and 42.1% for the general psychology test (SD = 12.3%, range = 7–73%). There was a small but significant positive correlation between scores on the two tests ($r = 0.18$, $p < 0.001$). Scores on both the abnormal ($r = 0.15$, $p < 0.05$) and general ($r = 0.34$, $p < 0.0001$) tests correlated significantly with the number of psychology courses completed by the participants. The general psychology test score also correlated significantly with participants' age ($r = 0.27$, $p < 0.0001$), number of completed criminology courses ($r = 0.16$, $p < 0.05$), and completed sociology courses ($r = 0.23$, $p < 0.001$). Neither the abnormal psychology test score ($r = 0.05$, $p = 0.45$) nor the general psychology test score ($r = 0.01$, $p = 0.85$) correlated significantly with total profiling accuracy.

Data Preparation

Prior to the primary analyses, some of the variables were re-coded as categorical variables that could be used as independent variables (IVs) in multivariate analyses of variance (MANOVAs). Although the re-coded variables were subject variables, they meet the assumptions for MANOVA because they are normally distributed, and it can be assumed that the values of these variables are representative of the college student population as a whole (i.e., there is no reason to believe that this sample is biased with respect to these variables). Because the abnormal psychology and general psychology test scores correlated significantly with each other, and because neither one correlated significantly with profiling accuracy, the test scores were combined for each participant. The combined score also did not correlate significantly with total profiling accuracy ($r = 0.04$, $p = 0.54$). Therefore, to determine whether the highest and lowest test scores influenced profiling accuracy, the participants' scores were categorized based on whether they were 1 SD or more above the mean ($n = 51$) or 1 SD or more below the mean ($n = 45$). This recategorization resulted in a reduced number of participants whose data could be analyzed for this psychology test variable ($N = 96$).

The number of psychology classes completed by the participants ranged from 0 to 16; the number of psychology classes completed did not significantly correlate with total profiling accuracy ($r = -0.05$, $p = 0.47$). Because most of the participants had not completed any psychology courses, participants were categorized into one of two groups: those who had not completed any psychology courses ($n = 68$) and those who completed one or more psychology classes ($n = 28$).

Profiling Accuracy

Profiling accuracy was defined by the number of correct responses on the offender characteristics questionnaire. Each participant had a total accuracy score as well as an accuracy score for each of the five offender characteristic areas: physical, cognitive, offense behaviors, history and habits, and other. Overall, participants showed a modest degree of accuracy. Physical accuracy had a possible 4 correct responses (participant M = 3.83, SD = 0.95, range = 2–6). Cognitive accuracy had a possible 5 correct responses (participant M = 3.29, SD = 0.94, range = 0–5). Offense accuracy had a possible 7 correct responses (participant M = 4.27, SD = 1.30, range = 1–7). History and habits accuracy had a possible 6 correct responses (participant M = 2.05, SD = 1.00, range = 0–4). Accuracy on the Pinizotto and Finkel question (adult convictions) only had 1 possible correct response (participant M = 0.36, SD = 0.48, range = 0–1). Total accuracy would have yielded 24 correct responses (participant M = 13.81, SD = 2.37, range = 5–19). Variables influencing profiling accuracy were examined through a series of MANOVAs using Pillai's trace criterion.

A MANCOVA was conducted with psychology major (yes, $n = 46$; no, $n = 216$) and sex (female, $n = 184$; male, $n = 78$) as the independent variables with the combined psychology test score (as a continuous variable) as the covariate. The 6 accuracy scores were the dependent variables. There was not a significant multivariate effect for psychology major [$F(6, 252) = 1.99$, $p = 0.07$, $\eta^2 = 0.05$], although the effect approached significance. Major accounted for 5% of the variance in profiling accuracy. There was not a multivariate effect for sex [$F(6, 252) < 1$], and no multivariate interaction [$F(6, 252) < 1$]. The covariate was not significant [$F(6, 252) = 1.27$, $p = 0.27$, $\eta^2 = 0.03$].

Despite the lack of significance in the multivariate tests, the between-subjects effects were examined, but only the significant findings are reported. A significant effect was found for psychology major on offense behavior accuracy [$F(1, 257) = 4.42$, $p = 0.04$, $\eta^2 = 0.02$]. Specifically, psychology majors were less accurate on offense behaviors (M = 3.93, SD = 1.36) than nonpsychology majors (M = 4.35, SD = 1.28). A significant effect was also found for psychology major on total accuracy [$F(1, 257) = 11.15$, $p = 0.001$, $\eta^2 = 0.04$]. Psychology majors were less accurate overall (M = 12.78, SD = 2.88) than nonpsychology majors (M = 14.03, SD = 2.19). The psychology test score had a significant effect on history and habits accuracy [$F(1, 257) = 4.56$,

$p = 0.03$, $\eta^2 = 0.02$]. According to a correlation test, higher test scores correlated with greater history and habits accuracy; therefore, the psychology test score variable (re-coded into a categorical variable) was used in subsequent analyses.

A MANOVA was conducted with sex (females, $n = 71$; males, $n = 25$) and psychology test score (1 SD or more above the mean, $n = 45$; 1 SD or more below the mean, $n = 51$) as the independent variables with the 6 accuracy scores as the dependent variables. The multivariate tests revealed no effects for sex [$F(6, 87) = 1.97$, $p = 0.08$, $\eta^2 = 0.12$] or psychology test [$F(6, 87) = 1.06$, $p = 0.39$, $\eta^2 = 0.07$], and there was not a significant multivariate interaction [$F(6, 87) = 1.25$, $p = 0.29$, $\eta^2 = 0.08$]. However, it should be noted that sex approached significance and accounted for 12% of the variance in profiling accuracy.

Despite the lack of significant findings in the multivariate tests, the between-subjects effects were examined. Only the significant findings are reported. There was a significant effect of sex on physical accuracy [$F(1, 92) = 4.60$, $p = 0.04$, $\eta^2 = 0.05$]. Specifically, females were more accurate (M = 4.00, SD = 0.87) than males (M = 3.56, SD = 0.92). There was a significant interaction between sex and psychology test on cognitive accuracy [$F(1, 92) = 5.10$, $p = 0.03$]. This interaction accounted for 5% of the variance in profiling accuracy of the offender's cognitive characteristics ($\eta^2 = 0.05$). Females with higher scores on the psychology test were more accurate (M = 3.62, SD = 1.04) than females with lower scores (M = 3.23, SD = 0.90), whereas males with lower scores on the psychology test were more accurate (M = 3.58, SD = 0.90) than males with higher scores (M = 3.00, SD = 0.71).

Another MANOVA was conducted with sex (females, $n = 71$; males, $n = 25$), psychology test (1 SD or more above the mean, $n = 45$; 1 SD or more below the mean, $n = 51$), and psychology major (yes, $n = 19$; no, $n = 77$) as the independent variables with the 6 accuracy scores as the dependent variables. The multivariate effect for sex approached significance [$F(6, 84) = 2.20$, $p = 0.051$] and accounted for 14% of the variance in profiling accuracy ($\eta^2 = 0.14$). However, there was not a significant multivariate effect for psychology test [$F(6, 84) < 1$] or psychology major [$F(6, 84) < 1$]. There was not a significant multivariate interaction between psychology major and psychology test [$F(6, 84) < 1$], psychology test and sex [$F(6, 84) < 1$], or psychology major and sex [$F(6, 84) = 1.21$, $p = 0.31$, $\eta^2 = 0.08$] (the three-way interaction was not analyzed due to inadequate numbers).

Despite the lack of significance in the multivariate tests, the between-subjects effects were examined. Only the significant findings are reported. There were significant effects for sex on physical accuracy [$F(1, 89) = 5.18$, $p = 0.03$,

$\eta^2 = 0.06$], cognitive accuracy [$F(1, 89) = 4.53$, $p = 0.04$, $\eta^2 = 0.05$], and total accuracy [$F(1, 89) = 5.54$, $p = 0.02$, $\eta^2 = 0.06$]. Specifically, females were more accurate than males in physical accuracy (females, M = 4.00, SD = 0.86; males, M = 3.56, SD = 0.92), cognitive accuracy (females, M = 3.41, SD = 0.98; males, M = 3.28, SD = 0.84), and total accuracy (females, M = 13.99, SD = 2.19; males, M = 13.32, SD = 2.61). There was a significant interaction between psychology major and sex in cognitive accuracy [$F(1, 89) = 4.21$, $p = 0.04$]. This interaction accounted for 5% of the variance in profiling accuracy of the offenders' cognitive characteristics ($\eta^2 = 0.05$). Female psychology majors (M = 3.71, SD = 0.85) were more accurate than female nonpsychology majors (M = 3.31, SD = 1.01) and all males. Male psychology majors (M = 2.00, SD = 0) were less accurate than male nonpsychology majors (M = 3.39, SD = 0.78).

A final MANOVA was conducted with sex (females, $n = 71$; males, $n = 25$), psychology test (1 SD or more above the mean, $n = 45$; 1 SD or more below the mean, $n = 51$), and completed psychology classes (none, $n = 68$; one or more, $n = 28$) as the independent variables with the 6 accuracy scores as the dependent variables. The multivariate effect for sex approached significance [$F(6, 83) = 2.17$, $p = 0.054$] and accounted for 14% of the variance in profiling accuracy ($\eta^2 = 0.14$). There was not a significant multivariate effect for psychology test [$F(6, 83) = 1.30$, $p = 0.27$, $\eta^2 = 0.09$] or completed psychology classes [$F(6, 83) < 1$]. There was not a significant multivariate interaction between sex and psychology test [$F(6, 83) = 1.24$, $p = 0.29$, $\eta^2 = 0.08$], sex and completed psychology classes [$F(6, 83) = 1.02$, $p = 0.42$, $\eta^2 = 0.07$], or psychology test and completed psychology classes [$F(6, 83) = 1.51$, $p = 0.34$, $\eta^2 = 0.08$]. There was not a significant multivariate three-way interaction between sex, psychology test, and completed psychology classes [$F(6, 83) = 1.13$, $p = 0.36$, $\eta^2 = 0.08$].

Despite the lack of significance in the multivariate tests, the between-subjects results were examined, but only the significant findings are reported. There was a significant effect of sex on physical accuracy [$F(1, 88) = 8.51$, $p = 0.004$, $\eta^2 = 0.09$]. Females were more accurate (M = 4.00, SD = 0.86) than males (M = 3.56, SD = 0.92) on profiling physical characteristics. Psychology test score had a significant effect on history and habits accuracy [$F(1, 88) = 4.92$, $p = 0.03$, $\eta^2 = 0.05$]. Participants with high scores on the psychology test were more accurate (M = 2.16, SD = 0.90) in profiling history and habits than participants with low scores (M = 1.80, SD = 1.17). There was a significant interaction between sex and completed psychology classes on physical accuracy [$F(1, 88) = 3.95$, $p = 0.05$]. This interaction accounted for 4% of the variance in profiling accuracy of the offender's physical characteristics ($\eta^2 = 0.04$).

Females who had completed psychology classes were more accurate (M = 4.27, SD = 0.70) than females who had not completed psychology classes (M = 3.88, SD = 0.90). Females were more accurate than males, regardless of the number of psychology classes. Among males, those who completed one or more psychology classes were about as accurate (M = 3.50, SD = 1.23) as males who did not complete any psychology classes (M = 3.58, SD = 0.84).

DISCUSSION

This research specifically examined the influence of college-level psychological knowledge and education on profiling accuracy. Past research has compared various professions such as police, psychologists, and professional profilers or compared years of investigative experience (7–10). This was the first study specifically examining whether a foundation in psychology, independent of profession, influences accurate profiles.

Contrary to expectations, most academic indicators did not correlate with accurate profiling scores. Overall GPA, psychology GPA, and the number of completed psychology, sociology, or criminology courses did not correlate with profiling accuracy. Because there were no correlations found, further analysis was not completed with these continuous variables. The multivariate tests found no significant multivariate effects for the IVs (psychology major, sex, psychology test, number of psychology courses), suggesting that the IVs do not influence accuracy across all profiling domains. The between subjects analyses did yield some significant effects, indicating that certain IVs have an impact on specific aspects of profiling accuracy.

Sex, psychology knowledge (as measured by the psychology test), and psychology background (as measured by completed psychology courses and major) affected aspects of profiling accuracy. Females were more accurate than males overall and when profiling the physical and cognitive characteristics of the offender. This finding was not expected because past research has not examined sex or given any suggestions that sex might affect profiling. As expected, psychology knowledge positively affected profiling accuracy. Specifically, participants who scored higher on the psychology tests were more accurate than low scorers when profiling the history and habits of the offender. Contrary to expectation, psychology background did not improve profiling accuracy. The number of psychology courses did not affect accuracy. In addition, nonpsychology majors were more accurate than psychology majors overall and when profiling offense behaviors. These results suggest that psychology knowledge is more important than psychology background in determining profiling accuracy.

These findings were clarified by three interactions. Two-way interactions were found between sex and psychology knowledge, major, and completed psychology classes. For females, psychology knowledge and background as measured by being a psychology major were associated with greater accuracy for profiling cognitive characteristics. For females, psychology background as measured by the number of classes was also associated with greater accuracy for profiling physical characteristics. In contrast, psychology knowledge did not affect the profiling accuracy of males. Psychology background as measured by major was associated with less accurate profiling of cognitive characteristics for males. Similarly, for males, psychology background as measured by the number of classes was associated with less accurate profiling of physical characteristics. Overall, for females, psychology knowledge and background enhance accurate profiling of the offender's cognitive and physical characteristics, whereas these factors decreased or had no impact on the profiling accuracy of males.

This study's findings about female profilers are consistent with those of Kocsis et al., who found that psychologists are more accurate in profiling physical characteristics, offense behaviors, and cognitive characteristics than the police *(8)*. Because the profilers in the current study were undergraduates, the current study suggests that the superior profiling accuracy of the psychologists in the Kocsis et al. study is not due to graduate-level knowledge and training alone (the accuracy results reported by Kocsis et al. are comparable to those obtained in the current study). Our findings about male profilers are consistent with those of Pinizzotto and Finkel, who did not find psychologists to be more accurate than FBI profilers *(6)*. Perhaps the conflicting results of the past research are due in part to the sex of the participants in those studies.

A possible explanation for the increased profiling accuracy of females who scored high on the psychology test is that females might score higher in general on this psychology test, which would mean that the real difference in profiling accuracy was due to psychology knowledge and not to the combination of sex and knowledge. However, a *t*-test with sex as the IV and the psychology test score (as a continuous variable) as the dependent variable (DV) found no significant difference for sex. A second test, a chi-squared analysis, was undertaken with sex as the IV and psychology test score group (1 SD above and 1 SD below) as the DV. Again, there was not a significant difference for sex. Therefore, improved profiling accuracy among females with greater psychology knowledge is not due to psychology knowledge alone.

A possible explanation for the increased profiling accuracy of females who are psychology majors and males who are nonpsychology majors is that intelligent females may choose psychology as a major, whereas intelligent males may choose other fields as majors. In other words, this suggests that it is overall aptitude that predicts profiling accuracy rather than sex or major. However, this is negated first by the fact that neither GPA nor psychology test score alone significantly predicted profiling accuracy. There could be something about sex or major, or a combination of those variables, that influences aptitude, which in turn influences profiling accuracy. To test this, two ANOVAs were run, each with sex and psychology major as the IVs. One was run with psychology test score (as a continuous variable) as the DV, and one was run with GPA as the DV. There were no significant effects for either analysis, which negates the hypothesis that smarter males pick nonpsychology majors and smarter females pick psychology as a major (assuming that GPA can be used as a measure of aptitude). These findings suggest that it is not simply aptitude that accounts for profiling accuracy. There is something specific to sex combined with psychology knowledge and background that influences profiling accuracy.

This study had strengths that set it apart from past research, but it also has a number of limitations. The murder case used in this study was not the same case used in past research. The case description was compiled from information found in archival newspaper articles. Although complete case information could not be obtained, the available articles did provide several factual points about the case and the offender. Previous profiling accuracy research by Kocsis et al. *(7,8)* used investigating police officers to provide the correct answers to a select few profiling questions based on their experience with the offender and the investigation. Pinizzotto and Finkel noticeably deleted important details, such as information about the victim and crime scene, from the cases used in their profiling research as requested by the original investigators who solved the actual cases *(6)*. This current study was based only on factual information available from publicly available archival sources. The advantages of using this method were that naiveté about psychological characteristics or potentially biased opinions of a police investigator did not influence the profile. The disadvantages of this method were the unavailability of all of the crime scene information for the murders and the possibility of inaccurate reporting from the archival sources. The results of profiling research would indeed be more valid and reliable if totally unedited replicas of solved police investigations could be provided to the participants.

Another limitation in this research was the reliance on self-reporting to obtain academic grades of the participants; self-reporting can be influenced by inaccurate memory. Some participants spontaneously reported during the experiment that they were having difficulty remembering information such as their GPA, the number of completed psychology classes, or the final grade associated with specific psychology classes. When this occurred, the participants were asked to do their best and report what they remember. It is not known how many participants had this difficulty. Possible memory confounds were limited when the participants' data were divided into groups based on whether they completed any courses. In addition, psychology GPA and overall GPA were not analyzed beyond correlational tests.

Still another limitation related to the test used to assess the participants' psychological knowledge. The psychology test was not a standardized test but was a typical classroom test in general and abnormal psychology classes. Using a standardized test such as the subject GRE test may have been a more reliable and generalizable indicator of psychological knowledge. However, using such a test would be time-consuming, expensive, and not necessarily a good indicator of psychological knowledge in a specialty area such as abnormal or clinical psychology. The test used in this study focused more on these areas of psychology.

Collecting comparable samples was a challenge. The sample size was unequal for levels of education and sex, and there were more nonpsychology majors than psychology majors. According to the power analysis, only 120 subjects were needed to have enough power to detect moderate effects *(12)*; but after collecting data from this number of participants, the distribution of majors and class rank was heavily skewed to female freshmen nonpsychology majors. An attempt to even out this distribution was made by increasing the number of participants, but sample sizes remained unequal. Specifically, there were not enough males or psychology majors, which impairs the ability to generalize the results.

This research is important because there is little research in the area of profiling accuracy, even though profiling is heavily relied upon as an investigative tool. It is important to be able to understand the factors that lead to accurate profiles and what area of knowledge or experience would be important to expand or develop in profilers.

The question remains about the factors that contribute to accurate profiles. This study suggests that sex, psychological knowledge, and psychological education are contributing factors. The research also shows the need to continue to evaluate factors influencing accurate profiles. Suggestions for future research are to examine psychological knowledge in graduate students who are beginning to train in psychological evaluations and assessments. Perhaps graduate training in psychology would have a stronger influence on profiling accuracy.

It would be valuable to examine the effects of training on profiling. Pinizzotto and Finkel found that profilers affiliated with the FBI are more accurate than psychologists, detectives, or students, which may be due to the profiling training that is specific to the FBI. The psychologists and students chosen for their study were naive about criminal investigations, but the detectives were not. It seems that the specific FBI training was the obvious difference between the detectives who had had many years of experience and the two groups of FBI profilers. Other research suggests that experience should not have played a role in accuracy *(8)*. Therefore, years of experience of the FBI profilers should not have been a factor. The educational or experiential background may be irrelevant if training alone determines accurate profiles. Further research should examine this possibility.

CONCLUSION

This study expanded the existing profiling accuracy research and discovered previously unexamined variables that seem to influence profiling accuracy. This research found that sex, psychological knowledge, and psychological education have an impact on profiling accuracy. Although a background in psychology seems to improve profiling accuracy for females, especially when profiling the physical and cognitive characteristics of the offender, it does not help males. This study has provided new and important findings to the literature on profiling accuracy, but further research is needed to understand more fully the influence of sex and psychology knowledge and background on profiling accuracy.

REFERENCES

1. FBI (2002). Uniform crime reports. Retrieved June 8, 2004, from http://www.fbi.gov/ucr/02cius.htm.
2. Wrightsman, L. S., Nietzel, M. T., & Fortune, W. H. (1998). Identification and evaluation of criminal suspects. In: *Psychology & the Legal System* (pp. 206–235). Pacific Grove, CA: Brooks/Cole.
3. Ault, R. L., & Reese, J. T. (1980). A psychological assessment of crime profiling. *FBI Law Enforcement Bulletin, 49,* 22–25.
4. Killinger, G. G., & Cromwell, P. F. (1975). *Issues in Law Enforcement* (p. 212). Boston: Holbrook Press.
5. Hazelwood, R. R., & Burgess, A. W. (1987). An introduction to the serial rapist research by the FBI. *FBI Law Enforcement Journal, 56,* 16–24.
6. Pinizzotto, A. J., & Finkel, N. J. (1990). Criminal personality profiling: an outcome and process study. *Law & Human Behavior, 14,* 215–233.
7. Kocsis, R. N, Hayes, A. F., & Irwin, H. J. (2002). Investigative experience and accuracy in psychological profiling of a violent crime. *Journal of Interpersonal Violence, 17,* 811–823.
8. Kocsis, R. N., Hayes, A. F., Irwin, H. J., & Nunn, R. (2000). Expertise in psychological profiling: a comparative assessment. *Journal of Interpersonal Violence, 15,* 311–331.

9. Kocsis, R. N. (2003). Criminal psychological profiling: validities and abilities. *International Journal of Offender Therapy & Comparative Criminology*, 47, 126–144.
10. Kocsis, R. N. (2004). Psychological profiling in serial arson offenses: a comparative assessment of skills and accuracy. *Criminal Justice and Behavior*, 31(3), 341–361.
11. Jacquin, K. M. (2004). Psychology test pool. Unpublished.
12. Cohen, J. (1988). *Statistical Power Analysis for the Behavioral Sciences* (2nd ed.). Hillsdale, NJ: Lawrence Erlbaum Associates.

Chapter 16

Profiling and Professionalization of Criminal Investigation

Jeffrey B. Bumgarner

Abstract

Any vocation that evolves into a profession necessarily proceeds through a multistep process. The process includes the creation of a full-time occupation, establishment of a training school reflecting and expanding the profession's theoretical underpinnings, formation of professional associations, and formation of a code of ethics. Many criminal justice scholars and practitioners argue that policing has evolved into a profession. Furthermore, some scholars and practitioners specifically point to the sophistication of modern criminal investigative techniques, including the use of criminal profiling techniques, as evidence of law enforcement's professional status. However, upon consideration of profiling as a professional subspecialty of criminal investigation, one is compelled to conclude that criminal profiling does not contribute significantly to the notion of policing as a profession.

INTRODUCTION

In recent years, criminal profiling—and particularly behavioral profiling—has gained prominent attention and notoriety in the Western world. During the past two decades in the United States, for example, there have been many novels, television shows, and movies predicated on the use of behavioral profiling to catch the criminal. Thomas Harris' fictional Hannibal Lector—the

From: *Serial Murder and the Psychology of Violent Crimes*
Edited by: R. N. Kocsis © Humana Press, Totowa, NJ

sociopath physician who figures prominently in most of Harris' novels (and later, movies)—has begat a cottage industry of yarns and scripts that pit the law enforcer protagonist against some clever but mentally deranged arch-villain, and profiling is the chief tool for deduction.

While behavioral profiling has taken off in the pop culture, something else important has been going on in law enforcement as well—the profession-alization of policing. The U.S. Department of Education historically classified policing as something other than a profession. With the grouping of law enforcement training programs under the "trade and industrial" category by the U.S. Department of Education, policing has shared vocational recognition with carpentry, masonry, cosmetology, and auto mechanics, among others (1). Today, however, there is resistance against placing law enforcement side by side with the trades on the vocational continuum. Many argue that policing is more akin to law, medicine, teaching, ordained ministry, and other professions.

This chapter explores the degree to which the growing interest and use of behavioral profiling contributes to the notion of policing as a profession by way of its association with criminal investigative practices. Along the way, the question of whether behavioral profiling even belongs to the family of law enforcement practice (as criminal investigation clearly does) is considered.

For years, law enforcement as an occupation has wrestled with its shape, form, and nature. Contemporary law enforcement officers and administrators are usually pretty quick to self-identify as "professionals." The very term "profession" has some rather attractive connotations. In addition to generally commanding higher salaries and social status—as physicians and attorneys do—there is an implication that the occupation is difficult and reserved only for an elite few who have conquered the requisite knowledge, skill and ability.

There is also the connotation of good performance in the term "profession." When someone does a job well (any job), it is often said that he or she did a professional job. For example, Griffin (2) identified five ingredients to police professionalism: integrity, intellect, initiative, industry (i.e., work ethic), and impact (i.e., influence). These are all laudable traits, of course, but do they go to the essence of professionalism?

Consider the statements: "Hey, the bathroom looks great. The plumber did a real professional job." "The roof looks great. You must have had the shingles done professionally." These types of statements are made all the time without regard for the fact that plumbing and roofing are not professions; they are crafts. Indeed historically, police work was thought of along the lines of a trade or craft. For well over a century since the first modern Western police force was established by Sir Robert Peel (i.e., London's Metropolitan Police) the occupation of law enforcement certainly fit the rubric of craftsmanship.

Police craftsmanship was first described by Wilson *(3)*, and later by Crank *(4)*, Bumgarner *(5)*, and others. Members of a trade or craft can be characterized by many things. Chief among theses characteristics is the tendency to learn by apprenticeship. The training of police officers on how to do their jobs has always placed its greatest emphasis on field training. Apprenticeship is the notion that a police officer learns his or her line of work by working under the direction of other seasoned veterans who know what they are doing. Those who deem this kind of learning as being of far greater importance and usefulness than formal education tend to view law enforcement as a craft.

Craftsmanship also assigns greater importance to oral traditions than to written records. Knowledge is passed down, not written down. As John Crank noted in his seminal work on police culture *(6)*, it is through oral tradition and war stories that officers learn about the organization for which they work, the expectations of colleagues, and the kind and quality of work that is valued (and that which is not) by coworkers, managers, and the public.

PROFESSIONALISM DEFINED

Wilensky *(7)* identified four structural tendencies that occupations consistently pursue as they become a profession. These tendencies are sequential.

- Creation of a full-time occupation
- Establishment of a training school (which eventually becomes affiliated with established universities) reflecting the knowledge base of the field and efforts by early leaders to improve the field
- Formation of professional associations
- Formation of a code of ethics

Morgan restated Wilensky's classic framework but overlaid on it the notion of a pulling sociological dynamic. He wrote *(8,* p. 19):

> ...the sociological perspective emphasizes three sets of factors that pull a practice along the professional status continuum. First, professions arise in response to a social demand for a body of esoteric knowledge and skills.... Second, the knowledge must flow from a body of consistent and integrated theory. Finally, a guild is created to monitor the creation and application of the special fund of esoteric knowledge in skills.

To the extent that criminal profiling is a dimension of law enforcement professional practice—specifically, criminal investigation—one would expect to find that criminal profiling has contributed to police work's march through Wilensky's sequence. Given the serious and threatening nature of offenders generally targeted by profiling, one might expect to observe the field of law enforcement taking ownership of criminal profiling in an effort to shore up the dynamic of social demand. If profiling actually contributes to the capture of violent serial offenders, society will perceive a need for it and demand it.

CREATION OF FULL-TIME OCCUPATION

Law enforcement as a nonmilitary, full-time vocation is only a couple of centuries old. The science and art of criminal investigation as a standard specialized activity of civilian law enforcement is even younger than that. Indeed, it is the presence of criminal investigation in the repertoire of police activity that helps distinguish policing as a profession. However, has the development of the practice of criminal profiling furthered the professionalization of criminal investigation and policing?

Brent Turvey described criminal profiling as a subcategory of criminal investigation. He noted that the term "criminal profiling" is often used interchangeably with behavioral profiling, psychological profiling, offender profiling, and others. In all cases, the application being discussed here is "the process of inferring distinctive personality characteristics of individuals responsible for committing criminal acts" (9, p. 1). One might add that this process is done in the law enforcement context; it is not for clinical or academic reasons but for solving crime. In other words, if behavioral profiling is fundamentally an activity of professional law enforcement, then inferring personality characteristics of criminals is not the end—it is a means.

That having been said, there are different types of profiling that result in different utilizations. Peter Ainsworth, by drawing from the work of Wilson and colleagues (10), described different types of profiling, including crime scene analysis and diagnostic evaluation. Crime scene analysis is the approach that is commonly portrayed in the cinema, on television, and in novels. It is also the very approach that has been commonly used by U.S. Federal Bureau of Investigation (FBI) profilers who work high-visibility and perplexing violent crime cases. With this approach, investigators attempt to connect behavioral evidence at a crime scene with personality typologies—typologies, by the way, which are not necessarily rooted in solid theoretical study or literature (11).

By contrast, diagnostic evaluation, as a profiling approach, relies on the judgment of clinical practitioners (i.e., trained psychologists and psychiatrists) to uncover the motives behind a criminal's behavior. This approach is more solidly rooted in the behavioral and medical sciences. Law enforcement may certainly make use of diagnostic evaluation to the extent that understanding motive helps solve crime, but diagnostic evaluation is not the province of criminal investigators themselves any more than an autopsy is. As such, diagnostic evaluation does not contribute to the professionalization of law enforcement *per se*. Rather, diagnostic evaluation advances the mental health professions.

Still another profiling approach is that of David Canter's investigative psychology. Canter's thorough use of psychological theory to build a theory base for explaining criminal activity is as rigorous, scientifically speaking, as diagnostic evaluation. Although Canter's work is clearly concerned with uncovering truth by the police investigator, he delves deep into the clinical literature to explain not only offender behavior but victim and police behavior as well *(12)*.

Criminal profiling as a subcategory of professional criminal investigation often is thought to have its modern roots in the most professional of criminal investigative organizations—the FBI. During the early 1970s, FBI special agents Howard Teten and Pat Mullany developed and delivered training courses on profiling techniques as an investigative tool. They also developed training that incorporated principles of abnormal psychology for successfully negotiating during hostage situations *(9)*.

In 1972 the FBI developed the Behavioral Science Unit (BSU) at the FBI Academy in Quantico, VA. At the BSU, Teten, Mullany, and other modern profiling pioneers worked to develop offender profiles—particularly for serial murderers—by interviewing offenders and classifying their behaviors and traits against what they did as criminals. In 1985, the profiling function of the BSU (presently called the Behavioral Analysis Unit) came under the auspices of the FBI's National Center for the Analysis of Violent Crime (NCAVC), but their work continued. During the past three decades, the FBI has employed profiling techniques (with varying degrees of success) to investigate a variety of famous cases, including the Unabomber, the Olympic Park bombing in Atlanta, the Washington, DC area sniper case, the anthrax letters case, and many other federal, state, and local cases.

Today, the FBI is just one of many law enforcement agencies with behavioral profiling units. Many other federal law enforcement agencies have profiling units, or at least profiling personnel, of their own. Furthermore, many states have profiling units in their primary investigative agency. Outside of the United States, several nations have enthusiastically set up profiling units in their own national and regional police agencies, including Australia, Canada, England, and The Netherlands *(9)*.

Of course, criminal profiling has been used to resolve mysteries even prior to the 1970s. For example in 1957, psychiatrist James Brussel developed a profile of a serial arsonist in New York City (the "Mad Bomber"), which turned out to be extremely accurate. Brussel correctly described the arsonist, who turned out to be George Metesky, as heavy set, middle-aged, Catholic, foreign-born, single, and a meticulous dresser *(13)*.

Campbell and DeVeni *(13)* pointed out that criminal profiling is similar to the model used by mental health clinicians when diagnosing conditions and drawing up treatment plans. The process includes the collection of data, assessment of that data, and formulation of hypotheses; one or more profiles are then developed and tested, and the results are reported.

To the extent that profiling follows a clinical model, one might ask whether profiling is genuinely the province of professional law enforcers, or are police profilers merely the psychological equivalents of midwives—laypersons peripherally permitted to engage in medicine so long as they do not hurt anyone.

ESTABLISHMENT OF TRAINING SCHOOLS AND A THEORY BASE

Professions can be distinguished from other vocations in that professions require more than mere technical competence *(14)*. Professions utilize a systematic body of knowledge that encompasses both the theoretical and applied *(15)*. Furthermore, the knowledge base of professions should always be expanding through observation and experimentation *(16)*.

Academe, for better or worse, is the steward of professional knowledge and literature. Some scholars have expressed concern about quality in professional education housed in universities but in a different way by voicing concern for the pragmatic capacity (or lack thereof) of professional schools *(14)*. They note the tendency of universities to fill the professional school vacancies with faculty exhibiting scholarly credentials but often failing to demonstrate practical knowledge or experience. As Rosenstein said in connection with a study of the Engineering School at UCLA after observing a trend of hiring strictly on the basis of academic credentials *(17*, p. 7):

> [T]he long-term consequence for the professions is evident, for it is apparent that the professional schools cannot play the science game and survive.... If professional schools have nothing more to teach than science or mathematics or even humanities, it is doubtful that they can do a better job than the respective schools of science, mathematics, or humanities.

What is the appropriate mix of theoretical and applied knowledge in professional law enforcement education? Moreover, insofar as criminal profiling is concerned, should the discipline of criminal justice or police science take ownership of the knowledge?

As far back as 1931, the National Commission on Law Observance and Enforcement, established by President Herbert Hoover and commonly known as the Wickersham Commission, urged that all police officers have college degrees *(18).* The Commission's position on police education was reiterated by the International Association of Chiefs of Police in 1965 when it stated: "Generally, it is conceded that today's law enforcement officer has a need for higher education. It is also generally agreed that within the next few years law enforcement officers will find higher education imperative" *(19).*

If criminal profiling is a practice that contributes to the professional status of law enforcement, one would expect to witness a serious effort by criminal justice and police science academic programs to develop and deliver profiling curricula. However, to date, profiling does not figure prominently in such programs.

In a stratified random sampling of criminal justice and law enforcement baccalaureate programs in the United States, 66 programs were initially identified to be examined for the presence of criminal profiling curriculum. Of the 66 colleges and universities, 16 were eliminated because they did not offer a basic criminal investigation course as a part of their curriculum. It was thought that programs so overly theoretical in criminology that no course in criminal investigation was offered could not be construed as sufficiently applied or preprofessional to expect that subspecialized criminal investigative topics would also be offered.

Of the remaining 50 colleges and universities offering criminal justice or police science degrees, only 10% offered courses primarily devoted to behavioral profiling. Some of the programs did offer other courses related to profiling, such as forensic psychology, but the overall numbers were still small. The percentage of criminal justice programs offering various courses are summarized below.

Randomly Sampled Criminal Justice Programs Offering Advanced Investigation-Related Courses in Addition to a Basic Criminal Investigation Course

Criminal investigation	100%
Behavioral profiling	10%
Advanced criminal investigation	12%
Forensic science	38%
Forensic psychology	22%
Serial crimes	8%
Homicide investigation	8%
Crime scene investigation	16%
Other investigation courses	2%

Although anecdotal, these figures suggest that no real impetus yet exists among criminal justice and law enforcement programs to include behavioral profiling or similar courses as a staple in the curriculum. Certainly one must recognize that criminal justice, as an academic discipline, serves as a prepro-fessional track of study for more than just would-be police officers and investi-gators. Indeed, people interested in corrections, the court system, law, and other career paths major in criminal justice. However, the interest among criminal justice majors in law enforcement careers has driven the discipline to offer growing numbers of policing-related courses.

The trend in law enforcement hiring at all levels has clearly moved toward the requirement of at least some college-level criminal justice education. As police chiefs and others who hire law enforcement officers become more comfortable with the banner of professionalization, there is a growing reluctance to hire just anybody—even with a college degree in another discipline—because doing so conveys the message that law enforcement is not a profession. Doing so suggests that no particular college coursework in the field is necessary because anyone can do the job. A growing number of police managers and line officers no longer think that is true. Rather, they maintain the parochial (i.e., professional) belief that there is a criminal justice body of knowledge of which police officers should have a command and that knowledge cannot be had by simply riding around with a field training officer for 2 months.

If criminal justice programs have become a primary vehicle of profes-sional education for prospective law enforcement officers, then what must be made of the absence of profiling courses in criminal justice curricula? The reluctance to deliver criminal profiling courses even when other inves-tigation and criminalistics courses are being offered suggests the discipline's low identification and comfort level with criminal profiling. There are many possible explanations why university criminal justice programs have not widely embraced profiling as a disciplinary prong. Chief among them is the dubious degree of academic rigor associated with profiling. Kocsis and Palermo *(20)* found that there continues to be few scholarly, empirical data suggesting that profiling consistently works as a criminal investigative tool. Furthermore, they noted that any effort to build the theory base through scholarship tends to be met with resistance and close-mindedness by profilers themselves unless the research in question happens to support their presuppositions *(20)*. In other words, the practitioner's perspective on profiling tends to be agenda-laden and unwilling to permit academe to take it wherever the data lead. Hence, criminal justice academe may, in turn, have decided that this lack of scholarly rigor warrants a limited role, if any, for profiling in criminal justice curriculum.

FORMATION OF PROFESSIONAL ASSOCIATIONS

A necessary trait for any genuine professional is that his or her occupational values and identity are shaped by professional associations and the standards of the profession. Professions are relatively homogeneous communities whose members share identity, values, definitions of role, and interests *(21,22)*.

The evolutionary development of professional and disciplinary associations tends to be similar across all professions *(23)*. For membership, one begins with a self-identified interest or practice in the subject. Early in a profession's development, congeniality may be put above competence when admitting new members.

In the case of criminal profiling, the emphasis on growing the membership may explain the current multidisciplinary nature of the field. Everyone is welcome—criminal investigators, psychologists, psychiatrists, and profiling consultants. However, over time, as the group achieves standing as representing an occupational specialty or intellectual discipline, "the standard tendency is for technical criteria of membership to be given increasing prominence, at the expense of well disposed amateurs.... What a professional association, adopting technical qualifications for fully authentic membership, loses by way of friendly discourse among a group of common believers it is likely to gain by the recognition of membership as an authenticating agency for its constituency" *(23, p. 115)*.

According to Azzaretto *(24)*, professional certification is one way a profession demonstrates its authority and legitimacy on its members. Professional certification is a voluntary process regulated by the profession to advance the competence of individual practitioners and to enhance the prestige of the profession. To become certified, one must master a body of knowledge and a set of competence qualifiers identified by the regulating professional association, followed by submitting to a regulatory mechanism set up by the profession to gauge practitioner proficiency *(24,25)*.

A related characteristic of professions is the trait of self-regulation (i.e., practitioners judging practitioners). Moore stated that there is a "strong and normatively supported tendency to emphasize the collegiality of the occupation" *(23, p. 109)* among the professions, especially those still attempting to gain full professional status. Consider that professionals frequently label their peers as "colleague," "fellow," and "brother." In fact, peace officers frequently speak of their "brothers and sisters" in law enforcement. When an officer is killed in the line of duty, expressions such as "our fallen brother" are common *(26)*.

There are several legitimate purposes of self-regulation. These purposes include preserving and enhancing standards, enhancing occupational prestige, controlling the number of authenticated practitioners to reduce competition and increase income, and finally to protect a particular orthodoxy within the profession from alternatives *(23)*. Macdonald *(27)* affirmed these purposes when discussing the objectives of any profession. He said the chief objective of a profession is to ensure a monopoly of service, which is accomplished through the culmination of a profession's secondary objectives—namely, establishing an exclusive jurisdiction of service, producing professionals by regulating and tailoring recruitment practices, and maintaining a monopoly of professional education.

Self-regulation is closely tied to the authority and jurisdiction of the professional to practice. Professionals must reign over themselves because laypersons are not qualified to do so. After all, it is unreasonable to expect or permit a lay person to judge the practice of a professional when that layperson is not qualified to engage in the very practice being judged.

The universality of professional authority was described by Greenwood *(28)* as the primary distinction between professions and other occupations. It is the professional who is always right, not the customer. This is because society has been convinced of a profession's domain and expertise and therefore agrees to the professional's exclusive jurisdiction and authority in his or her element.

The primary mechanism for the promotion and lobbying for a profession's exclusive jurisdiction is the professional association. This is also the primary mechanism for self-regulation. When a professional association effectively polices its members, its stature as the face of the profession to society is enhanced. In law enforcement, the International Association of Chiefs of Police (IACP) has attempted to serve as the association for the field. Although the IACP does transcend national borders, its membership is comprised of police administrators rather than the whole of law enforcement. Additionally, it competes with many other professional associations attempting to represent the discipline or some corner of it. In the United States, these associations include the National Sheriffs Association (NSA), the Federal Law Enforcement Officer Association (FLEOA), the National Association of Police Organizations (NAPO), and the Fraternal Order of Police (FOP), to name a few.

In 1999, several practitioners and academicians in the field of criminal profiling founded the Academy of Behavioral Profiling (ABP). The ABP describes itself as follows *(29)*.

The Academy of Behavioral Profiling is a professional association dedicated to the application of evidence based criminal profiling techniques within investigative and legal venues. The Academy is committed to the development and promotion of multi-disciplinary education and training, practice standards, and peer review for those who engage in evidence based criminal profiling. The Academy aims to foster the development of a class of practitioners capable of raising the discipline of evidence based behavioral profiling to the status of a profession.

In this statement, the ABP recognizes that behavioral profiling is multi-disciplinary in nature. It further acknowledges that profiling, in and of itself, has not yet attained the status of a profession. However, through developing practitioners and the creation and dissemination of behavioral profiling's own literature (by way of the ABP's *Journal of Behavioral Profiling*), the ABP hopes to elevate profiling to professional status.

The creation of the ABP is arguably an important step in Wilensky's professionalization process. However, with only about 100 members worldwide, the ABP's authoritative reach regarding the practice of criminal profiling is currently limited. Time will tell if either law enforcement or psychology/psychiatry will relinquish perceived control of profiling as it moves toward a profession in its own right.

The degree to which professional law enforcement can currently claim criminal profiling as a component part is debatable. Kocsis and colleagues *(30)* conducted a study in which the relative accuracy of profiling ability was gauged across different professional groups. Among the groups assessed were professional profilers, psychologists, and police officers/investigators. Profilers consisted of persons who had actually consulted in the past for law enforcement in developing psychological profiles of offenders. The police officer group included Australian police officers with at least 5 years of experience, including investigative experience. The psychologists group consisted of professional psychologists in Australia who had never studied criminal psychology.

The findings of the study indicated that the professional profilers were able to outperform the other groups in the study. In other words, professional profilers were better at profiling. This is not surprising given that professional profilers immerse themselves in the relevant elements of both psychology and criminal investigation. Interestingly, however, the study also suggested that psychologists with no forensic training were able to construct criminal profiles more accurately than police officers. The authors noted the logical implication, which is that psychological training and experience generally (i.e., expertise in general human behavior) was more useful in the practice of criminal profiling than training and experience in police work, including criminal investigation. Although some would argue that criminal profiling is a professional subspecialty of criminal investigation, this study seems to strike a blow against that notion.

FORMATION OF A CODE OF ETHICS

All professions proclaim ethical absolutes. Generally, the drive to be ethical is rooted in a professional's service orientation. Professionals believe in the indispensability of the profession and hold to the view that the work performed is beneficial to the public *(31)*. In addition to society's deference to the authority of professional expertise, society permits a profession to be a monopoly because it is convinced that the profession is ethical and altruistic. Admittedly, at some point in the evolution of professions, society is no longer in a position to revoke the monopoly status it granted a particular profession because there are no alternatives for the service, regardless of the perceived existence or deficiency of ethics. Law is a good example of that. A professional's service orientation relates directly to his or her character. Smith *(32)* ably described the importance of character to the true professional.

> [For the professional] character means embracing and employing in personal and professional life high moral principles and ethical values despite client demands and economic pressures; insisting on professional independence and retaining...the ability to say 'no'; living and practicing with integrity; dealing honestly with our clients and others and giving true value for our professional services.

The service ideal of the professional is articulated in the profession's code of conduct or code of ethics. Any legitimate code of ethics contains rules to protect the clients and defines practice or conduct that is incompetent or immoral *(7)*.

The presumed parent professions of profiling—psychology, psychiatry, law enforcement—all have their own existing codes of ethics. The codes of ethics disseminated by the American Psychological Association (APA) and American Medical Association (AMA) have authority over their respective practitioners, including those engaged in criminal profiling. The law enforcement code of ethics does not have similar reach and authority. The commonly accepted code for law enforcement was developed by the International Association of Chiefs of Police (IACP) during the 1950s. However, there is no universal sanction for violating the code (e.g., revocation of one's peace officer license). Additionally, many law enforcement agencies have adopted their own codes of ethics and ignore the IACP code altogether. The FBI is a case in point.

The upshot of this is that law enforcement officers are left to their own devices, ethically speaking. Short of illegal or unconstitutional conduct, a criminal investigator need only please his or her own conscience and that of his or her supervisor. This fact somewhat mitigates against the notion that law enforcement can legitimately be considered a unified profession at all. That aside, there are important implications for profiling.

Many authors have written about how criminal profiling, when abused or misused, can cause harm. Where harm unnecessarily occurs, ethics are implicated. Brent Turvey (9) summarized the potential harm in profiling: delaying apprehension of an offender because of false leads; delaying apprehension of an offender because of false suspects; delaying apprehension of an offender by falsely eliminated viable suspects; and harming the personal life of an individual by implicating his or her guilt in a crime due to a profile.

Of the four errors Turvey identified, the last is the most nefarious. What is more, we have seen this scenario play out many times. Cases that come to mind include Richard Jewell, who was wrongly implicated in the Atlanta/Olympic Park bombing and Steven Hatfield, the scientist who was implicated in the anthrax letter case. In both cases, these individuals fit into profiles developed by the FBI, and their identities as "persons of interest" were leaked to the press. Jewell was unceremoniously cleared without so much as an apology. Regarding Hatfield, the FBI was unable to firm up a case against him and appears to have moved on—but not before leaving a perpetual cloud of suspicion over him that will probably never permit his life to be the same again. This kind of conduct is covered by the Law Enforcement Code of Ethics; but as previously mentioned, the code has limited authority.

Interestingly, the above misconduct and other ethical gaffs identified by Turvey are, in the author's view, addressed in the ABP's code of ethics. Furthermore, a three-tiered sanction scheme is in place for violations. Ultimately, public censure and expulsion from the ABP could result from repeated violations. The existence of the ABP's code of ethics is further evidence of the practice moving toward a profession in its own right. Given the lack of universality or consequences for misconduct in the law enforcement code, the assertion by the professional criminal investigative community that profiling is their province is somewhat unconvincing.

CONCLUSION

Although occupational labels such as tradesman, craftsman, paraprofessional, and technician are not pejorative, recent generations of law enforcement officers have exerted significant effort to avoid them in favor of professional status. Likewise, profilers as an occupational group distinct from law enforcement have begun to self-identify as professionals and have taken overt steps to fit the professional caste. In fact, there is a tendency today to identify virtually any and every vocation as a profession and to ascribe best practices within that vocation as being "professional."

Morgan *(8)*, who paired society's dynamic pull with Wilensky's structural tendencies of occupations becoming professions, suggested that in the absence of pull, occupations may still seek professional status through political influence. He wrote *(8,* p. 19):

> While sociologists emphasize the factors that pull a set of practices toward professional status, political scientists emphasize the use of instrumental power that is needed to push a set of practices in to the status of a profession. According to this view, a practice acquires the status of a profession once the group successfully mobilizes sufficient political power to be delegated the authority to monopolize control over the marketplace. Pushed to its extreme, this view reduces professional associations to just another vested interest group."

Morgan would describe the claims of professional status by many occupations as suspect if they took the political track rather than the sociological track in their occupational evolution. Given a continuing affinity toward characteristics of craftsmanship in the law enforcement community, the frequent use of the professional label for policing may be due to "political pushing" as described by Morgan.

On the other hand, there do appear to be genuine professional developments taking place in the arena of criminal or behavioral profiling. This fact suggests that profiling either already belongs to an established profession (e.g., psychology or medicine) and is merely a developing specialty, or it is evolving into a profession in its own right. Although embracing the development of profiling's growing (albeit slowly) theoretical and literature base (in contrast to mere formulas) might have enhanced the argument for police professionalism at one time, law enforcement's adherence to craftsman-like traits has prevented it from doing so. Of course, this does not mean that law enforcement can never become a profession. Arguably, police work may have already reached the status of a profession, or has nearly done so. However, with a gulf between policing/criminal investigative education and profiling education in the colleges and universities, and given different ethical standards and sanctions governing police work and profiling, it appears the latter can claim no significant role in the professionalization of the former.

REFERENCES

1. Calhoun, C. C., & Finch, A. V. (1982). *Vocational Education: Concepts and Operations*. Belmont, CA: Wadsworth.
2. Griffin, N. C. (1998). The five I's of police professionalism: a model for front-line leadership. *Police Chief*, November, 24–31.

3. Wilson, J. Q. (1968). *Varieties of Police Behavior: The Management of Law and Order in Eight Communities.* Cambridge, MA: Harvard University Press.
4. Crank, J. P. (1990). Police: professionals or craftsmen? *Journal of Criminal Justice,* 18, 333–349.
5. Bumgarner, J. (2002). An assessment of the perceptions of policing as a profession among two-year and four-year criminal justice and law enforcement students. *Journal of Criminal Justice Sciences,* 13, 313–334.
6. Crank, J. P. (1998). *Understanding Police Culture.* Cincinnati, OH: Anderson Publishing.
7. Wilensky, H. L. (1964). The professionalization of everyone? *American Journal of Sociology,* 70(2), 137–158.
8. Morgan, D. F. (1994). The role of liberal arts in professional education. In: Brody, C., & Wallace, J. (Eds.), *Ethical and Social Issues in Professional Education.* Albany, NY: SUNY Press.
9. Turvey, B. (1999). *Criminal Profiling: An Introduction to Behavioral Evidence Analysis.* San Diego, CA: Academic Press.
10. Wilson, P., Lincoln, R., & Kocsis, R. (1997). Validity, utility, and ethics of profiling for serial violent and sexual offenses. *Psychiatry, Psychology, and Law,* 4, 1–11.
11. Ainsworth, P. B. (2001). *Offender Profiling and Crime Analysis.* Portland, OR: Willan Publishing.
12. Canter, D. V., & Alison, L. J. (1997). *Criminal Detection and the Psychology of Crime.* Brookfield, VT: Ashgate Publishing.
13. Campbell, J. H., & DeVeni, D. (Ed.). (2004). *Profilers.* Amherst, NY: Prometheus.
14. Mayhew, L. B., & Ford, P. J. (1974). *Reform in Graduate and Professional Education.* San Francisco: Jossey-Bass.
15. Brody, C. M., & Wallace, J. (Eds.). (1994). *Ethical and Social Issues in Professional Education.* Albany, NY: SUNY Press.
16. McGlothlin, W. J. (1964). *The Professional Schools.* New York: The Center for Applied Research in Education.
17. Rosenstein, A. B. (1969*). A Study of Progression and Professional Education.* Los Angeles: University of California Press.
18. Wickersham, G. (1931). *Report on Lawlessness in Law Enforcement.* Washington, DC: National Commission on Law Observance and Enforcement. Retrieved from http://www.lexisnexis.com/academic/guides/jurisprudence/wickersham.asp.
19. Crockett, T. S., & Stinchcomg, J. D. (1968). *Guidelines for Law Enforcement Education Programs in Community and Junior Colleges.* Washington, DC: American Association of Junior Colleges.
20. Kocsis, R. N., & Palermo, G. B. (2005). Ten major problems with criminal profiling. *American Journal of Forensic Psychiatry,* 26(2), 1–25.
21. Goode, W. J. (1957). Community within a community: the professions. *American Sociological Review,* 22, 194–200.
22. Bucher, R., & Strauss, A. (1961). Professions in process. *American Journal of Sociology,* 66(4), 325–334.

23. Moore, W. E. (1970). *The Professions: Roles and Rules.* New York: Russell Sage Foundation.
24. Azzaretto, J. F. (1992). Quality control in continuing professional education: accountability, effectiveness, and regulation. In: Hunt, E. S. (Ed.), *Professional Workers as Learners.* Washington, DC: U.S. Department of Education, Office of Educational Research and Improvement.
25. Galbraith, M. W., & Gilley, J. W. (1985). An examination of professional certification. *Lifelong Learning: An Omnibus of Practice and Research,* 9(2), 12–15.
26. Bumgarner, J. (2001). Police professionalism: an occupational misnomer? *Great Plaines Sociologist* 13(1), 63–87.
27. Macdonald, K. M. (1995). *The Sociology of the Professions.* London: Sage.
28. Greenwood, E. (1957). Attributes of a profession. *Social Work,* 2(3), 44–55.
29. Academy of Behavioral Profiling. *About the ABP.* Retrieved from: http://www.profiling.org/abp_about.html.
30. Kocsis, R. N., Irwin, H., Hayes, A. F., & Nunn, R. (2000). Criminal psychological profiling in violent crime investigations: a comparative assessment of accuracy. *Journal of Interpersonal Violence,* 15, 311–331.
31. Hall, R. H. (1968). Professionalization and bureaucratization. *American Sociological Review,* 33(1), 92–104.
32. Smith, W. R. (1998). Professionalism? What's that? *Florida Bar Journal,* 72(5), 28–37.

Index